In Search of an Inca

IDENTITY AND UTOPIA IN T

In Search of an Inca examines how people in the
the Incas to question and rethink colonialism a
the Spanish conquest in the sixteenth century ur
It stresses the recurrence of the "Andean utopia,
the precolonial past as an era of harmony, justice, and prosperity and the foundation for political and social agendas for the future. In this award-winning work, Alberto Flores Galindo highlights how different groups imagined the pre-Hispanic world as a model for a new society. These included those conquered by the Spanish in the sixteenth century but also rebels in the colonial and modern era and a heterogeneous group of intellectuals and dissenters. A sweeping and accessible history of the Andes over the past 500 years, *In Search of an Inca* offers important reflections on and grounds for comparison of memory, utopianism, and resistance.

Alberto Flores Galindo was an acclaimed historian and social critic who died in 1990 at age 40. *In Search of an Inca* won the prestigious Cuban Casa de las Américas Prize in 1986 and the Clarence Haring Prize from the American Historical Association in 1991. It is now in its fifth edition in Peru and has been published in Cuba, Mexico, and Italy. Flores Galindo was the author or editor of numerous other books, director of various scholarly journals, and recipient of many fellowships and honors. He received his doctoral degree from L'Ecole des Hautes Études en Sciences Sociales (Paris) and taught at the Pontificia Universidad Católica del Perú in Lima.

Carlos Aguirre is Associate Professor of History at the University of Oregon. He obtained his PhD degree at the University of Minnesota in 1996. In 1999 he was awarded a John Simon Guggenheim Fellowship. He is the author or coeditor of nine books, most recently *Dénle duro que no siente: Poder y transgresión en el Perú republicano* (2008).

Charles F. Walker is a Professor of History and Director of the Hemispheric Institute on the Americas at the University of California, Davis. His books include *Shaky Colonialism: The 1746 Earthquake-Tsunami in Lima, Peru and Its Long Aftermath* (2008) and *Smoldering Ashes: Cuzco and the Creation of Republican Peru, 1780–1840* (1999).

Willie Hiatt is Assistant Professor of History at Long Island University, C.W. Post Campus. He completed his PhD in history in 2009 at the University of California, Davis. His dissertation is entitled "The Rarefied Air of the Modern: Aviation and Peruvian Participation in World History, 1910–1950."

New Approaches to the Americas

Edited by Stuart Schwartz, *Yale University*

Also published in the series:

Arnold J. Bauer, *Goods, Power, History: Latin America's Material Culture*
Laird Bergad, *The Comparative Histories of Slavery in Brazil, Cuba, and the United States*
Noble David Cook, *Born to Die: Disease and New World Conquest, 1492–1650*
Júnia Ferreira Furtado, *Chica da Silva: A Brazilian Slave of the Eighteenth Century*
Sandra Lauderdale Graham, *Caetana Says No: Women's Stories from a Brazilian Slave Society*
Herbert S. Klein, *The Atlantic Slave Trade*
Robert M. Levine, *Father of the Poor? Vargas and His Era*
J. R. McNeill, *Mosquito Empires: Ecology, Epidemics, and Revolutions in the Caribbean, 1620–1914*
Shawn William Miller, *An Environmental History of Latin America*
Susan Socolow, *The Women of Colonial Latin America*

In Search of an Inca

Identity and Utopia in the Andes

Alberto Flores Galindo

Edited and translated by

Carlos Aguirre
University of Oregon

Charles F. Walker
University of California, Davis

Willie Hiatt
Long Island University, C.W. Post Campus

Cambridge University Press

CAMBRIDGE UNIVERSITY PRESS
Cambridge, New York, Melbourne, Madrid, Cape Town, Singapore,
São Paulo, Delhi, Dubai, Tokyo, Mexico City

Cambridge University Press
32 Avenue of the Americas, New York, NY 10013-2473, USA

www.cambridge.org
Information on this title: www.cambridge.org/9780521598613

First published in English 2010

Printed in the United States of America

A catalog record for this publication is available from the British Library.

Library of Congress Cataloging in Publication data

In search of an Inca : identity and utopia in the Andes /
Alberto Flores Galindo ... [et al.].
p. cm. – (New approaches to the Americas)
Includes bibliographical references and index.
ISBN 978-0-521-59134-8 (hardback)
1. Incas–Social life and customs. 2. Incas–Politics and government. 3. Inca philosophy.
4. Peru–History–Conquest, 1522–1548. 5. Peru–Colonization.
6. Spain–Colonies–America. I. Flores Galindo, Alberto. II. Title. III. Series.
F3429.3.S6I5 2010
985′.02–dc22 2010012784

ISBN 978-0-521-59134-8 Hardback
ISBN 978-0-521-59861-3 Paperback

Contents

List of Illustrations

Figure

Maps

List of Tables

Editors' Introduction

CARLOS AGUIRRE AND CHARLES F. WALKER

Alberto Flores Galindo: Historian and Public Intellectual

"A storm swept the world in 1968." That is how noted activist and writer Tariq Ali summarized the wave of protests and mobilizations that shook Paris and Berkeley, Mexico City and Prague, London and Chicago in that extraordinary year.[1] Two ideas are most frequently associated with those events: revolution and utopia. Radical and revolutionary change seemed just around the corner, although it was not always the change Marxists and socialists had dreamed about. This time the agenda for change included ideas and practices about sex, religion, culture, gender paradigms, generational relations, art, drugs, and music, not only (or mainly) working-class emancipation, and the pursuit of socialism. Although its importance is hard to deny, the legacy of 1968 is still a matter of dispute: was it truly revolutionary and emancipatory, or merely a frivolous and superficial outburst by spoiled kids in blue jeans?[2]

[1] Tariq Ali, "Where has all the rage gone?," *The Guardian*, March 22, 2008.

[2] For overviews of 1968 and the 1960s more generally, see Mark Kurlansky, *1968: The Year That Rocked the World* (New York: Ballantine Books, 2004), and Gerard J. DeGroot, *The Sixties Unplugged: A Kaleidoscopic History of a Disorderly Decade* (Cambridge, MA: Harvard University Press, 2008). For Latin America, Diana Sorensen, *A Turbulent Decade Remembered: Scenes from the Latin American Sixties* (Stanford, CA: Stanford University Press, 2007), and Jeffrey Gould, "Solidarity under Siege: The Latin American 1968," *American Historical Review* 114, 2 (April 2009), 348–75. For the case of Peru, see Eduardo Arroyo, "La generación del 68," *Los caminos del laberinto* 3 (April 1986), 41–7, and Alberto Flores Galindo, "Generación del 68: Ilusión y realidad," *Márgenes* 1, 1 (1987), 101–23.

Changes in the world and at home affected a new generation of radicalized students in Peru. The Cuban revolution and the recent death of Che Guevara; anticolonial struggles in Africa; the civil rights and anti–Vietnam war movements in the United States; the writings of Sartre, Fanon, Freire, and Marcuse; guerrilla movements in Latin America; the nationalistic reforms implemented by the Peruvian military government that came to power in October 1968; and the initial formulations of Liberation Theology all helped define the ideological contours of a generation of students and, less often, workers. Heeding the call to "go to the masses" (*acercarse al pueblo*), they engaged in "revolutionary" activities, even if these were often limited to militancy in small, semiclandestine parties, distributing fliers in factories, and endless theoretical debates that deployed the canonical works of Marx, Lenin, Mao, and Guevara as weapons not only to destroy capitalism and imperialism, but also (and sometimes especially) to discredit competing factions on the left.[3]

A young, relatively shy, and brilliant student at the still small and elitist Catholic University in Lima could not remain indifferent to these developments. Alberto Flores Galindo began his undergraduate education in 1966 and quickly immersed himself in the exciting political and intellectual climate. Born in 1949 to a middle-class family and educated at a private Catholic school, Tito (as he was called by those who knew him) was an avid reader as a child and later developed a deep social consciousness and a seemingly endless intellectual curiosity. He enrolled in the History undergraduate program at the Catholic University, then largely a bastion of political conservatism and historiographical traditionalism. Searching for new intellectual challenges, he took courses with Liberation Theology founder Gustavo Gutiérrez, a relationship that helped him rethink religion, spirituality, and the connection between intellectuals and the oppressed and marginalized sectors of society. The works of Jean Paul Sartre, Antonio Gramsci, and especially Peruvian José Carlos Mariátegui introduced Flores Galindo to Marxism. He participated in reading and discussion groups and established friendships and contacts beyond the walls of the Catholic University and the rather small community of historians and history

[3] Maruja Martínez, *Entre el amor y la furia. Crónicas y testimonio* (Lima: SUR, 1997); Eduardo Cáceres, "Introducción," in Alberto Flores Galindo, *Obras Completas*, vol. 1 (Lima: Fundación Andina / SUR, 1993), xi–xxxvii.

students.[4] Not surprisingly, he became an unequivocal militant of the left, first through radicalized but relatively small groups – FRES (Socialist Students Front), MIR (Leftist Revolutionary Movement), and VR (Revolutionary Vanguard) – and later as an independent and critical public intellectual. Socialism in those years, he asserted, "was more a myth than a proposal or a project, but it possessed the mobilizing passion to promote a sort of 'march to the people' ... that took many university students to peasant communities, mining camps, sugarcane cooperatives, urban slums, and especially factories."[5]

For Flores Galindo, the emancipation of the oppressed and the construction of a socialist society were intimately connected to the intellectual and ideological battles over the knowledge and interpretation of the past. Like Mariátegui, Gramsci, Walter Benjamin, or E. P. Thompson, Flores Galindo saw himself as an intellectual whose mission was to question the status quo, contribute to the forging of a new society, and help rethink the past as a weapon in the ideological and political battles needed to move socialism forward. He viewed history as one of the most important battlefields, and he never ceased looking at the past with a critical eye or engaging in hard-fought polemics against those who, in his view, manipulated it in the service of a conservative agenda.[6] However, Flores Galindo did not merely "apply" Marxist theory to the reconstruction of the past to produce superficial and ideological accounts to serve a political agenda, as was common in those days. Rather, he was a rigorous and creative historian whose work was grounded in solid archival research and a nondogmatic use of theory, Marxist and others.

The counterpoint between past and present and between theory and archival research was a signature throughout his fertile intellectual career. His first monograph explored the political organization, mobilization, and struggle of Andean mine workers (1900–30). Influenced by recent labor history, Flores Galindo examined not only the exploitation

[4] Literature was always one of his passions. In the 1970s he coedited a literary magazine with renowned poets Marco Marcos and José Watanabe.

[5] Flores Galindo, "Generación del 68," 104.

[6] On numerous occasions he attacked the view of history as a "dialogue with the dead," for it would mean that "we stop thinking about the present, we amputate our future, and transform historians into guardians of a cemetery." Alberto Flores Galindo, "Para una historia inteligente," *El Caballo Rojo* 157 (April 15, 1983), 15.

of Cerro de Pasco Copper Corporation workers, but also the role daily life and culture played in working-class consciousness.[7] Next he employed French *Annales* school methodology, including the *longue durée* and the use of the "region" as a unit of historical analysis, in a study of Arequipa. He focused on the economic exchanges and commercial circuits that articulated the "Andean south" between the eighteenth and twentieth centuries, but he also remained mindful of the actors (landowners, merchants, and peasants) behind those processes.[8] Flores Galindo consciously attempted to de-center the formulation of historical problems in Peru by adopting a regional and rural perspective. "The Andean south" ("el sur Andino") was central to this effort and informed most of his subsequent work and that of many historians. In addition, *Arequipa y el sur andino* briefly but convincingly critiqued Dependency Theory, still fashionable among Peruvian and Latin American intellectuals and scholars in the second half of the 1970s.

In the years between these books came significant personal and political changes. After completing his undergraduate degree at the Catholic University in 1971, he spent two years in Paris (1972–74) studying under the direction of Italian historian Ruggiero Romano.[9] He also became acquainted with prominent French historians such as Fernand Braudel and Pierre Vilar.[10] Once back in Lima, he started teaching at the Catholic University and participating in public debates. He developed a close, almost obsessive relationship with the printing and publishing world, writing articles on a variety of topics for newspapers, literary supplements, and academic journals, which reflected his intellectual and political interests and his passionate engagement with debates in the public sphere. He became a public intellectual compelled "to speak truth to power" and used any available forum and space (the labor union and the university podium, the modest student-owned magazine, and

[7] Alberto Flores Galindo, *Los mineros de la Cerro de Pasco, 1900–1930. Un intento de caracterización social* (Lima: Pontificia Universidad Católica del Perú, 1974).

[8] Alberto Flores Galindo, *Arequipa y el Sur Andino. Ensayo de historia regional, siglos XVIII-XX* (Lima: Editorial Horizonte, 1977).

[9] See his personal testimony of this relationship in "Ruggiero Romano, el viajero," *El Caballo Rojo* 167 (July 24, 1983), 13.

[10] In the first footnote of *Arequipa y el sur andino*, he recognized the work of French historians Pierre Vilar, François Furet, and Pierre Goubert as informing his approach to "regional history."

the more established academic journal) to make his work visible and his voice heard.[11]

Two historical figures began to attract Flores Galindo's attention: Tupac Amaru, the leader of a massive 1780 anticolonial Andean rebellion, and Mariátegui, the founder of Peruvian Marxism and one of the most important Marxist intellectuals of the twentieth century. It is not difficult to identify some of the motivations behind this interest. The military government that took over in 1968 used Tupac Amaru as a symbol of its alleged emancipatory program, as a "precursor" of its "military revolution," a notion that Flores Galindo and most of the Peruvian left found debatable. Historicizing Tupac Amaru would help demystify his role and legacy by answering a deceptively simple question: "What does Tupac Amaru II represent in colonial history? Or in other words, was the 1780 insurrection a mere rural riot, a hopeless rebellion, a revolution, an ethnic expression, or a national movement?"[12] Flores Galindo also asked why Peru, a tumultuous viceroyalty and country with much insurgency, had never experienced a revolution. From 1975 on he wrote various articles and edited an anthology of essays on Tupac Amaru and began to use the concept of *utopia* to refer to a host of ideas and projects behind insurrectionary movements.

Flores Galindo's interest in the study of Mariátegui, on the other hand, came mostly from his engagement in debates within the Peruvian left. How should the left respond to the military appropriation of "revolution" and "socialism"? What was the place of indigenous peoples in a socialist project? What was the relationship between the construction of socialism and the so-called national problem, that is, the idea that Peru had not "completed" its formation as a nation? And more urgently, what was the "revolutionary agent" that would carry on socialist transformations? Leftist intellectuals passionately debated these issues, all of which concerned Mariátegui in the 1920s. Although many commentators tended to canonize Mariátegui and make him the "precursor" of various branches of the Peruvian left, Flores Galindo aimed to historicize

[11] On this, see Carlos Aguirre, "Cultura política de izquierda y cultura impresa en el Perú contemporáneo (1968–1990): Alberto Flores Galindo y la formación de un intelectual público," *Histórica* (Lima) 31, 1 (2007), 171–204.

[12] Alberto Flores Galindo, "Presentación," in Flores Galindo, ed., *Sociedad colonial y sublevaciones populares. Túpac Amaru II – 1780. Antología* (Lima: Retablo de papel ediciones, 1976), 7.

Mariátegui and illuminate the person, his circumstances, and the ways in which his intellectual method might inspire new ways of thinking about Peruvian society. He did that in a series of articles and in two important books, the first with friend and collaborator Manuel Burga – a multilayered study of Peru's history between 1895 and 1930 – and the second a superb intellectual and political biography of Mariátegui.[13] In the latter he tried to understand Mariátegui's personal and intellectual developments in the context of his struggles against dogmatic Marxism, the Komintern, and APRA's reformist nationalism.[14] For Flores Galindo, Mariátegui offered a guide, not a prescription, for rethinking the relationship between a socialist project, indigenous peoples, and the national question in Peru.

Tupac Amaru and Mariátegui represented, in the eyes of Flores Galindo, attempts to navigate against the current, projects of radical social transformation, and alternative visions of the nation. These ultimately unsuccessful projects most clearly articulated in Peru the related themes of utopia and revolution that characterized the spirit of 1968. Those themes reappeared, widely amplified, when in 1980 a Maoist movement known as Shining Path started an insurrection allegedly under the guidance of Mariátegui's thought.[15] Shining Path promised to make communism a reality – not only in Peru but in the entire world – through the "correct" application of revolutionary violence. Utopian communism, unapologetic revolutionary violence, and the transformation of a small and isolated guerrilla group in the heart of Andean rural societies to a nationwide threat to the Peruvian state challenged leftist intellectuals and parties that once again engaged in urgent debates about the relationship between revolution, socialism, and Andean peoples and cultures. Few intellectuals were better equipped to tackle those issues than Flores Galindo. His most ambitious contribution was the

[13] Manuel Burga and Alberto Flores Galindo, *Apogeo y crisis de la república aristocrática* (Lima: Ediciones Rikchay Peru, 1980); Alberto Flores Galindo, *La agonía de Mariátegui. La polémica con la Komintern* (Lima: DESCO, 1980).

[14] APRA (American Popular Revolutionary Alliance) was a movement founded in 1924 by Peruvian ideologist Víctor Raúl Haya de la Torre. Although initially Mariátegui and Haya de la Torre were ideologically close and collaborated on various projects, a radical rupture took place in 1928 when Mariátegui clearly defined his socialist option.

[15] Although its official name was "Communist Party of Peru," the movement led by philosopher Abimael Guzmán was widely known as "Sendero Luminoso" (Shining Path). It started its armed insurrection in May 1980.

notion of "Andean utopia," a concept that he would use as a thread into the fractured history of Peru from the Spanish conquest to the present. We will come back to this.

The 1980s were a decade of dizzying intellectual productivity for Flores Galindo. Besides the texts that later made up *In Search of an Inca*, his output included numerous essays, edited volumes, and books on a variety of topics, all while he continued teaching, lecturing, consolidating a center of socialist studies (SUR), and directing *Márgenes*, a journal of cultural and political commentary. He completed his doctoral thesis in 1983, a social history of Lima in the transition from colonialism to independence, which was published as a book in 1984.[16] *Aristocracia y plebe*, a highly innovative study of the class structure and social dynamics of Lima, attempted to explain why, at a time when riots, rebellions, and other social movements shook the Andean region, the capital of the Viceroyalty of Peru remained relatively quiet. He found the explanation in Lima's peculiar class structure and the confluence of vertical forms of despotism, social control, and horizontal manifestations of violence and tension among the lower orders.

By the late 1980s, Flores Galindo had embarked on a major study of José María Arguedas (1911–69), the Peruvian anthropologist and writer who in his view best represented the dilemmas and tensions of Peruvian society. Arguedas, the son of a mestizo lawyer, was raised among indigenous servants, grew up speaking Quechua, and later attempted to depict Peru's fractured reality in ethnographic and fictional works. He also struggled against depression until committing suicide in 1969. As many other authors have suggested, Arguedas's oeuvre offers a fascinating laboratory in which to explore Andean culture and its conflictive relationship with the "western" world, precisely the central theme in Flores Galindo's own historical work, particularly in *In Search of an Inca*. Arguedas, wrote Flores Galindo, "is one of those exceptional characters who, in his linguistic trajectory and his work as a writer, condensed the tensions and preoccupations of a given society." In addition, Flores Galindo found in Arguedas's work a peculiar "precursor and futurist" content, a sort of visionary "anticipation" of the paths that Peruvian society would (or could) take.[17] Unfortunately,

[16] Alberto Flores Galindo, *Aristocracia y plebe. Estructura de clases y sociedad colonial, Lima 1760–1830* (Lima: Mosca Azul Editores, 1984).

[17] These citations come from one of the two manuscript essays that Flores Galindo wrote about Arguedas and that were published posthumously: "Arguedas y la

Flores Galindo's sudden illness in February 1989 and death in March 1990, at age 40, interrupted this project.

Dozens of publications in Peru and elsewhere mourned his passing and the tragic loss to brain cancer of a brilliant thinker in the prime of his life. Many noted a gaping hole in intellectual and political circles at a critical moment when the Shining Path guerrilla movement was escalating its violent campaigns and targeting union leaders, leftists, and community activists; when leftist parties (and socialism on a world scale) entered into profound crisis; and when Peruvian society began to suffer from Alberto Fujimori's ruthless dictatorship. Flores Galindo's voice had been leading the fight against these forces.[18]

Andean Utopia as History and Memory

Flores Galindo developed the notion of "Andean utopia" in collaboration with Manuel Burga. It emerged in 1978 when the two were discussing millenarianism and messianism in the Andes while working on their respective projects and coauthoring *Apogeo y crisis de la república aristocrática*.[19] Financial support from UNESCO later funded a long-term project on the Andean utopia. In 1982 they coauthored "The Andean Utopia: Ideology and Peasant Struggle in the Andes, 16th–20th Centuries," and although their collaboration continued, divergent interpretations led to the publication of two different books.[20] Flores Galindo published *Buscando un Inca. Identidad y utopía en los Andes*

utopía andina" and "Los últimos años de Arguedas," both included in his *Obras Completas*, vol. 6 (Lima: SUR, 2007), quotes from pages 395 and 392, respectively.

[18] His articles and essays of this period are included in volume 6 of his *Obras Completas*, "Escritos 1983–1990" (Lima: SUR, 2007). "Homenaje a Alberto Flores Galindo. 'Otro Mundo es Posible,'" a special issue of *Libros y Artes* (Lima) 11 (September 2005), includes a loving collection of essays about Flores Galindo.

[19] Manuel Burga, *La historia y los historiadores en el Perú* (Lima: Universidad Nacional Mayor de San Marcos/Universidad Inca Garcilaso de la Vega, 2005), 116. An early formulation of some of the ideas connected to "Andean utopia" appeared in Alberto Flores Galindo, "La nación como utopía. Túpac Amaru 1780," *Debates en Sociología* (Lima) 1, 1 (1977), 139–57. The first time "Andean utopia" appeared in print was in Flores Galindo's "Utopía andina y socialismo," *Cultura popular* (Lima) 2 (1981).

[20] Alberto Flores Galindo and Manuel Burga, "La utopía andina. Ideología y lucha campesina en los Andes. Siglos XVI-XX," *Allpanchis* (Cuzco) 20 (1982), 85–101.

in 1986, two years before Burga's *Nacimiento de una utopia. Muerte y resurrección en los Andes.*[21]

In Search of an Inca is a sweeping reinterpretation of key developments in Peruvian history covering more than 500 years. In Flores Galindo's view, the relationship between Andean societies and the western world shaped the entire period and articulated Peru's central historical problem. The ways in which Andean people rationalized, coped with, and responded to challenges generated by that encounter are central to his work. Peru's historical and contemporary social, racial, and regional fractures or divisions resulted from an asymmetrical, traumatic, and conflictive relationship between those two worlds. To understand the historical formation of those fissures and contribute to a political project to overcome them, Flores Galindo identified the recurrence of the Andean utopia, that is, the idealized depiction of the pre-Hispanic past, especially the Inca Empire, as an era of social justice, harmony, and prosperity. The Andean utopia functioned not only as a discourse about "the past" but also as the foundation for extremely relevant political and social agendas for the future. Various historical actors imagined the social and political structures of the pre-Hispanic Andean world – or at least what they considered as such – as models for their societies. The ideal society of the future was thus a return to a glorious past. "A distinctive feature of the Andean utopia," according to Flores Galindo, was that "the ideal city did not exist outside history or at the remote beginning of time. On the contrary, it was a real historic fact that had a name (Tahuantinsuyo), a ruling class (the Incas), and a capital (Cuzco)."[22]

Flores Galindo found this construction in the writings of Guaman Poma and Garcilaso de la Vega, in religious practices that resisted Catholic evangelization, and among the masses who followed Tupac Amaru's call for rebellion in the 1780s. He identified it as a mobilizing force behind indigenous and peasant unrest in the 1920s and 1960s and as inspiration for various forms of political discourse and agency in the 20th century (including Marxism, Aprismo, and others). And he saw it in José María Arguedas's literary expressions of the beauty and tragedy of Andean cultures and in the messianic and authoritarian undertones

[21] The first edition of Flores Galindo's book was published by Casa de las Américas (Havana, 1986). The first edition of Burga's book was published by Instituto de Apoyo Agrario (Lima, 1988).

[22] See Chapter 1.

of the Maoist movement known as Shining Path. He did not postulate equivalency between these constructions, nor did he suggest that the Andean utopia was a rigid and inflexible set of beliefs uniformly appropriated by different historical agents. In fact, he insisted that it was more appropriate to talk about "Andean utopias," for the plural reflected the contested and wide-ranging nature of these constructions. But he did see in all those formulations instruments with which "people without hope" (the vanquished, the subaltern, the oppressed) "challenge[d] a history that condemned them to the margins."[23]

In Search of an Inca therefore scrutinizes history and memory in the pursuit of an understanding of past and contemporary Andean people and culture. It looks at myths, dreams, memories, and imaginaries, but also at the ways in which they informed concrete political projects and actions. No other book had ever attempted such an ambitious interpretive framework to understand Andean societies.

Flores Galindo wrote the book not as a scholarly monograph but as a series of connected and independent essays, many of which were first published in journals or collective volumes and later revised for inclusion in this book. The urgency of releasing some of these materials in the context of intense ideological debates and rather dramatic political conditions in Peru explains the peculiar composition of *In Search of an Inca*. But it is also related to the author's following in the steps of many other Peruvian intellectuals and historians – Mariátegui, Jorge Basadre, Pablo Macera, and Raúl Porras Barrenechea, to mention but a few – who made ample use of the essay genre to produce influential works.[24] Flores Galindo's use of the essayist style helps explain the virtues and the shortcomings of this volume. It allowed Flores Galindo the freedom to cover hundreds of years of Peruvian history, combine different methodological

[23] See Chapter 11, 247.

[24] Flores Galindo highlighted Mariátegui's preference for the essay form: "Mariátegui was not an essayist by default or because he was unable to develop an alternative approach to national reality. He chose that option early on." Flores Galindo, "Marxismo y religion. Para situar a Mariátegui," *Obras completas*, vol. 6, 97–103, quote from 98. This tradition extends to other Latin American countries and has been frequently studied as an important genre with its own intellectual characteristics and narrative strategies. On this, see two books by Liliana Weinberg, *El ensayo. Entre el paraíso y el infierno* (Mexico City: Universidad Nacional Autónoma de México, 2002) and *Pensar el ensayo* (Mexico City: Siglo XXI, 2007).

traditions (history, ethnography, psychoanalysis, cultural and literary studies), and make ample and creative use of secondary materials. His talent as a historian and writer is displayed in the brilliance of these pages and in the sharpness of his observations about a wide variety of historical topics. As several critics have pointed out, however, the essayist style led to an uneven treatment of the book's many topics and to some flaws in his arguments, as we will see.[25]

Intellectual and Methodological Dialogues

The concept of Andean utopia introduced new themes and novel methodologies to Peruvian historical and social scientific circles. Nonetheless, Burga and Flores Galindo built upon and contributed to Peruvian debates of the 1980s or those of the "Generation of 1968." In discussions that varied widely in tone and sophistication, the left debated violence, revolution, and the role of the indigenous peasantry in a class society. Flores Galindo participated actively, stressing the need for the Peruvian left to return to Mariátegui's "heterodox" Marxism. He underlined Mariátegui's sensitivity to religion and culture and his attentiveness to the peculiarities of Peruvian reality, particularly its indigenous majority and pre-Colombian past. Flores Galindo pushed the left to avoid dogma and imagine creative possibilities for political action. With its focus on how Andean people and others conceived of or invented the Incas to rethink and change the present, *In Search of an Inca* addressed keystone issues of the left while nudging the debate toward history and questions of identity, the imaginary, and representation. Flores Galindo never abandoned his quest to reinvigorate Marxism and wrest it from the hands of those who saw it as a fundamentalist doctrine rather than a creative tool for interpretation and change. While challenging Eurocentrism, he sought to use Marxism and other theoretical schools of thought to interpret and transform Peru.

Flores Galindo's opening to interdisciplinary research, editorship of *Allpanchis* (1978–82), and long-standing position on the editorial board of *Revista Andina* – journals based in the highland city of Cuzco – put him in close contact with anthropological and ethnohistorical studies of the Andes. He was convinced of the need to overcome the unfortunate

[25] The reader will also notice a few cases of repetition of certain arguments in different chapters.

divide between Lima and the provinces and between anthropologists and historians. *In Search of an Inca* reflects Flores Galindo's familiarity with scholarship on the Quechua language, rituals, archaeology, and the precolonial period, topics that most Lima historians in this period did not study. At the same time, Flores Galindo sharply criticized the tendency – common among some ethnohistorians and anthropologists – to think of Andean societies and people as homogenous, frozen in time, and trapped in the mental structures of "Andean thought." In the introduction to this book and in several other works, he chastised some scholars for wanting to put Andean people into an "impossible museum."[26]

Flores Galindo did not just build on and recast Peruvian and Andean debates. He also incorporated readings and discussions on memory, utopianism, tradition, and modernity, making his own contributions to each. In doing so, he borrowed from a wide array of authors, intellectual traditions, and academic fields and called upon an eclectic selection of readings to develop his arguments. Besides the *Annales* school, innovative cultural historians such as Italian Carlo Ginzburg, unconventional Marxist thinkers such as Benjamin, and rediscovered authors such as Russian philosopher and semiotician Mikhael Bakhtin (1895–1975) were especially important. The Italian thinker Gramsci (1891–1937) proved influential, particularly as Flores Galindo explored Mariátegui, a Gramsci contemporary with whom he shared a similar unorthodox reading of Marxism and tragic life.[27] *Mentalités* studies and the work of English Marxist historians and other members of the New Left also were part of his intellectual repertoire. Flores Galindo built on Thompson to refine views on Andean uprisings, particularly Thompson's critique of interpretations of peasant outbreaks as mere "spasmodic" reactions to material woes. He clearly appreciated Thompson's able pen, political engagement, and effort to create culturalist definitions of class.[28] Studies on popular ideologies by historians Christopher Hill, Eric Hobsbawm, and George Rudé were also influential.

[26] See page 2.

[27] It is important to mention the influence of Argentine writer José Aricó in Flores Galindo's "Gramscian turn" and his rethinking of Mariátegui. See, especially, José Aricó, editor, *Mariátegui y los orígenes del marxismo latinoamericano* (Mexico City: Siglo XXI Editores, 1978).

[28] See his article "La historia y el tiempo. Miseria de la teoría," *El Caballo Rojo* 112 (July 4, 1982), 10, for a brief appraisal of Thompson's historiographical and political contributions.

Writing *In Search of an Inca* in the early and mid-1980s brought Flores Galindo into contact with many of the same subjects as Cultural Studies and Subaltern Studies, two schools of thought then in gestation. His attention to lower-class agency; the cultural dimensions of subaltern experiences; and societal forms of consent, control, and cultural domination paralleled the work of cultural critics such as Stuart Hall, Dick Hebdige, and Paul Gilroy. Flores Galindo was familiar with some of them – through Spanish or French translations – but his work betrayed a confluence of approaches and styles more than a Cultural Studies or Subaltern Studies "influence." Ranajit Guha published *Elementary Aspects of Peasant Insurgency in Colonial India* in 1983, and *Selected Subaltern Studies*, edited by Guha and Gayatri Chakravorty Spivak, appeared in 1988.[29] They were not widely read in Peru or elsewhere when Flores Galindo was drafting his ideas and were not translated into Spanish until the 1990s.[30] Readers familiar with these and other authors will recognize that Flores Galindo also questioned and reworked Marxism and other western narratives and sought alternative voices, discourses, and paths. Like Guha, Chatterjee, Chakrabarty, and others, Flores Galindo read colonial documentation against the grain to counter conventional interpretations of the Conquest and the "defeat" of indigenous people. He also looked beyond the traditional notion of the archive, incorporating oral traditions, contemporary rituals, and other sources.

The Andean Utopia under Debate

When Flores Galindo published the first edition of *In Search of an Inca*, he already enjoyed prestige in Peru and, to a certain extent, in academic circles in Spain, France, and the United States. *In Search of an Inca* consolidated his reputation, especially after he won the prestigious Cuban Casa de las Américas Essay Prize in 1986 and (posthumously) the Clarence Haring Prize in 1991 from the American Historical Association.[31]

[29] Ranajit Guha, *Elementary Aspects of Peasant Insurgency in Colonial India* (Delhi: Oxford University Press, 1983); Ranajit Guha and Gayatri Chakravorty Spivak, editors, *Selected Subaltern Studies* (New York: Oxford University Press, 1988).

[30] The first Spanish translation of some of Guha's and his collaborators' work was Silvia Rivera Cusicanqui and Rossana Barragán, editors, *Debates Post Coloniales: Una Introducción a los Estudios de la Subalternidad* (La Paz: Editorial Historias, SEPHIS, and Ediciones Aruwiyiri, 1997).

[31] This is a prize awarded to the "Latin American author who has written what is considered the best book in Latin American history in the previous five years."

The book has appeared in five editions in Lima and has been published in Cuba, Mexico, and Italy.[32]

Reviewers in Peru and elsewhere have lauded *In Search of an Inca* for its originality, breadth, importance, and style. They applauded Flores Galindo's search for utopias in the plural and his broad notion of messianic, millenarian, and other counter-hegemonic movements. Although this ample interpretation of Andean utopias made writing (and reading) *In Search of an Inca* more challenging, it allowed him to explore a variety of uses and inventions of the Incas and avoid a restrictive definition that overlooked the creative and heterogeneous invocation of the pre-Colombian past.[33]

In Search of an Inca had a great impact in Peru, and virtually every Peruvian intellectual considers it to be one of the essential books, if not *the* essential book, on Peru in recent decades. Nelson Manrique, a historian and close friend of Flores Galindo, cited its "surprising reception" in terms of the passion it provoked and the "amplitude" of the debate it prompted.[34] In a review of key works of Peruvian historiography and sociology since the 1960s, Sinesio López – after calling Flores Galindo "the greatest historian of the 1970s generation" as well as "the historian of the vanquished" – praised *In Search of an Inca* as "the most serious attempt" at understanding Andean world dynamics through the study of "internal social and political changes and the enormous repertoire of its cultural imaginary, which gave it its unity and identity."[35] Peruvian sociologist Gonzalo Portocarrero called Flores Galindo's work

[32] After the initial Cuban edition that consisted of six chapters, there were two subsequent enlarged editions in Lima (Instituto de Apoyo Agrario, 1987, and Editorial Horizonte and Instituto de Apoyo Agrario, 1988), with eight and eleven chapters, respectively. The book was reprinted in 1993 in Mexico (Grijalbo/Conaculta) and in 1994 and 2005 in Peru, by Editorial Horizonte and SUR, respectively. The Italian translation appeared as *Perù: identità e utopia. Cercando un inca* (Firenze: Ponte Alle Grazie, 1991), translated by Maria Antonietta Peccianti and with a preface by Ruggiero Romano.

[33] Magdalena Chocano, "Presentación," Alberto Flores Galindo, *Los Rostros de la plebe* (Barcelona: Editorial Crítica, 2001); Eduardo Cáceres Valdivia, "'No hay tal lugar': Utopía, ucronía, e historia," *Márgenes* (Lima) 17 (2000), 11–27.

[34] Nelson Manrique, "Historia y Utopía en los Andes," *Debates de Sociología* (Lima) 12–14 (1986–88), 201–11, quote from 202.

[35] Sinesio López, "La reinvención de la historia desde abajo," *Libros & Artes* (Lima) 22–3 (2009), 1–12, quotes from 8, 9, and 10.

on Andean utopia "an intellectual tour de force" that built upon and continued earlier contributions by Mariátegui and Arguedas.[36]

Not surprisingly, the book generated intense debates even among intellectuals close to Flores Galindo's own political and academic circles. Much of the criticism targeted his treatment of the most recent periods in Peruvian history. Anthropologist Carlos Iván Degregori, for instance, contended that the argument lost power as it moved into the 20th century. According to Degregori, Flores Galindo found few examples of the Andean utopia in recent decades, specifically after the weakening of the peasant movement in the 1960s. Degregori faulted his characterization of tradition and modernity as polar opposites and his failure to understand how vast societal changes since the 1960s, with the spread of technology, modern media, and markets, affected or weakened "the search for an Inca."[37] In contrast, anthropologist Henrique Urbano questioned his understanding of the early colonial period. Ever critical, Urbano censured Flores Galindo for overlooking the European roots of Andean messianism, which led to a misunderstanding of key figures such as Guaman Poma and Garcilaso de la Vega, and for an overly capacious definition of utopia. On this latter point, Urbano argued that if any idealization of the past is utopianism, then virtually every author in early modern Europe created utopias.[38] Manrique questioned Flores Galindo's evidence for the "pan-Andean" nature of the Andean utopia and argued for a more geographically restricted understanding. In addition, Manrique found that after the Tupac Amaru rebellion, which he describes as the "apotheosis" of the Andean utopia, its traces are more difficult to document.[39]

The political undertones of the book also generated heated discussions. Flores Galindo vehemently denied promoting the Andean utopia

[36] Gonzalo Portocarrero, "La hazaña como deber: perfil de Alberto Flores Galindo," August 7, 2005 (http://gonzaloportocarrero.blogsome.com/2005/08/27/la-hazana-como-deber-perfil-de-alberto-flores-galindo/).

[37] Carlos Iván Degregori, "Otro mundo es posible," *Libros & Artes* (Lima) 11 (2005), 11–13.

[38] Henrique Urbano, "Representaciones colectivas y arqueología mental en los Andes," *Allpanchis* (Cuzco) 17, 20 (1982), 33–83, esp. 48–52. See also his review in *Revista Andina* 4, 1 (1986), 282–4.

[39] Manrique, "Historia y utopia en los Andes," 205, 207. In a commentary written in 1988, Flores Galindo actually concurred with these observations. See "La utopía andina: esperanza y proyecto," in his *Tiempo de plagas* (Lima: El Caballo Rojo Ediciones, 1988), 248–54.

for socialist or neo-indigenista projects.[40] He noted its limitations as a foundation for transformative alternatives and underlined the authoritarian impulses behind some of its variants. Although he clearly sympathized with some of the people who embraced the Andean utopia, he recognized that it could not sustain an alternative project for contemporary Peru: "It should be clear, therefore, that we are not advocating the Andean utopia. History should liberate us from the past, not seal us off – as Aníbal Quijano argued – within 'longue durée' prisons of ideas."[41] Thus, despite the title, *In Search of an Inca* pushed social scientists, intellectuals, and readers to abandon the pursuit of a pristine Inca past, its remnants in the present, or a project for the future inspired by its traces. Instead, they should explore the creative appropriation, re-creation, and synthesis of the multiple cultural influences that make up Andean societies. It was time to stop searching for an Inca, Flores Galindo asserted, and to embrace instead "modern socialism," the only way to channel passions and dreams toward the construction of a better future.[42]

Indeed, Flores Galindo never retreated from his socialist convictions. At a time when the left was in crisis and many leftist intellectuals were abandoning socialism, he remained stubbornly loyal to the ideals that inspired him and his generation two decades before. "I continue to believe that the ideals that gave rise to socialism – justice, freedom, humanity – are still alive," he stated in his final intellectual manifesto. But socialism, he warned, had a future only "if we are capable of rethinking it and imagining it with new contents." For him, socialism should not be confined to just one path, one already traced; echoing Mariátegui, he saw socialism as "a challenge to creativity" ("un desafío para la creatividad"). In addition – and here the influence of thinkers such as Thompson is clear – socialism meant forging "a new morality and new values." He questioned intellectuals and militants who had lost their capacity to "feel the rage" ("sentir la indignación") when confronted with the injustices of capitalism or the violence of authoritarian

[40] See, among others, Mario Vargas Llosa, "Una crítica marxista de la utopía andina," in *José María Arguedas y las ficciones del indigenismo* (Mexico City: Fondo de Cultura Económica, 1996), 289–95.

[41] See page 248.

[42] His views are clearly stated in the interview "Redescubriendo lo andino," in Carlos Arroyo editor, *Encuentros. Historia y movimientos sociales en el Perú* (Lima: MemoriAngosta, 1989), 139–44; see also his prologue, "El rescate de la tradición," 9–21.

solutions such as Shining Path.[43] Many pages of *In Search of an Inca*, especially in the later chapters, can be read as an enraged indictment of the fallacies of Peruvian democracy, the various forms of social and racial discrimination inflicted upon the most vulnerable sectors of Peruvian society, and the egregious violations of human rights committed in the name of counterterrorism efforts.

Was Flores Galindo a utopian thinker? No doubt. He founded his entire intellectual project on the pursuit of a utopia – not the Andean utopia but a socialist one. That was his lifelong project. As anthropologist Nancy Postero has written, "If we think of utopia as a consciously constructed political vision for the future, rather than a fruitless return to a fictitious past, then perhaps utopias are just what are needed in the Andes."[44] Flores Galindo would have agreed.

Flores Galindo's work has proven fertile and inspirational in different fields – history, literary and cultural studies, anthropology – even if authors do not always agree with his premises. The notion of Andean utopia has served as a framework to understand different historical moments, literary trends, and contemporary political developments in Andean societies.[45] Twenty-five years after its first edition, *In Search of an Inca* continues to awe the reader with its brilliance, scope, and depth, as well as its magisterial combination of historical analysis and political commentary. It will continue to inspire students of the Andes for decades to come. We are certain this translation will help attract wide attention among English-speaking readers.

[43] The quotes are taken from his farewell letter, "Reencontremos la dimensión utópica," reproduced in Flores Galindo, *Obras Completas*, vol. 6, 381–90.

[44] Nancy Postero, "Andean Utopias in Evo Morales's Bolivia," *Latin American and Caribbean Ethnic Studies* 2 (April 1, 2007), 1–28, quote from 21.

[45] Wilfredo Kapsoli, *Ayllus del Sol. Anarquismo y utopía andina* (Lima: Tarea, 1984); Miguel Angel Huamán, *Poesía y utopía andina* (Lima: Desco, 1988); Rodrigo Montoya, *De la utopía andina al socialismo mágico: antropología, historia y política en el Perú* (Lima: Instituto Nacional de Cultura, 2005); Carlos García-Bedoya, "Garcilaso y la utopía andina" (unpublished manuscript); Miguel Giusti, "¿Utopía del mercado o utopía andina? Sobre la filosofía y la comprensión de la realidad nacional," *Areté* (Lima) 1, 1 (1989), 147–63; Postero, "Andean Utopias."

In Search of an Inca

Introduction

Historian Jorge Basadre used to say that the greatest legacy of twentieth-century Peruvian intellectuals was the growing consciousness about Indians. The assertion is irrefutable. Indians have inspired novelists and poets and motivated vibrant essays, political diatribes, and in-depth research about the past. But this discovery of the obvious, of those who have been the majority in our history, was initially subversive in a racist country that attempted to condemn its peasants to silence. Those who did not share this contested idea had two options: combat it, or attempt to assimilate it. Hard-line Hispanicists, oligarchic and ultramontane intellectuals associated with the Seville historiographical school – products of Francisco Franco's authoritarianism of the 1940s and 1950s – took the first approach. The second option interested a later, more cosmopolitan intelligentsia, one influenced by North American anthropology that sought an alternative to the threatening spread of Marxism. These *indigenistas*, some of whom feared that Indians could invade Lima, converted them into "Andeans": people on the margins of history, static, inward looking, necessarily sheltered from modernity, immobile and passive, singular and abstract. A logical spin-off was the proposed creation of a great museum in which Andean culture would end up as objects, isolated and immunized, inside a showcase.

Not everyone who has used the term *Andean* (*andino*) accepted these concepts. We should not discard it. It allows us, for example, to cast off the racist connotations implied by the term *Indian* (*indio*). It conjures the image of a civilization and includes not just peasants but urban residents and mestizos as well. It encompasses the coast and the Andes, transcends contemporary national boundaries, and underscores connections among Peruvian, Bolivian, and Ecuadorian history. What is the

Andean? Above all it was an ancient culture that should be thought of in terms similar to those used for Greece, Egypt, or China. This requires a new conceptualization that discards all mythification. History offers one path: it is a search for links between ideas, myths, dreams, and objects and the people who produce and consume them, who live them and are animated by them. We should abandon the placid terrain of free-floating ideas and find struggles and conflicts, people and social classes, and problems of power and violence in society. Andean people have not spent their history closed up in an impossible museum.

Indians and peasants are not the only people in this book. The Andean utopia also inspired Creoles and mestizos such as Gabriel Aguilar or José María Arguedas, a writer who lived the problem of identity even more intensely. Neither Indian nor Spanish, these middle sectors continue to see a reflection of themselves in the supposed national face of Peru. From diverse circumstances, Garcilaso de la Vega, Tupac Amaru II, and Juan Santos Atahualpa elaborated different versions of the Andean utopia.[1] We therefore must speak of Andean utopias, just as we must speak of Andean peoples. The plural allows us to abandon abstractions and more effectively approach historical reality. But we should view this reality not only from the outside but from life experiences and subjectivities. For this reason, the characters' dreams occupy a central place in this book.

We must avoid a misunderstanding: Aguilar, Arguedas, and myriad others interest us not as so-called authentic interpreters of the Indian but rather for what they were, thus avoiding the false problem of their representativeness. We cannot write the history of a collective idea such as the Andean utopia, as I understand it, without individuals and their biographies.

[1] There are two historical characters in this book who bear the name Tupac Amaru. The first one, always referred to as Tupac Amaru I, led the resistance against the Spaniards in Vilcabamba and was executed in 1572. The second one, referred to as Tupac Amaru II or simply Tupac Amaru, led the anti-colonial rebellion in Cuzco in 1780. His name was José Gabriel Condorcanqui, although he increasingly added Tupac Amaru from whom he claimed descent. [Editors' Note]

CHAPTER 1

Europe and the Land of the Incas

THE ANDEAN UTOPIA

To Inés and Gerardo

An asymmetric relationship between the Andes and Europe began in the sixteenth century. It can be summarized in the meeting of two curves on a graph: that of the plummeting indigenous population and that of the increasing importation of livestock, which occupied the space left by people. Violence and coercion dominated. But as the historian Ruggiero Romano reminded us, these exchanges were particularly complex: the ships that arrived with sugarcane, grapevines, oxen, plows, and Mediterranean and African people also transported ideas and conceptions of the world that some condemned as heresy in Europe. Alongside the breakdown of their worldviews, Andean people attempted to understand the cataclysm of the colonial conquest, to comprehend the Spanish conquerors and, above all, themselves. Identity and utopia were two dimensions of the same problem.

The Utopia Today

The Andes were the site of an ancient civilization. Between 8000 and 6000 B.C., the inhabitants of the high plains and coastal valleys began the slow process of plant domestication that opened the door to high culture. The first pan-Andean unification effort did not take place until the first millennium B.C., from a sanctuary deep in the heart of the central Andes, Chavín de Huantar. This process, marked by radical independence, was only interrupted by the European invasion. Without any cultural exchange with Central America or other areas, Andean people developed key crops such as potatoes, corn, and coca and camelid livestock (llamas and alpacas) and discovered ceramics, weaving, stonework, agricultural terraces, and irrigation canals.[1]

Despite their isolation, they did not build a homogenous and cohesive world. Throughout their autonomous history, regional kingdoms and dominions predominated, whereas empires are rather recent. A state did not exercise control over the entire cultural area until the arrival of the Incas, who expanded in rapid yet fragile fashion from Cuzco around the fourteenth century. With the coming of the Spanish and the fall of the Inca state, diverse ethnic groups such as the Huancas, Chocorvos, Lupacas, and Chancas reappeared with different languages and customs and often with deep rivalries resulting from a long history of conflicts.

By reducing all Andean people to the common condition of Indian or colonized, the European invasion unintentionally created a cohesive native society, even as the Spanish administration sought to maintain old conflicts and introduce new ones, such as that between *comuneros* (people who lived in Indian towns) and *colonos* (servants assigned to haciendas). Despite the strict legal boundaries between Indians and Spaniards – who were supposed to form separate and autonomous republics – the relationship between victors and vanquished produced an ambivalent offspring: mestizos, often scorned by both parents. Creoles or Spaniards born in the Americas, multiple ethnic groups of the jungle, and African and Asian slaves and forced labor made this highly heterogeneous society even more diverse. This is one of the most suggestive aspects of contemporary Peru, a country of "all the bloods" in the words of José María Arguedas. These traditions, however, have never cohered and often have not coexisted. Conflicts and rivalries produced a subterranean but effective racism that provoked disdain, suspicion, and aggression among the lower classes, revealed for instance in daily interactions between blacks and Indians. Here, colonial domination found a solid base.[2] The protagonists' social conscience also expressed this fragmentation. For example, despite a common past, peasants today

[1] The reference comes from an unpublished text by John Murra, cited in Luis Lumbreras, *Arqueología de la América andina* (Lima: Milla Batres, 1981), 33: "Andean civilization has developed independently of other civilization centers. This is greatly relevant for the social sciences because there are very few such cases in history."

[2] In a previous book, *Aristocracia y plebe*, I examined these conflicts in Lima, a city that had the discouraging image of a society without alternatives. Alberto Flores Galindo, *Aristocracia y plebe. Lima, 1760–1830. Estructura de clases y sociedad colonial* (Lima: Mosca Azul, 1984).

do not define themselves as Andeans or Indians but instead rely on the name of their birthplace, such as a town or ravine, as Rodrigo Montoya observed in Ayacucho and César Fonseca in Huánuco. Consciousness is local. In the central Andes, anthropologist Henri Favre found three ethnic groups (Asto, Chunku, and Laraw) who lived next to each other but did not communicate because of unintelligible variants of Quechua and Kawki.[3] The idea of an unchanging, harmonious, and homogenous Andean person thus reflects an invented or desired history, wishful thinking, not the reality of a fragmented world.

The Andean utopia was the project – or, better yet, projects – that confronted this reality, an attempt to reverse dependency and fragmentation, to search for an alternative path in the encounter between memory and the imaginary: the rebuilding of Inca society and the return of the Inca ruler. It was an effort to find in the reconstruction of the past a solution to their identity problems. That is why in Peru, to the surprise of a Swedish researcher, "it has been considered useful to employ the Incas not only in ideological discussions but also in contemporary political debates."[4] References to the Incas are common in speeches. No one is surprised when people offer ancient technology or presumed moral principles as answers to contemporary problems. There is a predisposition to think in terms of *la longue durée*. The past weighs on the present, and neither the right nor the left is free of its grip. The conservative Acción Popular party based its doctrine on an imaginary Inca philosophy. Parties on the left almost invariably begin with an energetic debate over what pre-Hispanic societies were and how to define them in Marxist terms. Everyone feels obligated to begin there. A different rhythm seems to operate in the Andes, one that stresses continuities. Although it is evident that the Inca Empire collapsed upon its first contact with the west, the same is not true of culture.

The *indigenista* historian Luis E. Valcárcel contended that Andean civilization "transformed a country ill-suited for agriculture into an agricultural country, a tremendous enterprise that persisted through Spanish rule up until today. That is why the study of Ancient Peru is so relevant today and why what we are studying are things that still exist and

3 Henri Favre, "Introducción," in Danièle Lavallée and Michèle Julien, *Asto: curacazgo prehispánico en los Andes Centrales* (Lima: Instituto de Estudios Peruanos, 1983), 13 ff.

4 Ake Wedin, *El concepto de lo incaico y las fuentes* (Upsala: Scandinavian University Books, 1996), 21.

which we learn through ethnological studies. There is a rigorous link between ancient and contemporary Peru."[5] No European could describe Greece or Rome in the same terms. Historian Friedrich Katz pointed out a noteworthy difference between the Aztecs and the Incas: in Mexico there is no equivalent historical memory to that of the Andes. There is no Aztec Utopia.[6] In Mexico, the Virgin of Guadalupe has the place held in Peru by the imperial past and ancient monarchs. Perhaps this is because Mexico is more integrated than Peru, the percentage of mestizos is higher, and peasants have directly intervened in the national project, first during the Wars of Independence and then in the 1910 Mexican Revolution. In contrast, although revolts and rebellions were common in the Peruvian Andes, peasants never entered the capital or took over the Governmental Palace. Except for the Tupac Amaru project (1780) and Juan Santos Atahualpa's adventure in the jungle (1742), no guerrilla movement emerged in Peru to rival those of Villa and Zapata. Subjected to domination, Andean peoples used memory as a mechanism to preserve (or build) their identity. They had to be more than peasants. They were also Indians with their own rituals and customs.

Is this pure rhetoric? Are these ideological constructions, in the most negative understanding of the term, or intellectual mystification along the lines of Valcárcel? The Incas have an important place in popular culture. Despite what some textbook authors write, teachers and students in Peru are convinced that the Inca Empire was an egalitarian society with no hunger or injustice, and thus a paradigm for today's world. This explains the popularity of Louis Baudin's *A Socialist Empire: The Incas of Peru*, published in French in 1928. The title was essential to its reception. Although Baudin was a conservative lawyer who wrote the book to criticize socialism as an oppressive regime, Peruvians who spoke of Inca socialism obviously did so from a different perspective.

A sociological study of the teaching of history in Lima found that most interviewees had a clearly positive view of the Inca Empire. The students were from prosperous sectors (children of businessmen and

[5] Luis Valcárcel, *Etnohistoria del Perú Antiguo* (Lima: Universidad Nacional Mayor de San Marcos, 1964), 17. *Indigenismo* refers to an artistic and political movement that aimed at defending Indians' rights and promoting the defense of their culture. *Indigenistas* were almost always not indigenous [Editors' note].

[6] Friedrich Katz, *The Ancient American Civilizations* (London: Weidenfeld and Nicholson, 1969), 332.

Table 1.1. *Perceptions of the Inca Empire among Lima Students (1985)*

Characteristics	Answers	Percentage of Surveyed Students	Percentage of Responses
Just	272	55.96	26.00
Happy	151	36.06	14.43
Tyrannical	155	31.89	14.81
Injust	187	38.47	17.87
Harmonious	283	58.23	27.05

Source: Survey conducted by the research team on "Teaching and Representation of Peruvian History," directed by Gonzalo Portocarrero, Universidad Católica, Lima.

well-paid professionals) as well as poorer groups (the marginal and unemployed). The nine schools studied were located in the urban core as well as in shantytowns and other poorer areas of the capital. Students could select one or more of five possible characterizations of the Inca Empire. Table 1.1 indicates the total number for each term, the percentages of students who selected it, and the percentage of the total.

The two most selected options were "just" and "harmonious." The Inca Empire is a sort of inverted image of Peruvian reality: it appears to be the opposite of the dramatic injustice and inequalities of Peru today. The three options that could be deemed positive add up to 68 percent, the vast majority. It is likely that the percentage would be even higher in provincial and rural schools. The survey allowed students to make an ethical assessment from the present, which is not such an unusual invitation in Peru. On the contrary, it is a common attitude among students and professors who regard the past as something quite close.

Different historical memories exist in Peru. Professionals – university graduates interested in erudite research – write one type. There is also a sort of informal history practiced by self-taught provincial authors who write the history of their town or place of origin. Finally, there is oral remembrance, in which memory takes on mythical dimensions. Between 1953 and 1972, researchers found fifteen versions of the Inkarri myth in Andean towns. According to this myth, the Conquest figuratively chopped off the Inca's head and separated it from his body. When head and body are reunited, the period of disorder, confusion, and darkness that Europeans initiated will end, and Andean people, *runas*, will recover their history. Informants between the ages of twenty-five and eighty – the majority elderly – from Ayacucho (8), Puno (3), Cuzco (2), Arequipa (1), and Ancash (1) told the story in the Quechua language.[7] Similar accounts circulated among the Shipibo and Ashani in the Amazon (stories about the beheaded Inca or the three Incas) and among fishermen in coastal Chimbote (visions of the Inca).

The Inkarri myth appears in other manifestations of Andean popular culture: Inca dances such as those performed in the high plateau; representations of Atahualpa's capture or death in the towns of Pomabamba, Bolognesi, Cajatambo, Chancay, and Daniel Carrión provinces in the central sierra; the dance of the Pallas (the Inca's women) and the Captain (Pizarro) in Huánuco, Dos de Mayo, Huamalíes, and Cajatambo; ritual battles between the defenders of the Inca and those who personify Pizarro and his forces, such as those in the Morochucos area (Ayacucho); and bullfights called Turupukllay, which take place mainly in highland communities in Apurímac and Cuzco, in which the bull enters the ring with a condor tied to its back, symbolizing the encounter between the world of above and the world below, between the west and the Andes.[8] These locations provide an idea of the geographical diffusion of contemporary Andean culture. Dances, bullfights, and performances form part of popular festivals celebrated over several days in honor of a patron saint or the town's anniversary, often during July and August, the dry winter in the Andes. Mapping these popular expressions indicates that they take place in the most backward parts of the country, areas where most of the indigenous population and the highest number of peasant communities persist. There is a clear correlation between Andean culture and poverty.

An idea similar to the Inkarri myth appeared to inspire a Quechua story entitled "The Pongo's Dream," translated and published by José María Arguedas. An hacienda peon, humiliated by the owner, imagines himself covered in excrement. The story ends with the landowner licking the peon. It is the old and universal peasant dream in which reality is

7 Rodolfo Masías and Flavio Vera, "El mito del Inkarri como manifestación de la utopía andina," unpublished ms. Other versions of the Inkarri myth have been found since 1972. For some examples, see *Anthropológica* (Lima) II, 2 (1984), particularly the articles by Juan Ossio, Alejandro Vivanco, and Eduardo Fernández.

8 Carlos Mendívil, *Los Morochucos y Ayacucho tradicional* (Lima: Editorial Litográfica La Confianza, 1968). See also Fanni Muñoz, "Cultura popular andina: el Turupukllay," BA thesis, Pontificia Universidad Católica del Perú, 1984. Professor Víctor Domínguez Condeso of the Universidad Hermilio Valdizán in Huánuco furnished information.

inverted, but in the Andes, where class conflicts are mixed with ethnic and cultural clashes, it appears to be infused with intense violence.[9]

The myth of Inkarri travels from popular culture to the city and academic circles, where anthropologists disseminate it. After 1968, when a nationalist military government erupted on the political scene, Inkarri became the name of a festival and appeared in handicrafts, in posters, and on book covers. For contestatory painter Armando Williams, Inkarri was a funereal mummy about to be untied; in the eyes of artist Juan Javier Salazar, it was a microbus (a peculiar form of transportation in Lima) descending from the Andes within the incendiary frame of a box of matches.[10] Intellectuals read the myth as the portent of a violent revolution, like the sound of the underground river that emerged at the end of José María Arguedas's novel *All the Bloods* (1964). The only way to compensate for the terrible injustice of the conquest was to transfer Indians' fears to whites. According to Arguedas, "Social classes also have a particularly deep cultural foundation in Andean Peru. When they fight – and they do it barbarously – it is not just economic interests that drive the struggle; other deep and violent spiritual forces inflame the different sides, agitating them with implacable force, with incessant and unavoidable violence."[11] Is this a description of Andean reality or the sentiments of a mestizo such as Arguedas? In most of his texts about peasant communities and popular art, Arguedas seems to be inclined to think about progress, modernization, and slow change achieved harmoniously: the mestizos of the Mantaro Valley became the prototype of the future. But in his fiction, where the narrator allows himself to unleash his imagination, mestizos seem to fade away, leaving only Indians and whites, with violence becoming the only available language. No change other than a true social cataclysm is possible. In this last case it is a matter of transforming quotidian and inner hatred or fury into a gigantic fire, a transforming force. Arguedas, thus, presents two images of Peru.[12] This ambivalence also appeared in Arguedas's political

[9] José María Arguedas, "The Pongo's Dream," in Orin Starn et al., eds., *The Peru Reader* (Durham: Duke University Press, 2005), 2nd edition, 273–8 [Editors' note].

[10] Gustavo Buntinx, "Mirar desde el otro lado. El mito de Inkarri, de la tradición oral a la plástica erudita," unpublished ms., Pontificia Universidad Católica del Perú, Graduate School in Social Sciences.

[11] José María Arguedas, "La novela y el problema de la expresión literaria en el Perú," in *Yawar Fiesta* (Lima: Editorial Horizonte, 1980), 9 [Editors' Note].

[12] See Chapter 9, "The Boiling Point."

sympathies: sometimes he supported reformist options, but at other times he sided with the more radical tendencies of the new left.

The history of the Andean utopia is a conflictive narrative, similar to Arguedas's soul. Complex and diverse like the society that has created it, the Andean utopia emerges at the intersection of popular and elite cultures, writing and oral stories, hopes and fears. It is a question of tracing not only the lineage of an idea, but above all the passions and practices that have accompanied it. In the Andes, utopia alternates between intense periods when mass movements converge, followed by moments of marginalization and oblivion. It is not a linear history; on the contrary, it is several histories. The image of the Inca and Tahuantinsuyo depend on the groups or classes that create it. Thus, for a large landowner such as Lizares Quiñones it was a way to conceal local power groups under the banner of Inca federalism (1919), whereas in the work of Valcárcel its content favored peasants.

Andean Utopia

What is utopia in the Andes? Let's clear up one misunderstanding. In common language "utopia" and "impossible" are synonyms, ideas that can never be achieved, distant from everyday life. The less realistic they are, the more closely they fit the definition. The term "utopia" is a neologism but, unlike many others, it has a birth certificate. It was born in 1516, when Thomas More published *Utopia*. Another misunderstanding is to link More's book with the Incas. In 1516 Pizarro had not even set foot on the Peruvian coast. Moreover, when writing his book, More did not refer to an existing society but instead to one that had no grounding in time or space. His book does not refer to a happy land but to a city that is outside history, the product of an intellectual construction. For some, his notion of a country without a location constituted a useful model to understand their own society through contrast; for others, it was an instrument of social criticism that signaled the errors and deficiencies of their time.

Utopia inaugurated a literary genre. After More came Tomasso Campanella, Francis Bacon, and other authors who wrote texts with three fundamental features: an imaginary storyline with no reference to a concrete place, a global and totalizing depiction of society, and the development of ideas or proposals through daily life. A city, an island, or a country was depicted through a meticulous and fictitious description of customs, streets, schedules, and day-to-day living. As

Bronislaw Baczko stated, "Utopia sought to place reason in the imaginary."[13] Over time it developed into a contestatory genre. Inconformity with the present led intellectuals to construct a society outside history: *Eu-topos* – without place. Some utopian writers defined it as "a way of dreaming while awake."[14] It represented the imagination, but controlled and guided by critical reasoning.

Utopia's popularity did not derive only from More and his followers. This style of confronting reality existed earlier "in practice." European peasant societies persistently and eagerly envisioned a place where social differences did not exist and everyone was equal. People in England and France evoked the time of Adam and Eve, when supposedly everyone worked and there were no lords. In Poland and other countries east of the Elba River, this world was not so far off in time but coexisted with the present. It was located on the other side of the mountains, beyond the horizon. In other places such as Renaissance Italy as described by Carlo Ginzburg, never-never land was an imaginary place where rivers flowed with milk, crisp bread grew on trees, absolute freedom reigned, and everyone drank, loved, and enjoyed life without limits, breaking the barriers that lord and Church sought to impose: the kingdom of naked, happy men and women, the country of Cocagne.[15] These dreams inserted themselves into towns' everyday life and enjoyed a privileged time for their insertion: carnival, when rank was inverted, the lower orders took over public plazas, and all hierarchies provoked laughter and ridicule. In other words, everything was permitted. Carnival, a central element to popular culture, avoided the risk of direct confrontations but kept alive, in its festivities and rituals, practical utopias.[16]

Baczko argued that utopias have not had a linear, uninterrupted history. There are times, "hot periods," when the genre spreads. The discovery of the Americas was one. Utopia crossed paths with a related intellectual current: millenarianism. This term also had a precise date of birth: the year 1000, when many believed that the end of the world was at hand. The idea was linked to the Christian notion that history would come to an end: the final judgment, resurrection, the condemnation of

[13] Bronislaw Baczko, *Lumiéres de l'utopie* (Paris: Payot, 1978), 32.

[14] Jean Servier, *La utopía* (Mexico City: Fondo de Cultura Económica, 1982), 18.

[15] Carlo Ginzburg, *The Cheese and the Worms: the Cosmos of a Sixteenth-Century Miller* (New York: Penguin, 1982).

[16] Mikhail Bakhtin, *Rabelais and His World* (Bloomington: Indiana University Press, 1984).

some and the salvation of others, to culminate in humanity's encounter with God. A Calabrian monk, Joachim of Fiore (1145–1202), turned the apocalyptic themes that formed part of the daily fears and hopes of medieval times into a "prophetic system," even putting it into writing. He divided history into three parts: the age of the Father, which had passed and corresponded to the Old Testament; the present or the age of the Son; and the future, the age of the Holy Spirit. In reality, the last period had already begun but required the defeat of the Anti-Christ for its culmination. Despite being condemned as heresy (or perhaps because of it), his system became "the most influential one known to Europe until the appearance of Marxism."[17] Elsewhere, these ideas were well received among some in the Franciscan order.

For the wretched, sick, crippled, poor, and destitute, those who had nothing, millenarianism reminded them that heaven would be theirs. Another age awaited them when all their suffering would be compensated with interest because they would be the chosen ones; no rich person would be invited to the celestial banquet. According to Church doctrine, millenarianism introduced heretical elements: salvation was an earthly matter; it occurred right here, and it even had a precise year. The end of time was not distant but, instead, close; one possible signal was humanity's suffering. The apocalypse required divine intervention in history, a miracle that could be incarnated in a person or envoy such as the angels who would sound the final trumpet; a new prophet able to lead the people to the promised land; or a messiah who needed mankind's help to triumph over the forces of evil.[18]

Some saw the effort to hasten the end of time and the struggle against injustice and poverty as one and the same. In their eyes, there was no justification for the existence of rich people; they were agents of evil. Revolutionary millenarianism sustained peasant revolts and rebellions, the most important of which was that of Thomas Münzer in 1525, an episode of the peasant wars in Germany where the violent dream of an egalitarian peasant society emerged and sought to level society from below. Another current, "elitist apocalypsism," flourished within intellectual circles and opted for nonviolent means such as extreme

[17] Norman Cohn, *The Pursuit of the Millennium: Revolutionary Millenarians and Mystical Anarchists of the Middle Ages* (Oxford: Oxford University Press, 1970), 108.

[18] On millenarianism, see Jean Delumeau, *La peur en Occident* (Paris: Fayard, 1978), 262 ff; Josep Fontana, *Historia* (Barcelona: Editorial Crítica, 1982), 37, 274.

piety, self-mortification, and flagellation to approach the holy. Central Europe was the base of the most radical currents of millenarianism. Messianic spiritualism prospered in the Iberian Peninsula at a time when social conflicts (the expulsion of Moriscos and Jews and subsequently the 1520–22 Revolt of the Comuneros) coincided with the discovery and conquest of America. Cardinal Cisneros, the reformer of the regular clergy in Ferdinand and Isabel's Spain, tolerated "apocalyptic mysticism." The idea spread that monks and nuns should imitate Christ's poverty. Shoeless men dressed in rags had founded the Church, so it was necessary to return to poverty. The poor were exalted not only in prayer or as a pretext for charity (and thus to earn indulgences) but as Christian models. In a book entitled *Agonía del tránsito de la muerte* (1537), Alejo Venegas appropriated a metaphor from Saint Paul to compare Christianity with a body whose head was Christ.[19] If the faithful distanced themselves from spirituality – and thus from the poor – the head separated from the body. This was a familiar theme in Spain, an area "dense in prophecies." It is not difficult to find these images in Inkarri tales, but let's not get ahead of the story.

New World/End of the World: Marcel Bataillon noted the correspondence between these two terms many years ago.[20] A new land was being discovered where the duty of any Christian, vital in order to reach the end of history, could be achieved: evangelization. Everyone should know the divine message and either follow or reject it. Outside of Christianity, men were Jews, Muslims, or Gentiles. The inhabitants of America were the latter. Taking the message to Indians meant the end of a cycle. That is why Franciscan missionary Gerónimo de Mendieta considered the Spanish monarchs the greatest princes of the New Testament: they would convert all humanity and were the messiahs of the Final Judgment. In another version, Indians were one of Israel's lost ten tribes, who, according to the prophecy, would reappear precisely on the day of the Final Judgment.

America was not only the stimulus of millenarian hopes but also the site of their realization. Christopher Columbus himself believed in earthly Paradise and – with an unquestioned certitude in the face of

[19] Américo Castro, *Aspectos del vivir hispánico* (Santiago de Chile: Cruz del Sur, 1944), 40–1.

[20] Marcel Bataillon, *Études sur le Portugal au temps de l'humanisme* (Coimbra: Por ordem da Universidade, 1970).

concrete experiences – confirmed the sighting of golden rivers, cyclops, men with tails, mermaids, and Amazons in the new lands.[21] Here is the distant origin of the mermaids who seem so dissonant in the mural paintings of Andean colonial churches. Introduced in Spain in 1473, printing presses helped popularize chivalric novels such as *Tirant lo Blanch, El caballero Cifar, Amadís, Palmerín*, and *Sergas de Esplandián*. These men were ready for action, models of bravery and nobility, able to confront the most difficult challenges, demonstrating that to be young was to "have faith in the impossible."[22] The conquistadors brought these books in their bags and relied on them to interpret the American landscape. When the printing press reached Lima (1584), nine of these novels, along with books of piety and religious texts, were among the first published.

New ideas, many of them persecuted in Europe, also arrived and found refuge and the unexpected opportunity for fulfillment in the new continent. In the words of historian Antonio Domínguez Ortiz, "America was an escape, the refuge for those in Spain who for different motives were not well looked upon."[23] Franciscans who embarked for Mexico, Quito, Chile, and, of course, Peru brought millenarianism to America. In the sixteenth century, they constituted the most numerous order in the new lands, with 2,782 friars. Next were the Dominicans with 1,579, and third were the Jesuits with only 133. They disembarked in a territory where the question of conquest was under debate. Did Spain have the right to take possession of these lands? Juan Ginés de Sepúlveda and Francisco López de Gómara defended the Spanish civilizing mission; Francisco de Vitoria preferred evangelization without war; and the Dominican Bartolomé de Las Casas developed the harshest critique of the exploitation of Indians. To get close to the Indians was to get close to the poor.

A distant disciple of Las Casas, the Dominican Francisco de la Cruz, foretold in the Peruvian capital the destruction of Spain and the fulfillment of the millennium in the Indies. He wanted to transform the church from Lima, proposing polygamy for the faithful, perpetual *encomiendas* for creoles (people of European descent born in the

[21] Tzvetan Todorov, *The Conquest of America* (New York: Harper Colophon, 1985), 15–17.

[22] Irving Leonard, *Books of the Brave* (Berkeley: University of California Press, 1992), 27.

[23] Antonio Domínguez Ortiz, *Los judeoconversos en España y América* (Madrid: Istmo, 1978), 131.

Americas), and marriage for the clergy.[24] He put theory into practice: He had a lover with whom he had a child. The Inquisition tried him for this as well as his ideas and condemned him to burn at the stake in 1578. The Jesuit Luis López, who appeared in the same trial, considered Spanish rule temporary, until a Peruvian prince emerged.[25] The Franciscan Gonzalo Tenorio (1602–82) was less radical but noted that a dying Christ had turned his head toward the west, turning his back on Rome and Spain, and that the Virgin Mary had channeled the River of Grace in the direction of Peru. Indians were therefore destined to assume the same role as the people of Israel in the Old Testament.[26]

The comparison between America and the chosen people had another source, underground and hidden; the discovery coincided with the expulsion of the Jews from the Iberian Peninsula. After a stay in Portugal, some victims of this diaspora embarked for America, where they took new names and assumed new identities. At the beginning of the sixteenth century, Lima became home to an important group of Portuguese merchants with medium and large fortunes. One of them, Pedro León Portocarrero, wrote a chronicle that remained anonymous for centuries.[27] The merchants, who secretly observed the Sabbath and other religious practices that the Inquisition deemed Talmudic, endured the same fate as Francisco de la Cruz. In a sort of pogrom, the Inquisition imprisoned and tried seventeen of them in 1635 and eighty-one the following year.[28] By then the Portuguese or Jews resided not only in Lima but in provincial towns as well.

After 1518 the Spanish limited foreigners' access to "impede the entry of heretics." However, there were always clandestine entries and the possibility of buying a royal license by bribing Spanish officials.

[24] Encomiendas were groups of Indians given to Spanish conquistadors as rewards for their services to the crown [Editors' note].

[25] Mario Góngora, *Estudios de historia de las ideas y de historia social* (Valparaíso: Universidad Católica, 1980), 21.

[26] John Phelan, *The Millennial Kingdom of the Franciscans in the New World. A Study of the Writings of Gerónimo de Mendieta (1525–1604)* (Berkeley: University of California Press, 1956), 24–5, 100–1; Marcel Bataillon, "La herejía de fray Francisco de la Cruz y la reacción antilascasiana," *Estudios sobre Bartolomé de Las Casas* (Barcelona: Ediciones Península, 1976), 365–7.

[27] Guillermo Lohmann Villena, "Una incógnita despejada: la identidad del judio portugués autor de la 'Discrición General del Piru,'" *Revista de Indias*, 119–22 (1970), 315–82.

[28] Domínguez Ortiz, *Los judeoconversos*, 139–40.

Table 1.2. *Foreigners in Peru (1532–1560)*

Place of Origin	Number
Portugal	171
Mediterranean (Italy and islands)	240
Europe (North and Central)	59
England and France	7
Undetermined	39
Total	516

Source: James Lockhart, *Spanish Peru, 1532–1560. A Social History* (Madison: University of Wisconsin Press, 1968), 242.

In 1566 and 1599 authorities raided those in the Indies without such a license, but with little success. In the first thirty years of colonization, about 4,000 to 6,000 Europeans entered Peru; more than 500 were not Spaniards.

These foreigners frequently worked in a maritime trade, to the point that *sailor* was almost a synonym for *Italian* or *Greek*. On land, some such as Pedro de Candia became artillerymen, whereas others were merchants. The Portuguese community included Jews whose contacts in the Iberian Peninsula allowed them big profits for bringing slaves from Africa. Although Toribio Medina argued that the first Jews arrived only after 1580, *conversos* or *marranos*, "new Christians," were present from the time of Atahualpa's capture in 1532. The number of foreigners was probably much higher than the table indicates. Many pretended to be Spaniards, especially those who had reasons to be cautious. The identity of a captain named Gregorio Zapata was discovered only after he made a fortune in Potosi and returned to his homeland: he was Emir Cigala, a Turk.[29]

For Jews, millenarists, and all those rejected by the Old World, America seemed like a place to fulfill dreams. The conviction grew that "Europe creates the ideas; and America perfects them by materializing them."[30] It was ideal territory for practical utopias. When Pizarro's forces pushed across the Andes, some chroniclers believed they had found a land without hunger or poverty, where abundance reigned. They came from Europe, a continent subject to the scourge of periodic agrarian

[29] José Luis Martínez, *Pasajeros de Indias* (Madrid: Alianza Editorial, 1983); Juan José Vega, *Los conversos en el inicio del Perú moderno* (Lima: Editorial Todo el Perú, 1981).

[30] Phelan, *The Millennial Kingdom*, 73.

crises, where years of good crops alternated with lean years, propitious for the spread of diseases and increased mortality. These men, who had horses and gunpowder but had left a hungry continent with frequent food shortages, were amazed to see *tambos* (storage centers) and food conservation systems. More published *Utopia* sixteen years before the Spanish entered Cajamarca, but his readers – those curious enough to read a chronicle of the conquest – might easily have confused his place outside of time and space with the land of the Incas.

The Death of the Inca

Peru's conquistadors were not rich men armed with titles and confidence about their lineage. Although backed by great fortunes such as that of the merchant Espinoza, most of the men on horseback or on foot were peasants, artisans, and ordinary gentlemen (*hidalgos*, the lower ranks of the nobility). Others were those without a trade who came to the new territories to make a name through their own work, to become someone, to increase their worth.[31] Rigidly stratified Iberian society blocked social mobility, because birth determined the course of every biography. In the Indies, by contrast, one's efforts and experiences provided what parents did not bequeath. Reality surpassed all expectations: in Peru they managed to conquer a kingdom for themselves, so they envisioned their own fiefdoms.

The death of Inca Atahualpa was a central moment in the history of the Spanish conquest. Atahualpa was captured in November 1532, and the Spanish sentenced him to the garrote in July 1533. It was not a death to be easily forgotten, for the Inca was a king, no less than Suleyman the Magnificent or Charles V – a prince, a man of a higher estate supposedly superior to his executioners. Perhaps Spanish fear of Inca troops rescuing the monarch or the need for definitive victory explained their harsh sentence, but there was also the peculiar mix of disdain and resentment that conquistadors might feel toward a defeated king (the historian Pablo Macera has suggested this). But for this very reason, the decision was not easy. The conquistadors came from a hierarchical society. Perhaps because in Peru and in Europe regicide was an extreme and exceptional act, some Spaniards considered the Inca's death a dishonor for them and expressed their doubts. For Hernando Pizarro, Pedro Cataño, and

[31] José Durand, *La transformación social del conquistador* (Mexico City: Porrúa y Obregón, 1953).

others, killing Atahualpa "was the worst deed that the Spaniards have done in this entire empire of the Indies."[32]

Upon Atahualpa's death, Peru was left without a king, and Charles V was far away. As the years passed, more than 500 of the 4,000 or so Spaniards had encomiendas. They won land and Indians in battle and aspired to become "an all powerful military nobility."[33] The idea of autonomy formed the backdrop for battles between Spanish administrators such as the first viceroy, Núnez de Vela, or the Visitador La Gasca, and conquistadors such as Gonzalo Pizarro, Diego de Centeno, or Francisco de Carvajal.

Curiously, the first mention of the idea of the Inca in sixteenth-century documents referred to a Spaniard, not an Indian. In 1548, Gonzalo Pizarro entered Cuzco just as he was organizing his men to battle the crown in a full-scale rebellion. Indians of different neighborhoods and tribes allegedly acclaimed him, calling him Inca. Perhaps it was not spontaneous. His right-hand man, Carvajal, who had promised to place "the crown of this Empire" on Pizarro's head, might have incited them.[34] Pizarro would ascend to royalty – which he supposedly deserved – on effort and not on ancestral lineage. The king was not eternal, and a friar linked to rebel *encomenderos* preached that providence could designate a replacement. The group even raised a banner with a GP monogram (Gonzalo Pizarro) with a crown on top. Foreigners, including Portuguese, Italians, and Germans, were among the most enthusiastic about a new monarchy, and a contemporary historian believes that there could have been heretics among them. A rumor circulated that Gonzalo Pizarro planned to marry a princess of royal Inca descent, his niece Francisca Pizarro Yupanqui. It was not true but, even as a fabrication, someone had come up with the idea of an alliance between conquistadors and conquered, colonizers and colonized.[35]

The conquest broadened the victors' consciousness to unimaginable extremes and permitted them to conceive of the new kingdom. Everything seemed possible and permitted. In 1559, Lope de Aguirre took

[32] José Antonio del Busto, *La hueste perulera* (Lima: Pontificia Universidad Católica del Perú, 1981), 52.

[33] Efraín Trelles, *Lucas Martínez Vegazo: funcionamiento de una encomienda peruana inicial* (Lima: Pontificia Universidad Católica del Perú, 1983), 82.

[34] Guillermo Lohmann Villena, *Las ideas jurídico-políticas en la rebelión de Gonzalo Pizarro* (Valladolid: Casa-Museo de Colón, 1977), 82.

[35] Francisca Pizarro Yupanqui was the daughter of Inés Yupanqui, Atahualpa's sister, and Francisco Pizarro [Editors' Note].

these ideas to their final consequences. This conquistador who arrived late in Peru, a man without wealth or luck, beaten up physically according to the chroniclers, decided after a failed search for the land of cinnamon to challenge the king in the middle of the jungle. He proclaimed himself a traitor and announced in a letter to the king a permanent war against the Spanish monarchy. No rules governed him, a man without a king; he owned all lives. Aguirre unleashed a bloodbath in his delirious trajectory through the Amazon jungle to areas near the Atlantic in what is today Venezuela. Other Spaniards viewed this Basque, killed in 1561, as a "sort of apocalyptic being," the incarnation of the Antichrist, and a living sign of the Final Judgment.[36]

In the 1560s a rumor circulated in Peru that Charles V, influenced by Las Casas, was considering abandoning the Indies. Although appearing in texts written by Las Casas's enemies, the story spread – and was considered verisimilar – that Peru would remain under the orders of a native monarch overseen from Spain in something like a protectorate. Many historians sanctioned this as true; of course, it was not. How did it gain credibility? Marcel Bataillon used the anecdote to suggest a reflection:

> A difference between Mexico and Peru is evident. Who could imagine resuscitating the Aztec sovereigns' abolished authority to apply Las Casas's doctrine of a protectorate in New Spain [Mexico], imposing an indigenous sovereign over the supreme power of the King of Castile and León, "the emperor of many kings"? The case of Peru was different. The immediate predecessors of Francisco de Toledo [Viceroy of Peru from 1569 to 1581], following royal orders, had tried to peacefully coopt the "Inca" rebel of Vilcabamba.[37]

As we will see, the Inca monarchy took refuge in Vilcabamba and in some ways still existed in Peru. There was an additional difference with Mexico: Peru was the site of a war between encomenderos that questioned the monarchy and royal authorities.

[36] José Antonio del Busto, *Lope de Aguirre* (Lima: Editorial Universitaria, 1965), 154.

[37] Marcel Bataillon, *Estudios sobre Bartolomé de Las Casas* (Barcelona: Ediciones Península, 1976), 354–5.

Everything seemed up for discussion in the 1560s.[38] Las Casas counted on informants in the plateau near Lake Titicaca. His ideas were known in Peru, and even though encomenderos were his fiercest enemies, years later when conquistadors began to die, some aging conquistadors-encomenderos expressed regret and others requested the return of property to Indians. Guillermo Lohmann Villena called this "Las Casas's legacy."[39] Guilt assaulted the victors. Fearing punishment (hell or purgatory), many elderly conquistadors took stock of their lives and saw a negative balance sheet. The idea of giving back to the usurped emerged in their wills.

Wills are private documents, written by men who sense death approaching. Relatives know about them and notaries store them. But, besides private wills, rumors always existed in this story. The idea emerged within the republic of Spaniards (to use the jurist Matienzo's term) that domination by Pizarro's descendents was open to question.

Oral and Written Utopias

The conquest was a true cataclysm for the defeated. The brutal demographic decline of the indigenous population due to diseases and the new workload was the most visible indicator. The encounter with Europeans meant death. Despite past exaggeration, prudent calculations by demographer David N. Cook put Peru's 1530 population at about 9 million, which plummeted to an Indian population of 601,645 by 1620.[40] Population decline worried the Spanish because Indians were the richest resource of these new territories; without them, the Spanish could not extract Potosí minerals cheaply. The Spanish established their colonial system not on the fringes but in the very center of the new territories. The goal was not to create markets for European goods but to extract primary products, which, given the technology of the era, required a massive workforce. They established mines with cities and haciendas around them. Following the pattern of Castilian communities, they organized Indians into towns. There they could watch, control, and

38 Guillermo Lohmann Villena, *Gobierno del Perú* (Lima: Instituto Francés de Estudios Andinos, 1971).

39 "La estela lascasiana" in the original [Editors' note].

40 Noble David Cook, *Demographic Collapse: Indian Peru, 1502–1620* (Cambridge: Cambridge University Press, 1981), 114.

mobilize them for the *mita* labor draft and for religious services. The Indians became the dominated.

How could they understand this cataclysm? The period of disarray and shock does not appear to have lasted long. A clear choice emerged from the very beginning: accept or reject the conquest. The first option implied admitting that European victory prompted the decline of Andean Gods and the collapse of all their myths. The Christian God was more powerful and there was no alternative but to assimilate, accept the new lords' customs and rituals, dress like them, and learn Spanish and even Spanish legislation.[41] Indians who served as translators took this route. One of them in the Huamanga area was the future chronicler Guaman Poma de Ayala.[42]

According to the invaders' discourse, if a handful of adventurers could defeat the Inca and his army, it was only because they carried the cross. By the same token, if Indians were defeated, it was because they had sinned and needed to purge their faults. The Spanish introduced their notion of guilt to the Americas and used it to dominate the souls of the defeated. Demons and evil beings populated the European imagination of the period. Saint Michael's decapitation of the dragon accompanied the transformation of the apostle Saint James (Santiago) from "Moor Killer" into "Indian Killer." Both fought alongside Pizarro. As human beings, Indians were not exempt from original sin. Idolatrous practices, abhorrent customs, sexual practices, family structure, religious rituals, and presumed human sacrifices were all sinful. That explained why the Spanish had to defeat them irredeemably.[43]

Obviously, there are other explanations for Atahualpa's tragedy. We cannot overlook the impact (more psychological than real) of firearms and military differences: on one side the Incas, an army whose vast numbers were subject to a vertical and despotic line of command; on the other side the Spanish, whose specialized soldiers (artillery, infantry,

[41] Steve Stern, "El Taki Onqoy y la sociedad andina (Huamanga, siglo XVI)," *Allpanchis* (Cuzco), XVI, 19 (1992), 49–77.

[42] Felipe Guaman Poma de Ayala (ca. 1535 to ca. 1615) was the author of the famous *Nueva coronica y buen gobierno*, a beautifully illustrated 1,188-page letter to the king of Spain in which he criticized aspects of colonial government, proposed a series of reforms, and offered an interpretation of Andean history. A digital copy of the manuscript is available at http://www.kb.dk/permalink/2006/poma/info/en/frontpage.htm [Editors' note].

[43] Gonzalo Portocarrero, "Castigo sin culpa, culpa sin castigo," *Debates en Sociología* (Lima) 11 (1985), 53–103.

cavalry, trumpeter) exercised their own initiative within a carefully coordinated battle plan under different rules of warfare. For Atahualpa, whose subjects were not even permitted to look him directly in the face, it was inconceivable that people he deemed inferior assaulted and imprisoned him by surprise. Traps and treachery were part of the conquistadors' arsenal, but for the stunned Indians, the possibility of imprisoning an Inca was unimaginable. This is the origin of the trauma that continues to mark the memory of the first encounter between Europe and the Andes, between Pizarro and Atahualpa.[44]

However, Andean cosmovision permitted another understanding of the conquest. The concept of *pachacuti* existed in the pre-Hispanic Andean mental universe. Some traditional chroniclers and historians believed it was the name of a governor, equivalent to Cesar, Pericles, or the Babylonian King Nabucodonosor, but the characteristics attributed to him suggest another possible meaning. His disruption of the country and introduction of new habits, it is believed, made him a reformer or transformer of the world. Garcilaso de la Vega, Blas Valera, and Las Casas viewed him as an individual. For others, perhaps people closer to the indigenous world such as Guaman Poma, pachacuti was at once a telluric force, a cataclysm, a new epoch, and a punishment. Argentine researcher José Imbelloni, author of an indispensable book on this subject, argued that etymologically pachacuti meant "to transform the earth," the transition from one 500-year cycle to another. For Martín de Morúa, it meant "turning the soil" as well as "to take away and disinherit one's own worth."[45] These are not necessarily incompatible meanings. They alluded to the transition from one age to another and its result, the inversion of the world. Mochica (200 B.C.–700) ceramics with the shield and the truncheon attacking the warrior represented the world upside down.[46]

With evangelization and the passing of time, pachacuti developed features that combined the horrors of the Conquest with Biblical passages. Hunger and thirst, plagues, death, suffering and pain, and the fluctuation between years of drought and incessant rains increasingly characterized the post-Conquest period. The conquest was a pachacuti – the inversion of order – for many Andean people. The Incas imagined

[44] Nathan Wachtel, *La vision des vaincus* (Paris: Gallimard, 1971), 55–6.

[45] José Imbelloni, *Pachacuti IX* (Buenos Aires: Editorial Humanior, 1976), 84.

[46] Anne Marie Hocquenghem, "Moche: mito, rito y actualidad," *Allpanchis* (Cuzco) 23, XX (1984), 145.

a world above and a world below, heaven and earth, hananpacha and hurinpacha (*pacha* meaning universe). This cosmological order was duplicated on other levels. Cuzco, the empire's capital, was divided into two neighborhoods – upper and lower – and the division in halves was characteristic of every town. The empire, in turn, was comprised of four *suyos*. Within this duality, its parts were both opposite and necessary to each other, and to preserve both and maintain equilibrium was the necessary guarantee that the social order would work.[47] Complementary parts conserved equilibrium. Heaven required earth just as men required divinities.

The Spanish apparently could join one of these halves, but the relationship they created with Indians was asymmetrical and coercive. They sought to superimpose an exclusive deity that demanded dedication and sacrifice and did not follow reciprocity rules. Some Ayacucho peasants still harbor this image of Christ. Andean people could understand all this as the inauguration of night and disorder, the inversion of reality, the world upside down. But Andean cosmovision was not necessarily antagonistic to Christianity. Andean people did not imagine a world created from nothing; they thought that the universe had always existed. In contrast to Christianity, there was not one but several gods, who limited themselves to "clarifying, establishing, and defining" the shape, characteristics, and functions of the cosmos.[48] Andean religion was not dogmatic and intolerant, and the doors of the pantheon were not necessarily closed to Christ, the Virgin, and saints, allowing the convergence between pre-Hispanic divinities and Christian representations. For example, Christ on the crucifix assumed the obscure features of a subterranean deity such as Pachacamac, including the ability to make the ground shake.[49] The Miracle Christ in Lima, the Luren Christ in Ica, and the Lord of the Trembler in Cuzco also exemplified this juxtaposition. This led to the images of Christ as poor and Christ as Indian, such as those found on the walls of the San Cristóbal de Rapaz church, probably painted by a mestizo between 1722 and 1761: Christ

[47] Tom Zuidema, *The Ceque System of Cuzco. The Social Organization of the Capital of the Inca* (Leiden: E. J. Brill, 1964); María Rostworowski, *Estructuras andinas del poder* (Lima: Instituto de Estudios Peruanos, 1983). Duality was one of the key social and mental principles of the Tahuantinsuyo, the others being the division into three and the decimal system.

[48] Julio C. Tello, "Wira Kocha," *Inca* (Lima) 1, 1–3 (1923), 93–320; 583–606.

[49] Conversations and visits to Lima churches with Anne Marie Hocquenghem were very helpful for understanding these concepts.

is depicted as whipped and tortured by Jews dressed like Spaniards.[50] These images inspired contemporary artisans of Cuzco's San Blas neighborhood such as Edilberto Mérida, who sculpted a long-necked Christ frozen in agony, and appear frequently in the small canvases painted by anonymous Andean artists.[51]

Father Jorge Lira compiled from peasants of the southern Andes Quechua Catholic hymn songs composed sometime in the eighteenth or nineteenth century. Among them was "Apu Inca Atawalpaman" (to the Inca Lord Atahualpa), a funeral song that evoked the Old Testament book of Jeremiah to recount the " Inca people's catastrophe."[52]

> They place Atahualpa in a shroud
> His beloved head wrapped up
> By the horrendous enemy.

But it was not an orthodox Christian sermon. The defeated may have been naturally inclined to integrate the more marginal elements of Christianity such as millenarianism. The Inkarri myth seems to have been part of a broader cycle: the three ages of the world, in which that of the Father corresponded to the time of the Gentiles (that is, when Andean people did not know the true religion); the time of the Son corresponded to Spanish rule, with suffering similar to that of Christ at Calvary; and the time of the Holy Spirit, when peasants would recover their land. There are similar stories with some variations from Huánuco, Huancavelica, Ayacucho, and Cuzco.[53] The pachacuti of the Conquest merged with the second age of Joachimism, an intermediate period that someday will end. From a cyclical vision, Andean people moved to a linear one, that is, from the eternal present to eschatology. Henrique Urbano called this shift the transition from myth to utopia.[54] It is also a shift from dualism to tripartition, I would argue. But let's not get ahead

[50] Arturo Ruiz Estrada, "El arte andino colonial de Rapaz," *Boletín de Lima* (Lima), 5, 28 (1983), 46.

[51] Pablo Macera, *Pintores populares andinos* (Lima: Banco de los Andes, 1980).

[52] Jorge Lira and J. M. B. Farfán, "Himnos quechuas católicos cuzqueños," *Folklore Americano* (Lima) 3, 3 (1955), prologue by José María Arguedas.

[53] Fernando Fuenzalida, Henrique Urbano, and Manuel Marzal have researched Joachimism in the Andes.

[54] Henrique Urbano, "Discurso mítico y discurso utópico en los Andes," *Allpanchis* (Cuzco) 10 (1977), 3–14 and his "Representaciones colectivas y arqueología mental en los Andes," *Allpanchis* (Cuzco) 20 (1982), 33–83. In this latter issue of *Allpanchis*, see Manuel Burga and Alberto Flores Galindo, "La utopía andina," 85–101.

of the story. The introduction of millenarianism was a prolonged process and was not universally accepted.

The Taqui Onqoy was a decisive moment in the construction of the Andean utopia. It literally means the "dance sickness," the name inspired by the jolts and convulsions that followers of this salvation movement experienced. Miraculously reconverted to Andean culture, they decided to reconcile with their gods, follow the orders of indigenous priests, and break with whites' customs. It was the 1560s, and the movement's organizers apparently sought to incite the entire kingdom against the Spanish. The first followers were recruited in the Pampas River basin near Ayacucho, whose access to the Inca holdout of Vilcabamba prompted some to wonder if there was a connection with Inca resistance. Taqui Onqoy followers, however, did not want to return to the time of the Incas but instead preached the resurrection of *huacas* or local divinities: a return to the time before the Incas.[55]

For common Andean people, the Inca Empire had been truly despotic and oppressive. In 1560, historical memory associated the Incas with war, the forced subjection of the *yanaconas* to work the land of the Cuzco aristocracy, and the massive transfer of people to new settlements under the *mitimaes* system. This latter system uprooted peasants of the Pampas River themselves, helping explain why ethnic groups such as the Huancas of the central Andes saw the Spanish as possible liberators from Cuzco oppression. They quickly became disillusioned, but Conquest atrocities did not make them forget those of the Incas.

The Taqui Onqoy represented a significant change. It was not an ethnic group that fought to return to the previous system. Instead, priests spoke of the resurrection of all huacas, from Quito to Cuzco. The two most important were Pachacamac on the coast near Lima and that of Lake Titicaca on the Aymara plateau. It never became more than a project. According to one account, a priest who did not respect the confidentiality of confession betrayed the rebels. What actually happened was that the leaders, convinced of divine support, did not attempt to hide sermons and conversions. It was thus not difficult to capture those involved. The Spanish detected 8,000 active participants in an area with approximately 150,000 people.[56]

[55] Juan Ossio, ed., *Ideología mesiánica del mundo andino* (Lima: Ignacio Prado Pastor, 1973).

[56] Stern, "El Taki Onqoy," 53. See also his *Peru's Indian Peoples and the Challenge of Spanish Conquest: Huamanga to 1640* (Madison: University of Wisconsin Press, 1982).

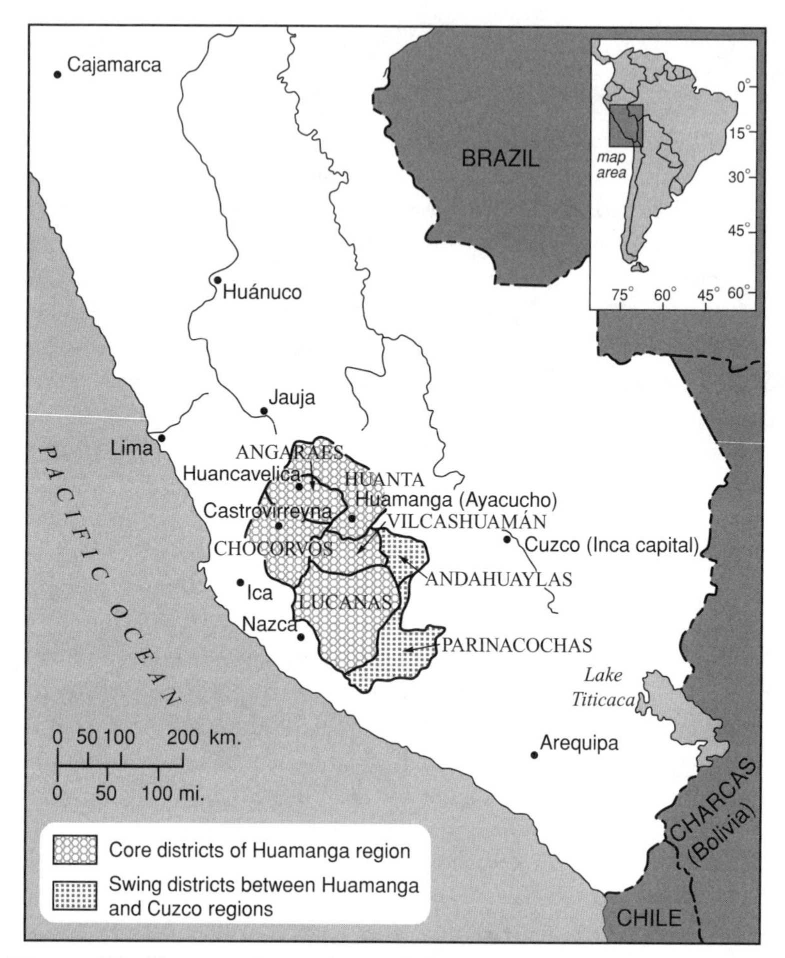

Map 1.1. The Huamanga Region (c. 1600). *Source:* Steve Stern, *Peru's Indian People and the Challenge of Spanish Conquest. Huamanga to 1640.* (From Cartographic Laboratory, University of Wisconsin Press, Madison, 1982.)

The resurrection of the huacas did not end there. Similar uprisings, although not centrally organized, hatched in other areas in what today are the departments of Abancay, Cuzco, Puno, and Arequipa. In the 1590 Moro Onqoy movement, witnesses referred to the apparition of the Inca or of his envoys sent to "liberate Indians from death."[57]

[57] A key text for these topics is Marco Curatola, "Mito y milenarismo en los Andes: del Taqui Onkoy a Inkarri," *Allpanchis* (Cuzco) 10 (1977), 69.

Conquest and death became synonymous as a result of wars, epidemics, and new workloads. In the minds of the defeated, Potosí was a monster that trapped bodies in the depths of the earth. Violence was a conscious weapon of domination. Every Spanish settlement began with the construction of gallows; the Indians' minority status and fear of uprisings provoked Spanish cruelty toward them. That a Cajamarca encomendero's dogs persecuted and ripped Indians apart was not an isolated incident. There was unnecessary loss of life from the moment of Atahualpa's capture in Cajamarca, an episode that lived in memory as carnage. Captain Cristóbal de Mena estimated that the Spanish massacred 6,000 to 7,000 Indians.[58] Another mortal danger arrived that transcends human will. Diseases spread with the ships and their rats, and the viruses arrived even before Pizarro's forces; any contact between European and Indian might cause contagion. Christianity privileged oral transmission and sacred texts, preaching and sermons, confession and absolution, but it also brought physical death to bodies that, in contrast to the Old World, were not sufficiently immunized.

This new religion, represented by the sinister image of a skeleton, also brought a message to which Indians were receptive. After his crucifixion, agony, and death, Christ rose to heaven on the third day. Bodies could revive, and death was not irreversible. The promise of resurrection at the end of time existed.

The idea of the Inca's return did not appear spontaneously in Andean culture, nor was it a mechanical reaction to colonial domination. Andean people previously reconstructed the past and transformed it into an alternative to the present. This was and is a distinctive feature of the Andean utopia; the ideal city did not exist outside history or at the remote beginning of time. On the contrary, it was a real historic fact that had a name (Tahuantinsuyo); a ruling class (the Incas); and a capital (Cuzco). Andean people changed the particulars of this construction to imagine a kingdom without hunger, without exploitation, and where they ruled once again. It represented the end of disorder and darkness. Inca became an organizing idea or principle.

The trajectory of these concepts originated in the Vilcabamba mountains, where the surviving Inca royal family took refuge, dedicated to an impossible resistance against the Spanish or to the negotiation of cogovernment or a Spanish protectorate. They debated whether to

[58] Portocarrero, "Castigo sin culpa."

collaborate or confront. Unlike Taqui Onqoy followers, they did not reject everything western but instead integrated it into their project: they used horses and firearms and read Spanish. One of the Vilcabamba monarchs, Titu Cusi Yupanqui, became a Christian. This encouraged some Cuzco mestizos to consider rising up "to suppress encomiendas, to proclaim Titu Cusi Yupanqui ruler in Vilcabamba, and to bring back Inca governance without getting rid of the best from western culture."[59] One of them, Juan Arias Maldonado, was supposed to stab the Viceroy. The Vilcabamba forces were denounced and persecuted. These events promoted the rumor that Titu Cusi Yupanqui was destined to be both Inca and King, because he would be the monarch of Indians and mestizos. Thus a project emerged of a Peru without Spaniards in which the conquered and the offspring of the Conquest would coexist. In 1570 in Vilcabamba, Titu Cusi Yupanqui began to dictate to a friar a chronicle or account to prove his legitimate rights over Peru, but his death interrupted the text. Indians blamed the friar for assassinating him, and they demanded that whether or not the accusation was true, he resurrect Titu Cusi Yupanqui. The friar tried but failed. The anecdote is interesting because as Urbano has posited, it shows that Inkarri implied the Christian notion of resurrection, an aspect of the Apocalypse that Andean thinking rapidly assimilated.

The history of the Vilcabamba Incas ended with Tupac Amaru I imprisoned by Viceroy Toledo and killed in Cuzco's Plaza de Armas in 1572. In contrast to Pizarro's garroting in Cajamarca, it was a public act in which those in attendance saw the executioner sever the head and display it. To dispel any doubts, the head remained on a pike while the body was buried in the Cathedral. Historian José Antonio del Busto argued that this was the moment when the idea of Inkarri was born. Tradition maintains that the head, instead of rotting, became more beautiful every day. When Indians began to venerate it, the *corregidor* (the local Spanish authority) sent it to Lima. But the process is actually more complex. Inkarri resulted from the convergence among the event itself (the death of Tupac Amaru I), Christian discourse about the mystical body of the Church, and popular traditions. Only then did the popular version of the Andean utopia, which went back to Taqui Onqoy, amalgamate with the aristocratic one, which originated in Vilcabamba. Franklin Pease suggested that the Inkarri myth began to circulate at the

[59] José Antonio del Busto, *Historia General del Perú* (Lima: Librería Studium, 1978), 379.

beginning of the seventeenth century.[60] This seems plausible. At that point the myth made it into writing.

This brings us to mestizos: children of the conquest, young people who should have been privileged because of their father or mother. However, when the Spanish decided to rebuild families, break with concubines, and replace Indian women with Spanish women, they ended up rejecting mestizos. For their mothers, this first generation of mestizos conveyed the memory of defeat as well as disdain due to their supposed rape. Deemed "natural children" or bastards, mestizos not only lacked a trade but in fact could not practice one. They joined the bands of vagabonds whose only option was to search for ever more scarce land or join the armies that fought rebellious Indians such as the Mapuche. They received the generic name of "Guzmanes." Mestizos who did not risk their lives in this way ended up like the son of Cajamarca trumpeter Pedro de Alconchel and of an anonymous indigenous peasant woman: a drunk who led a poor and miserable existence in the little town of Mala.[61] When one colonial official called them "men of destroyed lives," he was not exaggerating. For them, identity was an unbearably distressing matter. Mutinies always found a few mestizos willing to participate. They spurred on Titu Cusi Yupanqui, and it is possible that some witnessed in despair the execution of Tupac Amaru I.

Garcilaso was mestizo. Born in Cuzco in 1539, he left for Spain in 1560 when he was twenty and tried by every means possible to integrate into the victors' world. He wanted to be European, practiced warfare and the arts, fought the Moors in Southern Spain, and sought fame as an historian of Spanish Florida. He demanded the recognition of his father's service to the crown and the restitution of goods belonging to his mother, an Inca princess named Isabel Chimpu Ocllo. He failed.[62] As an old man, alone and frustrated, he took refuge in the small Andalucian town of Montilla and began a different task: writing the history of his land in an attempt to make sense of his own misfortunes, to convert failure into creativity. Exile and the proximity of death fostered nostalgic yearning. He undertook a history of the Incas, the conquest, and the civil wars among conquistadors. The aspiration to follow the facts, respect sources, and tell the truth guided his story, as well as the belief that history

[60] Franklin Pease, *El Dios creador andino* (Lima: Mosca Azul Editores, 1973).
[61] Del Busto, *La hueste perulera*, 183–4.
[62] Aurelio Miró Quesada, *El Inca Garcilaso y otros estudios garcilasistas* (Madrid: Ediciones Cultura Hispánica, 1971).

could provide ethical models. He was a "Platonic historian," convinced that the past could be the basis for political discourse pertinent to the future.[63] Eagerness to immerse himself in European culture led him to Leo Hebraeus, a neoplatonic Jewish author decisive in utopian thought and the author of the *Dialoghi de amore*, which Garcilaso translated into Spanish, his first literary work. It continued to influence him years later when he wrote *Royal Commentaries of the Incas*, a two-volume book that covered the history of the Incas and the conquest of Peru. This was a controversial text aimed to counter the pro-Toledo chroniclers. Under the inspiration of this viceroy who defeated the Vilcabamba resistance, these writers disseminated an image of the Andean past that, contrary to that of Las Casas, sought to justify the Conquest. Toledo recruited Pedro Sarmiento de Gamboa, the author of *Historia Indica*, in which the Incas appear to have taken power only recently, as tyrants and usurpers, expanding their empire through force at the cost of the rights of older and more traditional monarchs. The Incas had seized power, and the conquistadors therefore did not have to recognize their rights. Expelling the Incas righted a previous injustice. But there was more to the Toledo discourse: the Incas were idolatrous, existed side by side with the devil, performed human sacrifices, and, finally, practiced sodomy.

Garcilaso challenged this vision of the Conquest, arguing that before the Incas there was no civilization in the Andes, only hordes and scattered chiefdoms over which Cuzco imposed a sense of organization. The Incas introduced agriculture and patiently created an empire using warfare only in extreme cases, relying instead on persuasion and exchange. According to Garcilaso, the Incas were the Romans of the new world. And just as the Romans prepared the ancient world for Christianity, Cuzco rulers prepared their imperial subjects to receive the Christian message. Reflecting Renaissance admiration for antiquity, this discourse implied converting the Tahuantinsuyo into a golden age.[64]

In writing his history, Garcilaso proudly assumed his identity as a mestizo ("I proclaim it out loud," he would say) and included the name Inca in his signature. Traditional history has viewed his *Royal Commentaries* as a harmonious conciliation between Spain and the Andes. Is this interpretation valid? The elegy to the Tahuantinsuyo contains a critique of the Spanish, effective even if indirect and muffled. In contrast to the

[63] José Durand, *El Inca Garcilaso, clásico de América* (Mexico City: SepSetentas, 1976).

[64] I borrow ideas developed by Pierre Duviols.

Europeans, the Incas achieved nonviolent conquests; unlike Toledo, who decapitated Tupac Amaru I, they respected the rules of legitimate succession. Garcilaso ended his book precisely with the death of this monarch: "So ended the Inca, the legitimate heir to the empire by the direct male line from the first Inca Manco Cápac to himself."[65] For Garcilaso, the Spanish were usurpers; the notion of restoring the empire to its legitimate rulers was established. The publication of parts I and II of the *Royal Commentaries* in 1607 and 1619 completed the birth of the Andean utopia: from practice and desire, sometimes clear, sometimes hazy, it became a written discourse. It is possible to connect, as Pierre Duviols noted, Garcilaso with Vilcabamba.

It was not a successful text at first. When Garcilaso died in 1616, half the first print run was in his library. But editions increased in the following years. During the seventeenth and eighteenth centuries, seventeen editions (complete or partial) appeared in print, ten in French, four in Spanish, two in English, and one in German. Garcilaso's skills as a writer helped, but utopian resonances also played a role. In 1800, the Madrid editor of the Royal Commentaries wrote in his prologue: "I must confess that I am surprised that this type of work, sought after by the nation's sages, fancied by the curious, praised, translated, and published many times by foreigners, all sworn enemies of Spain's glory, ends up becoming scarce."[66]

Garcilaso found fervent readers in the Andes among the *kurakas* (ethnic leaders) and descendents of the Cuzco aristocracy. They accepted and disseminated the list of Incas found in the *Royal Commentaries*, casting the Andean past in European political terms. The Inca was a king. The dual system meant that the Inca Empire was not a monarchy but a "diarchy": the Incas represented one of two existing parallel dynasties, one in each Cuzco neighborhood. This dual system was not prolonged in Vilcabamba, and it did not exist for Garcilaso. In the eighteenth century, when Andeans awaited or sought the return of the Inca, they always conjured it in the singular: one individual, one character who legitimately formed part of the empire and who took on messianic

[65] Garcilaso de la Vega, El Inca, *Royal Commentaries of the Incas and General History of Peru. Part Two*, translated with an introduction by Harold V. Livermore (Austin: University of Texas Press, 1966), 1482.

[66] Alberto Tauro, "Bibliografía del Inca Garcilaso de la Vega," *Documenta* (Lima) IV (1965), 337–47.

features. Although Tupac Amaru II took along a copy of the *Royal Commentaries* on trips, we only need his letters and proclamations to see that the idea of imperial restoration inspired him. Garcilaso entered oral culture through the indigenous aristocracy, who discussed his book. Some arguments found their way into lawsuits and genealogical charts that Inca descendents, invented or real, created throughout the eighteenth century.

Garcilaso enjoyed a parallel if belated fame in Europe. Miguel de Cervantes was apparently the first to turn to his work, in *The Travels of Persiles* and *Sigismunda* (1617). The theater was another outlet. The *Royal Commentaries* influenced Pedro Calderón de la Barca's *La aurora de Copacabana* and Tirso de Molina's *Amazonas en las Indias*. Garcilaso's presence was even more evident in Cristóbal María Cortés's *Atahualpa*, published in Madrid in 1784. The Incas appeared in one of Voltaire's novels. Eighteenth-century utopian thinkers saw this land, distant in time and space, as an exceptionally happy society.[67] The Andean utopia assumed universal dimensions. The Incas became Garcilaso's re-created people and not Sarmiento de Gamboa's shady monarchs.

Garcilaso's list of fourteen Inca rulers became official. It appeared in a 1740 engraving by don Alonso de la Cueva and, a hundred years later, in Justo Sahuaraura's *Recuerdos de la monarquía peruana*. As a *Cuzqueño*, Sahuaraura left out Atahualpa, the Quito Inca, and included Manco Inca, Sayri Tupac, and Tupac Amaru I, the Vilcabamba monarchs. He did not follow but rather reinterpreted Garcilaso.[68]

AN IMAGINARY SPACE: PAITITI

The discovery and conquest of America significantly advanced cartography: it was necessary to determine precisely the shapes and dimensions of these new territories. But alongside these supposedly rigorous calculations, an imaginary geography, a sort of conquistador oneiric horizon, also emerged. The conquistadors were determined to find Atlantis

[67] Guillermo Lohmann Villena, "Francisco Pizarro en el teatro clásico español," *Arbor* (Madrid) 5 (1946), 425–34; María Cristóbal Cortés, *Atahualpa* (Madrid: Por Don Antonio de Sancha, 1784); Aurelio Miró Quesada, *Cervantes, Tirso y el Perú* (Lima: Editorial Huascarán, 1978), 102.

[68] Sahuaraura's text, written in 1838, was published in Paris in 1850. A handsome edition that includes a facsimile of the manuscript has been published as Don Justo Apu Sahuaraura Inca, *Recuerdos de la monarquía peruana o bosquejo de la historia de los Incas* (Lima: Fundación Telefónica, 2001) [Editors' note].

with Sarmiento de Gamboa, to reminisce about the lost island of San Anselmo with Las Casas, and to search for the isle of San Brandan. As expeditions entered more distant and inhospitable territories, new lands emerged, almost as compensation: Dabaybe, the Esmeralda Mines, la Laguna del Sol, la Gran Noticia, el Reino del Sol. El Dorado was the most renowned, a golden land where wealth abounded and was within reach, populated by Amazons. Orellana and the expedition that explored and named the Amazon River were convinced El Dorado existed. In 1550, this quest led Captain Juan Pérez de Guevara to Moyobamba, which permitted access to the jungle from northern Peru. Chroniclers claimed that some natives who came from the east and whom the Spanish called "Brasile Indians" confirmed the existence of El Dorado. Another account claimed that a Cuzco authority, fleeing from the Chancas ethnic group in the time of Pachacutec (1438–1471/72), founded a kingdom in the middle of the jungle.[69] Might another Cuzco exist?

Cuzco also obsessed the conquistadors of Paraguay, at the other end of South America. Hernando de Ribera reached Asunción in 1544 and declared his discovery of a sun temple in a land populated by Amazons. Several expeditions were organized. One claimed to glimpse the Andes when climbing the Pilcomayo Mountain; another alleged to have discovered a kingdom that Manco Inca founded. In reality, Spanish visions blended with Tupi-Guarani myths about the "land without evil" that spurred pilgrimages to the west. On the other side of the Andes, the Vilcabamba resistance raised the traditional notion that the city of Cuzco had a double, an idea that the dual system in which Andean thought was inscribed made possible. Before the arrival of the conquistadors, that second imperial city appeared to be Tumibamba, in the north, in what became the kingdom of Quito. But with Vilcabamba, the second city passed to the jungle.

Paititi emerged from the convergence of three cultural traditions: Andean duality, Spanish dreams, and Tupi-Guarani myths.[70] Little by little its location became more precise, to the point that it was said to be in the Peruvian department of Madre de Dios, near the modern border

[69] José Antonio del Busto, *Pacificación del Perú* (Lima: Librería Studium, 1984), 218–19 and 37–8.

[70] Thierry Saignes, "El Piamonte de los Andes meridionales: estado de la cuestión y problemas relativos a su ocupación en los siglos XVI y XVII," *Boletín del Instituto Francés de Estudios Andinos* (Lima) X, 3–4 (1981), 141–85.

with Brazil and Bolivia. From the sixteenth century on, an increasing array of arguments claimed to confirm its existence. Today the topic of Paititi forms part of everyday beliefs in Cuzco, found in mythical stories as well as in *mistis*' convictions.[71] The search for Paititi continues to stimulate laborious expeditions and the use of aerial photography, and people think every new archeological site is the Great Paititi.

During the seventeenth century the Amazon region was the scene of another imaginary place: paradise. In 1650, a Lima-based savant named León Pinelo wrote a weighty text full of biblical citations and Hebrew sources that attempted to show that earthly paradise was located near where the Marañón and Amazon rivers met. Alongside the citations he included observations of flora and fauna. Doubts persist about León Pinelo's Jewish origins – which Raúl Porras Barrenechea confirmed but Lohmann Villena denied – and his parents might have been Portuguese *conversos*. Regardless, his ideas seem to have sprung from Hebrew conceptions. Although the text did not appear in print until the twentieth century, intellectuals did not ignore it.[72] In the mid-eighteenth century, José Eusebio Llano Zapata alluded directly to his theories, which incidentally were not just Pinelo's. In 1651, a Franciscan and enthusiastic reader of Garcilaso wrote a chronicle that also referred to paradise:

> Finally, the multitude of rivers and springs of crystalline water that flow on golden sand and precious stones made many believe that Terrestrial Paradise was found in this quarter of the new world, particularly in light of the temperance and smoothness of the wind, the freshness, greenery, and beauty of the trees, the currents and sweetness of the water, the variety of birds with their feathered adornments and the harmony of their songs, the gracious and happy disposition of the land, part of which, if it's not Paradise, at least enjoys its properties; and don Christopher Columbus was such a great astrologer that he knew for certain that Paradise was located at the ends of this part of the world.[73]

[71] Misti is a Quechua term that refers to non-Indian, higher-status individuals in Andean societies [Editors' note].

[72] Compare the prologue by Raúl Porras Barrenechea to *El paraíso en el Nuevo Mundo* (Lima: Concejo Provincial, 1943) and Guillermo Lohmann Villena, *El gran canciller de Indias* (Seville: Escuela de Estudios Hispanoamericanos, 1953).

[73] Fray Diego Córdova y Salinas, *Crónica franciscana de las provincias del Perú* (Washington, D.C.: Academy of American Franciscan History, 1957). For a

The Franciscans who took the Christian message to the jungle must have done so with paradise in mind. They founded missions in two regions: the Gran Pajonal in the central jungle, with the Ocopa Convent as the center of operations, and in the south in the Puno province of Carabaya, with Cuzco as the point of departure. In 1677 missionaries found Carabaya natives with Inca clothing they acquired when the Incas fled to the jungle. In another settlement, natives presented themselves as Inca subjects, to whom they gave gold and feathers. The Franciscans also heard accounts of the Inca's death and began to ask about Paititi. An old man responded that it was the name of a river near where the Incas live "in a very large settlement."[74]

The jungle began to assume a prominent place in the colonial imagination. Its vegetation, animals, and colors appeared frequently in mural paintings and graced the dome in Arequipa's Compañía Church. Gustavo Buntinx hypothesized that the *papagayo* parrot, associated at times with Indian nobles, occasionally symbolized Paititi. Winged images found on the walls of the Andahuaylillas temple in Cuzco further demonstrated the prevalence of jungle imagery. A route to the jungle passed near Andahuaylillas, through Paucartambo, where in the eighteenth century, highland peasants met the Piros-chontaquiros, an ethnic group of merchants and warriors who navigated rivers to collect jungle goods and trade with Andean people in an annual fair.

It was a Piros Indian who led an unusual pilgrim from Cuzco to the Gran Pajonal, the Franciscans' other mission territory. The pilgrim called himself Juan Santos Atahualpa, wore a painted tunic, kept his hair short like the Indians of Quito, and chewed coca leaves. In 1742 rumors began to circulate that he could make the ground shake, proclaimed heresies, sought the expulsion of Spaniards, including friars, and wanted to organize an uprising of all the Amazon natives, allied with Andean people, to establish a new kingdom.[75] He claimed to descend from Atahualpa and that he embodied the Holy Spirit, thus his name. This

key study of changing mentalities within religious orders, see Bernard Lavallé, *Recherches sur l'apparition de la conscience créole dans la Vice-royauté du Pérou* (Lille, France: Atelier national de reproduction des théses, 1982).

[74] Michele Colin, *Le Cuzco la fin du XVIII et au debut du XVIII siécles* (Paris: Institut des Hautes Etudes de l'Amerique Latine, 1966), 110–11.

[75] Stefano Varese, *Salt of the Mountain: Campa Asháninka History and Resistance in the Peruvian Jungle*, translated by Susan Giersbach Rascón (Norman: University of Oklahoma Press, 2002); Mario Castro Arenas, *La rebelión de San Juan Santos* (Lima: Milla Batres, 1973), 24. See the review of this latter book by Simeón

cosmovision was a peculiar amalgam of millenarianism and Andean beliefs: "There are only three kingdoms in this world, Spain, Angola, and his own and he did not set out to steal another kingdom – the Spanish came to steal his; but the Spaniards' time has run out and his time has arrived."[76] Time was up – one age ended and another one began. The Spanish had severed Atahualpa's head and taken it to Europe; they had snatched a throne that did not belong to them and now it must return to the Incas' true descendents. Juan Santos's kingdom took in the jungle and the Andes.

Between 1743 and 1756 Juan Santos Atahualpa's followers battled the Tarma corregidor's troops and then the Viceroy's. Colonial forces organized five expeditions, all of which Juan Santos answered with incursions from the jungle into the central Andes. Indigenous peasants and even some mestizos and blacks joined the natives. The Spanish did not manage to defeat Juan Santos, but they impeded new incursions. A Franciscan summarized the uprising: "In all of the tapestry of events around this uprising, our forces did not make a single wise move or achieve any success."[77] The movement expelled the friars from the jungle, to which no western man could return until the middle of the nineteenth century. However, in 1756 Juan Santos's trail was lost: according to tradition, he rose to heaven leaving a trail of smoke.

The jungle thus shifted from an imaginary place in the Andean utopia to the epicenter of a social movement, the only one the Spanish could not defeat. That it was the only successful uprising reinforced the idea that the Incas persisted in the jungle. Some researchers explained the standoff by alluding to the jungle's marginality in the colonial economy. Although it is true that his base was not a vital area or close to important cities such as Cuzco, Juan Santos threatened central Andean mining and the cities of Jauja and Huancayo in the Mantaro Valley, a military rearguard and Lima's breadbasket. A more plausible explanation for his success should consider the rebels themselves, who enjoyed an ideological cohesion not found in other rebellions. Regardless of ethnic and cultural differences, they came from the same social group

Orellana, "La rebelión de Juan Santos o Juan Santos el rebelde," *Anales Científicos de la Universidad del Centro del Perú* (Huancayo) 3 (1974), 513–51.

[76] Fray Bernardino Izaguirre, *Misiones franciscanas* (Lima: Talleres Gráficos de la Penitenciaría, 1923), 118.

[77] Ibid., 163.

and were equally poor Indians or natives. Finally, there was no major difference between the leader and the masses: Juan Santos became just another man in the Gran Pajonal.[78]

Paititi gained complete verisimilitude by the middle of the eighteenth century. It encouraged the Huarochiri rebels outside of Lima in 1750; thirty years later Tupac Amaru II declared himself the Gran Paititi sovereign; and in 1790, Juan Pablo Viscardo y Guzmán, a Jesuit expatriate in Italy who conspired against Spanish rule, was convinced that an "Inca deputy" had formed a "considerable state" in the jungle.

Utopia Represented

In 1952 the Bolivian writer Jesús Lara found the manuscript of a play about the conquest entitled *The Tragedy of Atahualpa's Death*. The copy was dated 1871 in Chayanta, but the original was probably much older, perhaps dating to the late seventeenth century. The play finishes when Pizarro offers the Inca's head to the king. Before that, Pizarro only moved his lips, expressing the radical lack of communication between the two worlds. He pronounces a few words in the final scene, displaying pride in his accomplishment, but he is stunned when Spain, that is, the king, tells him: "Why did you do this?/The face that you have brought me/Is my own." The king is the Inca, the Andean Inkarri. The play ends with a curse: Pizarro will be thrown into fire, his descendents killed, and his possessions destroyed, "that nothing remain/of this vile traitor."[79]

According to the chronicler Arzáns y Vela, the first performance of the Inca's death took place in 1555 in Potosí. But he was writing in 1705, and it doesn't seem plausible that the Incas would be exalted at such an early time, given that memory of the Andean past did not yet reside in collective memory. Miguel Cabello de Balboa, it is argued, wrote several plays between 1550 and 1588, among them *La comedia del Cuzco*, which possibly had "fabulous indigenous history" as its theme.[80]

78 See also Alfred Métraux, *Religión y magias indígenas en América del Sur* (Madrid: Aguilar, 1967).

79 Raúl Meneses, *Teatro quechua colonial* (Lima: Edubanco, 1982), 504.

80 Guillermo Lohmann Villena, *El arte dramático en Lima* (Seville: Escuela de Estudios Hispanoamericanos, 1945) and the same author's "Las comedias de Corpus Christi en Lima en 1635 y 1636," *Mar del Sur* (Lima) 11 (1950), 21–3.

It was not until 1659 that a precise date could be given. On December 23, in Lima's Plaza,

> the Inca king appeared and fought with two other kings until he conquered them and took over the fort. Then the three kings, with dignity, offered the key to the [Spanish] prince who was portrayed on a float. Then all the Indians of this kingdom came out to the plaza, each in his own native dress. There were more than two thousand and the plaza appeared to be covered with a variety of flowers as all the Indians were elaborately costumed and with much finery.[81]

This passage from Mugaburu's *Diary of Lima* recalls the Corpus Christi procession in Cuzco, captured in sixteen paintings dating from the late seventeenth century. They portray members of the indigenous aristocracy dressed in traditional style with luxury and pride. By then, the prolonged siege against Andean culture had ended; the Spanish instead opted for tolerance. The extirpation of idolatry campaigns in the Andes east of Lima had ceased, and evangelizers concluded that Indians were Christians. The Spanish no longer imprisoned folk healers; some Europeans even noted that they could cure, although using different methods than those taught at San Marcos University. These circumstances, which clearly did not exist in 1555, allowed the utopia to become public.

By 1666 conspiracies, small outbreaks of violence, and failed rebellions had taken place in different and far-flung sites such as Quito, Lima, and Tucumán. In Lima, a man with the curious name of Gabriel Manco Capac who had played the role of Inca in a festival was one of the rebel leaders. He was detained but managed to escape from the city jail before the trial and was later seen wandering around Huancayo. There, Huanca kurakas and peasants who a century before had been steadfast allies of the conquistadors readily embraced his preaching.[82] An ideological change had taken place that reached collective mentalities. The kurakas and indigenous aristocracy began to create genealogies that stretched back to the last Incas: in this stratum of wealthy, Spanish-speaking Indians, the search for ancestors kept memory alive. A similar process occurred

[81] Josephe and Francisco Mugaburu, *Chronicle of Colonial Lima: The Diary of Josephe and Francisco Mugaburu, 1640–1697*, translated by Robert R. Miller (Norman: University of Oklahoma Press, 1975), 54.

[82] Franklin Pease, "Andean Messianism" (Public lecture, Lima, 1985).

in distant towns such as Ocros, Otuco, and Acas, where two phenomena converged: a clandestine hierarchy of indigenous priests who conserved links to the past, and the Vecosina ritual, where songs and dances referred to, in the words of an extirpator, histories and relics.[83]

The memory of the Incas entered public discourse, a process that culminated in the eighteenth century. The past emerged in murals, paintings, and the designs on *qeros* or drinking vessels that José Tamayo Herrera called a compendium of daily life. It appeared in a new symbolism (angels with harquebuses that recalled the pre-Hispanic lightning bolt); the reading of Garcilaso; performances of the Inca's capture presented in Cajamarca, Huacho, and Cuzco; images of Huascar and Atahualpa; and, finally, in "end of time" prophesies. Utopia assumed a pan-Andean dimension. Its territory stretched from Quito to Tucumán, from small towns such as Huacho to the Amazon frontier. Not everyone, however, awaited the Inca's return. The utopia's territory spread outward but fragmented into small islands and archipelagos. The utopian ideas circulated not only among Indians but also creoles, Spaniards, natives of the central jungle, and mestizos, although obviously it did not become consensual. By the end of the eighteenth century, segments of colonial society maintained the hope of uniting in a revolution and expelling all Spaniards. The utopia burst into spaces previously reserved for the dominators' discourse. A description of eighteenth-century Lima recognized that unusual paintings about "the history of the Indians and their Incas, by Cuzco painters" adorned the walls of the cabildo or municipality, a symbol of the capital's Spanish population. These paintings were probably intended for a different audience and place, given their evident didactic content: "[T]o illustrate the theme they represented, they included captions coming out of the people's mouths where you could write what you wanted them to say."[84]

In 1659 a theater group staged a fight between kings in Lima, highlighting another path the Andean utopia took. It reached the theater in small towns through popular performances such as allegorical religious works and other plays staged in Church atriums, particularly during Corpus Christi and its octave, June 7 and 14. Works such as "Doce pares de Francia" or the fight between "Moors and Christians" reached

[83] Lorenzo Huertas, *La religion en una sociedad rural andina (siglo XVII)* (Ayacucho: Universidad Nacional San Cristóbal de Huamanga, 1981), 52.

[84] Armando Nieto, "Una descripción del Perú en el siglo XVIII," *Boletín del Instituto Riva Agüero* (Lima) 12 (1982–83), 268.

the Andes and came into contact with indigenous dances (*taquis*) such as those held in Cuzco in 1610 to celebrate San Ignacio de Loyola's canonization and battles "done in jest" that Father Acosta observed in many towns.[85] But the battle between Moors and Christians presented a favorable image of the Conquest by venerating the victors; in the end, reconciliation was the only option, that is, the recognition of defeat. According to Ricardo Palma, when these battles were staged in Lima in 1830, the Moors ended up singing: "We are now Christians/ we are now friends/ we now all have/ baptism water."[86]

In Andean towns such as Pampacocha, peasants still depict the legend of Charlemagne, but the Inca and Pizarro replace medieval European knights and Cajamarca supplants Roncesvalles, one ambush for another.[87] The change of characters delivers a different message: a critique of the conquest, the painful and even aggressive memory of the Inca. We see this variation in paintings that represented the Moors killed by Saint James or Santiago as Indians or recast the fight between Moors and Christians as a battle between Indians and Spaniards. The enemies were close at hand.

In some towns these performances replaced ancient rituals. Today, many patron saint festivals depict the Inca's capture; food, drink, dance, performances, fireworks, and bands all form part of this version of carnival. Other towns maintain the ritual that repeats the millennial encounter between shepherds and farmers, *llacuaces* and *huaris*.[88] Ethnographic observations and research in Lima's Archbishop Archive led Manuel Burga to hypothesize that theater substituted ritual, just as utopia substituted myth.[89]

[85] Arturo Jiménez Borja, "Coreografía colonial," *Mar del Sur* (Lima) II, 7 (1949), 31–41.

[86] Marcel Bataillon, "Por un inventario de las fiestas de moros y cristianos: otro toque de atención," *Mar del Sur* (Lima) II, 8 (1949), 3. In Huamachuco, the Nusta-Inca dance is called the "Turks Dance." Turk (*turco*) is used as a synonym of Moor.

[87] María Angélica Ruiz, "Carlomagno y los doce pares de Francia, en la comunidad Pampacocha Yaso," BA thesis, Pontificia Universidad Católica del Perú, 1978.

[88] Pierre Duviols, "Huari y Llacuaz. Agricultores y pastores. Un dualismo prehispánico de oposición y complementariedad," *Revista del Museo Nacional* (Lima) XXXIX (1973), 393–414.

[89] Manuel Burga, "Una crisis de identidad: mito, ritual y memoria en los Andes centrales (siglo XVII)," in his *Nacimiento de una utopía* (Lima: Instituto de Apoyo Agrario, 1988), 123–96.

Utopia and Conflicts

Cuzco's Archaeological Museum, the Museo Inka, has an anonymous painting entitled "The beheading of don Juan de Atahualpa in Cajamarca," whose tonality is similar to that of some qeros. It is small, comparable to the painting of Huascar's death in Arequipa's Archaeological Museum. The Spanish must have destroyed many similar paintings after the 1781 defeat of Tupac Amaru II, when their prohibition of artistic representation of the Incas forced them underground. What is worth noting is Atahualpa's "beheading." In the Chayanta drama seen previously, he also ends up beheaded. The chronicles, however, confirm that he was strangled with the garrote. What happened was that popular memory confused Atahualpa with Tupac Amaru I, who was truly the last Inca. This fusion took hold in the beginning of the seventeenth century, when Guaman Poma de Ayala included in his *Nueva coronica y buen gobierno* a drawing of a conquistador in Cajamarca using a hammer and dagger to chop off the Inca's head. His account, which captured the provincial and local version of Peruvian history, remained unpublished and unknown until the twentieth century.[90]

Theater groups from the colonial period until today have staged Atahualpa's death. In 1890 the Pallas or Inca women, who form part of these choreographies today, still danced in Lima around Christmas time.[91] It was performed in Puno at the beginning of the twentieth century.[92] Today it is limited to towns in the central Andes, and its outcome varies. Whereas in some places the Inca is still decapitated or has his throat slit (Aquia and Ambar), or an animal's neck is symbolically torn off, in other towns the play ends with the capture of Atahualpa, his rescue, or a conciliatory hug between the Inca and Pizarro.[93] The outcome depends on whether it is a mestizo or Indian town.

90 Enrique Gonzales Carré and Fermín Tivera, *Antiguos dioses y nuevos conflictos andinos* (Ayacucho: Universidad Nacional San Cristóbal de Huamanga, 1983).

91 Carlos Prince, *Lima antigua. Fiestas religiosas y profanas* (Lima: Imprenta Universal de C. Prince, 1890), 20.

92 Wilfredo Kapsoli, *Ayllus del sol. Anarquismo y utopía andina* (Lima: Tarea, 1984), 115.

93 Ana Baldocería, "Degollación del Inca Atahualpa en Ambar," *La Crónica*, Suplemento Cultural (Lima), August, 11 1985; Francisco Iriarte et al., *Dramas coloniales en el Perú actual* (Lima: Universidad Inca Garcilaso de la Vega, 1985); Nathan Watchtel, *La vision des vaincus. Les Indiens du Perou devant la Conquete espagnole* (Paris: Gallimard, 1971).

The Chiquián festival also demonstrates that the Andean utopia is beset by conflicts.[94] Chiquián, a town of 6,000 and the capital of the Bolognesi province in the department of Ancash, is located at the end of a ravine off the small road that runs from the highlands of Conococha to Huaraz. The festival honors Saint Rose of Lima and includes mass, a procession, two bullfights, and the capture of the Inca. As many as 1,000 visitors travel to Chiquián for the weeklong celebration. Cows, pigs, and rams are slaughtered to feed everyone, and sweets and bread are made for every meal. Participants consume endless amounts of beer and a local drink, the chinguirito, alcohol mixed with herbs and hot water. Organizers spend thousands, and leading families proudly take on their duties and enthusiastically receive visitors. According to them, the festival is democratic, nobody is excluded, and everyone can dance and drink in any house. The festival seems to transmit the image of a mestizo country, in which opposing sides have reconciled and the western and the Andean have merged. Conflicts don't exist. In the end, the Inca and the Captain (the name given to Pizarro) embrace and dance in the latter's house. The next day in the plaza they preside over a traditional Spanish-style bullfight in which local volunteers join a Lima bullfighter.

The Captain is the most important character in the festival. It is also the most expensive, but every year people fight for this post within the cargo system. In 1984, a wealthy truck driver portrayed the Captain, and a much less affluent man who also worked in transportation played the Inca. The latter's features were much more indigenous, and during the festival, relatives and friends from nearby towns such as Mangas visited his house. In contrast, the town's elite and visitors from Lima (merchants, professionals, and teachers) filled the Captain's house. From the beginning of the twentieth century through the 1960s, Chiquián was the home of a powerful group of owners of livestock haciendas. Their power over small towns and Indian communities stretched from the Pativilca River all the way to the coast. The local story is that an invasive wild grass brought from Africa, *kikuyu*, destroyed pastures. The

[94] Manuel Burga and I participated in the festival in 1984. Although they might disagree with my observations, I want to thank Elías James, the Captain, and Gaudencio Romero, the Inca. See also Héctor Martínez, "Vicos: las fiestas en la integración y desintegración cultural," *Revista del Museo Nacional de Historia* (Lima), XXVIII (1959), 190–247; Emilio Mendizábal, "La fiesta en Pachitea andina," *Folklore Americano* (Lima), XIII (1965), 141–227.

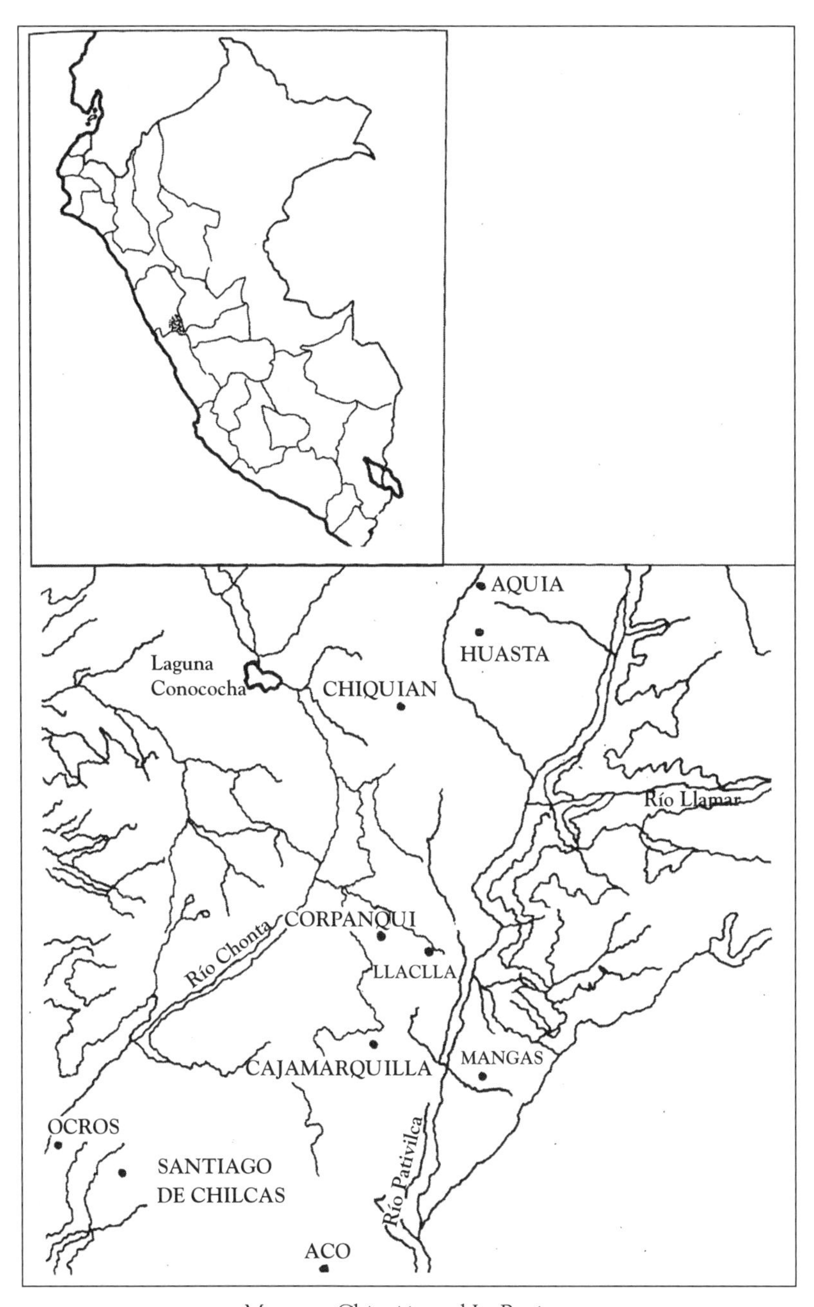

Map 1.2. Chiquián and Its Region.

1969 Agrarian Reform finished off the landowners, who were already losing power. They left the area, closed up their houses, and joined Lima's middle classes. In a symbolic act, the Velasco Alvarado regime that initiated the reform ceded one of these houses to teachers. In the end, battles between members of the left and the APRA political party left the house in shambles. The remains located in Chiquián's main plaza stand as a symbol of the landowners' decline. The other houses remain closed all year except for the last week of August, when mistis or their children arrive for the festival. They mingle, although with certain limits, with the very people who seek to fill the vacuum: the town's middle sectors, who need cohesion and prestige to consolidate their power.

While Chiquián has fallen into a seemingly irreversible decline, nearby towns have thrived. Technology has improved their livestock, and they produce high-quality cheese that trucks take to the coastal city of Huacho. They no longer need to pass through Chiquián to go to the coast, so other towns now challenge its dominance; Ocros, an overwhelmingly peasant town, aspires to become the provincial capital. Here they also celebrate the Inca's capture, but in the end he is rescued. In no way is he a secondary or scorned character.

In light of these conflicts and tensions, Chiquián's festival is an opportunity to preserve the town's prestige and confirm, despite recent history, its hegemonic position. The festival cultivates reciprocal ties and kinship relations: courtships and marriages ensue that allow some to rise socially or a few to join the ranks of the nouveau riche. Perhaps these power relations explain the expenditures and the relationship between mistis and Indians throughout the festival. They do not mingle. The doors are open for visitors from Lima or Huaraz but not for all peasants, with the exception of the Inca and his entourage. Indians can only watch, stay in the doorway, or perhaps enter the front patio. This correlates with the relationship between the Inca and the Captain, whose meeting in the plaza marks the beginning of the festival's main days. A type of persecution then takes place as they separately visit authorities' houses. Whereas the Captain goes into the living room or *sala*, the Inca goes no farther than the front patio.

The festival must not have been like this in the past. In the early twentieth century, when a renowned bandit from the area, Luis Pardo, played the role of the Inca, it was the most important character. Vestiges of this are still evident in the Inca's clothing and accessories, which include a type of crown, an ax, and embroidered cloth like those in late eighteenth-century drawings by Bishop Martínez de Compañón. In addition, Rumiñahui, supposedly Atahualpa's general, accompanies the Inca, and both have a group of *pallas* or female dancers. According to mistis, these women seek romantic adventures and often end up pregnant. According to the women themselves, it's a sacrifice requiring fasting and abstinence to pay thanks for a miracle or request the help of Saint Rose: they feel that they incarnate the Inca's imperial virgins rather than the Inca's concubines. Their dress is particularly colorful and changes with each day and each celebration. Their Spanish and Quechua songs not only provide music but also serve as the festival's guiding force. The Chiquián woman who prepares the pallas and teaches and directs the songs is actually the director of the entire performance. She received the position from her mother and is preparing her daughter to take over one day.

The Inca used to be the main character in Chiquián and still is in Carhuamayo, Roca, and Aquia. He lost this position when mistis took over the performance and saw it as an instrument of power. But in 1984 the situation is not so clear. Events inside and outside of Chiquián have brought mistis' power into question. This explains the tension in the festival. When they meet – the Inca's court, with its string instruments and the pallas' soft voices, and the Captain's court, on horseback, with its loud wind instruments – national conciliation seems to go up in smoke. Violence takes the stage.

The ritual battle between followers of the Inca and the Captain takes place on the day of the capture; the former are on foot and the latter on horseback. They proceed from the outskirts down the main street to downtown and then to the plaza, where the bullfight is held the following day, all the while throwing rock-hard sugar candies at the rival groups. Up to this point they follow the chroniclers' version of Atahualpa's capture: the night before, the Captain and his groups, just like Pizarro and his forces, don't sleep. They enter on horseback and begin persecution of the Inca around 4 P.M. Firecrackers and blazing flares, blaring clarinets and trumpets, and gunpowder, smoke, and general confusion set the stage for his capture in the plaza. Tensions spill over in a struggle that pays little attention to historical fidelity. The fight between the Captain and the Inca ends up in a free-for-all, with everyone fighting everyone: Limeños against locals, rich against poor, whites and mestizos on one side and Indians on the other. They move from tossing hard candy to fighting. National integration falls by the wayside when one member of the Captain's entourage uses the

Peruvian flag as a lance to charge people who try to drag him off his horse and hit him. Tempers flare. A horse charges the crowd, and people bring out their whips. They are supposed to go around the Plaza twice, but Limeños who don't know the ritual push the Captain into the Inca, and the former hits and captures the latter. This was not in the script. The Inca is angry and does not go to the celebration later that day. The next day, however, he puts his anger aside and attends the bullfight.

Ending with the bullfight, where next year's Captain is selected, is a way to assert that Spanish is the fundamental element in Peruvian culture. Mestizaje does not mean equilibrium but the imposition of some over others. This historical discourse affirms Chiquián's domination over neighboring towns, but a performance in which the quotidian disrupts historical narrative reveals just how precarious the situation is. The biography of the Andean utopia does not exist outside class struggle, and a contestatory discourse becomes the discourse of domination. Unlike Cuzco's mestizos in 1569, Chiquián's mestizos in 1984 cannot imagine Peru without Spaniards or whites.

THE INVENTION OF THE FUTURE

The Andean utopia is a collective creation that emerged after the sixteenth century. It would be absurd to consider it an unaltered prolongation of pre-Hispanic Andean thought. The concept of disjunction, which derives from iconographic analysis, can help us illuminate it. The term refers to the situation in which, in the context of cultural domination, the vanquished appropriate forms introduced by the victors but give them new content, producing something wholly new.[95] They don't repeat discourse others attempt to impose on them, nor do they continue with their own conceptualizations. To understand the cataclysm of the Peruvian conquest, Andean people had to refurbish their mental tools. Mythical thought did not allow them to place themselves in a radically different world, nor could they assume orthodox Christianity. The characters might be the same – Christ, the Holy Spirit, the king – but the final product was undoubtedly original. America not only put into effect European ideas but also produced its own.

George Kubler introduced the notion of disjunction into Andean history, and Francisco Stastny developed it in his studies of popular art.

[95] Erwin Panofski, *Renacimiento y renacimientos en el arte occidental* (Madrid: Alianza Editorial, 1975).

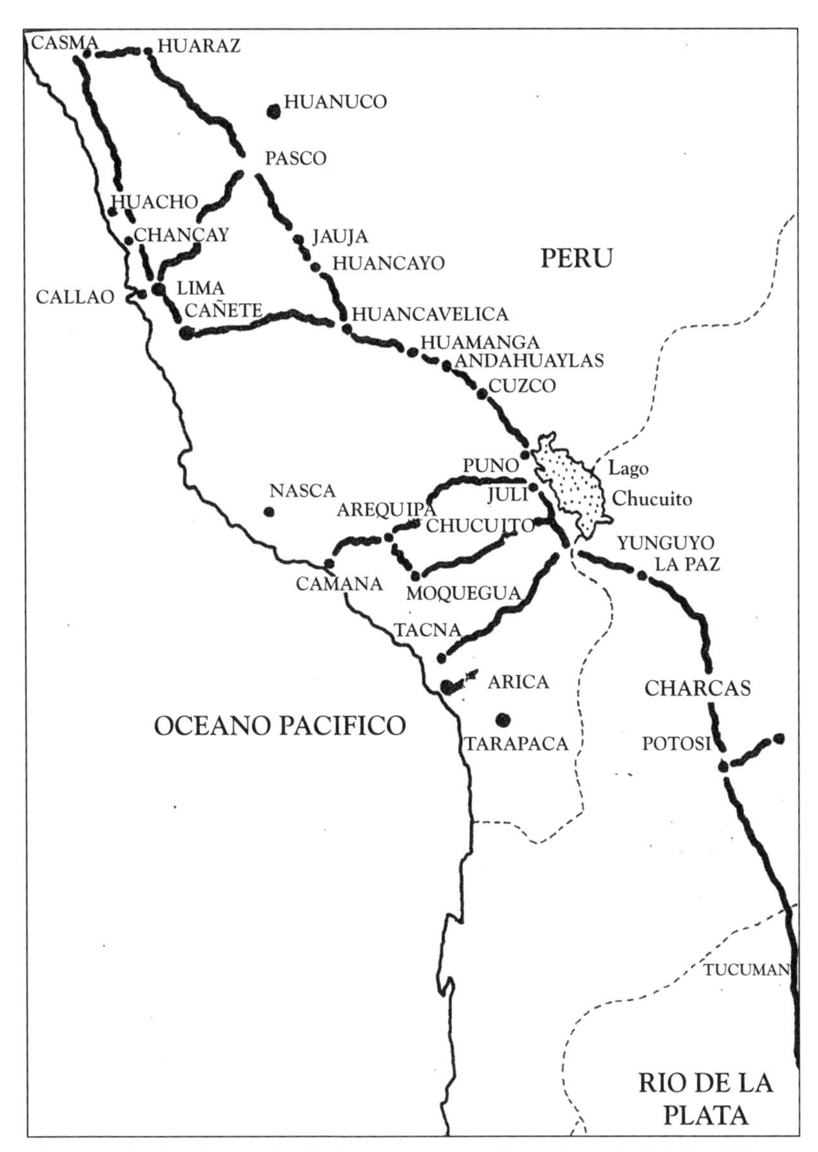

Map 1.3. Andean Routes (18th Century). *Source:* Emilio Mendizábal, "La difusión, aculturación y reinterpretación a través de las cajas de imaginero ayacuchanas," *Folklore Americano* (Lima) XI, 11-12 (1963).

The latter author showed how contemporary weavings, engraved gourds, silverwork, painted wood, and ceramics express not the assimilation of western and Andean traditions but instead innovation and invention. The result is neither repetition nor replicas but something different.

The *retablos* are the best example that Stastny provides: "[T]hey include different protectors of autochthonous species such as condors and other birds, messengers of the mountain spirits, *Apus*, and the protectors, that is the huacas, of the European animals, the saints whose role is to facilitate the integration of external livestock into the indigenous cosmos, where all animals already have their huacas."[96] Retablo is the Peruvian name for a type of image box divided in two: Catholic saints generally appear on top, protected by the wings of a condor, while scenes of animals, branding rituals, or a misti or peasant are on the bottom. It is the world of above and below: the representation of the cosmos. The retablo is a portable altar, an easily transportable sacred place that can be carried to rituals in the countryside or placed in homes. Its history goes back to the saint boxes that the conquistadors brought. The first retablos were made in the early eighteenth century, but they were much larger than those of today, and the saints were sculpted in stone or wood. They shrank over time and acquired the shape of a small box in the nineteenth century. Residents in Ayacucho and in other areas of the central and southern Andes used them in livestock branding rituals, and muleteers helped disseminate them. Their area of diffusion correlates to the map of the Andean utopia and that of the great Andean trade route that since the eighteenth century linked Lima and Buenos Aires, the Pacific and Atlantic oceans.[97] Cities such as Puno, Cuzco, Huamanga, and Huancayo where artisans established themselves and created artistic traditions constituted the route's key stops. Peasants who sought this portable huaca, muleteers who transported them, and clever artisans who made them all played a role in the history of the retablo.[98] In the end, the retablo loses its resemblance to Spanish saint boxes. The word is still European, but it designates a new object, just like the Andean utopia.

Definitions are only complete at the end and should thus appear in the conclusions rather than the introduction. The Andean utopia has three dimensions: not only does it attempt to understand the past or provide an alternative to the present, but it also seeks to discern

[96] Francisco Stastny, *Las artes populares del Perú* (Madrid: Edubanco, 1981), 58.

[97] Emilio Mendizábal, "La difusión, aculturación y reinterpretación a través de las cajas de imaginero ayacuchanas," *Folklore Americano* (Lima) XI, 11–12 (1963), 115–34.

[98] Pablo Macera, *Retablos andinos* (Lima: Universidad Nacional Mayor de San Marcos, 1981).

the future. What happened is as important as what will happen. It announces that someday the time of the mistis will end and a new age will begin.

Mythical stories have the same capacity for synthesis and condensation as dreams do. What in an academic history book would require several volumes and in a textbook many pages – a narrative about Peruvian history from the Conquest until today – is summarized in the "myth of the three ages" collected by Father Manuel Marzal in Urcos:

> In the second age God created the world of Jesus Christ, which is today's world and that will come to an end. God created the present generation in three categories. First, the Qollas who live near the lakeshore. They always come here in search of food as they are fishermen. Second, the Inkas, who lived in the great city of Cuzco. They were very powerful and could do grandiose things, such as cities, roads, and forts, but God did not grant them the great power of reading. When the mistis arrived, the Incas fled towards Father (*Tayta*) Paititi, escaping to the hills and hiding with their wives in the high plateaus that the mistis couldn't reach. That is why they live in the most solitary and inhospitable plateaus, which is divine punishment for the sins they committed. Third, the mistis, God's last children, the *chanas*, who can do what they want because God tolerates their sins; also, they know how to read.[99]

EIGHTEENTH-CENTURY ANDEAN ROUTES

The preceding story does not display a cyclical view of history. Time is linear, and one period substitutes another. The circle is broken; there is no eternal return. Nor does it offer archetypes or models. Instead, its anonymous authors search for historical events and offer divine will as a general explanation. Is it a millenarian text? Can we draw an uninterrupted line between Joachim of Fiore and Urcos and other Andean towns? New elements created in the Americas, such as Paititi, as well

[99] Manuel Marzal, "Funciones religiosas del mito en el mundo andino cuzqueño," *Debates en Antropología* (Lima) 4 (1979), 12. [Editors' note: Although Flores Galindo has the word *chama* in the original, it is actually *chana*, which comes from *chanacuy*, the last child in Quechua. We thank Gisela Cánepa and Juan Ossio for clarifying this.]

as older, pre-Hispanic ones, fill this story. The three categories of the second age appear to correspond to the three-way organization of Inca kinship, each with different social roles. First, Collana: the founders, the authorities, aristocrats, found in the first world, the world of above, *hanansaya*. Second, Payan, the other half, *hurinsaya*, the peasant population, secondary relatives of the *Collana*. Third, Cayao: foreigners, who live apart from the first two and provide secondary wives.[100] In the Urcos story, the Incas are Collana: they live in Cuzco, that is, in the "great city." Aymaras, who live outside the city as peasants or shepherds, are Payan. Finally, the mistis as foreigners are equal to the Cayao. These categories don't reflect reality but were instruments that helped pre-Hispanic Andean people understand their society. That was how they thought the world was organized and how it should work. The Conquest completely disrupted this scheme. According to historian Jan Szeminski, the Spaniards should have been Cayao but "on the contrary, acted like Qollana."[101] Those on the fringes of the cosmos, on the lowest scale, moved to the top. Reality inverted. An incomprehensible and total power appeared: The mistis "did whatever they felt like."

We need other explanations to understand the turmoil of the conquest, for traditional Andean thought reached its limits. The vanquished had to turn to the victors' religion, from which the Urcos story takes the notion of guilt: the Incas were defeated because of their sins. Over time, the introduction of rural schools, the increase in literacy, and other similar phenomena must have led to ignorance of writing as an additional explanation. Andean people blamed themselves and their cultural deficiencies for the defeat. An obvious lesson emerges: abandon Andean culture and assume that of the victors. Schools were a constant demand in twentieth-century peasant struggles, at times as important as land or payment in salary.[102] The story suggests a seemingly negative but ambivalent view of Andean people. Yes, the mistis triumphed, but the Incas didn't disappear. They still exist. They took refuge in distant, isolated areas, in the high plateaus or the jungle where Paititi,

[100] Tom Zuidema, "Mito e historia en el antiguo Perú," *Allpanchis* (Cuzco) 10 (1977), 10 ff.

[101] Jan Szeminski, *La utopía tupamarista* (Lima: Pontificia Universidad Católica del Perú, 1984), 91, 125.

[102] Rodrigo Montoya, "El factor étnico y el desarrollo" (Cuzco: Centro de Estudios Rurales Andinos Bartolomé de las Casas, 1985), mimeograph.

Cuzco's double, was located. It was an uncertain triumph. According to a narrative that also belongs to the Inkarri cycle, Paititi was also the city of large dimensions, radiant light, and abundant bread to where the Incas fled.[103] The Promised Land was there, beyond the mountains, somewhere in the jungle.

The Urcos story of the three ages of creation does not end with mistis' domination. The peasant storyteller immediately adds, "[T]he world will end in the year 2000." Here, the Andean utopia encounters other eschatological images that circulate in the Andes today. In Iquitos, the Brothers of the Cross prepare for the final hour, and in other jungle areas those who live along the river await the great flood. In Lima, the preacher Ezequiel Ataucusi gains followers for his new "Israelite Church" and calls on them to prepare for a return to the times of the Old Testament. Followers dress the way schoolbooks portray the prophets. In Ayacucho, people interpreted recent earthquakes as signs that the earth could not bear so much suffering. In the northern cities of Chiclayo and Trujillo, rumors about the end of the world accompanied unusually heavy rains and flooding. Lima's shantytowns enthusiastically embrace miraculous images, the appearance of the Messiah's face in trees, saints, and preachers. In his novel *The War of the End of the World*, Mario Vargas Llosa reconstructed a Brazilian messianic rebellion that struggled against its time. He didn't have to go that far. "O conselheiro," the man who traveled across the southern plains of Brasil, also lived among us. That past was present in Peru.[104]

Today, in addition to many evangelical churches, there are in Peru about 100 religious groups that the Catholic Church considers sects. Some have important international connections, and it is plausible that United States political groups greet them with enthusiasm if not more direct support: Mysticism could be a political antidote, and traditional messianism can serve as a containing wall against the progressive elements of Christianity. But other groups emerged spontaneously, eager to escape stifling reality or offer ways to make sense of the disorder and worsening injustice that the economic crisis prompted in recent years and to confirm hope in the face of discouragement. They seem to suggest that there is an alternative, even if in an imaginary and distant jungle kingdom that could be reached through a long pilgrimage.

103 Ossio ed., *Ideología mesiánica*, 494.

104 Mario Vargas Llosa, *The War of the End of the World*, translated by Helen R. Lane (New York: Farrar Straus Giroux, 1984).

Between the second and third ages, according to the Urcos story, there is a terrible transition in which "men with two heads, animals with five legs and many other things" will appear. Cataclysms and the arrival of antichrists are announced. The story ends with these words: "After everything, the third age will come, that of the third person, God the Holy Spirit, and other beings will inhabit the earth." The mistis are not eternal. They will perish like the Incas and, as anyone from the sixteenth century would say, "the earth will belong to others."

CHAPTER 2

COMMUNITIES AND DOCTRINES

THE STRUGGLE FOR SOULS (CENTRAL ANDES, 1608–1666)

Andean societies did not have horses or the wheel and obviously could not invent the coach. The pre-Hispanic world thus lacked classic symbols of hierarchy, status, and power. The historian Pablo Macera has subtly observed that all Andean people – rich or poor, lords or peasants – went on foot. Lacking visible status symbols such as horses and coaches, those who held political or religious power in the Andes had to create a complex symbolic apparatus. Relative military precariousness forced an exaggerated growth of religious mechanisms to ensure domination through fervor or, more frequently, fear. The crusading spirit of the Spanish meant that the "spiritual conquest" of the Indies would prolong military conquest. One chapter of this story was written in the early seventeenth century in the Peruvian central highlands, but the dispute between indigenous and Christian priests echoed in other parts of the Andes, including the viceregal capital, Lima, and the northern coast.

Throughout history, those who bear injustice and marginality have always envisioned societies without inequalities. They place them outside history, at the end of time or the beginning of everything, in some distant place on the other side of the mountains, in a time when Adam and Eve lived in paradise and lords and peasants didn't exist. Andean people identified this alternative with the land of the Incas: Popular memory recreated the empire. It converted a relatively brief period of Andean history, when the Inca imposed state coercion on towns and regions, into an extended period when hunger did not exist, people shared goods, and epidemics did not strike. It was the image of the colonial world inverted. However, this paradigm did not automatically emerge as a reflexive response to conquest. Rather, elements of Andean and western thought flowed together or confronted one another: myth and history, oral tradition and writing, peasants and priests, popular culture and intellectuals. It also emerged from social conflicts. Scholars have tended to pay more attention to overt struggles such as mutinies, rebellions, and uprisings, but other confrontations – constant, intense, yet not so bloody – took place. This was the case of the area under the jurisdiction of the Lima Archdiocese in the first half of the seventeenth century, specifically in the towns that now make up the provinces of Huarochirí, Canta, Cajatambo, Bolognesi, Pasco, Ambo, and Dos de Mayo in the central Andes.

The existence of medium-sized mines and textile mills or *obrajes* meant that the Spanish had a greater presence among the central Andes' Indian population than in the south. This area became Lima's breadbasket, where muleteers transported goods to the capital along various routes supported by *tambos* or storage houses. Movement of goods and people helps explain the relatively high percentage of mestizos and the prevalence of Spanish over Quechua in the region. But *mestizaje* did not spell the end of Indian communities. On the contrary, today's central Andes departments of Ancash and Junín have a relatively high number of Indian peasant communities. Of the 2,716 communities recognized by the state in 1976, more than 700 were located in these two departments.

There is an evident relationship between the Andean utopia and peasant communities.[1] If we mapped the principal manifestations of the utopia, it would include places where stories about the *Inkarri* and the world's three ages have been uncovered, such as all those towns in the Bolognesi and Cajatambo provinces that still stage the Capture of the Inca. Although most take place in August, these performances do not follow the same script. In some places, the Inca embraces Pizarro; in others, he ends up decapitated, imprisoned, or rescued. Despite the differences, the performance generally projects the discourse of Peru as a mestizo country, privileging the western over the indigenous.

In 1976, forty-two recognized peasant communities existed in the Bolognesi Province, ten of which had sought and received recognition by the Office of Indian Affairs soon after it was first possible, between 1926 and 1930. Representatives from towns such as Aqía, Congas, Huasta, and Copa traveled to Lima with documents and titles in hand. Centuries earlier priests from Lima, often Jesuits, visited those same towns as part of the "extirpation of idolatry" campaigns. They set out to

[1] See the previous chapter.

interrogate indigenous *hechiceros* or sorcerers, destroy huacas and places of worship, seize idols, and discover clandestine cemeteries. The clash between two cultures prolonged the era of the Conquest. Those same towns answered the state's call for official recognition in the 1920s because they were more attentive to what was happening in the capital and also could fulfill the requirements: that they had their titles and papers in order was a sign of literacy and also expressed a historical consciousness linked to the land and the knowledge of town boundaries. Communities defined their identity and constructed a historical memory as part of a unique regional history created in the midst of cultural conflicts.

Between 1610 and 1660, the Spanish unleashed three idolatry extirpation campaigns in the central Andes. They began with a seemingly anecdotal incident. In 1608, a creole priest trained by Cuzco Jesuits, who had lived in the town of San Damián (Huarochirí) for eleven years, discovered that a hidden adoration of two ancient pre-Hispanic divinities, Pariacaca and Chaupiñamocc, lurked within the Virgin of the Assumption celebration held for five days each August. The Spanish had converted Indians to Christianity in appearance only. Father Francisco de Avila preached, took confession, and with the help of informants arrested Hernando Paucar, who "had become an idolatrous priest and was very feared and venerated among his kind."[2] Authorities took Paucar to Lima, along with his idols or *conopas*. In December, workers built a stage in the Plaza Mayor for an *auto de fe* and invited all of the city's population and nearby Indians. With a theatric performance befitting baroque piety, idolatry campaigns began.

The Archbishopry and colonial administrators supported Father Avila. Church and state collaborated in an undertaking that most believed required the participation of the religious orders, particularly the Jesuits. At the beginning of the seventeenth century authorities in Spain and the Americas imposed absolutist, exclusionary policies that sought integration by eliminating and suppressing all that was strange and different. They persecuted beggars and the poor, attempting to confine them, and displayed anxiety about the mentally ill, which anticipated the establishment of insane asylums. These campaigns also included enclosures and fears, the persecution of Jews, and the expulsion of people of Muslim heritage in Spain. Authorities took these measures

2 Rubén Vargas Ugarte, *Historia General del Perú*, vol. 3 (Barcelona: Milla Batres, 1966), 129.

to the extreme in the Americas not just because of the distance separating metropolis and colony and the desire to imitate Spain, but also because they perceived foreigners' presence within the colonies – the Portuguese, for example, or the Dutch ships that threatened Callao (including Spielbergen, the pirate) and even burnt down the town of Paita – as a dangerous threat. Indians, already the equivalent of poor Europeans, assumed the social standing of Jews. The extirpation campaign took the Inquisition as its model, as Pierre Duviols has argued.[3] It's also true, however, as Manuel Marzal responded, that idolatrous Indians were not executed. Authorities did not seek to suppress them but to get rid of what the extirpators considered idols and demons and to reconcile them with true faith: that is, dominate their souls.

In a society where political power was closely linked to the sacred, control over souls was a privileged terrain. Domination demanded the use and manipulation of magical and religious elements. Local indigenous authorities, kurakas, who increased their identification with their towns by assuming additional roles as healers and even shamans, understood this well.[4] Furthermore, in the seventeenth century, religious delirium spread among the Spanish, expressed in processions, flagellations such as those attributed to Lima's Saint Rose, and San Francisco Solano's preaching. While the extirpators roamed the central Andes searching for sorcerers, San Francisco Solano wandered the streets of Lima, crucifix in hand, seeking penitents. Rumors of his prophecies of imminent cataclysm proved credible when earthquakes rocked Arequipa, Arica, and Lima.

Idolatry campaigns followed the procedures that Avila had tried out in Huarochirí. The priests – Avendaño, Hernández Príncipe, and Bernardo de Noboa, among others – arrived, preached, took confession, interrogated Indians and mestizos, and sought informants. Divine punishments such as pain, illness, and even death awaited those who did not collaborate. But risks and threats lurked on the other side as well.

3 The key study is Pierre Duviols, *La lutte contre les religions autochtones dans le Pérou Colonial* (Lima: Instituto Francés de Estudios Andinos, 1971). See also Karen Spalding, "Resistencia y adaptación: el gobierno colonial y las élites nativas," *Allpanchis* (Cuzco) 17–18 (1981), 5–21, as well as studies by Luis Basto Girón, Manuel Burga, Guillermo Cock, Lorenzo Huertas, and Irene Silverblatt.

4 See the work of Luis Millones on magic, witchcraft, and power in the Andes, including "Medicina y magia: propuesta para un análisis de los materiales andinos," *Boletín del Instituto Francés de Estudios Andinos* (Lima) XIII, 3–4 (1983), 63–8.

In 1613, in a town between Huancavelica and Ayacucho, a lightning bolt destroyed a church just as priests arrived, an event that could be interpreted as evidence of the wrath of a pre-Hispanic divinity. When the Jesuits inspected the ruined temple they found a huaca behind the altar and a clandestine cemetery below the floor. They interpreted the lightning bolt differently than Andean people did.[5]

In the Lima sierra, the extirpators agreed with their Huancavelica counterparts that Indians only simulated Christianity. There was a different, underground world, where appearances did not match reality. Although they demand critical reading, and the events they refer to must be analyzed from both sides, records in Lima's Archbishop Archive help us reconstruct this dark side of the moon.

In the European countryside, the Church dominated the faithful by controlling daily life and ideological discourse. They changed the pagan calendar, dedicated specific days to Christ and saints, and organized festivals and rituals. They named the faithful based on the calendar of saints' days, making the population more uniform and generating identities. Extirpators therefore were surprised to find that the idolatrous had dropped their Christian names and acquired new identities: "some of them don't use their baptismal saint's names, but instead those given to the gentiles by the sorcerers."[6]

Andean peoples chose to use their own names, but also their own clothes. In their reencounter with traditional rituals, Andean people wore clothing from the time of the "gentiles." These *conversos* (or *re-conversos*) also avoided Spanish food and relied solely on native plants and animals. They turned to corn, guinea pigs, and llamas and gave up wheat and wine – essential for mass – and "Castilian lamb or pork that they call *raccha micuna* which is prohibited food."[7] Coca leaves occupied a preferential place in ritual. Andeans poured *chicha* or corn beer on the ground as an offering to mother earth and used guinea pigs as a divination tool, to discover illnesses, and as sacrificial lambs.

5 Carlos Romero, "Idolatría de los indios huachos y yauyos," *Revista Histórica* (Lima), 6, 2 (1918), 191.

6 Pierre Duviols, *Cultura andina y represión: procesos y visitas de idolatrías y hechicerías. Cajatambo s. XVIII* (Cuzco: Centro Bartolomé de Las Casas, 1986), 164. Duviols published documents from the Lima Archbishopry Archive relating to the Cajatambo province.

7 Duviols, *Cultura andina*, 164. [Editors' note: The meaning of *raccha* is unclear; *micuna* means food in Quechua.]

In Europe, the Church controlled the major events in every Christian's life. Besides baptism, priests also consecrated marriages and accompanied the faithful through last rites. In the Andes, idolatrous towns used a parallel wedding system and a different cemetery, generally a site of a pre-Hispanic place of worship called *machay*, "cavern," "cave," or "grotto" in Quechua. Archaeologist Pedro Villar Córdova identified three types of caverns that served as rooms for habitation, worship, or burials.[8] Transferring the dead from the Catholic temple to the machay, a cemetery and a sacred place, represented for Andean people a re-encounter with their traditions and ancestors and, in this way, with the world of their divinities.

The Andean pantheon was heterogeneous. There were diverse gods who in their organization appeared to follow the hierarchy of *panacas* (royal lineage), *ayllus* (kinship groups), and regions.[9] Men who permitted communication between the sacred and the profane were "religious specialists" whom the extirpators called witches or sorcerers but whose followers considered true priests. Their local name was *camachicos*, but they were also called Huacapúllac (he who speaks with the huaca), Laicca, or Auqillo (father or old man).[10] Besides presiding over rituals, they practiced divining and curing.

Diviners predicted harvests, weather, and approaching cataclysms. They read dreams. They observed spiders and toads, symbols of the underworld, and guinea pig innards. People sought indigenous priests about the risks of an upcoming trip or the whereabouts of a lost mule or other animal. These priests also detected and cured ailments. According to Basto Girón, there were three types of hechiceros or sorcerers: "[T]hose who harmed people's health and property; those who focused on amorous relationships; and, finally, the healers, *curanderos*."[11] In other words, those devoted to good and those devoted to evil. According to a testimony published by Duviols,

> that's what this witness said he heard, that some guy named Marcaguaman, whose first name he didn't know, from the town of

[8] Pedro Villar Córdova, *Las culturas prehispánicas en el departamento de Lima* (Lima: np, 1935), 110.

[9] I am following here the work of Maria Rostworowski and Manuel Burga.

[10] Joseph de Arriaga, *La extirpación de la idolatría en el Perú* (Lima: Imp. Sanmarti, 1920), 32.

[11] Luis Basto Girón, *Salud y enfermedad en el campesino peruano* (Lima: Universidad Nacional Mayor de San Marcos, 1957), 65.

> Machaca, and a priest and cantor named García are *cauchus queta runamicuc* who kill people and these sorcerers' children always inherit this trade from their fathers; and he also heard and it's also publicly known that Lucas julca [sic] from the town of Chilcas is the biggest indoctrinator.[12]

According to this testimony, indigenous priests succeeded into the position and were divided into various strata. Other testimonies, however, suggest that there was a minimal division of labor. Those who organized a machay were also healers and fortune-tellers. Unlike Catholic priests, indigenous priests worked with good and evil. Some gained followers from as far away as Huacho, a coastal town, but most plied their trade locally, in small towns, and on their own.

This culture paralleled Christian religiosity but not the institutional apparatus of the church. That there were indigenous priests but not indigenous bishops suggests that the conflicts centered on the battle between indigenous priests (healers, fortune tellers, etc.) and a town's Catholic priest, the *doctrinero*. The indigenous priest or healer was also sometimes the kuraka, as was the case in Huarochirí, Ayacucho, and elsewhere in the central Andes.[13] One town's documents indicate that traditional rituals were held in the kuraka's house, whereas elsewhere they took place in what was called the communal house. This direct link to or coexistence with political power – represented by the kurakas – undoubtedly bolstered idolatrous practices. Some extirpators blamed the spread of idolatry on priests' abandonment of small towns or the far-flung extension of some parishes. Kurakas and local priests fought not only over religion but also over indigenous labor and the towns' negligible surplus.

The fact that a diversity of actors practiced idolatry without a concerted plan and that sorcerers were dispersed throughout the Andes made it difficult to repress. Isolation and lack of organization, however, cost practitioners a common strategy to resist the coordinated efforts of colonial administrators, local priests, and religious orders. In this case, absolutism swept away local autonomy.

Indians' relationship with Christianity was ambivalent. In some cases, they attempted a complete break; in others, they simulated some

[12] Duviols, *Cultura andina*, 171–2.

[13] Luis Millones, "Shamanismo y política en el Perú colonial: los curacas de Ayacucho," *Histórica* (Lima) 8, 2 (1984), 131–49; Spalding, "Resistencia y adaptación."

Christian ways to avoid detection. They buried the dead in churches but then secretly took them to the machay at night. They participated in celebrations of Christ, saints, and virgins, but practiced other types of rituals in the midst of dancing and drinking. They tolerantly incorporated Catholic practices, as additional manifestations of the sacred. Polytheism absorbed monotheism.

A 1619 document from the province of Cajatambo shows that authorities imprisoned 22,511, absolved 20,893, and tried or accused 1,618 priests or sorcerers. Every man or woman, young and old, seemed to be a suspect. How did indigenous priests attract so many followers over such a large area? How was it that they became superior to Catholic priests? Documents offer an answer. Indigenous priests knew how to mediate conversation between Andean gods and people. Idols were not silent. Rituals and sacrifices made mummies (*mallquis*), amulets (*conopas*), and sacred sites (huacas and *adoratorios*) relevant to everyone's daily life. Indigenous priests did not preach from the pulpit or demand self-incrimination from the confessional. Andean religiosity addressed immediate and practical problems such as finding a lost animal, impeding a neighbor's threats, and especially protecting precarious lives besieged by frequent disasters such as earthquakes, landslides, and epidemics. People consulted indigenous priests primarily about health problems. Hernando de Hacaspoma, an Indian from Cajatambo, said that "he taught the people not to venerate God, the Lord, or his saints because they are for the Spanish, they were their Gods and Creators, just golden painted sticks who did not speak and did not respond to Indians' requests, unlike their ancient *guamancama* and other idols and malquis who if you consulted and made them a sacrifice, would answer your request."[14] Indigenous divinities offered greater protection against illnesses, frost, plagues, and even the Spaniards' affronts.

Around 1618, a devastating measles outbreak struck Lima and its hinterland. Smallpox hit Cajatambo numerous times. Alongside physical illnesses such as *uta* or leishmaniasis, asthma, venereal diseases, and mange, we must consider psychological and cultural maladies such as the evil eye, the evil wind, lightning strikes, and deep fear or panic. Threats, anguish, and tension reigned in the indigenous world.[15]

[14] Duviols, *Cultura Andina*, 145.

[15] Hugo Pereyra, "Sublevaciones, obrajes e idolatrías en el Corregimiento de Cajatambo durante los siglos XVI y XVII," BA thesis, Pontificia Universidad Católica del Perú, 1986, and, by the same author, "Mita obrajera, idolatría y

The Spanish also admitted that idols spoke, but they understood them as incarnations of the devil, as evidence of evil's domination over Indians' souls. Amidst the extirpation campaigns – which could be considered a true crusade – Catholic priests seem to have been overwhelmed by thoughts of devils and the anxious need for exorcism. Therefore, not all of the written European testimonies should be accepted. The notable increase in cases against idolaters was more a barometer of Spaniards' religiosity than a measure of contemporary indigenous mentalities. The fact that they diminished after 1670 and virtually disappeared in the eighteenth century does not necessarily mean extirpators won and Indians had converted.

What instruments did those fighting idolatry use? Confession and preaching were useful in the first foray, but recovering souls was a lengthy task. More than words were required to keep the sheep in the pen. Duviols emphasized two key institutions: jails and schools. Viceroy Francisco de Borja y Aragón, the Prince of Esquilache, founded both in 1617. The Santa Cruz jail housed those considered "dogmatizers." The school was for *caciques*, underlining the link between religion and political power in Andean towns. Both were located in Lima's Indian neighborhood, el Cercado. The jail housed forty prisoners in 1620, whereas the year before twenty-one students began the Cacique school. The number of new students fluctuated from six in 1627 and one in 1628 to fourteen in 1632. Thirty years later, the numbers began to decrease irreversibly. Only one new student entered in 1644, and in subsequent years no more than one a year. The rise and fall of the number of extirpation of idolatry trials paralleled that of the number of incoming students.

Jesuit priests ran the school. Authorities frequently called upon them for inspections (*visitas*) of Andean towns and for extirpation campaigns. They played a similar role in Europe at the beginning of the seventeenth century during the Counter-Reformation. They imposed true faith in rural areas, combated heresy, and sought Christian unity.[16] In Peru, Jesuits (priests, students, and novices) increased from 241 in 1594 to 342 in 1610 and were probably one of the most numerous orders.[17] The decline of extirpation campaigns coincided with their 1658 retreat from

rebelión en San Juan de Churín (1663)," *Boletín del Instituto Riva Agüero* (Lima) 13 (1984–85), 209–44.

[16] Ginzburg, *The Cheese and the Worms*, 126.

[17] Rubén Vargas Ugarte, *Historia de la iglesia en el Perú* (Burgos: Aldecoa, 1959), II, 235.

Table 2.1. *Distribution of Cases of Extirpation of Idolatry, 1600–1749 Archive of the Archbishopric of Lima*

1600–09	1
1610–19	4
1620–29	4
1630–39	1
1640–49	7
1650–59	5
1660–69	66
1670–79	6
1680–89	4
1690–99	13
1700–09	3
1710–19	2
1720–29	6
1730–39	2
1740–49	1
Total	135

Source: Manuel Burga, "La crisis de la identidad andina: mito, ritual y memoria en los Andes centrales" (unpublished ms., University of Wisconsin, 1984).

the Chavín parish in the Conchucos area, bordering Cajatambo. Why did they retreat and change paths? Probably because the church believed that Indians were already converted to Christianity, which depended not so much on practice but on the recognition of a hierarchical institution.

Authorities used the Lima jail and school for the more recalcitrant cases and the rural elite. For other souls, however, authorities turned to religious brotherhoods or sodalities (*cofradías*) and parishes. The *visitadores*, those in charge of the visitas, sought to create as many cofradías as possible in the towns they visited. Around 1619, the Lima Archdiocese had 250 such brotherhoods, with 36 percent dedicated to the Virgin and 21 percent to the Lord. In the same area, 159 *doctrinas* or parishes existed in 1664, managed by 111 clerics and 78 *religiosos*.[18] Parishes

[18] Manuel Marzal, *La tranformación religiosa peruana* (Lima: Pontificia Universidad Católica del Perú, 1983). This is an important historiographical work that is key to understanding what could be called the orthodox version of these events. [Editors' note: "Clerics" were the secular priests, whereas "religiosos" pertained to religious orders].

Table 2.2. *Students in the School of Caciques (Admitted) 1618–1680*

1618	17
1619	21
1620	9
1621	4
1622	3
1623	4
1624	5
1625	11
1626	3
1627	6
1628	1
1629	6
1630	3
1631	8
1632	14
1633	5
1634	12
1635	1
1636	11
1637	10
1638	15
1639	9
1640	4
1641	13
1642	22
1643	9
1644	6
1645	8
1646	7
1647	4
1648	3
1649	4
1650	14
1651	13
1652	9
1653	9
1654	7
1655	11
1656	6
1657	7
1658	12
1659	4

(*continued*)

Table 2.2. *(Continued)*

1660	9
1662	8
1663	5
1664	1
1665	1
1666	2
1667	2
1668	0
1669	1
1670	3
1671	1
1672	2
1673	0
1674	0
1675	1
1676	0
1677	2
1678	1
1679	2
1680	5

Source: "Colegio de Caciques," *Inca* (Lima), I, 4 (Oct–Dec. 1923), 800–9.

obviously permitted a closer relationship between authority (the priest) and subject (the parishioner).

The parishes were not merely spatial divisions for religious work. Bernard Lavallé and Antonio Acosta have documented that parishes, although smaller than the political jurisdictions called *corregimientos*, could provide greater and steadier income.[19] Priests serving rural parishes, usually members of the regular clergy, controlled the labor force and were key players in providing workers for textile mills and mines. They also counted on *sínodos* or royal stipends as well as fees from holy sacraments, masses, and burials. Father Avila, it is worth recalling, led the parish where the Spanish first denounced idolatry. Before he made his accusations to great fanfare in Lima's Plaza Mayor,

[19] Lavallé, *Recherches sur l'apparition*; Antonio Acosta, "El pleito de indios de San Damián (Huarochirí) contra Francisco de Avila. 1607," *Historiografía y bibliografía americanistas* (Seville) XXIII (1979), 3–33.

Huarochirí Indians took him to court for economic extortion.[20] Many of the extirpators were *doctrineros*, the heads of parishes. Although political, religious, and ideological motives played a role, we can't dismiss mundane material reasons, because dominating souls produced considerable economic dividends.

Religious doctrine took hold in rural communities. The church organized the space and life of the faithful, but it had to make concessions. Priests started calling idolatry healing, allowed the use of herbs and guinea pigs to cure the ill, and tolerated coca leaves and chicha corn beer. Rituals became folkloric practices. That Catholic priests demonstrated more power than sorcerers but couldn't enlist them as allies indicates the limits of what until this point seemed like a church victory. It was a Christian land and a religious people with little religious vocation; there were creole and mulatto saints, but no Indian saints.

But this was not a monolithic confrontation between the Christian west and the Andean world. Events were much more complex. The discovery of idolatry was possible because there were local informants. At times, tips came from a rival town, but in most cases mestizos and creoles gave up the kuraka or the local camachicos. Religion always played a role: on one side someone threatened by an evil sorcerer turned to the church; on the other, a person blamed his abandonment of traditional ways for his child's evil eye. Rivals shared similarities, including the frequent lack of coherence.

Idolatry was a regional problem that did not make it to the north. The epidemic spared Jauja Valley and weakened as it moved south. Why didn't Ayacucho and Cuzco seem to have idolaters? Perhaps Christian forces were less anxious about their hegemony there than in the Lima Archdiocese and other areas near the capital. Spaniards, Indians, and mestizos also did not coexist as frequently in Cuzco, Ayacucho, and other rural areas as they did in Lima's hinterland.

Paradoxically, complex ethnic confrontations created the basis for collective identity. What authorities deemed sorcery united diverse ethnic groups and strata, who formed a part of popular culture that Indians, blacks, Spaniards, and mestizos recognized. The poor, marginal, and women of different skin color in Lima practiced sorcery. Catholic priests always saw this as the work of the devil, capable of assuming

[20] Acosta, "El pleito." See also the essays by Acosta and Lavallé in *Allpanchis* (Cuzco), 19 (1982).

the physical characteristics of the Inca, a logical association considering that they identified pre-Hispanic religiosity with evil. Perhaps the tendency in popular culture to invert dominant discourses explains why many came to view the devil positively. In seventeenth-century Lima, sorcerers such as María de Córdoba, a quarteroon, invoked Satan and Barabbas alongside the Inca and the colla.[21] Another mulatto woman, Petrona de Saavedra, invoked coca leaves and the Inca.

Female sorcerers in Lima also employed ceramic and metal idols extracted from ancient pre-Hispanic buildings. Evocation of the Inca thus drew strength from ancient objects. De Saavedra or de Córdoba, who employed this magic, came from cultural traditions distinct from those of indigenous people. Based in Lima, they descended from African slaves, and they must have mixed with Andean migrants in the city's poverty, its streets and alleys, where they learned of mud promontories and huacas that surrounded Lima. This is how a sort of popular identity emerged.

A 1662 trial involving the town of San Francisco de Magas suggests that Spaniards tolerated invocations of the Inca. After denying any relation with idols and denouncing a presumed indigenous priest as a con artist, the accused confessed that in a festival "he dressed like an Inca with two other Indians, Don García Ricapa, deceased, and Francisco Callan, and battled other Indians dressed like Spaniards." This text could be considered another birth certificate of the Andean utopia. An ancient ritual that recalled the confrontation between inhabitants of the higher elevations (*llacuaces*) and valleys (*huaris*), that is, between shepherds and farmers, was transformed in the second half of the seventeenth century into a theatrical representation of the Spanish-Andean encounter. In the central Andes, extirpation campaigns prolonged the conquest for another century. History became a problem of the present. Even though rebels invoked the Inca in an isolated uprising in Churín in 1633, the Spanish tolerated his representation. It was not just retreat and loss for the peasant world; parishes never fully subjugated Indians. Souls were difficult to control.[22]

Let's pause and sum up our journey thus far. Extirpators converted huacas, synonyms of the sacred in the Andes, into demons, which are

[21] María Emma Mannarelli, "Inquisición y mujeres: las hechiceras en el Perú durante el siglo XVII," *Revista Andina* (Cuzco) 3, 1 (1985), 146–7.

[22] Burga, "Una crisis de identidad."

later personified as Incas. Clandestine practice vindicated the devil and exalted or tolerated the Inca, a profane character only in appearance. The utopia, the hope for the return of the Incas, enmeshed in everyday life and ultimately offered a type of compromise to cultural conflict. On the Andean side, protagonists included priests, kurakas, and communities. The indigenous community did not just embody Indians as a corporate group but also became a political instrument.

Just as the Spanish tolerated the idea of the Inca, events forced acceptance of sorcery, by then considered healing or *curanderismo*, practiced not only in the central Andes and Lima but throughout the viceroyalty. It sought not only to heal people, but also to ease anxieties and tensions in a precarious and conflictive world. The *curioso* ("inquisitive"), the "sage," and the "healer," who could be Indian, mestizo, or white, man or woman, persisted alongside the priest. In 1762 authorities arrested a Spaniard in the town of Olmos, Motupe, and found "idolatry gear and other stuff."[23] Unlike a century earlier, systematic persecution of these practices did not ensue. Characters such as this appeared in the archives only when some serious problem prompted an investigation. In 1746 in Paiján, Trujillo, testimonies in an investigation about a mayor's death mentioned "a barber who can also heal" and "several practicing women." When the mayor became mysteriously ill, his family turned to both a mestiza, Antonia de Arce, and a priest who had medicine. They did not see them as alternatives; it was not a matter of picking one or the other.[24] This was not the case years later, in Eten, when in a peasant uprising against two priests, some suspected a man named Gabriel Carrillo "whom the Indians worship."[25] We don't find similar cases in the Piura, Chiclayo, and Trujillo archives, a possible sign of peaceful coexistence between priest and healer, parish and popular religion.[26] Idolatry extirpation, in the end, was not exactly a victory for the "true faith."

[23] Archivo Departamental de La Libertad, Corregimiento, Causas Criminales, Legajo 55, doc. 1147 (1762).

[24] Archivo Departamental de La Libertad, Corregimiento, Causas Criminales, expediente 2784.

[25] Archivo Departamental de La Libertad, Intendencia, Causas Criminales, Legajo 355, expediente 1408.

[26] The north coast continues to be the area where curanderismo or healing is most commonly practiced.

CHAPTER 3

The Spark and the Fire

JUAN SANTOS ATAHUALPA

To Juan, Isabel, and the friends of Cerdanyola

An apparently triumphant rebellion such as that of Juan Santos allows a discussion of the boundaries of the Andean utopia, its social and geographical limits, and its potential for changing the course of events. The history of the Andean utopia did not develop irreversibly or uniformly. We cannot study it in isolation from the men and women who assumed it as their own. In fact, we must write it in plural: the Andean utopias. Juan Santos' version of the Andean utopia differed from Tupac Amaru II's in the 1780s and that of the independence conspirators years later.

Juan Santos Atahualpa arrived in the town of Quispongo in late May 1742, just as the rainy season ended, and began to rabble-rouse in the Cerro de la Sal (Salt Mountain) mission area.[1] Little is known about Juan Santos. It's believed he was born between 1705 and 1710.[2] If true, he would have reached the jungle around age 30, which Christ showed was perhaps the best age for a messianic leader to begin preaching. Many suspect he was from Cuzco and that a Piro Indian had guided him to the jungle, whereas others say he was from Cajamarca. Some claim he had traveled to Europe and Africa. His detractors – almost always Franciscans – considered him a criminal and fugitive. These meager and contradictory references contrast with the comparatively well-documented rebellion that lasted years and resisted five royalist expeditions.

[1] Biblioteca Nacional del Perú (hereafter BNP), C. 4174 (1745).

[2] Simeón Orellana, "La rebelión de Juan Santos o Juan Santos el rebelde," *Anales Científicos de la Universidad del Centro del Perú* (Huancayo) 3 (1974), 517.

The lack of sources partially explains the many unknowns about Juan Santos. Most available sources are testimonies from the Franciscans themselves, whom the rebel leader dislodged from their missions. In no text does he directly give his version of the rebellion, which always comes to us filtered through emissaries, informants, and missionaries. Franciscan chroniclers and historians subsequently weighed in. Today, few researchers follow Varese, Orellano, and Lehnertz in the study of the Juan Santos rebellion, although Zoila Mendoza and Sara Mateos have attempted to reinterpret the few available documents and have even found new sources.[3] The primary and secondary sources are limited, forcing us to carefully organize what we have.

Who heeded Juan Santos' call for rebellion? First on the list were diverse ethnic groups from the central jungle, especially the Campa, Amuesha, Cashibos, Otentotes, and Maparis on the left side of the Ucayali River.[4] People from the highlands and from the ecological frontier between the Andes and the jungle, the high jungle or *ceja de selva*, also joined the native rebellion. People eked out a living on sugar haciendas as well as on other haciendas, farms, small plots of coca bushes, and sawmills.[5] The missions must also be considered. The Franciscans established population centers that followed the early colonial "reduction" model, premised on the belief that a "civilized" life – residing in houses near a church, with surrounding land distributed according to whether the native themselves, the community, or the convent cultivated it – must precede evangelization. In several of these missions' names we find a recurrent theme: Santa Cruz del Espiritu Santo (the Holy Cross of the Holy Spirit), Espiritu Santo de Anapati, Espiritu Santo de Centori. It could be symptomatic.

The Salt Mountain brought together the missions and tribes of the central jungle.[6] Located between Chanchamayo and Quimir, it drew natives searching for a scarce good indispensable for seasoning and food

[3] Zoila Mendoza, "La rebelión de Juan Santos Atahualpa: su singularidad y su proyección hacia la region andina," *Procesos* (Huancayo) 8 (1986), 13–31; Sara Mateos, "Un modelo de conversión franciscana: las misiones de Pangoa (siglos XVII y XVIII)," BA thesis, Pontifica Universidad Católica del Perú, 1987. Scarlett O'Phelan was the advisor for both studies.

[4] BNP, D 10641 (1818).

[5] Eduardo Fernández, *Para que nuestra historia no se pierda* (Lima: CIPA, 1986), 21.

[6] See Stefano Varese, *Salt of the Mountain: Campa Asháninka History and Resistance in the Peruvian Jungle*, translated by Susan Giersbach Rascón (Norman: University of Oklahoma Press, 2002).

conservation. Years after the uprising, a Franciscan friar stressed the mountain's strategic importance to Spanish authorities:

> [I]t's where the Indians go for salt, which they then take in canoes down river and inland; the Campa nation, dispersed but numerous, also gets its supply there. If your Majesty took control of it, he would benefit greatly without much expense as it will soon provide income; keeping twelve men there will allow him to subject this land; the missionaries' lives will be protected by simply ordering that Indians cannot take salt without written proof of their conversion.[7]

The central jungle was an ecologic, religious, and ethnic frontier zone. Different economic systems and cultures coexisted, and people entered and left in different directions using rivers and mountain trails. It was an excellent place to shelter uprooted people such as outsiders, those without a trade, and mestizos. In the bordering Andean zone, besides mines, haciendas, and Indian communities, some manufacturing centers could be found, such as the San Juan de Culpas textile mill that Juan Santos destroyed.[8] Indian and mestizo *forasteros*, people who had left their town of origin, were also present. According to one testimony, "you never asked them where they are from, where they come from, and why."[9] These outsiders came from different places such as Huancavelica, Castrovirreyna, Huamanga, Huanta, and even distant Cuzco and La Paz.

When the rebellion began, rumors spread that Juan Santos recruited Andean people, Indians as well as mestizos, for his "party."[10] Was it true? And if so, who were they? These are difficult questions to answer. But in Comas, near Runatullo, ten years after the outbreak of the rebellion, the Spanish detained three Andean people dressed as "*chunchos*" (a derogatory term for Amazon inhabitants) who asked about the powerful "Apu Inca" or Inca Lord. The rebels had already attacked Andamarca in August 1752, and the Spaniards feared a general offensive. The three detainees spoke so explicitly that it appears that they expected to find other followers or that the name of the Inca

7 BNP, 321, 182.

8 Mateos, "Un modelo," 56.

9 BNP, C336 (1772). Varese, *Salt of the Mountain*, was the first to point this out.

10 Francisco Loayza, *Juan Santos, el invencible* (Lima: Imp. Domingo Miranda, 1942), 51.

would easily attract recruits. This was not the case. They ended up in prison, tried and sentenced. The judges had no doubts about their guilt.

Their trials provide an entryway into the social profile of the rebels.[11] The first, Juan Lamberto, a twenty-six-year-old Indian, was from Maquiyauyo in Jauja. He was married and had no profession. It appears that rebels captured him and later he joined them voluntarily. The second, Julián Auqui, was also an Indian without a profession from Tambo, in Huanta. He did not know his age, but he appeared to be about thirty and was married to an Indian from Huanta. The third, Blas Ibarra from San Bartolomé, Cajatambo, was the oldest of the group, about forty, and married to a woman from Tarma. He was listed as a *cholo*.[12] The three referred to Juan Santos with extreme veneration. At the trial, they stated that no one could touch the Inca's food or step on his footprints and that he should be referred to as "Capac Inca son of God." For them, Spaniards and Jews were equivalent terms.[13] Their testimonies indicate that Juan Santos' followers included at least one Spaniard (a scribe from Lima), a mestizo from Cuzco (the overseer of the Ninabamba hacienda in La Convención), another mestizo from Concepción, some cultivators of coca, and some 600 Indian and mestizo archers, frontier people whose native Amazon attire included the *cushma*, a cotton tunic.

Four years later, officials arrested another Andean man, José Campos, and accused him of serving as the "the rebel's guide in Andamarca." The fact that he was a "mountain guide" makes the accusation plausible. Born in Andamarca itself, he was about thirty-five and married. In 1751, he joined the rebel troops in Metraro, where he worked picking coca leaves. The Spanish sent him to Lima and sentenced him to hard labor in the San Francisco Monastery bakery. Once his six-month sentence was over, he found work on a farm outside Lima as a day laborer. He returned to the capital after a few months; unable to find work, he went back to the highlands, staying a few months in Tarma, where he had a kuraka friend, and marrying a woman from Acobamba. Both went to Andamarca, and he soon rejoined the rebels.[14] His biographical sketch illustrates the

[11] Scarlett O'Phelan found the documents, and Sara Mateos used them in her thesis.

[12] The term *cholo* refers to a hispanicized Indian or a mestizo with visible indigenous features [Editors' note].

[13] Archivo General de la Nación (hereafter AGN), Lima, Real Audiencia, Causas Criminales, Leg. 15, cuad. 159, 1752.

[14] AGN, Real Audiencia, Causas Criminales, Leg. 18, cuad. 198, 1756.

geographical mobility of rebel supporters. They were born, married, and worked in different places. Juan Santos was not the only traveler.

The uprising rallied natives and Andean people in the name of the Inca. But beyond the name, Juan Santos preached a curious amalgam of Andean and Christian notions. Like many pre-Hispanic mythological figures, he was a divine envoy dressed in shabby clothing. He had the power to make the ground shake, and like many founding heroes of the Inca Empire, he came from a stone house and was one of four brothers and sisters. Mendoza points out that "it's noteworthy that Juan Santos alludes to having an older brother in Cuzco and two younger siblings who also stayed in Cuzco."[15] According to the document Loayza published, Juan Santos had as an archetype the characteristic hero of the *Antisuyo*, the Incan eastern quarter: the jungle basin east of Cuzco, an area whose supposed ferocity and abundance of plants, flowers, and fruits, many with healing powers, gave it magical resonance.[16]

These testimonies indicate that Juan Santos organized his ideas in threes. He referred to three groups (Indians, blacks, and Spaniards), three spatial divisions (his own, Angola, and Spain), and three periods, the last of which was that of the Holy Spirit, his own. His name was a synthesis of Andean and Christian elements: Santos (for the third element of the Holy Trinity, the Holy Spirit) and Atahualpa (the Inca supposedly decapitated and from whom the Spanish seized the empire). He was also called Juan Santos Atahualpa Apu Inca Huayna Cápac.

The importance of religion meant that the rebellion against Spaniards took place on at least two fronts. On one side were military confrontations between the viceroy's troops and the rapid, guerrilla-type forces of the natives. On the other, an intense religious struggle pitted Juan Santos against the Franciscans. Years earlier, the Franciscans' ability to perform miracles had attracted natives to the first missions. According to an often-repeated anecdote, natives resistant to Christianity left a newborn for dead in the bush. Friars brought the newborn back from the forest and baptized him; the child did not die. Whether historical fact or myth, it seemed to confirm the power of holy water to bring people into true life. Natives believed the missionaries had revived a stillborn baby. The idea that bodies could resuscitate

[15] This information appears in a document published by Loayza that refers to Juan Santos in his first appearance. Mendoza, "La rebelión," 16.

[16] Henrique Urbano, *Wiracocha y Ayar. Héroes y funciones en las sociedades andinas* (Cuzco: Centro Bartolomé de Las Casas, 1981), XXXII, 55.

persisted, making believers more receptive to Juan Santos' preaching that the Inca could return.

Making the ground shake was one of the Apu Inca's powers. On October 28, 1746, four years after the rebellion began, the ground trembled violently for three or four minutes in Lima, leaving "only twenty-five houses standing." The earthquake cracked church walls and virtually destroyed the Augustine and Mercedarian churches. One cathedral tower fell onto the other, both crashing into the dome. A bridge arch tumbled, and the viceroy's palace was left "without a salvageable room or office." The ground continued to shake until October 29 and forced much of the city's population to sleep outside.[17] Interpreting the catastrophe as a sign of divine wrath, people formed processions and performed acts of penitence. The earthquake was equally devastating in the neighboring port of Callao. The rough sea produced massive waves that crushed ships and docks. The rumor spread that the water might reach Lima's Central Plaza. The tsunami struck the entire central coast, including the Chancay, Huaura, Supe, and Pativilca valleys. Some believed that it fulfilled a prophecy attributed to Saint Rose of Lima about the disappearance of the Peruvian capital. In popular imagination, Saint Rose also predicted that the Inca Empire would return to its legitimate owners.

As mentioned, it was believed that Juan Santos could literally move the earth: "[A]s an envoy from heaven, he would shake the ground in his empire, to establish that of the Incas and expel the Spanish."[18] In November 1746, the Franciscans who battled the rebels in the central jungle received a letter that referred in detail to the catastrophe in the capital. It established a curious association between this event and Juan Santos: "[W]ith this and other atrocities the rebel's weapons moved terribly and gloriously."[19] According to the Apostolic Prefect of the Missions, a Franciscan, people in Satipo and "throughout the kingdom" felt the earthquake.[20]

Under these circumstances, more than one Franciscan must have recalled another prophecy, attributed to Friar José Vela, according to

[17] Manuel de Odriozola, *Terremotos: Colección de las relaciones de los más notables que ha sufrido esta capital y que la han arruinado* (Lima: Aurelio Alfaro, 1863), 38, 55.

[18] Loayza, *Juan Santos*, 67.

[19] Loayza, *Juan Santos*, 120.

[20] BNP, C 336 (1772).

which in 1742 "an abominable monster full of arrogance will emerge to crown himself King of this entire kingdom and of the New World of Peru."[21] This prophecy must have reached the ears of the natives, for whom Juan Santos might have been this monster, although for them he was more likely the Inca who returned "to recover the crown taken by Pizarro and other Spaniards who killed his father, the Inca, and sent his head to Spain."[22] In this new "dispute over souls," similar to the one that took place in the central Andes in the first half of the seventeenth century, ideas and concepts passed back and forth from one side to the other. For the Franciscans, recovering their missions was an opportunity for martyrdom, conducive to all types of miraculous events. Immersed in these anxieties, two Franciscans entered unprotected into the stronghold of the infidels. They were forced to retreat, and one drowned while fleeing across a river. The other one, Father Domingo García, made it across but ended up like an engraving in a devout religious book, pierced with arrows: "kneeling with his hands down and his eyes turned towards heaven, he was finished off with clubs."[23] He became a martyr, but the story did not end here. His attackers cut off his head and buried it in the town's church. When Spanish forces penetrated the area a month later, they excavated and found his head "fresh, with no decay or bad smell. . . . "[24] No one pointed out that salt might have helped preserve his remains. It was a very different mentality than that of today, but one similar to that of the enemy: the head separated from a body that later returned to life. That was the essence of the mythical stories about Inkarri, whose echoes are found in the figure of Juan Santos himself.

At first it seemed the new Apu Inca only opposed the Spanish, rallying against colonial exploitation and seeking to get rid of textile mills and bakeries (where prisoners faced brutal work conditions) but supporting Christianity, for he wore a cross and prayed in Latin. Later, he seemed to oppose only the Franciscans, prompting some to speculate about possible ties to the rival order, the Jesuits. Subsequently, some claimed Juan Santos rejected all clerics without exception and sought

[21] Fernando Rodríguez Tena, *Misiones de la Santa Provincia de los XII Apóstoles de Lima*, manuscript, 1779, Libro Segundo, 525.

[22] Izaguirre, *Misiones franciscanas*, 116.

[23] Loayza, *Juan Santos*, 78–9.

[24] BNP, C 4176 (1745), 157.

to replace them with "children of the Incas." But according to the testimony of two of the rebellion's recruits, the Indians Auqui and Lamberto, around 1750 Juan Santos resolutely rejected Christianity. He snatched the rosary away from one of them and insisted he denounce the lies with which priests indoctrinated. Juan Santos forced the other to marry again, this time to a different woman and in a peculiar ritual, apparently rejecting the validity of the Catholic ceremony. The rebellion apparently became more nativist over time, which was probably why it had minimal success in extending into the central Andes and recruiting creoles and mestizos.

Juan Santos did not want to confine the movement to the jungle. To the contrary, recovering his kingdom meant expelling the viceroy and crowning himself in Lima or Cuzco. Everyone who spoke with the rebel was convinced of this.[25] The rumor was considered believable and a true threat; fear spread. Friar José de Amich asserted that if Juan Santos left his refuge with 200 Indian archers, "a general Indian uprising in the kingdom's provinces" could ensue.[26] Some speculated about possible links between the rebel and the English. This alarming news reached Cuzco and writer Diego de Esquivel y Navia repeated it.[27] There was talk in Cuzco of a cousin of Juan Santos ruling in the Great Paititi. These fears – a mix of reality and fiction – must have influenced the prosecutor who charged Juan Santos' collaborators mentioned earlier. He worried that Indians and mestizos from outside the Amazon would reinforce "the great number of chunchos" and "ignite the spark that grows into a regrettable fire, the combustion of heretical errors; don't forget that the leader himself is an Indian from these very provinces, and it is a natural assumption that their shared condition leads his followers to believe in his errant ways, making a solution very difficult." But this did not happen. The spark was lit in the jungle, but it did not spread to the entire kingdom. Why not?

Many have insisted that Juan Santos was not defeated, which is certain. The Spanish could not capture him, decapitate him, or exhibit his remains. But in light of the leader's goals, the uprising was not exactly a triumph. It did not threaten Lima. After the attack on Andamarca, which he held for just three days, Santos returned to the jungle and did

[25] Orellana, "La rebelión," 521.

[26] Loayza, *Juan Santos*, 158.

[27] Diego de Esquivel y Navia, *Noticias cronológicas de la gran ciudad del Cuzco*, vol. 2 (Lima: Fundación Wiese, 1980), 277–8.

not leave again. Why didn't the fire ignite? Perhaps the name of the Inca did not have the resonance the prosecutor feared. The return of the Inca could rouse people in Cuzco, Huanta, or Cajatambo, but maybe not in the Andean area around the Salt Mountain. Comas, where the Spanish arrested three collaborators in 1752, was the entryway into the Mantaro Valley. The path they took from the jungle to Comas led to the Ocopa Convent, the Franciscan headquarters. The three rebels arrived talking about the Inca but were quickly charged and imprisoned. This was the region populated by the Huancas, allies of the Spanish against the people of Cuzco during the conquest. The name Atahualpa did not necessarily evoke positive memories. Juan Santos could enlist uprooted people, forastero Indians, and mestizo vagabonds, but not community Indians, the bulk of the region's population. As Nelson Manrique suggested, we need to map out the Andean utopia. The Inca still does not have positive connotations in the Mantaro Valley today and can even be the object of mockery, as occurs, for example, in the town of Sapallanga's festival.

If the fire did not spread, it was due, paradoxically, to the movement's success in the Salt Mountain region. Migrating natives and missionaries themselves perhaps brought the idea of the Inca and a mystified Andean history into the jungle. Even today the Shipibo speak of a quartered Inca and the Ashami refer to three Incas. Although the idea that the Inca could return and that it was necessary to rise up against the Spanish was acceptable to the natives, the need to undertake a long march from the Amazon to the Pacific coast was not. It is worth considering why people listened to and took seriously this pilgrim who arrived in Quisipongo in 1742.

When the Franciscans began to reestablish the missions in 1790, they observed that natives were hesitant to live in towns. Priests blamed it on the Indians' natural laziness. They understood this instinctive mobility, which both frightened and outraged them, as the polar opposite not only of Christianity, but of the human condition itself. At times, natives pretended to tolerate "civilization": "they set up their houses and fields and remain until the priest provides tools and then, with these supplies, they abandon the place for an area where fish and game are more abundant."[28] This quote suggests that the priests not only wanted to congregate them in towns but also to initiate them into agriculture.

[28] BNP, D 10641 (1818).

Perhaps this was the deepest conflict between Franciscans and natives: civilization versus savagery.

Savagery meant living in freedom. This is how the Cunivos, for example, lived prior to the friars' arrival:

> The Cunivo Indians are corpulent and usually go around naked ... They wear their hair short on the top and let it cover their ears. From the time they are little, they wear multicolored cotton bands around their ankles, knees, arms, wrists, and waists. Married women don't wear more than a cotton rag that covers their privates. Young women go completely naked. They don't spin and don't work other than in their small plots; they only wear the clothing that their husbands, fathers, or relatives steal from their enemies in their incursions. Men marry as many women as they want, and because the land is fertile and the women are happy with little food, it is easy to maintain them. These Indians are proud of their loyalty, bravery, and friendliness.[29]

They had a different family structure, a different sexual life, and a different daily rhythm. This lifestyle was based on a simple, rotating agricultural system, hunting, gathering, and fishing. The natives maintained an environmental equilibrium in a region poorly suited for sedentary, let alone intense, agriculture. They lived moving from one place to another and thus protected vegetation.

The friars and Spaniards did not take into account the peculiarities of the Amazon environment and quickly caused ecological depredation. But even more serious was the spread of epidemics and the high infant mortality rate, the latter the result of diseases, change in diet, new work regimes, and concentration in population centers. The great 1720 Andean epidemic reached the Salt Mountain. The mission population tended to decline in the following years, with strong fluctuations that indicate measles or smallpox outbreaks. In a 1732 speech justifying the missions, Friar Francisco de San Joseph admitted that about 12,000 baptized children had died in the previous twenty-two years. As in the initial years of the Conquest, death accompanied evangelization, a true contrast to the friars' promise of eternal life. The "resuscitation" of the

[29] José Amich, *Historia de las misiones del convento de Santa Rosa de Ocopa* (Lima: Milla Batres, 1975), 92–3.

newborn native could be recalled in this context. In 1739, the Amueshas reached, according to Fernando Santos, "their historical low point."[30]

Fernando Santos and Sara Mateos have shown that other uprisings took place in the Salt Mountain region before Juan Santos, all related to high mortality rates.[31] It is not an exaggeration to state that ethnic genocide took place there in the first half of the eighteenth century. The Spanish fought gods, altered lifestyles, and exterminated inhabitants. In 1736–37, the kuraka Ignacio Torote led natives in the Sonomoro Mission uprising against the friars. One of the fathers asked before dying, "Ignacio, why are you killing us?" Torote responded, "Because you and your people are killing us everyday with your sermons, taking away our freedom."[32] History repeated itself over and over in the Amazon. The fathers did not learn their lesson. When they returned, with the embers of rebellion barely out, epidemics also came back. In 1799 they founded Nuestra Señor del Pilar with a population of 130 Piros; only 42 remained in 1818. In reality, the friars could not change. Christian evangelization was essential to the imposition of the western world.

Juan Santos' success was rooted in his rejection of the western world, which became more radical over the years. At the same time, he identified himself more and more with natives. For them, victory was not crowning an Inca in Lima but instead the return to an earlier social order, so very close and, in some ways, so very accessible. It was only a question of destroying the missions, of not returning to them and living as before. During military confrontations with the Spanish, they maintained a degree of organization, but once Juan Santos was gone, they lost it completely. They scattered and returned to the status quo, able to fight among themselves but not against a qualitatively different military force. A Franciscan observed that "now that the insurgent as they called him is dead, nobody forces them to live in town: everyone retreats to live where he thinks best, with his closest relatives, removed from one another, a quarter or half league away, and the town or towns are deserted or covered over by the forest, or if they still exist, they only have three or four families."[33]

[30] Fernando Santos, "Epidemias y sublevaciones en el desarrollo demográfico de las misiones Amuesha del Cerro de la Sal, siglo XVIII," *Histórica* (Lima) XI, 1 (1987), 25–53, quote from 43.

[31] Santos, "Epidemias y sublevaciones," 85.

[32] Mateos, "Un modelo," 49.

[33] BNP, C 336 (1772).

Juan Santos' paradoxical mix of success and failure contains the same problem that we will find in 1780 with Tupac Amaru forces and later with other Andean rebellions: the inability to unify followers, that is, to build a social movement. To use the same words as the Spanish prosecutor, Andean Indians and Amazon natives did not share the "same nature," i.e., they did not have the same interests. Contradictory goals ultimately expressed not only different geographical spaces but also equally different times. They also manifested historical experiences lived differently depending on whether one was from the central or southern Andes. Elucidating these issues would help explain why a country such as Peru with an ancient peasant history that withstood such tough colonial impositions has not produced a successful social revolution. This task has been postponed from one generation to another.

In Peru, the option of a national revolution with broad participation against an external enemy has not worked. Tupac Amaru demonstrated this, albeit against his will. But leaders such as Juan Santos, who based their movements on a defined sector of the population, with a determined ethnic or class composition, also have failed. If we extend this parallel and compare the two rebellions' duration, we see that Juan Santos fared better than Tupac Amaru, but neither managed to find the Inca. Why? The answer is one of the keys to understanding Peru. It is an unsolved problem. Maybe we can find a solution if we stop being dominated by memories. Perhaps it's precisely a matter of not searching for an Inca.

CHAPTER 4

The Tupac Amaru Revolution and the Andean People

The 1780 Tupac Amaru rebellion was the most ambitious attempt to convert the Andean utopia into a political platform. Had it succeeded, Cuzco would be the capital of Peru, the Andes would dominate over the coast, rulers would descend from the colonial indigenous aristocracy, and neither the Indians nor their culture would have faced discrimination. Why did it fail? To answer this question, we need to contrast ideas and projects with human agents and their praxis.

> Amaro: A mythological being, in the form of a bull, that foretells *huaicos* [landslides] and disseminates desolation and death.[1]

An historian once called the uprising led by Tupac Amaru II in 1780 the "isolated scream from Tinta." It would be impossible to reach such a conclusion today, because it would reveal crass ignorance of Peru's eighteenth century. What began as an execution of a regional authority, a corregidor, snowballed into a mass movement that spread throughout the southern Andes, the culmination or high point of a prolonged cycle of rebellions that shook the century.

Most of these rebellions were spontaneous riots, short in duration. The fact that they occurred in isolation helps explain why we know so little about their leadership, organization, and ideological underpinnings. But alongside these events, more significant social movements rocked regional economic and social life. This was the case of Huarochirí in 1750 and 1783, both correctly interpreted as rebellions. Some of

[1] Carlos Camino Calderón, *Diccionario Folklórico del Perú* (Lima: Compañía de Impresiones y Publicidad, 1945), 15.

the uprisings were predominantly urban, such as fiscal protests in Arequipa, Cuzco, or Huaraz, to cite three examples from around 1780. The case of Tupac Amaru moved beyond all of them. In light of its social composition, objectives, and impact on colonial structures, it must be considered a revolution. The same can be said for the other great eighteenth-century rebellion, led by Juan Santos Atahualpa in the central jungle beginning in 1742. Whereas Juan Santos was never defeated (the Spanish would not return to the area inhabited by the Campas Indian group), the Tupac Amaru movement lasted only from November 1780 to May 1781, between the execution of the corregidor Antonio de Arriaga and that of Tupac Amaru II in Cuzco. The uprising, however, would continue in Puno and the highlands of Charcas (in present-day Bolivia) through July 1783, the date of Diego Cristóbal Tupac Amaru's execution.[2] Its defeat does not mean that the Tupac Amaru movement was not revolutionary; it just indicates a collective frustration.

The data from several studies give a total of 128 uprisings in the Andes during the eighteenth century, distributed in the following way: 10 in Ecuador, 107 in Peru, and 11 in Bolivia, although the numbers were probably greater in Ecuador and Bolivia.[3] The concentration in Peru reflects the careful research conducted there, particularly by Scarlett O'Phelan Godoy. In Peru's interior, the number of uprisings increased over time. A simple tally from the research of O'Phelan and Jürgen Golte provides the figures in Table 4.1.

Any statistic about rebellions must necessarily be treated carefully. The increase might be the result not so much of a changing social reality but of better sources, the presence of more cautious observers, or some other chance circumstance. Furthermore, by definition no rebellion is perfectly comparable with others. But alongside this increase

2 Diego Cristóbal Tupac Amaru was the cousin of Tupac Amaru II [Editors' note].

3 Segundo Moreno, *Sublevaciones indígenas en la Audiencia de Quito* (Bonn: Bonner Amerikanistische Studien, 1976); Boleslao Lewin, *La rebelión de Túpac Amaru y los orígenes de la independencia hispanoamericana* (Buenos Aires: Librería Hachette, 1957); Scarlett O'Phelan, "Túpac Amaru y las sublevaciones del siglo XVIII," in Alberto Flores Galindo, ed., *Túpac Amaru II – 1780. Sociedad colonial y sublevaciones populares* (Lima: INIDE, 1976), 67–81; Jürgen Golte, *Repartos y rebeliones* (Lima: Instituto de Estudios Peruanos, 1980). In a later work, O'Phelan registered as many as 140 uprisings. Scarlett O'Phelan, *Rebellions and Revolts in Eighteenth-Century Peru and Upper Peru* (Cologne-Vienna: Bohlau Verlag, 1985), 284–98.

Table 4.1. *Uprisings in Colonial Peru, 1730–1779*

Years	Number of Uprisings
1730–39	10
1740–49	5
1750–59	11
1760–69	20
1770–79	66

Sources: Golte, *Repartos y rebeliones*; O'Phelan, "Túpac Amaru y las sublevaciones del siglo XVIII."

in the number of uprisings, their social composition and spatial extension also changed. Geographically, they shifted from the north of the viceroyalty to the south: 61 of the 107 took place in what are today the provinces of Cuzco, Arequipa, Apurímac, and Ayacucho. Just in the 1770s, nine Cuzco corregidores were attacked. The south was one of the most densely populated regions, an overwhelmingly indigenous area, where commerce and mining increased in the second half of the eighteenth century. These facts frame a process, although they in no way fully explain it.

The Tupac Amaru revolution, however, was not just the culmination of a cycle. In some ways it was an exception. To understand it, the rebels' consciousness or ideas must be taken into account, as the uprising involved forming an army, designating authorities in liberated areas, collecting taxes, and producing decrees, bands, and proclamations disseminated throughout the southern Andes. All of this indicates that it was not a spontaneous or improvised event.

Perhaps the complexity of the Tupac Amaru movement lies in the fact that from the beginning it counted on an organization, a specific group of leaders, and a program for which to fight. In this sense, consciousness and historical will played a crucial role. Tupac Amaru outlined a program that challenged colonialism and the Lima aristocracy, focusing on three key points:

1. The expulsion of the Spanish or *chapetones*, as they were called with a clear derogatory sense. It was not enough to do away with the *corregimientos* and *repartos* (the forced sale of goods); the high court and the viceroy also needed to be abolished and all dependency on the Spanish monarchy broken.
2. The restitution of the Inca Empire. Reflecting his reading of Inca Garcilaso de la Vega, the rebel leader believed that the Inca

monarchy could be restored, placing the descendents of the Cuzco indigenous aristocracy on top.

3. The introduction of substantial economic changes: the suppression of the *mita* labor draft, the elimination of large haciendas, the abolition of custom houses and sales taxes or *alcabalas*, and free trade.

This program required the leadership of kurakas and Inca nobles, but to succeed, they needed both mass peasant support and the participation of other social groups, particularly creoles. Tupac Amaru sought to create, as Miguel Maticorena has shown, a new "body politic" in which creoles, mestizos, blacks, and Indians would coexist harmoniously, rupturing caste distinctions and creating racial solidarity among all non-Spaniards. The program had clear elements of what could be called a national movement.[4]

The idea of the Inca could unite all of the colonized against Spain: it constituted an organizing principle that would overcome the chaos and darkness imposed since the conquest. The Inca was not an abstract notion in the eighteenth century. Real or supposed descendents of the Inca aristocracy existed and could be seen in public spaces and celebrations. José Gabriel Condorcanqui Tupac Amaru was one of them. Some historians and anthropologists believed that Tupac Amaru (or Thupa Amaro, to use the spelling most frequently found in documents) was a pseudonym assumed by José Gabriel for its messianic resonance. The amaru is a subterranean divinity that emerges from lagoons in the form of a wild bull and foretells cataclysms, particularly the massive landslides or *huaicos* that strike the Andes in the rainy season from November through April (the time of the rebellion itself), when overflowing rivers and plummeting mud and rocks destroy everything in their path. But it turns out that this was the name of the Tungasuca kuraka, as seen in his baptism certificate. He was a legitimate descendent of the Inca royal family, a direct relative of Tupac Amaru I, the last Inca of Vilcabamba who was executed in 1572. Therefore, in addition to his journeys throughout the southern Andes, the other key antecedent to the rebellion was Tupac Amaru's lawsuit with the Betancourt family over who was the legitimate descendent.[5] The trial forced Tupac Amaru

[4] Flores Galindo refers here to the work of Miguel Maticorena, "El concepto de cuerpo de nación en el siglo XVIII," doctoral dissertation, Universidad Nacional Mayor de San Marcos, 1975 [Editors' note].

[5] Tupac Amaru was a merchant and muleteer whose business took him on frequent travels throughout the region [Editors' note].

to spend time in Lima in 1777, a number that, as we will see, had great significance.

Why did a revolution take place in Cuzco in 1780? Although peasants did not lead it, it is clear that without their massive participation, it would never have had such vast geographic impact: in just the four months that Tupac Amaru led the uprising, the rebels marched from Tinta toward Cuzco, then toward Cailloma, Lampa, and finally back to Cuzco. The participation of peasants, as well as the sympathy from Cuzco's artisans, means that it must be placed alongside other mass precapitalist revolutions such as the Fronde in France, the anti-Spanish revolution in Naples, and the 1640 Catalan revolt. Obviously, the term "revolution" cannot be limited to the contemporary world, as feudal societies or those in transition also generated popular revolutions. In light of this digression, we could ask a more precise question: why did a popular revolution begin in Cuzco in 1780? To answer, it's necessary to forgo any explanation that reduces the phenomenon to abstract notions such as "colonial exploitation." It's not a matter of depicting with somber tones the misery and destitution of the colonial period and then simply turning the page to describe the Tupac Amaru movement. The uprising didn't take place at just any moment: it had a precise date and setting. It's necessary to think about it historically, to follow the chronology and place it in a social totality. This is what Jürgen Golte – although with some flaws that will be noted – set out to do in his book *Repartos y rebeliones*.[6]

Golte's argument is impeccably clear: during the eighteenth century, the internal market expanded thanks to the efforts of Lima's large merchants who, given the small division of labor and (we should add) the meager circulation of money in the colonial economy, turned to compulsive measures to boost that small market. They relied on one mechanism based on the convergence of the colonial state and merchant capital: the corregidores' authority to force Indians to purchase goods through the reparto. They created a network that stretched all the way from Lima merchants (importers of metropolitan goods) to Indians, with the corregidor as the intermediary. The debts that this authority assumed to take office made the system work, guaranteeing, according to Golte, the extraction of profits from rural areas. Peasants who had to bear the scourge of the reparto ended up indebted and oftentimes were forced to migrate or to "sell" their labor in mines, textile mills,

[6] Golte, *Repartos*. For a critique of this book, see O'Phelan, *Rebellions*, 123.

and haciendas. The reparto thus generated both commodity and labor markets. Golte also concluded that the reparto eroded the traditional local economy, thereby constituting a type of bourgeois project.

Rebellions and repartos do seem to be closely linked: 77 percent of the uprisings included the abolition of the reparto as one of their objectives. These rebellions implied a rejection of colonialism but also of progress, in the sense that the term was beginning to assume in enlightened Europe, identified with the development of capital. Although Golte adds other observations about kurakas, Andean messianism, and the ambivalent role of the Church, the reader gets the impression that these are only the side dishes to a meal centered on the analysis of colonial economic structures. In fact, when he turns to analyze how the rebellions worked, the correlation becomes mechanical in that the uprisings are understood as simple reactions to exploitation. The historiography on social movements created, in the past, simple equations such as epidemics = rebellions, dearth = rebellions, or subsistence crisis = rebellions, to which we could add the Andean case in which, according to our reading of Golte, repartos = rebellions; that is, almost reflexive responses to exploitation, what's been called the "spasmodic theory of social movements."[7] According to this view, eighteenth-century peasants were enmeshed in structural conditions controlled from Lima or Europe that shaped their lives and granted them little room to maneuver, forcing them, in essence, to react instinctively through revolts, which ended up being a form of sterile rural "furies."

These comments, however, should not be exaggerated. Jürgen Golte recognizes the importance of non-economic factors in eighteenth-century uprisings, but the obsessive eagerness to present his thesis clearly and to make it irrefutable and the inevitable selection of one theme over others make him overlook changes in culture and collective mentalities that preceded the uprising, without which we could not understand *Indianos'* growing consciousness, expressed in this verse:[8]

> Our King Gabriel Inca lives
> We swear to him as King
> Because he is so according to law.

[7] This is a reference to the well-known critique offered by E. P. Thompson in "The Moral Economy of the English Crowd in the Eighteenth Century," *Past and Present* 50 (1971), 76–136 [Editors' note].

[8] Indianos is used here by Flores Galindo as synonymous with "born in the Indies," which includes Indians, creoles, castas, and other groups.

And he should receive what is his
All *Indianos* are ordered
To defend their rights
Because Charles III
Will kill and pluck everyone in spite.[9]

If triumphant, the Tupac Amaru revolution would have implied a radical transformation of colonial society. Building on some ideas of Emilio Choy, I noted elsewhere that as the uprising developed, Indians replaced other social groups, gaining hegemony and imposing their demands, in a clear confrontation with all things western.[10] The masses sought the return of the Inca Empire that popular imagination had reconstructed as an egalitarian society, a homogenous world made up of *runas* (Andean peasants) where powerful merchants, colonial authorities, haciendas, and mines didn't exist. Those who until then had been pariahs and impoverished would again decide their own fates: the classic image of popular revolutions as the inversion of reality, the world upside down. An opponent of the rebellion captured this sentiment in the following poem:

The world is either upside down
Or it has lost its mind
Because the judge was subjected to torture
and the defendant became judge.
He who is feet becomes head
The vile slave, a lord
The thief, a legislator
The creepy-crawly, a person
The Inca Crown, the Royal Crown
The monarch, a great traitor.[11]

Despite internal contradictions, the separatist sentiments of Tupac Amaru himself are undeniable. It's not by chance, as Christine Hünefeldt has shown, that the revolution began on Carlos III's birthday, and as though to avoid any doubt, the rebel leader proclaimed himself

[9] Rubén Vargas Ugarte, *Nuestro romancero* (Lima: Talleres Gráficos de Tipografía Peruana, 1951), 34.
[10] AGN, Derecho Indígena, Leg. XXIII, cuad. 643, Real Hacienda, Cuzco, 1781.
[11] Vargas Ugarte, *Nuestro romancero*, 140.

Inca-King in clear defiance of the Spanish monarchy.[12] In letters and proclamations, rebels compared the oppression of the Andean world with that of Israel, Spain with the tyrannical image of ancient Egypt, and they presented Indians as the chosen people in search of their homeland, of their country, and of a messiah as in the Old Testament. Images from the Judeo-Christian tradition supported concepts that were otherwise local. For the crown to become an Inca crown, a *mascaipacha*, it was necessary not only that exploitation became intolerable but that the rebels ground their efforts in a culture, in a conception of the world itself, created over many years and running against the current.[13]

The indigenous cultural world had penetrated the art world well before the eighteenth century. While from a western perspective the aesthetic quality of paintings fell, the quantity of paintings increased, becoming an artisan activity (often with repeated images such as the Lord of the Earthquakes) that incorporated indigenous color schemes as well as the Andean combination of multiple perspectives and the frequent depiction of the Inca dynasty. The principal Andean contribution, however, was to rejuvenate mural art, which spread from churches and convents to the quotidian world of haciendas and houses. José Tamayo has insisted on "the extraordinary graphic history" found in the qeros or ceremonial beakers that date from the Inca and colonial periods.[14] To put it briefly, in art as in other fields, indigenous culture was respected rather than scorned. A Cuzco noble was considered as important as a Spanish noble. One painting portrays with clear ostentation the 1572 wedding between don Martín de Loyola, governor of Chile, and doña Beatriz Ñusta, "Peruvian [Inca] heiress and princess," which unified the Inca royal family with the Loyola and Borja houses.

This can be better understood in light of the formation in the eighteenth century of a nucleus of families such as the Betancourts and Sahuarauras (Cuzco), Apoalayas (Jauja), and Choquehuancas (Puno) who expressed pride in their noble Inca genealogy, collecting material about their ancestors such as ingenious coats of arms. They could do this

[12] Christine Hünefeldt, "Sociedad y rebeliones campesinas entre 1780 y 1783," BA thesis, Universidad Nacional Mayor de San Marcos, 1977.

[13] Pablo Macera, "El indio y sus intérpretes peruanos del siglo XVIII," in *Trabajos de historia*, vol. 2 (Lima: Instituto Nacional de Cultura, 1977), 303–24.

[14] José Tamayo, *Historia del indigenismo cuzqueño* (Lima: Instituto Nacional de Cultura, 1980), 97. On popular culture, see Jorge Hidalgo, "Amarus y Cataris," *Chungara* (Tarapacá) 10 (1983), 117–38.

because, as was the case with Tupac Amaru, they had the resources to cover the expenses. The power of the Inca aristocracy was not a reward from the Spanish for serving as provincial authorities but instead derived at least partially from the fortunes they made in commerce (this was the case of Tupac Amaru) and the management of rural property and mines, as was the case with the kurakas of Acos, Acomayo, and Tinta. Although special high schools existed for the children of the indigenous nobility in Lima and Cuzco, the small number of students enrolled indicates that most of them relied on private education, avoiding ideological subjugation and allowing the teaching of aspects of European culture and Andean traditions. Tupac Amaru, who spoke Quechua and Spanish, knew Latin, was well versed in Garcilaso de la Vega's *Royal Commentaries*, and understood Andean messianic dreams and Christianity, was not an exception in the eighteenth century. To be Andean was above all a question of distancing oneself from the Spanish; without overlooking western contributions or achievements, they saw themselves as different than the Spanish. Llano Zapata was amazed by the Canta and Lurín kurakas who bragged about their royal Inca lineage. In the 1725 festivities for the proclamation of Louis I, Don Cristóbal de Apoalaya used his family's own adornments and jewelry to portray the Inca Lloque Yupanqui.[15]

What happened? It's not just a question of the indigenous elite. The old subordination of the republic of Indians under the republic of Spaniards, created around 1560, had changed and a new relationship emerged, in which sectors of the indigenous population differentiated themselves from peasants, engaged in new economic activities, formed dynasties, and began to accumulate wealth, often competing successfully with Spaniards. These economic processes, which can only be hypothesized until more research is conducted, weakened a supposedly rigid social structure based on the equivalence between caste and class. An Indian could only be a peasant and vice-versa. By the mid-eighteenth century, however, an Indian – proud of his background and conscious of his family and collective heritage – might lend money to a Spaniard, battle in the courts, acquire property, gain influence in local commerce, confront corregidores, and even challenge Lima's high court. An Indian could be noble and rich; Tupac Amaru said, "I am an Indian all over."

[15] Ella Dumbar Temple, "Los caciques Apoalaya," in *Actas y trabajos científicos del XXVII Congreso Internacional de Americanistas*, vol. 2 (Lima: Librería e Imprenta Gil, 1942), 463–8. See also Francisco Mostajo, "Los Chuquihuancas hasta la época de Túpac Amaru," in *Actas y trabajos científicos*, 411–20.

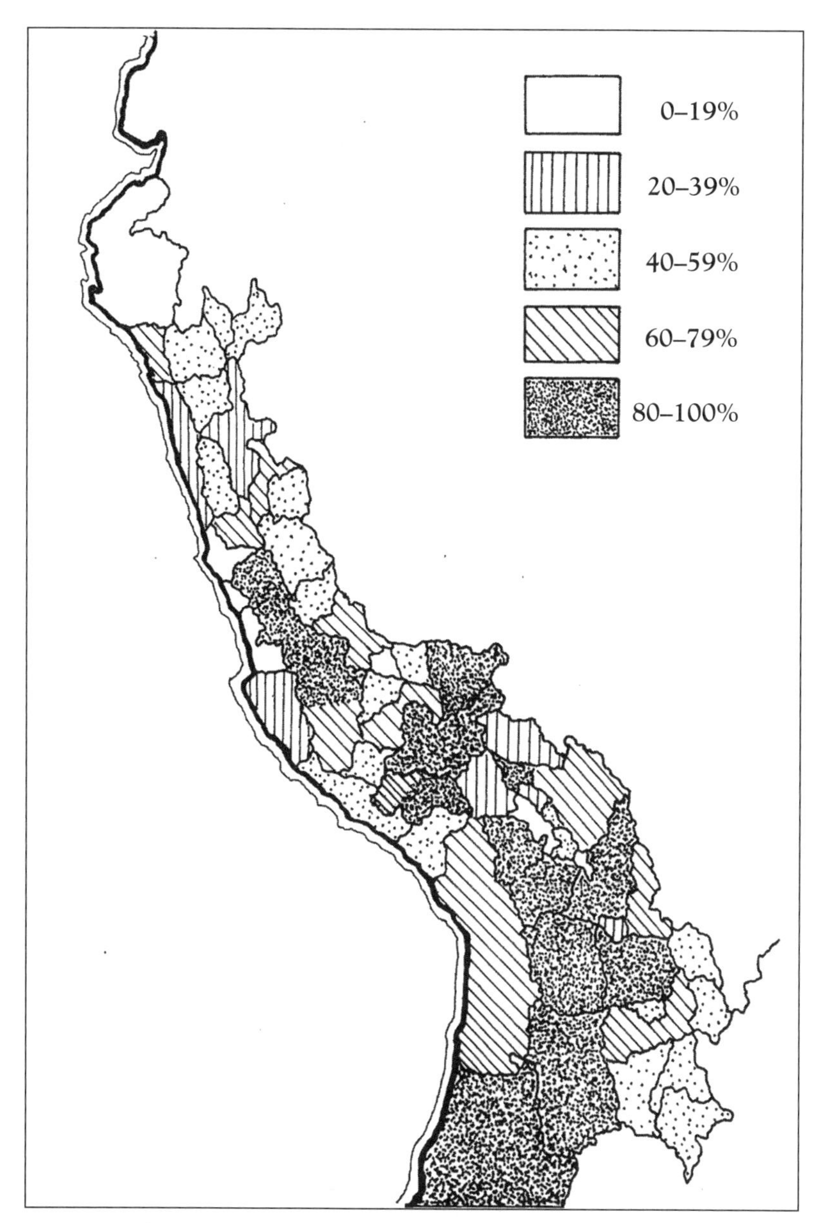

Map 4.1. Indigenous Population as a Proportion of the Total Population of the Viceroyalty of Peru (1780). *Source:* Jürgen Golte, *Repartos y rebeliones* (Lima: Instituto de Estudios Peruanos, 1980), 209.

The door was thus open for people to invert supposedly rigid social categories such as "feet" and "head," switching the world below for that above, subverting reality. All of this is too general, though: it is necessary to specify the different phases of native cultural renaissance and to flesh out its expansion in colonial society in order to portray the features of its principal followers and discover the mechanisms for its propagation. This is a difficult agenda for scholars, for this was a rural and largely oral culture accustomed to silence and submerged in an instinctive distrust.

The increase in internal trade in the eighteenth century might also reflect changes within the republic of Indians. In an important study on the colonial fiscal system, Javier Tord showed that all taxes related to commerce increased in Cuzco and Potosí but even more so in Oruro, La Paz, and Arequipa, most markedly between 1750 and 1790.[16] Was this just an expression of the increase in the reparto? The corregidores' economic activities certainly increased, but according to other sources, the reparto was not the only mechanism used by Lima's leading merchants. They created a trade network that involved provincial merchants and itinerant traders who were either indebted to Lima capital or received their goods on consignment.[17] These men plied their goods in the most diverse areas, reaching provincial cities as well as mining camps (Hualgayoc, Cerro de Pasco, Huarochirí, Cailloma), where they extended the network of debts that originated in Lima. It shouldn't be forgotten that silver and copper production increased in the eighteenth century, particularly in the territories of present-day Peru, where in 1790 more than 700 mines were in production with more than 8,000 workers (a number that perhaps should be multiplied by five, because these workers came with their families). One way or another, most mine owners ended up indebted to Lima's leading merchants, particularly when they needed supplies.[18] Few were like Pedro Abadía, who combined mining and trade.

Some medium and small provincial merchants managed to elude this tight, complicated trade network emanating from Lima, especially those such as Tupac Amaru or Tomás Catari (a leader of the simultaneous uprising in Charcas), who as Indians did not have to pay the alcabala

[16] Javier Tord, "Sociedad colonial y fiscalidad," *Apuntes* (Lima) 7 (1977), 3–28.

[17] I base this on the records of the Tribunal del Consulado. See Flores Galindo, *Aristocracia y plebe*.

[18] AGI, Lima, 692, "Matrícula de Mineros," August 4, 1790.

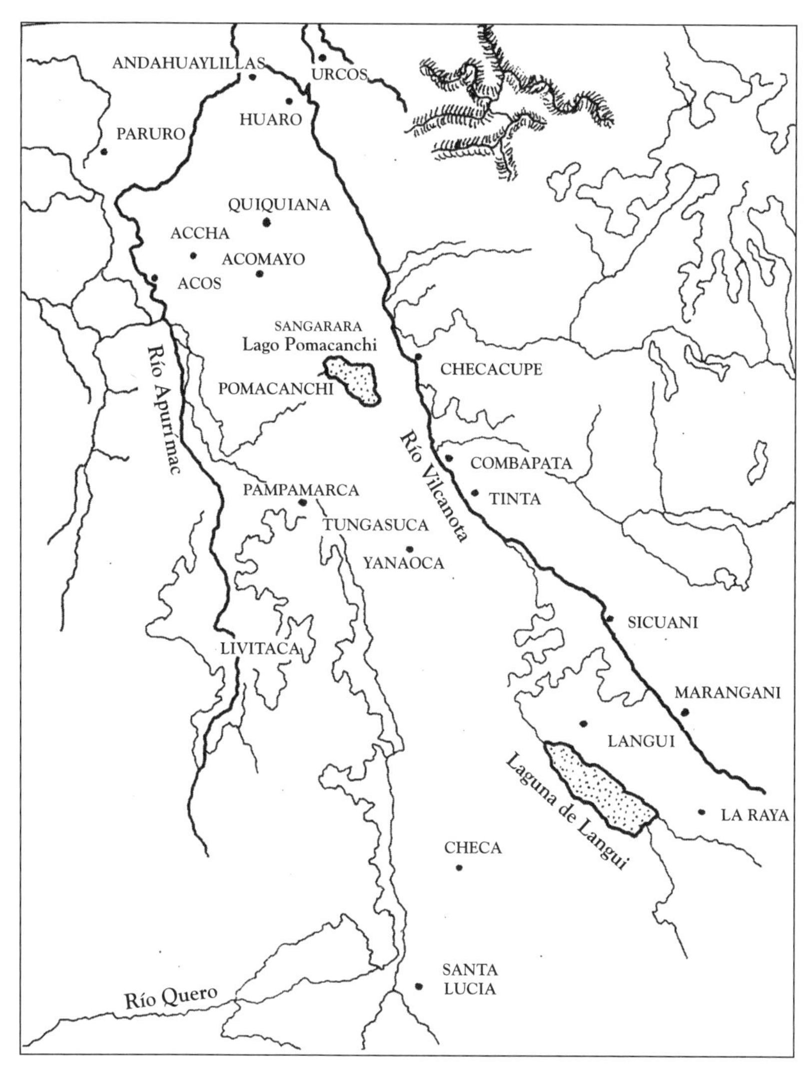

Map 4.2. Pro–Tupac Amaru Communities (1780).

or excise tax, confronted the great Lima merchants, and opposed the reparto. When in addition to being merchants they were also kurakas, they found themselves much better placed to challenge the corregidores. This way, a trade dispute could quickly become an anticolonial conflict and develop – in light of the alliance between powerful merchants and the bureaucracy – into what is often called class struggle.

It is difficult to understand trade competition between Lima and the provinces, essential in the Tupac Amaru conflict, without taking into account changes in the internal market. The stereotypical idea of a "general crisis" in eighteenth-century Peru was long ago cast aside. But was the expansion of the internal market only the reflection of the compulsive mechanisms used in the reparto? It's important to remember that the reparto was relatively weak in areas most affected by the rebellion (Cuzco, Lampa, Cailloma) when compared to regions such as Arequipa and Arica, where the reparto burden was much higher. Answering this question requires looking not only at the export economy (mining, sugar, and viticulture) but also and especially at production destined for local or regional markets. This is what María Isabel Remy and Luis Miguel Glave set out to do in their study of corn production in Ollantaytambo. Focused on one production center, the disproportionately large estate run by the Bethlemites, Silque, they show that it expanded its cultivated area and production and marketed its corn all the way to Upper Peru. The sugar produced in the Abancay hacienda of Pachachaca had a similar destination.[19] These observations, however, cannot be extrapolated to indigenous communities, so we need to examine what happened in Cuzco's indigenous communities in the eighteenth century.

Cuzco rebels came from towns in the Canas y Canchis and Quispicanchis districts, located in the mountainous areas that bordered with Puno and Arequipa and along the Vilcanota and Apurímac rivers, where towns such as Tinta, Tungasuca, Surimana, Pampamarca, and Acomayo can be found.[20] Most people registered as taxpayers (*contribuyentes*) owned land, whereas haciendas were not that common. The majority identified themselves as Indians: 83 percent in Quispicanchis and 90 percent in Canas. They lived equidistant from two important trade routes: the great longitudinal Andean route that linked Lima with Buenos Aires and thus Cuzco with Upper Peru and, on the other hand, the route that linked Cuzco and Arequipa. Unlike today's road that goes through Puno,

[19] Luis Miguel Glave and María Isabel Remy, "La producción de maíz en Ollantaytambo durante el siglo XVIII," *Allpanchis* (Cuzco) XIV (1980), 116.

[20] To determine the area most affected by the rebellion, its epicenter, where the core of the rebels came from, we used the following indicators: sites of key battles, the Tupac Amaru itinerary, and the distribution of the bodies of those executed on May 18, 1781 (Tupac Amaru and nine other leaders). Particularly useful was Juan de la Cruz Salas, *Vástagos del Inti* (Cuzco: Garcilaso, 1959), 109. See also Magnus Mörner and Efraín Trelles, "Un intento de calibrar las actitudes hacia la rebelión en el Cuzco durante la acción de Túpac Amaru," in *Dos ensayos analíticos sobre la rebelión de Túpac Amaru en el Cuzco* (Estocolmo: Instituto de Estudios Latinoamericanos, 1985).

this latter route stretched from Arequipa through the Majes Valley, Cailloma, and what are called the "upper provinces," reaching Cuzco via Tungasuca, where every September a fair took place that brought together peasants, muleteers, and traders from throughout the southern Andes.[21] Mule-driving was a central economic activity in the area. The mules came from Tucumán and found good pastureland in Tinta. This trade promoted local production: potatoes, corn, wheat, and cloth from small textile mills and workshops called *obrajes* and *obrajillos*. The former were large artisan production centers linked to haciendas, whereas the latter were small manufacturing centers within indigenous communities. It is difficult to provide precise figures about this textile production. One Cuzco historian asserts that there were 18 obrajes and 24 obrajillos, whereas Magnus Mörner claims there were 12 and 29, respectively. Canas y Canchis was known for its "cheap coarse woolen cloth," whereas Quispicanchis was not only the Collao granary but was also said to produce "much common cloth in several obrajes and infinite *chorrillos*."[22]

These towns do not seem to fit the image of the relentlessly miserable colonial conditions that some go out of their way to propagate. It's not a question of trying to revive the "pink legend" of Spanish beneficence but rather making the point that in some areas peasants could successfully resist the colonial system. Acomayo, which massively supported Tupac Amaru, was not a rundown village. At the end of the century, it produced corn, wheat, and fruit, supporting 3,000 inhabitants, 2,400 of them indigenous. In 1790, it only had two haciendas, both small. Even today four mills can be discerned, despite their abandonment in the past 200 years, testimony to the town's eighteenth-century splendor, when hundreds of mules connected the entire region.[23] This trade was "made up primarily of coca leaves."[24] People considered it a first-rate district.

[21] The fair was held between September 8 and October 4, celebrating the Christ of the Muleteers, who was venerated in the Tungasuca church. It attracted traders all the way from Majes to Tucumán in what is today Argentina. José Antonio Del Busto, *José Gabriel Túpac Amaru antes de su rebelión* (Lima: Pontificia Universidad Católica del Perú, 1981), 66.

[22] Archivo General de Indias (hereafter AGI), Mapas y planos, Perú, 94, 1986; Manuel Aparicio Vega, "Cartografía histórica cuzqueña," *Revista del Archivo Histórico del Cuzco* (Cuzco) XIII (1970), 185–202; Magnus Mörner, *Perfil de la sociedad rural del Cuzco a fines de la colonia* (Lima: Universidad del Pacífico, 1980).

[23] AGI, Cuzco, Legajo 35. "Estado de la provincia de Quispicanchis." Oropesa, October 19, 1786.

[24] AGI, Cuzco, Legajo 33, Inventory by Capitán Ramón de la Llave.

The neighboring town of Acos displayed similar characteristics. The kurakas of both towns, Tomasa Tito Condemayta and Marcos de la Torre, backed the Tupac Amaru rebels.

In 1781, the colonial state seized de la Torre's possessions, and so we know that he had a large house (that included fourteen paintings), mules, two stores, three smaller houses, and two haciendas, one of which produced wheat and had five plow oxen.[25] Here was another case of a provincial merchant who, as part of the indigenous aristocracy or as a politician, had become rich. Is it possible to find a fissure within rural Andean structures from which mercantilism emerged? Lima merchant capital was not mere profiteering, nor does it fit the characterization of a parasite, but those merchants who through hard work, and with or without compulsive mechanisms such as the reparto, began to develop a market did not question colonialism or servitude; in contrast, provincial merchants could not avoid confronting a system that oppressed them and even impeded them from becoming a recognized social group. Ironically, they were more reliable promoters of the internal market than were colonial bureaucrats.

Tinta, Tungasuca, and Acomayo were not just peasant towns. In addition to those who cultivated communal plots of land, artisans baked bread, had specialized jobs in textile mills, and worked in the ornamentation of churches; muleteers, small merchants, and some prosperous local families such as that of Tupac Amaru also need to be considered. Opposition to the corregimiento system and to the reparto unified them in a concrete way. They moved beyond this grievance – which would have produced just another eighteenth-century revolt – because this region lay at the crossroads of many routes, where travelers going to or from Cuzco, La Paz, Arequipa, Lima, or Buenos Aires could meet and where countless small inns and *chicha* or corn beer taverns helped spread news and information. Canas or Quispicanchis inhabitants did not fulfill the stereotype of a peasant attached to the land, immobile, and subject to a routine life. Their horizon transcended local mountains. Hacienda peasants found themselves in the opposite situation: these *yanaconas* remained subject to the servile rules that predominated in Andean haciendas. This was the case on the other side of the Vilcanota River, in the towns and villages of Paucartambo; toward the east, in Urubamba or Ollantaytambo, where the Silque hacienda was

[25] Biblioteca de la Academia de la Historia, Madrid, "Compendio Histórico," in Colección Mata Linares.

located; and in Abancay, an area that produced sugar and sugar-brandy (*aguardiente*). The Spanish mobilized Indians from all of these areas to break the rebels' siege of Cuzco in early 1781 and then to attack the Tupac Amaru towns. They were the center of the counterrevolution.

The rebellion recruited Indian followers from market-oriented communities. Beyond the subterranean confrontation between Lima and the provinces just summarized lay another conflict that gave the uprising an "antifeudal" element. Tupac Amaru referred specifically to large properties and attacked servitude. His proclamations against the mita would not only affect mines, because a mita for haciendas and obrajes also existed. He demanded the abolishment of all types of obligatory work benefiting Spaniards.

Some opponents of the rebellion blamed the growing freedom that Indians had gained in certain areas for the uprising itself. One letter from Cochabamba claimed that "if Indians had been kept in the servitude of the *yanaconazgo* system, subjected like slaves, without granting them so much freedom in their community lands and exemptions in their economic activities, as our Pious Monarch has granted them, we would not have suffered so much damage." Another deemed that the way to avoid further rebellion was "to not permit them to be so lazy or to have money, which only allows them to get drunk and rebel."[26] The historian Jorge Hidalgo noted that the idea of the return of the Inca was propagated in Cuzco's chicha taverns. Swayed by the feeling of complicity and freedom that a few drinks can provide, strangers discussed these topics over glasses of chicha or sugar brandy. The Spanish seemed to reason that an Indian with free time and money was a lost Indian.

In the years before the rebellion, the towns of Canas y Canchis and Quispicanchis were not peaceful. Not only did conflicts with corregidores, priests, and other local authorities flare, but other types of tensions were common, easily overlooked because they were longstanding and were virtually part of everyday life: disputes between communities over boundaries, fights within communities, lawsuits among family members, livestock rustling, and other crimes. There were also forms of private and daily violence that sometimes surfaced in face-to-face encounters during festivals and that often began with lovers' quarrels. Love was paradoxically the primary motive in

[26] Jan Szeminski, *La utopía tupamarista* (Lima: Pontificia Universidad Católica del Perú, 1984), 38–41.

homicides.[27] Physical violence was familiar, at times literally, to all the inhabitants of these provinces.

Violence was one of the most distinctive characteristics of the 1780 uprising. Historians who contend this rely on a 1784 report that calculated that 100,000 Indians and 10,000 Spaniards had died, a remarkable figure considering that the population of what became Peru and Bolivia did not reach 2 million.[28] The imprecision in the use of numbers in this pre-statistical era and the general unreliability of these figures about a unique war fought over an extensive territory must be taken into account. Some historians have questioned these figures, considering them too high. Luis Durand Flórez argues that a close examination of certain battles indicates that death rates were not that high. In Pucacuca, only three Spaniards were killed and twelve seriously wounded; in the Tupac Amaru victory of Condoruyo, led by Apaza, only nine Spanish officers and sixteen soldiers were killed and eighteen wounded.[29] So should we doubt these figures?

Tupac Amaru organized an army, but we cannot think of troops and weapons in the same way as we would for the royalists. It was more of a central nucleus, where the leaders and their closest followers promoted town uprisings. In the first few days, Tupac Amaru's itinerary included Yanaoca, Tungasuca, Quiquijana, Pomacanche, Sangarará, and Andahuaylillas, all in the direction of Cuzco. In November 1780, only one regular military confrontation with royalist forces took place. In other cases, Tupac Amaru sent emissaries, relied on decrees and proclamations, and searched for contacts in nearby towns to provoke uprisings. He would then make his entrance. This is what he sought to do in Cuzco, relying on creoles, noble Indians, and Bishop Moscoso himself. The delay while he waited for an uprising from within the city of Cuzco prolonged the siege and in the end explains why the rebels could not take it.[30]

Because there was not a clear demarcation between spontaneous uprisings in towns and Tupac Amaru's military campaigns, the historian

[27] Ward Stavig, "Violencia cotidiana de los naturales de Quispicanchis y Canas y Canchis en el siglo XVIII," *Revista Andina* (Cuzco) 3, 2 (1986), 451–68.

[28] Oscar Cornblit, "Levantamientos de masas en Perú y Bolivia," in Flores Galindo, ed., *Tupac Amaru II*, 131.

[29] Luis Durand, Flórez *Criollos en conflicto* (Lima: Universidad de Lima, 1985).

[30] Iván Hinojosa, "El nudo colonial: La violencia en el movimiento tupamarista," *Pasado y Presente* (Lima) 2–3 (1989), 73–82.

who examines these events without considering the peculiarities of the war encounters hundreds of battles, a figure that at first glance seems to support the official sources about the elevated number of Tupamarista troops. The Cuzco city council reported 60,000 rebels, although only 20,000 were present in the key battle of Sangarará.[31] This report and other documents, however, indicate that in contrast to the Spanish, they lacked discipline and weapons. It was difficult for a core group to impose rules on spontaneous insurgents. Spontaneity was inevitable and even necessary.

Tupac Amaru had at most six cannons and 200 harquebuses. Most of his men relied on lances, knives, slingshots, and rocks. The leadership did not have the money or the organization to arm supporters. The latter had to take weapons from Spaniards and, when that was impossible, convert their work tools or anything else, even rocks, into arms.

One thing is reality from afar, another is reality close up. From the royalists' perspective, the rebels were capable of destroying everything. One person used a graphic term to refer to the Tupamarista incursion into Oropesa: "[H]e and his troops entered and they razed (*taló*) all of this canyon's haciendas."[32] *Talar*: to not leave anything standing, to destroy everything. Rumors and exaggerations spread, first to hurry royalist reinforcements coming from Abancay or Lima and then to embellish their deeds. The Spanish imagined unequal battles where a handful of them faced thousands and thousands of Indians. Don Lorenzo Pérez Lechuga claimed that he and only 200 Spaniards defended Paucartambo against 11,000 Indians for seventeen days.[33] Scenes from the Conquest seemed to repeat themselves. Just as in the sixteenth century, those who told these stories forgot to mention their Indian collaborators.

The Merchant Guild in Lima armed and uniformed 1,000 soldiers. In the beginning of 1781, about 2,500 soldiers made up the columns that confronted Tupac Amaru.[34] A painting from the period depicts these troops camped out near the highlands of Langui, close to where Tupac Amaru would be captured: the infantry with harquebuses, the cavalry

[31] Colección Documental de la Independencia del Perú, *La rebelión de Túpac Amaru* (Lima: Comisión Nacional del Sesquicentenario de la Independencia del Peru, 1971), vol. II, 2.

[32] Archivo Departamental del Cuzco (hereafter ADC), Audiencia, Administrativo, 1807.

[33] ADC, Audiencia, Administrativo, 1803–04.

[34] Colección Documental de la Independencia del Perú, *La rebelión*, II, 2.

with sables and shields, and the artillery. They were superior to the rebels in firepower, although they were probably close to even with the rebels in numbers because groups of Indians mobilized by loyal kurakas, corregidores, or priests followed and aided every column of royalist soldiers. They sought to leave no embers lit, fearing that this massive fire, the Tupac Amaru rebellion, could be revived. They showed no pity toward insurgents and their relatives. In the words of a key Spanish authority, the judge Mata Linares, they wanted to clean "the fields of all weeds so that the little grain left would not perish." Although it's possible that more rebels than royalist soldiers died, the Spanish, despite their superiority, were not capable of organizing large massacres. The figure of 100,000 dead might be an exaggeration but nothing indicates that the number was small. On the contrary, military engagements were unusually intense in comparison to other conflicts.

It is important not only to know how many died but also how people took the lives of others, that is, the qualitative dimensions of violence. Testimonies insisted on rebel ferocity, overturning the stereotype of the timid Indian always ready to flee from firearms:

> An Indian with a lance embedded in his chest had the guts to pull it out with his own hands and then to chase the enemy until he stopped breathing; another one who had lost an eye to a lance chased the soldier who had wounded him with such energy that if another soldier had not killed him, he would have slain his adversary.[35]

In November 1780, Tupac Amaru forces assaulted Calca, sacking nearby haciendas and executing all Spaniards without exception: adults, children, the elderly, and women.[36] They were not content to kill them but rather wanted to demonstrate the supremacy of Indians over whites. They raped women, at times in public places and preferably places that had special significance for the Spanish, such as churches. One rebel in Calca "after killing an unfortunate white woman, her husband, and their children, took advantage of her physically inside the church."[37]

The victims seemed to be those reputed to be Spaniards. Who was a Spaniard? Szeminski argues that rebels considered Spanish anyone of

[35] Lewin, *La rebelión*, 474.

[36] ADC, Corregimiento, Causas criminales, Leg. 78, 1780–84.

[37] Szeminski, *La utopía*, 19.

light skin (called *puka kunka* in Quechua or red neck), who dressed in European style, or who owned property. This helps explain why in Calca rebels acted "without any apparent commiseration even with Indians themselves, their countrymen, who suffered the same fate [as Spaniards] just because they wore a shirt or other clothing that was similar to that of the Spanish."[38] Although Tupac Amaru attempted to protect priests and maintain good relations with the Catholic Church, rebels ransacked temple garments and ornaments.[39] They attacked twenty-five priests in Cuzco and Puno, killing six of them, and committed other sacrilegious acts. In some cases, rebels treated rich Indians the same as Spaniards: they destroyed the property of Antonia Chuquicamata in Azangaro and the house of the royalist kuraka Chillitupa in Oropesa.

According to verses falsely attributed to the rebels:

> The soldier will kill
> Mayors, Corregidores
> Rich, Poor, and Judges
> Or I am not Tupac Amaru.[40]

The rebellion's epicenter shifted over time from Cuzco to the altiplano, the high plateau to the south. Violence there, in the Collasuyo, was even more intense. In one area, it was "well known that not even infants are safe."[41] In March 1781, Tomás Callisaya, a member of Tupac Catari's inner circle, explicitly incorporated violence into the leadership's public discourse, and did so in the name of the Inca:

> The Sovereign Inca King orders that all Corregidores and their Administrators, Caciques, Collectors, and other dependents be run through with a knife, as well as all *Chapetones* [Spaniards], Creoles, women, children of either sex, and all people who are or appear to be Spaniards, or who dress in Spanish fashion. And if these people take refuge in a church or if some priest or other person impedes this or defends them from beheading, they will pay for it, the priests killed with a knife and the churches burnt.[42]

[38] ADC, Corregimiento, Causas Criminales, Leg. 78, 1780–84.
[39] For the case of Pampamarca, AGN, Real Hacienda, Cuzco, 1781, "Autos seguidos por don Antonio López de Sosa."
[40] Lewin, *La rebelión*, 433.
[41] Colección Documental de la Independencia, *La rebelión*, 802.
[42] Lewin, *La rebelión*, 492.

In the town of Sorata in August 1781, the church where some survivors took refuge was barely standing after three months of looting, killing, destruction, and fires. Andrés Tupac Amaru (nephew of the rebel leader) forced them out, separating Creoles from Spaniards and men from women. Rebels killed the men "without pity" and forced the women to wear peasant clothing, chew coca leaves, and go barefoot. Some of the rebels in Oruro seemed to understand the revolution as peasant and rural domination of cities: they wanted to burn down the town.[43] In Tapacarí, rebels hurled Spanish and even mestizo children from church towers. Similar events took place in the two sieges of La Paz, between March and October 1781.

The Great Rebellion of 1780–82

In any revolution it is necessary to define allies and enemies. At first, the demarcation seemed crystal clear: everyone born here against all the others; indianos against Europeans. But as events developed and violence spread, the dividing line shifted to insurgents versus royalists, one army against the other. "Insurgent" became an almost exclusive synonym for Indian, and "Spaniard" expanded to include all European, creoles, rich kurakas, and some mestizos. The fear of radical revolution prompted many to defend a system that, even if it did not benefit them, provided some minimum prerogatives. For the Spanish, "Tupamarista" became a synonym for any shabbily dressed and poor Indian. In Cuzco an Indian was arrested in 1781 "suspected of being a spy for Diego Tupac Amaru because of his appearance" when actually he was an Indian "who survived by begging and milling germinated corn for chicha."[44]

Massacring Spaniards was not tactically efficient. Tupac Amaru forces generated fear, but the better-organized viceroy's troops used terror more effectively, as Sebastian Segurola demonstrated in the siege of La Paz when he burned and ransacked settlements and then executed peasants. But rebel violence did not just respond to political strategy. Although it is impossible to imagine a revolution without violence, rebel brutality – decapitations, rapes, and mutilation – requires explanation.

Why did rebels kill Spaniards? In whose names did they commit these killings? Colonial exploitation, whites' disdain of Indians, the

[43] Fernando Cajías, "Los objetivos de la revolución indígena de 1781: el caso de Oruro," *Revista Andina* (Cuzco) 2 (1983), 417–18.

[44] ADC, Cabildo, Causas Criminales, 1780–82.

brutal injustice of the conquest, ethnic genocide, and other structural phenomena are essential as background. People and social classes, however, do not act mechanically: their acts are not simple reflex responses. They needed a worldview, an ideology, a moral code to bring them together.

For many, the violence seemed irrational, incomprehensible, and sterile:

> A Peru with everyone writhing
> So much treasure spent
> Some many towns ruined
> So many subjects dying
> So many poor cursing
> So much senseless war.[45]

Was it really an irrational response to exploitation, or was there a deeper reason?

Following Jan Szeminski's path, we can probe Andean mentalities.[46] The Spanish could be killed because they were heretics and not good Christians, and they didn't follow the norms they preached. This was conquest discourse inverted. Rebel texts referred to them as "impious" or "the excommunicated," placed them at the edge of humanity, or denied them humanity: Spaniards were the devil incarnate, anti-Christs and *pistacos*, the infernal, evil beings who emerged only to steal fat or blood.[47] One document stated that corregidores "come to suck and take advantage of blood and sweat."[48] Pistacos had to be killed through rituals so that they could not return and do even more damage.

Many rebels came from the Canas y Canchis province. A 1772 lawsuit suggested that the two halves of a town fought one another with intense violence in periodic ritual battles, representing the Inca concept

45 Aurelio Miró Quesada Sosa, ed., "La poesía de la emancipación," Colección Documental de la Independencia del Perú, XXIV (Lima: Comisión Nacional del Sesquicentenario de la Independencia del Peru, 1971), 163.

46 Szeminski, "Why kill the Spaniard? New perspectives on Andean insurrectionary ideology in the 18th century," in Steve J. Stern, ed., *Resistance, Rebellion, and Consciousness in the Andean Peasant World. 18th to 20th Centuries* (Madison: University of Wisconsin Press, 1987), 166–92.

47 The Ayacucho anthropologist Efraín Morote Best has studied the pistaco. See also Juan Ansión, *Desde el rincón de los muertos* (Lima: GREDES, 1987).

48 Szeminski, *La utopía*, 21.

of Hanan versus Hurin. It was not only a rite of passage but also a propitiatory one: blood spilled over the earth, wounded and dead foretold upcoming harvests. *Pachamama*, the mother earth, could not produce without sacrifices.[49] Ethnography and the chronicles demonstrate that the fights concluded with victors taking young women and virgins, opening them up like furrows in the fields; they needed to spill blood to become fertile. Human and agricultural fertility appeared closely related.

In 1780 time had run out: the Spanish era would end and the Incas would return. Resurrection of the dead and return of the defeated seemed near. Eschatological prophecies intensified in 1777. It was the year of the three 7s, the seven-day creation, the seven letters in God's name (Jehovah), the seven-part cycles (the ears of grain in Genesis, the days of the week), whereas 3 corresponded to the Holy Trinity. It was a perfect number: the end of one cycle and the beginning of another. "Don't you know that the time of the prophecy has arrived?" asks one witness cited by Miguel Maticorena.[50]

The end-of-the-world atmosphere dated from earlier in the century. Federica Barclay and Fernando Santos showed that the belief in the return of the Inca was related to physical calamities that struck Peru during the eighteenth century: the 1720 epidemic in Cuzco that devastated the Calca highlands and reached all the way to Lima ("one of the worst since its discovery"); torrential rains and floods that destroyed Zaña in 1727; the destructive 1746 earthquake in Lima, perhaps the worst in its long seismic history; and the 1779 and 1780 weather disturbances in southern Peru, where intense rainfall and flooding befell Arequipa and Cuzco itself.

But the apocalypse and the pachacuti or, better, the fusion of the two did not arrive on their own. Like crops, they needed pleas and sacrifices to make the earth open and for the weather to change. Killing Spaniards formed part of change as total inversion: the pachacuti was violent, it brought new suffering, it hurt as much as childbirth. The conviction in its arrival allowed people to overcome the worst challenges and explains Indians' bravery, which surprised and even dumbfounded Spaniards. We may even argue that through revolution, Canas y Canchis peasants projected their customary carnival ritual battles into the whole society and even the entire cosmos.

[49] Diana Hopkins, "Juegos de enemigos," *Allpanchis* (Cuzco) 20 (1982), 167–83.
[50] No citation given in the original [Editors' note].

Ritual battles were linked to another Andean element, human sacrifices, which dated at least to the Chavín period (900–200 B.C.). During the Inca empire, large pan-Andean ritual battles such as the Capacocha were performed, a yearly event in which people sent offerings from all corners of the empire, including children to be sacrificed. According to Pierre Duviols, "they collected an enormous number of natural or cultural products, with the number of human victims much higher than is commonly believed."[51] With the arrival of Christianity, these manifestations were not prohibited but were halted by Indians themselves. But their memory persisted a century later in the central sierra. Acos inhabitants remembered how to bury young people alive in homage to the Inca. In 1621 the people of Ocros "conserved a surprising memorial of this area's *capacochas*."[52] There are no reliable testimonies that would allow us to confirm the practice of human sacrifices in the seventeenth or eighteenth centuries.[53] Even if done secretly, they would be the exception. Were these rituals, which Christianity fought with such ferocity, lost and forgotten?

A revolution is the breakdown of order, a time when deferred and repressed notions emerge. Reviewing how the Tupac Amaru rebels ended up at odds with the Catholic Church and priests clarifies this. As discussed earlier, Tupac Amaru defended them. He counted on Bishop Moscoso and turned to Christian images to explain his ideas. Two priests always accompanied him. Yet his followers burned down a church in Sangarará where Spaniards had taken refuge and later exposed priests who collaborated with royalists. They withstood the excommunication of Tupac Amaru and other leaders, as well as Moscoso's possible treason, and responded by ransacking churches and, in the battle for La Paz, hanging friars. The revolution was a return to the past, the possibility of building a homogenous society, leveled from below and composed solely of Indians.

Tupac Amaru's initial plans were different. The Inca was a monarch who would set up a "national body," unifying all the inhabitants of Peru, seeking common rules to live by, and breaking with Europe. The

[51] Pierre Duviols, "La Capacocha," *Allpanchis* (Cuzco) 9 (1976), 13.

[52] Duviols, "La Capacocha," 42.

[53] Here I differ with Emma Velasco, "La K'apakocha, sacrificios humanos en el incarios," manuscript, Museo Nacional de Antropología y Arqueología, 4. Thanks to Manuel Burga I was later able to review the criminal trial of Lorenzo Rodríguez, accused of killing a young, white female for "some type of diabolic sacrifice." Archivo Departamental de Cajamarca, Corregimientos, 1759.

continuation of the church, the tithe, property (although not extensive ones), noble titles, and provisions for merchants were part of his political plan. Tupac Amaru would be king with the Cuzco bishop at his side. When he entered the Livitaca plaza in December 1780 and congregated its population, he was greeted with these words: "You are God and Lord and we ask you that there not be priests to bother us." He replied that it was impossible to fulfill their demand, because there would be no one "to assist them at the moment of death."[54]

Like other revolutionary leaders, Tupac Amaru found himself in a dilemma. In the words of Friedrich Engels, "What he *can* do is in contrast to all his action as hitherto practised, to all his principles, and to the present interests of the party; what he *ought* to do cannot be achieved."[55] The earlier Juan Santos insurrection built an impregnable base in the central jungle because it previously coalesced into a single movement. In the Tupac Amaru revolution two coexisting forces – indigenous aristocracy's national project and the class (or ethnic) project that emerged during the uprising – ended up clashing. At first, everyone seemed to accept Tupac Amaru's "political platform," but divergences emerged as the revolution and violence spread. Leaders sought to break with colonialism, initiate modernization, and expand trade; peasants believed they were gathered for a pachacuti, which so many signs had foretold.

Some Spaniards understood that the rebellion threatened all of them and the only way to win was to eradicate all rebels. In June 1781, after Tupac Amaru's death, one Fernando Saavedra sent a letter from Cuzco to Lima in which he described the situation as follows:

> [T]roops will have to camp here in winter because the Indians are tenacious and restless, particularly the rebel remnants who are harming the careless or those they kill or rob, and this is why another military campaign is necessary, to finish the extermination of these insolent people who are against all Spaniards (chapetones) and other mixed-blood people.[56]

Two elements found repeatedly in this story reappear in this letter: caste war and extermination.

[54] AGI, Cuzco, Leg. 29.

[55] Friedrich Engels, *The German Revolutions (The Peasant War in Germany)* (Chicago: University of Chicago Press, 1970), 104.

[56] AGN, Colección Moreyra, Letter from Fernando Saavedra, Cuzco, June 11, 1781.

In the following years, historical memory of the uprising separated the two rebel camps. While historians converted Tupac Amaru into a precursor of Peruvian independence and ignited a dreadful debate about his reformist or revolutionary character, oral tradition conserved the identification of the movement with the Andean world.[57] When the North American traveler George Squier passed through Cuzco around 1860, he heard a version of the rebellion that varied from the well-known story of corregidor José Antonio de Areche's execution. According to this version, the first thing Tupac Amaru did after initiating the rebellion in Tinta was take his followers

> to the ruins of the temple of Viracocha, and there, surrounded by black and rugged lava walls, and under the shadow of the crumbling sanctuary, with strange and solemn ceremonies and ancient invocations, he adjured the aid of the Spirit that had fought by the side of the young Viracocha on the plain of Yahuarpampa. For a time he was successful; the dead gods seemed to live once more, and the banner of the Incas, glowing anew with its iris blazon, appeared destined to float again above the massive walls of the great fortress of Cuzco. But treachery, more than force, ruined the cause of the Indian chieftain.[58]

[57] See Chapter 6, "Soldiers and Montoneros."

[58] E. George Squier, *Peru: Incidents of Travel and Exploration in the Land of the Incas* (London: Macmillan and Co., 1877), 415.

CHAPTER 5

Govern the World, Disrupt the World

Tupac Amaru's death ended the association between the Inca and the king (in the European sense) in the Andes. With a few exceptions such as the 1805 Aguilar and Ubalde conspiracy, no one any longer contemplated replacing the Bourbons with an Inca descendent. Monarchic concepts no longer formed part of the arsenal of opponents to colonial rule.

During the independence period (1808–25), therefore, the intellectual elite had to find a new political language. The Inca persisted in popular culture as a messianic character or organizing force and not as the heir of a dynasty.

This chapter attempts to address an issue raised by Ruggiero Romano: how to consider Peruvian historical problems within the larger framework of the formation and crisis of a trans-Atlantic empire.

On November 4, 1780, the kuraka Tupac Amaru II imprisoned corregidor Antonio de Arriaga, a Spanish provincial authority, near Tinta, a southern Andean town of about 2,000. Days later he executed him. Rebel leaders convoked kurakas from Cuzco and Puno and others throughout the region, without racial distinction, to present them with a plan to end stifling fiscal demands but also to expel Europeans and restore some type of Inca monarchy. Tupac Amaru's proclamations and decrees reached cities throughout the high plateau that stretched from Cuzco well into what became Bolivia. His forces destroyed haciendas and textile mills and surrounded but did not enter Cuzco. Five months later, however, Spanish soldiers captured Tupac Amaru. They executed him and eight accomplices in Cuzco's central plaza in May 1781.

This convulsive period began in Arequipa, before Tupac Amaru hanged the corregidor, when the urban plebe rose up against new taxes. Similar protests took place in La Paz and Cochabamba in the beginning of 1780, just when a conspiracy was uncovered in Cuzco. The Great Rebellion, as colonial authorities called it, did not end with the execution of Tupac Amaru II. Diego Cristóbal Tupac Amaru pushed on in Puno and what are now Bolivia, northern Argentina, and northern Chile. Tupac Catari laid siege to La Paz twice, for 109 and 64 days, respectively. The difficulties in confronting the rebels and the high cost of mobilizing troops (17,500 against Tupac Amaru alone) prompted the Spanish to sign a type of armistice with the rebels. The conflicts, however, continued. In June 1781, Felipe Velasco Tupac Inca, a character who considered himself Tupac Amaru's brother, attempted to organize a rebellion in Huarochirí, an Andean town just east of Lima. In August 1783, Diego Cristóbal was executed. All these events occurred in the course of three and a half years (see Maps 5.1 and 5.3). In the words of Alexander von Humboldt, "The great revolt in 1781 very nearly deprived the king of Spain of all the mountainous part of Peru, at a period when Great Britain lost nearly all her colonies in the continent of America."[1]

Rebel attacks and occupations, troop movements, and battles covered all the southern Andes, approximately 193,000 square miles. Boleslao Lewin calculated that the scenario of the rebels' direct actions encompassed 1,500 square miles, but Jan Szeminski contended that the "Tupamarista zone" was much larger.[2] This was not a marginal area in the colonial economy. The southern Andes were the very heart of Spanish holdings in South America.

Cities such as Arequipa, Cuzco, and La Paz, mines such as Potosí, and ports such as Arica helped articulate this economic zone, centered on the longitudinal route between Lima and Buenos Aires. Densely populated by Indians, the region had undergone growing economic differentiation since the previous century: products included coca from Cuzco's jungle as well as the Bolivian *yungas* (the warm valleys north of La Paz), sugar from Abancay, wine and brandy from Arequipa, wheat from Cochabamba, corn from Ollantaytambo, and textiles from the

[1] Alexander von Humboldt, *Political Essay on the Kingdom of Spain*, vol. 1, translated by John Black (London: Longman, Hurst, Rees, Orme, and Brown, 1814), 200.

[2] Lewin, *La rebelión*; Szeminski, *La utopía tupamarista*.

Map 5.1. The Tupac Amaru Revolutions in the Spanish Empire (South America, 1780–1783).

small mills of Cuzco's upper provinces. Commerce linked these areas as muleteers plied their goods, their work made easier by tambos or small inns and stores as well as annual fairs such as those in Copacabana, Tungasuca, and Cocharcas (see Map 5.2).

According to Boleslao Lewin, 100,000 Indians participated in the rebellions, 40,000 in the siege of La Paz alone. The number increases greatly if we consider that peasants who voluntarily joined or were drafted by the Tupac Amaru forces often brought their entire families, and if we add those caught up in events such as the siege of La Paz (23,000 inhabitants) and the 30,000 threatened by the rebels in the city of Cuzco. Yet we should not exaggerate the movement's strength

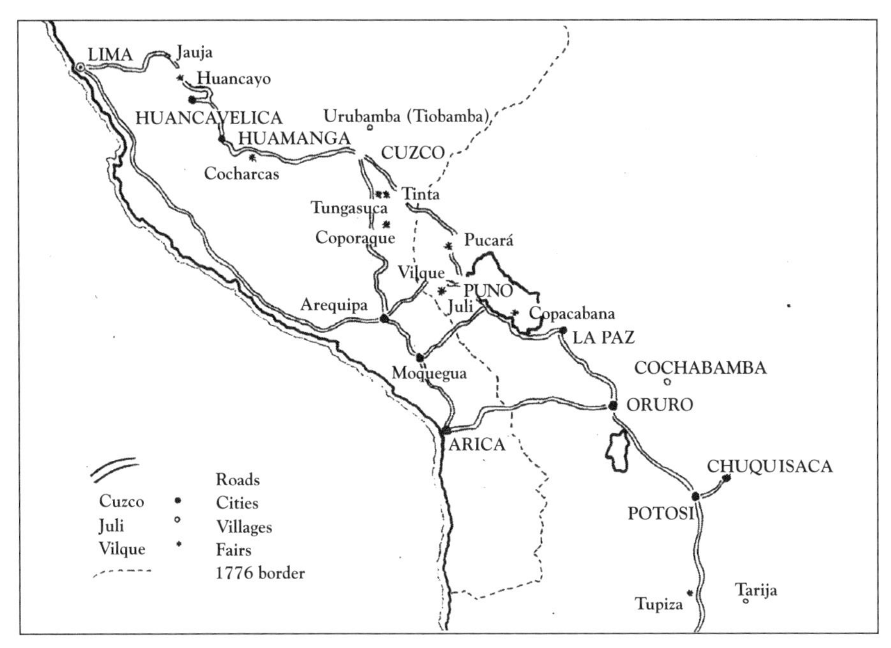

Map 5.2. The Andean South: Cities, Fairs, and Routes (Late 18th Century).

and numbers. There was no "Tupac Amaru zone" in the literal sense. Within a single region such as Cuzco provinces, there were rebel and loyalist towns and even neighborhoods. In Chucuito, Indians and mistis ended up on opposing sides. Moreover, although the region was the site of a conspiracy in 1770, and the 1780 leaders appeared to know one another – Tupac Amaru and Tupac Catari, both muleteers, crisscrossed one end of the southern Andes to the other – these distinctive events were not synchronized, and each rebellion ended up with its own characteristics.

Although everyone referred to Tupac Amaru II as the Inca, they understood his proclamations in different ways. Cuzqueños emphasized the need to protect the lives and property of creoles and mestizos; La Paz and Atacama inhabitants understood that the Inca ordered the extermination of all non-Indians. Leadership also varied. In Arequipa (January 1780) and Oruro (February 1781), it was creoles who commanded the uprisings with the support of an urban plebe made up of Indians and mestizos. Some historians suggest the existence of two rebellions: that of the Amarus, Cuzco and the Quechua, and that of the Cataris, the high plateau, and the Aymara. The multiple faces of the Tupamaristas

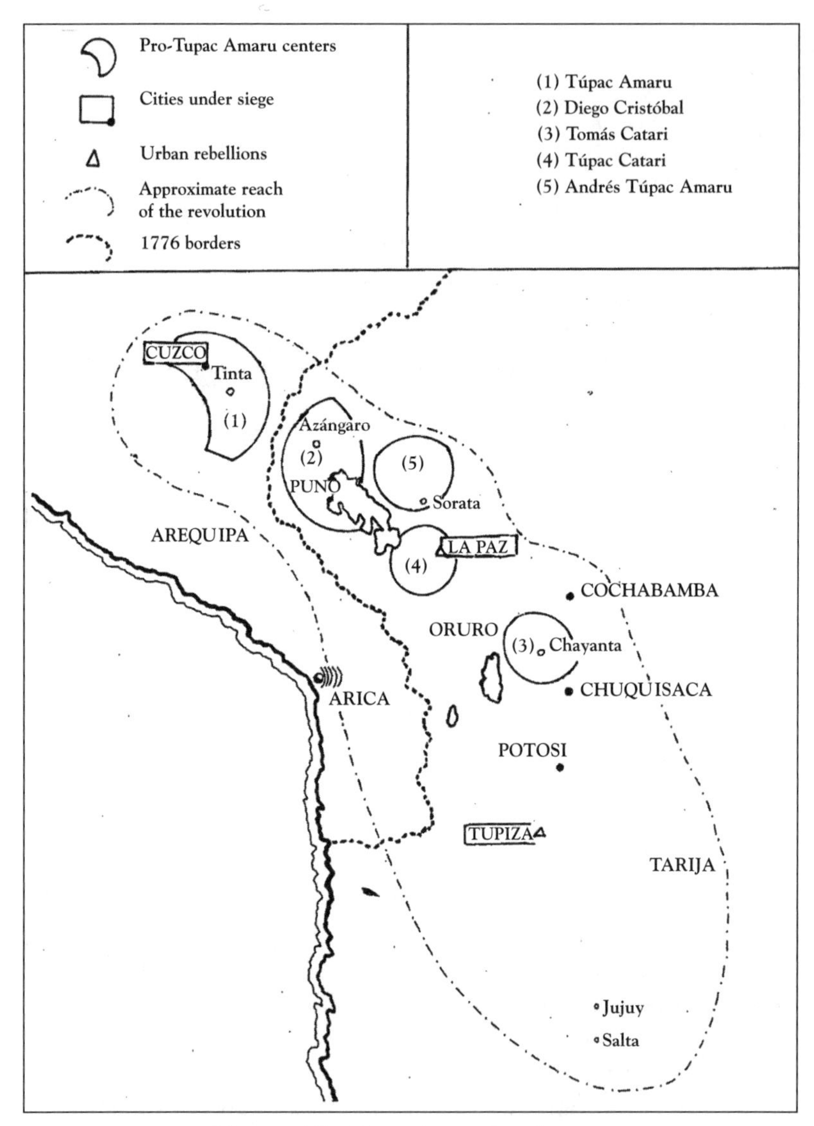

Map 5.3. The Tupac Amaru Revolutions.

allowed for a wide range of positions between the restoration of the Inca Empire on the one hand and the radical millenarist inversion of the world on the other.

Just as rebels proposed radical change to transform the world, the Bourbons, particularly Carlos III (who ruled from 1759 to 1788), sought to reorganize the administration to make the old colonial system more efficient. By the middle of the eighteenth century, the Spanish colonial system had remained largely unchanged for centuries, without significant modifications such as those in the Caribbean or in the British colonies. The metropolis extracted surplus from the colonies through its commercial monopoly, precious metal (Peruvian and Mexican silver), and taxes. It was a matter of "obtaining the largest possible amount of precious metals with the least cost for the metropolis."[3] Spanish America remained quite self-sufficient and was not a market for Spanish products, but this did not represent a serious obstacle for the functioning of the "colonial ancien régime."[4]

The distinction between colonizers and colonized, as seen in two separate republics in the sixteenth century, increasingly blurred over time. The Spanish based their colonial system not on the margins (the coast) as the Portuguese did in Africa or Asia but on the geographical center. They established mining centers, cities, and haciendas, all of which required not only functionaries but merchants, landlords, and colonizers who came to *hacer la América*. They mixed with indigenous people, and creoles and mestizos appeared. In small towns, whites became merchants and small landowners, called puka kunkas by Quechua Indians. As the colonizer-colonized distinction blurred, the area's colonial condition and dependency on Madrid also became murky. The colonial pact associated the situation of the Americas with that of peninsular areas such as Catalonia or the Basque country. Thus, Spanish and creoles could compete equally for the same positions. In the first half of the eighteenth century, the latter dominated in city councils, religious orders, and even the high court. According to this image, Peru was an integral part of the Spanish Empire, similar to the kingdom's other territories. The existence of a supposedly Inca aristocracy alongside a European counterpart (but integrated by a growing number of creoles) contributed to the illusion of equality.

Peru or Mexico did not pertain to Spain but directly to the crown of Castile. To understand the Hapsburg system in the Americas, Richard Morse adopted the Weberian notion of patrimonial society: at the top, the king, and from there a descending succession of hierarchies, set off

3 Tulio Halperin Donghi, *Historia contemporánea de América Latina* (Madrid: Alianza Editorial, 1969), 14.

4 Carlos Sempat Assadourian, *El sistema de la economía colonial* (Lima: Instituto de Estudios Peruanos, 1982); Eric Hobsbawm, *En torno a los orígenes de la revolución industrial* (Mexico City: Siglo XXI, 1971).

against one another in order to regulate and control each other, which prevented any secessionist risk but also made the system sluggish.[5] In this system, created after the defeat of the encomenderos, the king's authority rested on the alliance between crown and Church and unified the pyramid.[6] The political demarcation of colonial Peru expressed these notions in the territorial divisions of parishes, corregimientos, and curacazgos. Indians had to answer to priest, corregidor, and kuraka, their authority not clearly divided. Often the corregidor was also a merchant and the priest a landowner, whereas the kuraka could be both. Conflicts were frequent, and authorities ended up recriminating one another about who abused Indians the worst.

The Bourbon Reforms sent the patrimonial system into crisis.[7] The Spanish created two new South American Viceroyalties at the extremes of the massive Peruvian Viceroyalty: New Granada in 1739 and Río de la Plata in 1776. In 1767, they expelled the Jesuits, who had gained clear economic autonomy through their numerous haciendas and extensive urban real estate, and placed their properties under direct administration of the colonial state. The Bourbons restricted access to public positions to create a bureaucracy. As new authorities came from Spain, creoles began to lose positions. The power of visitadores or inspectors from Spain such as Areche and Manuel de Guirior challenged that of the viceroy. Deeming the mita labor draft and the head tax insufficient, Madrid created a tax on brandy (12.5 percent) and increased old taxes such as the alcabala (excise tax), which increased by 2 percent in 1772 and by 6 percent in 1776. The Spanish set up customhouses, modernized accounting methods, and attacked contraband and corruption, for which the patrimonial system had a propensity. John Lynch considered these reforms part of a "second conquest" of the Americas.[8] The reforms must have burdened local merchants, artisans, muleteers, and even Indian taxpayers with a level of aggression reminiscent of the Conquest. Authorities contemplated registering all Indians once again

5 Richard Morse, "The Heritage of Latin America," in Louis Hartz, ed., *The Founding of New Societies* (New York: Harcourt, Brace & World, 1964), 123–77.

6 In the 1540s, a rebellion against the Spanish crown organized by encomenderos and led by Gonzalo Pizarro was defeated by the Spanish loyalist forces [Editors' note].

7 Heraclio Bonilla, "El ordenamiento colonial," *Revista del Museo Nacional* (Lima) XLV (1981), 280.

8 John Lynch, *The Spanish-American Revolutions, 1808–1826* (London: Weidenfeld and Nicolson, 1973), 16.

to prevent tax evasion, including them in the alcabala excise tax, and forcing them to pay the tithe, or at least a percentage of it. The reforms affected everyone: "Spain was at last exercising 'classic' commercial imperialism."[9]

The reforms sought to strengthen the state and end private privileges and local autonomy. The metropolis had to centralize the colonies to make up for the chronic weakness of Spain's treasury. In the Americas, cities and ports had to dominate the hinterland.

What was the relationship between the Bourbon project and the Tupac Amaru Revolution? Scarlett O'Phelan presented two conclusions: that the reforms opened an "irreversible breach between colonial society and the Crown" and "accentuated regionalisms."[10] A number of insurrections broke out just years after the reforms' introduction. Were these "counter-Reform" movements, as some have suggested, or revolutions against enlightened despotism? The restoration of the Inca monarchy might seem like a traditional response to modernizing reforms, but social movements aren't spasmodic reactions. In the previous chapter, I questioned Jürgen Golte's model in which the reparto de mercancías (the forced sale of goods by the corregidor) prompted the eighteenth-century revolts, an interpretation that overlooked the Bourbon Reforms. For similar reasons we cannot accept the equation Bourbon Reforms = Andean rebellions.

To understand events in the southern Andes, we must examine the deep economic transformations that, along with political changes, reorganized colonial space. The official trade route between Lima and Portobelo, Panama (and from there overland to the Atlantic), ended in 1720 when ships began to go around Cape Horn to reach Pacific ports. The growth of Buenos Aires and the importation of slaves through its port indicated the imminent demise of Lima's commercial monopoly. The trade route that linked Buenos Aires with Tucumán, Salta, Jujuy, and Potosí gave Upper Peru a more direct link to Europe and broke its dependence on Lima. Behind the rivalry between Lima and Buenos Aires lay a deeper conflict between Pacific and Atlantic, that is, between the old and the new colonial systems.[11] The southern

[9] Timothy Anna, *Spain and the Loss of America* (Lincoln: University of Nebraska Press, 1983), 9.

[10] Scarlett O'Phelan Godoy, "Las reformas fiscales y su impacto en la sociedad colonial del bajo y Alto Perú," *Historia y Cultura* (Lima) 16 (1983), 27.

[11] Ralph Davis, *The Rise of the Atlantic Economies* (Ithaca: Cornell University Press, 1973), 170.

Andes ended up caught between two rival poles. The implementation of free trade in 1778 was an important moment in this conflict.

At the end of the eighteenth century, almost 80 percent of Potosí's imported goods came through Buenos Aires, but the domination of this nascent economic center should not be exaggerated. The other 20 percent still went through Arica. Lima merchants headed to this Pacific port from Callao and then inland toward Arequipa or up the Andes toward Oruro and ultimately La Paz and Potosí. Moreover, although Potosí was less self-sufficient than a century earlier, it still relied on American products; imports, whether from Buenos Aires or Lima, played a secondary role. Arequipa, Cuzco, and Lima provided more than 50 percent of these American-made goods destined for Potosí. The rest came from Río de la Plata.[12] The statistics suggest a conflict. Between two hegemonic poles, Buenos Aires and Lima, a unique southern Andean region emerged.

The region's intermediate location and the Lima-Buenos Aires rivalry were not the only reasons behind this emergence. The high percentage of goods attributed to Río de la Plata did not come from Buenos Aires but instead from areas that, although part of this viceroyalty, were closer to Potosí, such as its surrounding areas, Cochabamba, La Paz, and Puno. Furthermore, the creation of the Río de la Plata Viceroyalty supposedly set new boundaries on the Pacific and the Atlantic influence in the southern Andes, but did not take into account links between cities and regional fairs.

Potosí's mining recovery after 1740, the development of other mining centers, and population growth, particularly in urban areas, promoted commerce in the southern Andes, crisscrossed by muleteers. Some well-known cases illustrate this process: Cuzco haciendas such as Pachachaca (sugar) and Silque (corn) increased production. Textile mills did so as well. But the natural economy (i.e., little or no money) and a meager division of labor slowed production and trade and signaled the limits of a regional market. Enrique Tandeter and Nathan Wachtel argued that between 1759 and 1780, "Indians faced a saturated market and struggled to get the necessary money for the head tax or the *reparto*."[13]

The Indian population was much more concentrated in the southern Andes than in other colonial territories. The region held about

[12] Enrique Tandeter et al., "El Mercado de Potosí a fines del siglo XVIII," in Olivia Harris et al., eds., *La participación indígena en los mercados sur-andinos* (La Paz: Ceres, 1987), 187–9.

[13] Enrique Tandeter and Nathan Wachtel, *Precios y producción agraria. Potosí y Charcas en el siglo XVIII* (Buenos Aires: CEDES, 1984), 91.

one-third of Peru's population and, depending on the locality, Indians made up between 60 percent and almost 100 percent of the population. By 1780 the indigenous had to bear a dreadful one-two punch: economic crisis and political changes. Their response in this articulated space had a regional inflection. Potosí mines and cities such as Cuzco and La Paz were not just stopping points in the lengthy trade route between Lima and Buenos Aires; they had their own economic life that permitted what Tibor Wittman called "autonomism."[14] Local merchants such as the Ugarte, La Madrid, and Gutiérrez families worked alongside peasants and artisans, creating a degree of social density.[15] Indians tried their hand at commerce; some such as Tupac Amaru became influential, and others such as Julián Apaza (who became Tupac Catari) remained poor. The names of these merchants appeared in the trials against the 1780 rebels, and about eight muleteers were also accused of collaborating closely with Tupac Amaru. Professional middle sectors from Chuquisaca or Cuzco, including Creoles who joined the rebels and served as "scribes," also turned up in the trials.

These conditions allowed the emergence in the Southern Andes of an alternative project to colonial domination. The term "colonial domination" can only be used if a certain notion of king and monarchy was broken. Inadvertently, the Bourbons contributed to its breakdown. In the southern Andes a social group that claimed to incarnate the continuity of another dynasty hastened this process; it was the Inca versus the king. As one of Tupac Amaru's commanders, Ramón Ponce, declared in his confession, "Tupac Amaru said that the kingdom pertained to him, and his titles and commissions indicated he was the fourth grandson of the last Inca."[16]

At the beginning of the uprising, Tupac Amaru commissioned a painting in which he appeared adorned with symbols of Inca royalty. Peasants who visited him, inhabitants of towns where he passed, and even some priests who gave him a royal welcome (in Andahuaylillas, for example)

[14] Tibor Wittman, *Estudios históricos sobre Bolivia* (La Paz: Editorial El Siglo, 1975), 26.

[15] Scarlett O'Phelan Godoy, "Aduanas, mercado interno y élite comercial en el Cusco antes y después de la gran rebelión de 1780," *Apuntes* (Lima) 19 (1986), 53–72.

[16] *Colección Documental del Bicentenario de la Revolución Emancipadora de Túpac Amaru* [hereafter *Colección Documental del Bicentenario*] (Lima: Comisión Nacional del Bicentenario de la Rebelión Emancipadora de Túpac Amaru), III, 1, 594.

treated him like an Inca. They had to follow his orders because he was the Inca, confirmed by ancestry and divine powers, such as resuscitating in three days those who died serving him. A close group of collaborators – his wife, children, cousins, and other relatives – surrounded Tupac Amaru from the beginning. The Cuzco conspiracy earlier in 1780 allowed the Tupac Amaru forces to quickly establish a line of authority to replace the deposed Spaniards. In an effort to organize an army like that of the Spanish, rebel forces included "colonels" and "generals." This proved difficult.

Tupac Amaru, kurakas, and newly named authorities convoked Indians to join the rebel army. Indians who arrived, in some cases with wives and children, had to be armed, fed, and supplied coca leaves and alcohol. Furthermore, the European model required salaries. The insurrection disrupted commercial routes and normal supply channels; documents referred to "the many Indians in the roads."[17] Desertions, which were punished harshly, mounted as the months passed. Leaders instructed Ramón Ponce, the rebel cited previously, to "go back to that province and pick up everyone who is said to have deserted, Indians and Spaniards."[18]

The Tupamarista army reproduced the hierarchical structure of colonial society. The apparent restoration of the Inca monarchy indicated that the indigenous aristocracy incorporated certain patrimonial concepts. But alongside what could be called the regular rebel army, a series of spontaneous uprisings and a multitude of small confrontations took place. These increased as the months passed. In fact, as the revolution moved south, to the altiplano, these more spontaneous confrontations predominated. Whereas in Cuzco, Tupac Amaru made decisions through a "political hierarchy," in La Paz, Tupac Catari was "controlled by the principal Indians, organized in twenty-four councils that deliberated about the problems of the war and peace."[19] Groups and communities had already begun to make collective decisions. When the Tupamaristas reached the town of Pucará, they found that people had taken up arms against local authorities, clamoring "that they be allowed to pick the local judge, selecting don Ventura Merma

[17] Ibid., 650.

[18] Ibid., 570.

[19] Scarlett O'Phelan Godoy, "La rebelión de Túpac Amaru: organización interna, dirigencia y alianzas," *Histórica* (Lima) 3, 2 (1979), 89–121; Hidalgo, "Amarus y Cataris."

Huaypartupa."[20] In places such as these, a different way of organizing and making decisions emerged.

It disconcerted Spaniards that someone like Tupac Catari, who had no royal ancestry and was in fact a poor, common, shabbily dressed Indian who did not speak Spanish, assumed the title of viceroy. It was truly a world upside down. They understood Tupac Amaru much better. Some colonial authorities believed that just the name of the Inca attracted multitudes. Royal treatment came not only from Indians but also from Spanish followers. This helps explain the harshness of his sentence. His Majesty's scribe described Tupac Amaru's May 18, 1781, execution succinctly:

> One of the said executioners cut José Gabriel Tupa Amaro's tongue and then tied each arm and leg with strong rope, attaching the rope from each limb to one of the four horses whose riders faced the four corners of Cuzco's main Plaza; once the signal was given, the body of the traitor was torn into four parts. His head was sent to Tinta, one arm to Tungasuca, the other to the capital of Carabaya, one leg to Livitaca in Chumbivilcas, the other to Santa Rosa in Lampa, and the rest of his body to the Piccho peak, where his forces had tried to enter Cuzco. These remains as well as those of his wife were thrown into a fire, the ashes spread through the air.[21]

According to one witness, horses were unable to quarter his body, and so the executioner was forced to finish the job. Eight other prisoners were executed. The spectacle – or show (*función*) according to one document – lasted from 10 in the morning until past 5 in the afternoon. Inspector General Areche and the Judge Benito de la Mata Linares, the new authorities reforming colonial administration to increase crown revenues, orchestrated the execution. The cruelty was intended to terrify and teach Indians a lesson, to propagate fear. The execution took place in a society in which domination was increasingly based on coercion. Military expenditures and the number of army and militia soldiers increased after 1780. The militia had 4,200 members in 1760, 51,467 after the Tupac Amaru revolution, and 70,000 by 1816. The creation of a colonial army was one of the rebellion's consequences.[22]

20 *Colección Documental del Bicentenario*, III, 1, 590.

21 Ibid, 282.

22 Leon Campbell, *The Military and Society in Colonial Peru (1750–1810)* (Philadelphia: American Philosophical Society, 1978), 16, 218–19.

In his justification of the sentence, Areche noted that it addressed not only Tupac Amaru's "horrendous crime" of pretending to crown himself monarch, but also the fact that many people believed that his project was plausible, especially Indians, who treated him like a "lord, excellence, highness, and royalty." That is why the execution had to be public and his remains displayed in different towns to prove his death and refute "superstitions that led Indians to believe that it was impossible to impose the death sentence on him due to his elevated character, believing that he was from the main line of the Incas."[23]

Although Areche and other colonial authorities viewed Tupac Amaru as an imposter with fake titles and lineage, they acknowledged that the true problem was his treatment by potential subjects. Quartering was reserved for extreme cases, in crimes of lese-majesty, such as in France in 1757, when Robert-Francois Damiens attacked Louis XV. But for those who believed Tupac Amaru was an Inca, his remains were the incarnation of the Indian nation. Quartering and burning him symbolically destroyed the Inca royalty. When Diego Cristóbal agreed upon an armistice with the Spaniards, he gathered Tupac Amaru's remains – what was left of them – and buried them symbolically with great pomp in Cuzco's San Francisco Church. Soon after, Mata Linares arrested Diego Cristóbal and sentenced him to hang. Once he was dead, the Spanish quartered his body, laid waste to his house, and salted his fields.

Tupac Amaru's sentence prohibited the use of titles referring to the royal Incas, ordered the destruction of paintings depicting them, and demanded that Indians wear western clothing. Although Areche wanted to avoid the spread of "the implacable hatred of every European," the division between Spaniards and Indians was only accentuated. For Areche, stifling the rebellion was part of the reformist project that aimed to reorganize colonial administration. The existence of noble Indians and the use of Quechua were obstacles to a centralist project. But reforms jettisoned the very concepts that masked and sustained Spanish domination: patrimonialism and social hierarchies. Rebellions also tore apart these same ideas. The massacres of chapetones (a derogatory term for Spaniards), especially those who lived among Indians, radically separated the colonizers and colonized. Rebels as well as new Spanish authorities hastened the decline of a certain idea of the empire and the King.

[23] *Colección Documental del Bicentenario,* III, 1, 269.

Humboldt, whose quote began this chapter, traveled in the Americas between 1799 and 1804 and was in Peru about twenty years after the Tupac Amaru revolution. He arrived in the northern part of the viceroyalty and proceeded to Lima, where he spent a few days. Humboldt spoke with intellectuals and members of the local aristocracy, creoles and Spaniards. Concerned with the governing of the colonies and ethnic relations, he became interested in the "great disturbance" of 1780. Although Humboldt sympathized with the Indians and criticized the corregidores, after an informed analysis – he claimed to have documents signed by Tupac Amaru – he sided with the Spanish.[24]

Humboldt saw that rebels abandoned their initial objectives of restoring a dynasty. The uprising turned into a fierce caste war in which participants were forced to pick one side or the other, with no room for anything in between, and extermination was a distinct possibility. The struggle of Americans against Europeans became a struggle of Indians against whites, unifying peninsular Spaniards and creoles. Humboldt felt more affinity for the latter as the struggle represented "civilization" against "barbarism."

The same terms, civilization and barbarism, also appeared in Viceroy Agustín de Jáuregui's memoir (1780–84), when he tried to explain the rebellion beyond hatred toward the corregidores. He claimed that colonization had failed because "the Indians are generally and commonly inclined to their ancient barbaric customs and also to the veneration of the Incas."[25] Civilization and barbarism also underlay the reasoning of eminent intellectual Alonso Carrió de la Vandera as well as the "Lagos Report" (1786), which recommended forcing children of "principal Indians" to attend school to "civilize them" and prevent uprisings.[26] These works were part of a postrevolutionary literature produced by intellectuals and colonial authorities that oscillated between criticism and defense of the system.

In the contrast between civilization and barbarism, Charles Minguet identified all the problems of the colonial world, where a westernized

[24] Charles Minguet, *Alexandre von Humboldt* (Paris: Institut des Hautes Études de l'Amerique Latine, 1969).

[25] Agustín de Jáuregui, *Relación de Gobierno* (Madrid: Consejo Superior de Investigaciones Científicas, 1982), 193.

[26] "Informe Lagos," in Luis Durand Flórez, ed., *La revolución de los Tupac Amaru. Antología* (Lima: Comisión Nacional del Bicentenario, 1981), 381–484.

minority dominated an indigenous or mestizo majority and scorned and negated their traditions.[27] Civilization or barbarism was the central problem posed by the Tupac Amaru rebellions, one that forced consciousness of colonialism. A paradigm was born, one invoked repeatedly after independence to explain Latin America and the future of each of the region's countries.

[27] Minguet, *Alexandre von Humboldt*, 25.

CHAPTER 6

SOLDIERS AND MONTONEROS

The Andean utopia was not absent from creole discourse during the wars of independence, but just as peasants did not participate en masse, that discourse reduced the Incas to stereotypical topics and images. Creole military officers imagined themselves as an extension of the Inca past. The return of the Inca ended up limited to rural spaces – a clandestine, underground idea that blended with village folklore and the silent fears of the white population.

Between 1820 and 1824, loyalists and patriots clashed in Peruvian territory. As the former withdrew to the southern Andes and fortified their position, independence spread along the entire north coast at a speed that surprised even the most optimistic participants. Peru's political geography turned upside down. Previously, rebellion played out on the southern stage while the forces of order established a secure rearguard in the north. That was the scenario in 1780 and again in 1814, when three insurgent armies organized in Cuzco and marched toward Ayacucho, La Paz, and Arequipa. Six years later, attrition and regional economic decline altered the political context. The north and south – and to some extent the coast and sierra – marched to different political rhythms. The wars of independence and the fate of the Peruvian-Bolivian Confederation confirmed this polarization: southern cities Arequipa and Cuzco accepted the project of the Confederation, but northern counterparts Lima and Trujillo did not; they had also been on opposite sides during the final years of the wars of independence.

In 1820 the central sierra controlled the course of events between these opposing spaces. Traveler Robert Proctor was not exaggerating when he observed that the region was "in an excellent central situation both to threaten Lima and to defend Cuzco."[1] The Mantaro Valley's more than 247,000 acres served as the capital's breadbasket. A few years earlier, surrounding mines filled colonial coffers; in 1799 the area was home to no less than 60 percent of Peru's mining production. The extensive route that linked Pacific and Atlantic, Lima and Buenos Aires, passed through the valley, where muleteers and pack animals were a familiar part of the local landscape. All this contributed to premature "urbanization." However, unlike the great metropolis on the central coast, it encompassed several midsized population centers such as Reyes (now Junín) with 4,000 inhabitants, Huancayo with 8,000, Jauja with 10,000, and Cerro de Pasco, whose population fluctuated between 4,000 and 6,000. Travelers observed commercial development and precocious handicraft production. Twentieth-century research confirmed the image of a valley open to all exchanges, as manifested in the persistence of colonial-era fairs.[2]

The central valley saw six military campaigns, including incursions by Gen. Juan Antonio Álvarez de Arenales, Brigadier Mariano Ricafort, Viceroy José de La Serna, and Bolivarian troops on their way to confront loyalists in Junín. In August 1824, an estimated 6,800 soldiers filled the liberating army's ranks; loyalists numbered 7,000. Although unimpressive when compared with Napoleon's armies, these numbers were disproportionately large given the central sierra's low demographic density. Armies were veritable itinerant populations that had to be fed, and an improvised army in a country in ruins was synonymous with plunder.

Livestock appropriation, hacienda destruction, and assault on populations were frequent practices on both sides. To understand this aspect of war, we must remember that irregular troops fought alongside soldiers and created a peculiar army structure. The objective was to win over the local population. Arenales' expeditions had no other purpose than to incite towns into harassing the loyalist rearguard. However, independent leaders wished to avoid the massive and

1 Robert Proctor, *Narrative of a Journey Across the Cordillera of the Andes and of a Residence in Lima and Other Parts of Peru in the Years 1823 and 1824* (London: Archibald Constable and Co., 1825), 325.

2 José María Arguedas, *Estudio etnográfico de la feria de Huancayo* (Huancayo: Cuadernos de Investigación, Universidad Nacional del Centro del Perú, 1977); Nelson Manrique, *El desarrollo del mercado interior en la sierra central* (Lima: Taller de Estudios Andinos, 1978); and Nelson Manrique, *Mercado interno y región. La sierra central 1820–1930* (Lima: Desco, 1987), 25 ff.

uncontrollable popular participation that might duplicate the southern Andean massacres of 1780 and 1814, which were still fresh in memory. The ideal formula was the organization of armed groups with ties to local authorities and serving under patriot military command. The result was the formation of guerrillas who intervened in Junín and harassed loyalist movements. Loyalists, in turn, also formed their own "guerrilla bands." Independence struggles in the central sierra resembled civil war.

Poorly armed troops from the regional peasantry but recruited particularly among muleteers, vagabonds, and mine laborers spontaneously appeared alongside guerrillas. They attacked with no planning, lacked clear command, wore ragtag clothing, and improvised everything, even weapons. They were called *montoneros* because they went about in *montón* (loads or masses). Besides patriot and loyalist montoneros, some resorted to banditry and plundering and others protected towns from would-be pillagers.

Argentine general José de San Martín unleashed plundering the moment he disembarked in Pisco. In the neighboring Caucato hacienda, he enlisted 200 slaves and appropriated 750,000 pounds of sugar. Even though Chileans and Argentines comprised the liberating army, the Peruvian population did not view them as foreigners but instead showed increasing animosity toward the Spanish. Loyalist desertions rose, and officials' distrust extended beyond Europeans. Beginning in 1820, chapetones increasingly relied on violence to control the central sierra. A witness sent a letter to General Arenales from Huaral claiming that "within a month's time montoneros led by military men are capable of beating even the best armies."[3] That was only a slight exaggeration. Lack of local cooperation made plunder more frequent among – though not exclusive to – viceroy loyalists. When La Serna withdrew from Lima and moved to Jauja, his troops sacrificed 7,000 sheep from the Huarca hacienda in the Laros pass, burned and destroyed the owner's house, and seized "most of the sacred objects" from the chapel.[4] The ease with which Mantaro Valley towns declared independence exasperated the Spanish, who figured terror was the best weapon against patriot guerrillas and

[3] Rubén Vargas Ugarte, *Historia General del Perú* (Lima: Milla Batres, 1971), VI, 98.

[4] Ezequiel Beltrán, *Las guerrillas de Yauyos en la emancipación del Perú* (Lima: Editores Técnicos Asociados, 1977), 39.

montoneros. Loyalist pillaging degenerated into extermination. Carratalá began executing suspects and leveled entire towns. In December 1821, for example, he declared that Cangallo "be reduced to ashes and erased forever from the registry of towns."[5] To him, as to other loyalist generals, patriots were men without honor who came from the dregs of society.

Although Fernando VII conceded belligerent status and with it certain rights to patriots, in practice the loyalist army continued to view them as insurgents. Enrique Carrión's erudite history of the term "insurgent" showed how the history of words illuminates broader societal history. It appeared in 1776 in French to refer to North Americans revolting against the English. It entered Spanish in 1780 when Peruvian authorities needed a sufficiently abhorrent term for Tupac Amaru and his followers. The idea was to label them rebels, traitors, and apostates, to deprive them of rights. Denied political motivation as well, they could be captured or killed at government discretion.[6]

Patriots responded with such terms as *godo*, chapetón, *peninsular*, and *realista*, but the strongest was *sarracenos* ("Saracens"), that is, Moors, which evoked "foreigner" and "heretic." Its nationalistic and even older resonances recalled battles between Moors and Christians or the *Santiago matamoros* (St. James the Moor-Killer) from the Conquest. In 1820 in Moquegua, loyalist broadsheets mocking patriots asked, "Where will we go/fleeing the rage/of these Saracens/who have no pity?"[7] Saracen also connoted violence and savagery.

Montoneros were essential to patriot victory but were not from colonial society's highest echelons. Proctor encountered one on the road to Cerro de Pasco via Canta: "He was dressed in a coarse yellow jacket and high cap, with long trousers reaching far below his boots."[8] He looked Indian but more likely was mestizo. The montonero apparently decided not to attack only after Proctor assured him he was not Spanish. The best description came from William Miller, an English general who was fighting for the patriots when he encountered a group in the Junín

[5] Vargas Ugarte, *Historia General del Perú*, VI, 121.

[6] Enrique Carrión, "De la campaña verbal durante la independencia," *Boletín del Instituto Riva Agüero* (Lima) 12 (1982–83), 45, 55. In contemporary Peru, one could trace a similar history of the term *terrorist* as a substitute for guerrillero, but with the same meaning as insurgent.

[7] Ibid., 57.

[8] Proctor, *Narrative*, 311.

pampa (elevated plains):

> Some mounted on mules, others on horses, some wearing bearskin caps, others helmets, others chacos, and many with broad-brimmed *vicuña* beaver hats. Some wore feathers, but this finery was not general. Their garments were not less diversified. Hussar jackets, infantry coats, and scarlet pelisses stripped from slain royalists, were mingled with patriot uniforms... But there was uniformity for one piece of clothing: every man had a poncho, which he either wore in the usual manner, or tied around the waist like a sash, or dangling fantastically from the shoulder. Neither was there one amongst them without his lasso. Their arms were not less multiform than their clothing. Muskets, carbines, pistols, swords, bayonets, sabres, long knives, and lances or pikes, were the weapons with which chance had furnished them.[9]

All were "mounted men." Montoneros were part of a Mantaro Valley environment in which peasants were not tethered to the land. They owned their own parcels and could buy and sell products in local markets. Along with merchandise from Lima and Buenos Aires came news and cultural currents; many peasants in this mestizo region were literate. The valley produced a characteristic social type: the muleteer, "half adventurer, half traveling salesman (*trajinante*)."[10] Arenales's patriotic proclamations heralding elimination of tribute, expulsion of the Spanish, and the fight for liberty resonated in this milieu.

Patriots quickly noticed the veneration that Andean men professed for their past. Miller and others after him observed that many towns still mourned the Incas. The campaign newspaper *Los Andes Libres* characterized the war as a struggle to end creole and Indian misfortune. A writer used eighteenth-century rhetoric to argue that Peru's woes dated to the decapitation in Cuzco's Plaza de Armas of the "innocent prince Tupac Amaru, legitimate heir of the empire."[11] The prince was the last Vilcabamba Inca. The theme of restitution and monarchal legitimacy

[9] John Miller, *Memoirs of General Miller in the Service of the Republic of Peru*, 2nd ed., vol. 2 (London: Longman, Rees, Orme, Brown, and Green: 1829), 140.

[10] Dionisio Bernal, *La muliza* (Lima: Herrera Editores, 1978), 93. For these and other themes from central sierran history, see Waldemar Espinoza, *Enciclopedia Departamental de Junín* (Huancayo: Chipoco Editor, 1973).

[11] *Los Andes Libres* (Lima) 2, July 31, 1821.

resurfaced. In 1822 guerrillas and montoneros in Jauja fought "in the name of their father the Inca."[12]

The liberating army enjoyed the protection of Santa Rosa, a cult that had reached the Río de la Plata and whose image graced the hall of the Tucumán Congress in Buenos Aires.[13] In Lima, patriots found believers in the prophecy that the scepter would return to Inca hands after Spanish monarchs had reigned as long as the Incas before them.

While traveling through Huacho in 1820, Englishman William Bennet Stevenson observed the enduring power of memory in the region. Each year inhabitants depicted Pizarro's execution of the Inca Atahualpa: "[T]he whole [performance] is such a scene of distress, that I never witnessed it without mingling my tears with theirs. The Spanish authorities have endeavoured to prevent this exhibition, but without effect, although several royal orders have been issued for the purpose."[14] The representation did not evoke joy; contemplation and sadness were the prevailing sentiments. Similarly, Humboldt observed in 1802 in Cajamarca that "[w]herever the Peruvian Quichua language has extended, some traces of such expectations of the return of the Inca's sovereignty continue to exist."[15]

When Bolívar reached Cuzco he allowed the city's pervasive legend – the memory of the "golden kingdom" in which the sun turned to gold and Incas became viceroys and prefects – to envelop him.[16] Right away he evoked the "fable" of Garcilaso de la Vega and Bartolomé de Las Casas' *La destrucción de las Indias*. But apart from letters and proclamations, Bolívar also authored decrees. He abolished the title of Indian chieftain (kuraka) and transferred its functions to leaders "named by the central government." The glorification of the Inca empire did not impede the

[12] Jean Piel, "Las guerrillas indiennes dans les guerres d'indépendance du Pérou (1819–1824)," *Actes du XLII Congrès des Américanistes*, vol. III (September 1979), 10–16.

[13] Tomás Catanzaro, "El incanato y Santa Rosa en el Congreso de Tucumán de 1816," *El Comercio*, July 9, 1964, 2.

[14] W. B. Stevenson, *A Historical and Descriptive Narrative of Twenty Years' Residence in South America*, vol. I (London: Hurst, Robinson, and Co., 1829), 401.

[15] Alexander Von Humboldt, *Aspects of Nature in Different Lands and Different Climates; With Scientific Elucidations* (Philadelphia: Lea and Blanchard, 1849), 433. [Editors' note].

[16] Horacio Villanueva, *Simón Bolívar y el Cuzco* (Caracas: Biblioteca Venezolana de Historia, 1971), 30, 40. See also Villanueva, "La idea de los Incas como factor favorable a la Independencia," *Revista Universitaria* (Cuzco) 115 (1958), 137–58.

continuation of Bourbon policies against the indigenous aristocracy. The Incas became beings from a remote past, beautiful and distant like Greek gods.

To be sure, the past was not as relevant to liberators as it was, for example, to the Indians of Huacho. The Inca was a rhetorical figure to liberators. The past was transformed into nature, represented in images of the formidable Andes, and embodied in the sun, which appeared frequently on stamps and official documents. An 1825 allegorical painting by Cuzco artist Santiago Suárez featured a phrygian cap, symbolizing liberty, on a shield with the vanquishers of Junín and Ayacucho in the center: generals Gamarra, Lara, and Córdova to the left; Sucre, La Mar, and Miller to the right; and Bolívar in the center striking a Napoleonic pose. Below the liberator appeared the Sacsahuamán fortress, the sun, and on each side two eagles with open wings on top of two inverted lions. Finally on the lower part were the Inca queen (colla) and the Inca.[17] Eagles were a frequent imperial symbol. Suárez, however, proposed an unlikely marriage between empire and republic in depicting Bolívar as an extension of the Incas. Omitted were the three colonial centuries – depicted in patriotic speeches as a period of darkness, horror, and chains – in the desire to connect the present with supposedly national roots.

A similar theme appears in Marcos Chilli Tupa's 1837 painting in which the Inca dynasty culminates in the image of San Martín. In another dynastic representation in a private British collection, the forehead of each Inca carries two red and white feathers, the same colors as their vestments. After 1821 red and white symbolized the patria.[18]

In silent iconographic warfare, republican elites incorporated Andean motifs as their own. A Lima theater group staged a play about Atahualpa in 1827, just after independence. In a later play, *El pueblo y el tirano* (*The People and the Tyrant*) by romantic writer Carlos Augusto Salaverry, an Indian carrying a flag led a popular sixteenth-century

[17] Museo Inka, Casa del Almirante (Cuzco). Teresa Gisbert reproduced the painting in *Iconografía y mitos indígenas en el arte* (La Paz: Gisbert y Cía., 1980), figures 182 and 183.

[18] Gisbert dated the image to the early nineteenth century and Luis Eduardo Wuffarden and Gustavo Buntinx placed it after independence. In 1829 the following advertisement appeared in *Mercurio Peruano* (Lima): "In the store in the Portal de Botoneros No. 5 there are the most beautiful collections of painted paper ... the Incas." *Mercurio Peruano* (Lima), February 5, 1829. Juan Carlos Estenssoro supplied these references.

assault on the viceregal palace.[19] Although the republican future and the imperial past appeared together in fiction, not until the first decades of the twentieth century did real-life peasants see a reflection of themselves in the red and white flag. Beginning in the 1930s, popular mobilizations frequently employed the flag, and after 1945 it always preceded peasants who marched on to invade haciendas. Was that a late creole introduction? History is more complicated. The colors red and white were not chosen randomly; they appeared frequently in Andean representations such as in *qeros* or ceremonial cups.

The urgent need to mobilize Indians against Spaniards during the wars of independence explains attempts to connect Andean and western cultures. But these links were fragile and lacked cohesion. The challenge was to defeat the Spanish while avoiding a social revolution that might ignite a "caste war." Although montoneros embodied popular participation, their actions more closely resembled individualist social banditry than collective and spontaneous peasant insurrection. Even if the generals of Junín and Ayacucho did not admit it, fears of a wider rebellion were obvious to outsiders. In referring to Indians and whites in 1820, the traveler Alexander Caldcleugh observed: "There was no common interest, nothing but a mutual and disguised hatred. At times, however, these secret murmurings have given way to open rebellion."[20] He then recalled the rebellions that occurred after the "execution of the leader" – that is, Tupac Amaru II – and how boulders and stones launched from atop mountains killed many Spaniards during military marches. Some time later, in 1841, Swiss traveler Johann Jakob von Tschudi recalled hearing that Indians still possessed the weapons used against the Spanish and were awaiting the appropriate moment to employ them again.[21]

Inca discourse, however, did not eliminate political conflict. Even as late as 1828, some peasants chose to remain loyal to the king and squared off against the Republic. The Iquicha montoneros who first organized in 1780 to fight Tupac Amaru later mobilized under the command of José

[19] Raúl Porras, *Tres ensayos sobre Ricardo Palma* (Lima: Juan Mejía Baca, 1954), 39–40. Salaverry also produced a theatrical piece entitled "La conquista del Perú," staged in July 1858. *El Comercio* (Lima), August 4, 1858.

[20] Alexander Caldcleugh, *Travels in South America During the Years 1819–20-21* (London: John Murray, 1825), 69–70.

[21] Johann Jakob von Tschudi, *Travels in Peru, During the Years 1838–1842, on the Coast, in the Sierra, Across the Cordilleras and the Andes, into the Primeval Forests*, translated by Thomasina Ross (New York: Putnam, 1849), 478.

Antonio Navala Huachaca to fight the Angulo brothers.[22] The Spanish turned this Quechua-speaking Indian into a guerrilla commander, and his fame grew when the south became a loyalist stronghold. He continued fighting even after the Ayacucho surrender. With a strengthened hold in the upper reaches of Iquicha, he seized the city of Huanta on November 12, 1827, and then marched toward Ayacucho. Republican troops contained him only after bloody conflicts, although he continued fighting until 1839.[23]

Historian Lorenzo Huertas attributed this rebellion to loyalists who took refuge in the upper highlands (punas) after their defeat in Ayacucho. They mobilized Indians through coercion, forced them to enlist, and played on religious sentiment by calling the patriots heretics or Englishmen. Navala Huachaca signed a manifesto that in effect defended religion. A closer reading suggests that more than a defense of the king, the rebellion sought local autonomy. It was a curious alliance between Spaniards and indigenous inhabitants of Huanta and the punas to protect so-called common interests. They demanded

> ... the departure of the military bosses who are in this area, robbing, forcing themselves on married women and maidens, even violating the temples by force, and on top of that are despots, in light of all of this, your Honor, you should determine that they leave us and our business in peace, that they leave our commerce alone, and we will stay here to make sure that your honor determines that they do not harm our business and do not oppress anybody in Huanta or the punas... If not, it will be necessary to take the last life to defend religion and our families and interests. I promise it in the name of everyone, thus we declare. Signed: Pablo Guzmán and A. Navala Huachaca.[24]

The montoneros, who initially formed to serve patriot and loyalist armies, acquired autonomy and fought for other interests. In Huanta, they first served the king and later defended the region against soldier demands and abuses, whatever their political banner.

[22] *Informe de la comisión investigadora de los sucesos de Uchuraccay* (Lima: S.I., 1983), 47–8.

[23] Jorge Basadre, *Historia de la República del Perú*, vol. 1 (Lima: Editorial Universitaria, 1983), 201.

[24] Lorenzo Huertas, "Lucha de clases en Ayacucho 1700–1830," BA Thesis, Universidad Nacional Mayor de San Marcos, Lima, 1972, 88.

The January 1983 murder of eight journalists in the Iquicha community of Uchuraccay evoked those events. In the struggle against Shining Path guerrillas, the police and army resorted to methods similar to those the loyalists employed: they mobilized Indians against Indians. Apparently it was not difficult to find collaborators in Iquicha. Old rivalries between farmers and shepherds of highland communities appeared to underlie those events. Some Andean stories refer to battles fought in terms of the mythic figures of *huaris* and *llacuaces*. On one side were sedentary people established in sheltered fertile valleys; on the other were migrant shepherds who eased their precarious living conditions by controlling the high routes and passes that connected one valley to another.[25] It was community Indians (comuneros) of the Pampas River against Iquicha shepherds – patriots and loyalists, respectively. Political and ethnic rivalries coincided.

[25] Pierre Duviols, "Huari y Llacuaz. Agricultores y pastores. Un dualismo prehispánico de oposición y complementaridad," *Revista del Museo Nacional* (Lima) 39 (1973), 153–91.

CHAPTER 7

A Republic without Citizens

The following pages address the other side of the Andean utopia: racism, that peculiar manner of looking at "the other," a discourse on society that constitutes the very structure of daily life.[1]

> Topsy-turviness perpetuates itself: domination is propagated by the dominated.
>
> Theodor W. Adorno[2]

The Authoritarian Tradition

No Peruvian identifies himself as a racist. However, racial categories not only color our social perception but at times condition it. They are part of the very structure of professional groups, mass-media messages, and so-called beauty contests, to mention only a few examples from daily life. Few consider the racist content of a common census category such as "illiterate," a disparaging term that classifies as inferior those who choose not to speak Spanish.[3] Racism exists even if racial terms do not officially circulate in public. Even when veiled or denied, a phenomenon

1 This is a new version of a paper I first presented in July 1987 at a Latin American history colloquium organized by Hermes Tovar at the Universidad de Alcalá de Henares (Sigüenza, Spain). I have incorporated comments from Tovar, John Lynch, and others. The Social Science Research Council supported field work for this paper.

2 Theodor W. Adorno, *Minima Moralia: Reflections on a Damaged Life* (New York: Verso, 2005), 183. [Editors' note].

3 Juan Martínez Alier, *Los huacchilleros del Perú* (Paris: Ruedo Ibérico, 1973), 36.

is no less real.[4] One function of history is to bring us face to face with ourselves, to take us back to the formation of concepts and values we later wished to hide. In that sense, a psychoanalyst and an historian play a similar social role.

Racism is more than contempt and marginalization. It is an ideological discourse that underpins social domination and accepts the existence of races and the hierarchical relationship among them. Racist discourse in Peru structured itself around the relationship between whites and Indians and then disseminated to other groups. Colonial domination was the source of this paradigm. Before the Spanish set foot in Andean territory, runas or common Andean people belonged to diverse ethnic groups such as the Quechuas, Aymaras, Chocorvos, Chachapoyas, and Chancas. Conquest introduced the category of "Indian" and with it the forcible homogenization of the vanquished population and the reduction of diverse cultural expressions to what Henri Favre called a "subculture of dependence." Spanish domination did not always succeed against persistent Andean resistance. The fact that the Spanish established their colonial system at the epicenter of conquered territory required the insertion of the vanquished into the system of production, which in turn created an array of social problems. Increasing demand for mining labor underlay this system. Domingo de Santo Tomás was not the only one to assert that Indians, and not silver, were the New World's true riches.[5] The contrast between the ascending production curve and the falling demographic curve presented a great challenge for the Spanish. To avoid depopulation and maintain control over the

[4] The psychoanalyst Max Hernández has said that contemporary Lima is like a thinly veiled (*solapada*) South Africa. Jorge Eduardo Eielson has expressed this in similar terms: "If Lima seemed to some of us so horrible ... it was because we saw in it the countenance of an ill and prostrate organism called Peru. And this even though the old and comical cosmetics of a courtesan city wanted to hide it from us. For the rest of the Limeños of that time, Lima was instead a civilized, clean, orderly, and even for some, aristocratic city. But this aristocracy is like the white, Anglo-Saxon majority in Johannesburg, South Africa, even – it must be recognized – without the racist violence of the Afrikaners." Jorge Eduardo Eielson, "El respeto por la dignidad humana," *El Comercio* (Lima), February 14, 1988, Section D, 1.

[5] Domingo de Santo Tomás (1499–1570), a missionary friar, published the *Grammatica o arte de la lengua general de los indios de los Reynos del Perú* (Valladolid: Francisco Fernández de Córdova, 1560), the first Quechua grammatical text [Editors' note].

vanquished, colonialists imagined a dual society in which the Spanish formed one republic and Indians another.

Ethnic segmentation conditioned the organization of colonial urban space. The Spanish district in Lima, for example, was clearly set apart from its Indian counterpart. Parishes engaged in similar differentiation: There was one baptism registry for the Spanish, creoles, mestizos, castas, and blacks, and another for Indians. This division, however, was not rigid. A Spanish functionary completing an investigation in Cuzco at the beginning of the eighteenth century observed a population divided between Indians and mestizos on one side and Spanish on the other – the first were synonymous with "contemptible people," the other were "honorable neighbors."[6]

Later an Aristotelian conception of society emerged that likened society to a human body, a collection of organs with diverse but clearly hierarchical functions. The head served to think, the feet to walk. An inversion of the vertical relationship between them might create a monster. The fact that nature and society were considered fixed classified man in the same way as plants and animals. Not only did eighteenth-century economists and ultramontane priests espouse these ideas, but so did reformist writers such as José Baquíjano y Carrillo and other writers for *Mercurio Peruano*, the supposed instrument of the enlightened Peruvian elite. All believed hierarchical division was necessary to avoid disorder.[7] They imagined heaven as a peaceful, orderly hierarchy and represented hell as the very expression of chaos.

Colonial Peruvian society was much less integrated than its European counterparts and, because of that, people were categorized by fortune, culture, or ethnicity in addition to caste (*estamento*). A person might be classified in various ways depending on shifting criteria. Caste apparently was the most obvious, but it was ambiguous. On the one hand it alluded to ethnic classification; on the other hand it designated a specific group formed by all the variants of black mestizaje. There were at least nine classificatory terms for these "castes" (such as *mulato*, *sambo*, or *tercerón*), but "race tables" were not as common in Peru as in Mexico.[8]

6 Bernard Lavallé, *Le Marquis et le marchand* (Paris: Centre National de la Recherche Scientifique, 1987), 117.

7 Pablo Macera, *Trabajos de historia*, vol. 2 (Lima: Instituto Nacional de Cultura, 1977), 155.

8 Gregorio Cangas, "Miscelánea étnica," *Inca* (Lima) 1:4 (October–December 1923), 929–33; José Varallanos, *El cholo y el Perú* (Buenos Aires: Imprenta López, 1962). Anthropologist Fermín del Pino made this observation.

In colonial society a person might occupy one place according to his or her caste and another for income.[9] As the colonial order evolved, the initial identification between whites/colonizers and Indians/colonized blurred. In Indian towns such as Ollantaytambo, a class of poor whites – small merchants and even peasants – emerged.[10] On the opposite side an enduring indigenous aristocracy created an Indian sector that articulated with the structures of colonial domination through chieftainships (*kurakazgos*) and the so-called *cacique* schools. Beginning at the end of the seventeenth century, wealthy Indian families who understood Andean reciprocity and exchange, colonial legislation, and mercantile practices entered the world of *trajines* or overland commerce. They controlled commerce in the Collao (the area between Peru and what became Bolivia), owned mule trains, had money at their disposal, served as moneylenders, and acquired land.[11] Indian and peasant, therefore, were not necessarily synonymous. An Indian in the eighteenth century might be a noble like the Tupac Amaru or Apoalaya families or rich like the Betancourt, Choquehuanca, and the Huamanpuco clans. At mid-century three indigenous families controlled the extensive Mantaro Valley. A marital alliance with any of those families was not beneath Spaniards. That is not to say that social mobility during the colonial period was easy, but many managed to break free of perceived rigidity and immobility. The classificatory obsession did not always work.

The nebulous space between Indian and Spanish republics represented by the mestizo population complicated racial issues in the eighteenth century. Mestizos, a small minority in the sixteenth century, constituted 23 percent of the colonial population by 1786. They predominated in northern and central Peru – in Trujillo and Tarma, for example – and in urban settings. It is also important to consider African immigration in the racial mix. The slave minority was concentrated in central coastal valleys and especially in Lima, where it made up 25 percent of the population, and the outskirts of the capital. Demographic heterogeneity created within elite colonial discourse the idea of a "national body" that demanded equilibrium among its parts. Miguel

9 Szeminski, *La utopía tupamarista*.

10 Luis Miguel Glave and María Isabel Remy, *Estructura agraria y vida rural en una región andina. Ollantaytambo entre los siglos XVII y XIX* (Cuzco: Centro de Estudios Rurales Andinos Bartolomé de las Casas, 1983), 160.

11 Luis Miguel Glave, "Trajines: un capítulo en la formación del mercado interno colonial," *Revista Andina* (Cuzco) 1 (1983), 9–76.

Maticorena found this concept repeatedly in viceregal reports, proclamations, and verse. However, we should not confuse it with the idea of nation and nationalism that romantics later introduced. First of all, it was based on corporatist notions. When rural riots and uprisings became frequent, some colonial functionaries thought stability lay in balancing the large number of Indians with more Spaniards, mestizos, and blacks. In 1791 Viceroy Gil de Taboada could not conceive of a Peru without Indians, but he hoped that "for each Indian or his offspring there would be 5 and 1/8 people of other castes."[12]

The indigenous population was concentrated in the sierra because of demographic collapse in the sixteenth century, but even though there were regions of unequal development within colonial space, later imbalances were not yet apparent. Lima was the capital of that vast space. For all its efforts, Lima's mercantile aristocracy did not succeed in imposing its will on local elites in interior cities. The subterranean rivalry between the capital and provinces explained why anticolonial social movements also targeted Lima and its pretentious aristocracy. Regional interests permitted the unification of diverse social sectors ranging from creole middle sectors to the indigenous peasants whom Tupac Amaru rallied in 1780. But once unleashed, rebellion took on a life of its own. On March 13, 1781, Tupac Amaru signed an edict in Tinta that stated:

> In so far as the news has reached me that in the province of Chumbivilcas many excesses have been committed, with people killing one another, with Spaniards and Indians harming each other; I order and commission that from this day forward you live harmoniously, loving each other, living as God commanded, and upon not doing this I will punish you and condemn you to death by hanging.[13]

In most cases, however, his words went unheeded.

The victims of the Tupac Amaru rebellion were not the distant Lima aristocracy but rather the Spaniards and creoles from Cuzco (it was difficult to distinguish between them) and the Spanish living among

[12] Viceroy Gil de Taboada to Pedro de Lerna, February 5, 1791, cited in Carlos Deustua, *Las intendencias en el Perú* (Seville: Consejo Superior de Investigaciones Científicas, 1965), 210.

[13] *Colección Documental del Bicentenario*, II, vol. 1, 110.

Indians. The 50,000 or so victims, the violent deaths and massacres, the intense clashes that practically divided towns – all left traumatic memories. A literary obsession with Indians began. Tupac Amaru's defeat initiated the decline of the indigenous aristocracy, which was accused, rightly or wrongly, of collaboration with rebels. Officials abolished titles and in many cases expropriated possessions. Attributing the rebellion not only to economic factors such as repartos (the forced distribution and sale of goods in Indian communities) but also to cultural issues, the colonial administration attacked everything it considered Andean culture. Officials prohibited indigenous theater and painting, Garcilaso de la Vega's *Comentarios reales*, and the use of Quechua and traditional dress. Was this ethnocide? Non-Indians began to scorn the indigenous as much as fear them. Andean culture disappeared from public spaces and went underground. Racial distinctions acquired new importance. The need to correctly classify the colonial population motivated the 1786 census and the population rolls that provincial governors (*intendentes*) oversaw. Parishes joined this campaign.

Fear of another "caste war" like the 1780 rebellion generated true ethnic tension and spread through unexpected mechanisms. News of the Haitian Revolution in June 1793 and fears that Peruvian slaves in Lima and the coast might follow suit sowed panic. But in colonial society, ethnic boundaries did not only separate rich from poor. They also functioned within the "lower classes" themselves, pitting, for example, Indians against blacks. Whether spontaneous or fomented by colonial administration, ethnic rivalries represented a pillar of social equilibrium. Viceroy O'Higgins dismissed fears of a general rebellion by arguing that blacks and Indians had irreconcilable differences. Indeed, groups who ransacked coastal valleys recruited creoles, Spaniards, free blacks, black slaves, sambos, and mulatos, but only rarely Indians, who instead were frequently victims or informants. In Lima the rivalry played out even in the distribution of urban space: Indians occupied the *barrio del cercado* or walled town on the outskirts; blacks occupied the city's center or the San Lázaro neighborhood on the other side of the Rimac River. The product of white-black racial mixture predominated among city castes, whereas *chinos*, the result of black-Indian mixture, were the minority. Esteban de Terralla y Landa noted the "total abhorrence" that Indians and blacks professed for each other.[14] Even popular sectors internalized ethnic distinctions, demonstrating the efficacy of the caste system. More than

[14] Esteban de Terralla y Landa, *Lima por dentro y fuera* (Madrid: Imprenta de Villalpando, 1798), 99 [Editors' note].

simply ideological discourse, racism was an active part of daily colonial life.

The wars of independence interrupted the anti-indigenista cycle that began in 1780. Patriots admitted that indigenous troops made victory possible. Paradoxically, the idea of integrating Indians into the republic as citizens was one argument for abolishing the legal status of indigenous communities. What's more, the victors fancied themselves as extensions of the Incas. As Simón Bolívar wrote to Joaquín de Olmedo, "I arrived yesterday in the classical country of the Sun, of the Incas, of the fable, and of history."[15] The image of Inca monarchs returned to official iconography and appeared on canvases, coins, bills, and official seals. Hymns and epic poems evoked their memory. Yet lifeless images of the sun, the Andes, and highland lakes reduced Indians to mere abstractions and disembodied images. Beyond speeches, the idyllic encounter between creole troops and peasants began to dim. In the early 1820s the southern Andes – once the stage of the great Amaru and Catari rebellions – became a secure loyalist rearguard. If patriots emerged victorious in Ayacucho, loyalist priests in nearby Huanta harassed them with the support of peasants organized into guerrilla and montonero groups:

> As Indians are the ones who have behaved the worst and with most hostility in the district of Huanta, I have advised the governor to make them pay a third of the tribute owed the Spanish government in December, exempting the towns of Quinua, Acos Vinchos, and Huaichao of that tribute and the town of Quinua of all contributions because it treated us very well and gave the army whatever it had.[16]

The image of towns confronting each other played out time and again. Chaos was the most apt description for the new country. As Tomás de Heres described it to Bolívar, "Strictly speaking, Peru has no administration whatsoever; it is a ship in the cape with no sails and no rudder."[17] Bolívar absolutely agreed: "No one obeys anyone

[15] Reproduced in *Cartas del Libertador. Memorias del General O'Leary publicadas por orden del ilustre Americano General Guzmán Blanco* (Caracas: Imprenta y litografía del Gobierno Nacional, 1887), 81 [Editors' note].

[16] Vicente Lecuna, *Documentos referentes a la creación de Bolivia* (Caracas: Litografía del Comercio, 1924), letter from Sucre to the Minister of War, Huamanga, December 5, 1825, 26.

[17] Jorge Cornejo Bouroncle, *La confederación Perú-Boliviana* (Cuzco: Lib. Imp. H.G. Rozas Sucs., 1935), 8.

and everyone detests everyone else."[18] One explanation for the state of the republic was that independence caused the collapse of the colonial upper class. First, the Bourbon reforms and emergence of a rival Atlantic port, Buenos Aires, weakened the Lima aristocracy. Then elites lost control of Chile and Upper Peru. The elimination of repartos upset the commercial circuit. Finally, war destroyed the merchant marine, forced Spanish emigration to Brazil and the peninsula, and prompted hasty flight to Callao and the sierra behind loyalist armies. Lima merchants remained loyal to the crown almost to the end, so it was not surprising that the *Tribunal de Secuestros*, formed to manage the confiscation of royalist estates, seized many of their possessions.

The long list of Spanish emigrants included around fifty merchants. In the following years more than forty haciendas, most located on the central coast, ended up in the hands of the new state. When the First Constituent Assembly convened on September 20, 1822, to establish the legal foundation of the new republic, only nine merchants and a similar number of landowners figured among the ninety-one deputies. The majority were lawyers, doctors, ecclesiastics, and soldiers from the provincial middle sectors, a fragile social stratum that could not replace the colonial aristocracy. Early on, the power vacuum that accompanied radical political change was apparent. Before the first year was over, José de la Riva Agüero, an ex-conspirator and budding caudillo, mutinied against congress and inaugurated a long tradition of military coups. Antonio José de Sucre in turn ousted him in November 1823.

These events demonstrated the precariousness of democratic projects in Peru. In his *Memorias*, written in 1823 in Quito, Ecuador, Bernardo de Monteagudo claimed that profound ethnic differences coupled with the uneven distribution of wealth and other factors threatened "social existence." He was thinking not only of the separation between whites and Indians but also of diverse and opposing castes. The wars of independence deepened the colonial world's social fragmentation. In Lima and other places, Monteagudo observed "men who formed as many social subdivisions as there are variations in their color," which was incompatible with "democratic ideas."[19] The revolution did not significantly

[18] John Fisher, "La formación del Estado Peruano (1808–1824) y Simón Bolívar," in Inge Buisson, ed., *Problemas de la formación del Estado y la Nación en Hispanoamérica*. (Köln: Bohlau, 1984), 467.

[19] Bernardo Monteagudo, *Memoria sobre los principios políticos que seguí en la administración del Perú* . . . A.F.V. (Santiago, Chile: Imprenta Nacional, 1823), 18–19.

modify the structure of daily life. For the most radical participants, independence meant not only a break with Spain but also the liquidation of the colonial aristocracy. This came about as much from circumstances – the enduring crisis of those years – as from anti-Spanish efforts. In contrast, the colonial order survived in the domestic sphere, to which no one was paying attention. The republic inherited racial conflicts and marginalization.

Racist Discourse

The anarchic early years of the Republic followed the collapse of the colonial order. It was not possible for military caudillos in Peru to achieve political stability comparable to that of Diego Portales in Chile. After the Provisional Statute of 1821 came further guidelines created in 1822 and then the 1823, 1826, 1828, 1834, and 1839 constitutions. Mariscal Agustín Gamarra, one of the governors who achieved greatest stability during that period, weathered fourteen conspiracy plots against him. Historian Heraclio Bonilla called Peru a country adrift. The recomposition of the Peruvian upper class did not begin until the 1840s or 1850s, when customs income and guano exports permitted the rapid accumulation of family fortunes.

The so-called consolidation was a particularly important moment in the reconstitution of the upper class. The internal debt incurred during the wars of independence came due in 1850. Officials attempted to convert into cash the *papelitos* or little papers that patriot generals issued during the wars of independence to hacienda owners, merchants, muleteers, small property owners, and other victims of wartime confiscation, ranging from those with great fortunes to those who contributed a horse, mule, or meager crops to the cause. In time these promissory notes declined in value and passed from hand to hand. Speculators bought them up and then used their political influence to force the state to pay up. It finally paid off during Echenique's administration. A small group of fifty or so people with export commerce connections and clientelistic ties to the regime ended up as well-paid beneficiaries. This created a terrible scandal amid cries of forgery. The term *consolidado* entered the dictionary as a synonym for "swindle" (*estafa*) and "embezzlement" (*peculado*) at the expense of public funds. This scandal was one of the factors behind the uprising led by Ramón Castilla in 1855. Once in power, his administration abolished slavery and eliminated indigenous tribute, but the regime soon repeated the actions of the previous administration in debt payment, aggravated by similarly inflated indemnities to coastal owners for slave manumission. A new revolt, this one led by Manuel Ignacio de Vivanco, failed.[20]

Consolidados ended up squandering their fortunes. The reemergence of the Peruvian upper class was postponed several years until elites built on guano and export commerce. A rudimentary financial circuit permitted the flow of capital from commerce to export agriculture through the payment of bonds from the internal debt, slave manumission, and Banco Central Hipotecario loans. The loans overwhelmingly went to north and central coastal departments, where the expansion of sugarcane and cotton quickly altered valley landscapes. Mills and cotton gins went up, steam tractors arrived, and hydraulic works began. The Arequipa upper class complained when benefits did not trickle down to the south. In the latter half of the nineteenth century, the economic center of the country shifted from sierra to coast, and growth through export agriculture tipped the balance of national power toward Lima and the ports. In many ways the Peruvian coast was closer to Asia, the source of labor that sustained the so-called guano bourgeoisie, than to the Andean "hinterland."[21] Enormous profits did not foster a domestic labor market. Peruvian elites belatedly recognized geographic fragmentation and began to imagine a railroad network that connected coastal ports with the sierra.

A small roster of thirty families with names such as Aspíllaga, Ayulo, Barreda, Larco, and Pardo represented a particular type of Lima bourgeoisie, one armed with capital but not factories and workers. Among the few survivors from the colonial aristocracy were the Ramírez de Arellano family, which held on to some haciendas, and the Mariátegui family, which emerged afloat thanks to a daughter's marriage to Enrique Swayne y Wallace, an associate of a Liverpool firm. The latter was not the only foreigner to make a fortune. The upper class that emerged was small, young (one or two generations in Peru), and too European for a country whose majority population was indigenous. The brief and fleeting "consolidation" created a deep gulf between state and society. Scandals and the concentration of public money in few hands eroded public confidence in state administration. The disgruntled included small property owners, artisans, merchants, and intellectuals who had

[20] Alfonso Quiroz, *La deuda defraudada* (Lima: Instituto Nacional de Cultura, 1987).

[21] Flores Galindo is referring to the importation of thousands of Chinese coolies after 1849 [Editors' note].

their first political experience during the 1850 elections. They obtained nothing hopeful from their vote or from Castilla's uprising. Echoes of the European Revolution of 1848 infused some young people with hopes for a similar change in Peru, but it was not to be. Frustration and disillusion set in. This was not fertile soil for consensus. In the words of Jorge Basadre, the republic deepened the abyss between the Peru defined by laws and the real Peru.

How could a small group control a large, disarticulated, and troubled Peru? Colonial social order rested upon the idea of monarchy and the guarantee that peninsular armies opposed anyone who questioned the king. The republic constructed itself upon the loyalist army's debacle. Independence also created a rupture with the clergy, another important pillar of support for the colonial aristocracy. The Church hierarchy blessed the viceroy's troops to the very end, and a Pope Leon XII encyclical urged continued obedience to Ferdinand VII. The Vatican refused to recognize the new republic, and not until 1852 did it admit the first Peruvian legation into Rome. Nineteenth-century Peru, for one reason or another, was an increasingly secular society that demanded a temporal political order.

During the colonial period, three institutions permitted social domination in the interior: the corregidor, a Spanish provincial authority who administered justice; the kuraka, the indigenous authority who served as the conduit between the communities and the colonial administration; and the priest, who watched over souls and dispensed norms and values from the pulpit and the confessional booth. At the end of the eighteenth century intendentes replaced corregidores, and after independence, prefects supplanted intendentes. However, the republican state was unable to grant its functionaries the same support that the colonial state had provided. At the same time, its ties to the Church weakened. Clerical ranks dropped from 3,000 priests in 1820 to 2,400 in 1874, and foreigners began to predominate. Some orders, such as the Jesuits in 1767 and later the Bethlemites, disappeared altogether. Those orders had possessed some of the most extensive and efficient colonial agricultural haciendas. The number of Church properties declined. In the Puno province of Azángaro, only eleven of the forty Church haciendas and chaplaincies that existed in 1829 were still around a century later. By the middle of the nineteenth century, when the state abolished the tithe, the clergy's material foundation foundered. The Church lost power in the countryside, and the first abandoned churches appeared. Priests, whom indigenistas such as Narciso Aréstegui viewed as a scourge to Indians, saw their power wane. Officials suppressed kurakas after the defeat of Tupac Amaru, and Bolívar's 1824 decree in Cuzco did away with what was left. All this led Bartolomé Herrera to state in 1842 that "the principle of obedience perished in the struggle for emancipation."[22]

The disappearance of kurakas and corregidores, the decline of the clergy, and the weakness of republican police and bureaucratic apparatuses allowed landowners a newfound monopoly on local political power. In the nineteenth century a landowner might mobilize "his" Indians into montonero groups or private armies. The forces that participated alongside Vivanco, Castilla, and Echenique formed this way. To become the country's dominant group, the coastal upper class implicitly tolerated the private jurisdiction of interior landowners, which allowed them to exercise control over peasants. An asymmetrical reciprocity functioned within haciendas. The owner allowed his colonos usufruct rights to land and livestock in exchange for labor and/or products, and he provided coca, alcohol, protection, and exemption from military service. The term *gamonal*, a Peruvianism coined for those landowners, entered the social science mainstream to describe unprecedented political fragmentation and ruralization. Gamonal power derived from a combination of consensual and violent control mechanisms. Hardly an absentee landowner, a gamonal knew his peasants personally, spoke Quechua, and did not hesitate to use the whip or stocks. He combined racism with paternalism.[23]

Modernization during the guano period, which began in 1840 with the first fertilizer exports, almost inevitably increased servitude. The Lima and coastal bourgeoisie and traditional landowners of the interior shared power, a form of domination called the "oligarchic state." The term "oligarchy," depicting the minority and exclusive exercise of control, first appeared in print in 1877 in the title of a pamphlet by José Andrés Torres Paz, *La oligarquía y la crisis* (Oligarchy and Crisis).[24] It denounced a social class built from "money earned above all in guano," a group that "attempted to politically elevate itself on the ruins of detestable military *caudillaje*." Elite guano wealth contrasted starkly with

[22] Bartolomé Herrera, *Escritos y discursos*, vol. 1 (Lima: Librería Francesa Científica, 1929), 17–18. Herrera was a prominent conservative cleric and intellectual. The quoted line was part of his eulogy at the funeral of former president Agustín Gamarra in 1842 [Editors' note].

[23] For these themes see Chapter 8, "The Utopian Horizon."

[24] José Andrés Torres Paz, *La oligarquia y la crisis* (Lima: Imprenta del Teatro, 1877).

"the despair and degradation of the people." However, this was true only for Lima and parts of the coast. As the capital expanded and razed its colonial walls, cities such as Cuzco began an irreversible decline. In 1865 the traveler George Squier observed that

> infinitely less is known of Cuzco in Lima, today, than of Berlin; not one person in the capital has visited it, while hundreds have visited Paris; and the journey from Lima to New York may be made in less time, at a fourth of the cost, and a thousandth part of the trouble and fatigue, than it can be made from the same point to the proud but isolated city of the Sierra.[25]

According to an error-plagued census in 1876, Peru's population was almost 2,700,000, including an indigenous majority of 1,554,678, mostly in the sierra and rural areas; more than 500,000 mestizos; 371,195 whites; and a little more than 50,000 blacks and Asians, respectively. Indians posed a problem for whites, and not only for numerical reasons. A few years earlier Santiago Távara asked: "[A]nd these Indians whom we call citizens, of what use are they to the Republic?"[26] His response was not optimistic; he viewed Indians as distrustful, vile, base, dejected, fearful, and suspicious – that is, the passive and inert part of Peruvian society.

The author of history textbooks used in those times displayed a similar vision. Spaniard Sebastián Lorente (1813–84), a liberal thinker, most directly shaped the historical consciousness of Peruvian school children and literate adults. Lorente taught at Lima's Guadalupe School, founded Huancayo's Santa Isabel School (1851), and authored *Historia de la civilización peruana* and various manuals on the pre-Hispanic, conquest, colonial, and independence periods. Lorente's version of Peruvian history accepted racial difference, and he found in the ideas of Gobineau, by then common in Peru, the key to historical explanation. Distinguishing between oppressor and oppressed races allowed him to simultaneously pity Indians and reproach the "prosperity" and "madness" of their dominators. However, Indians were the very negation of change and modern progress, people utterly lacking

[25] E. G. Squier, "Among the Andes of Peru and Bolivia," *Harper's New Monthly Magazine* (New York), 37, 218 (July 1868), 145–65, quote from 162.

[26] Santiago Távara, *Emancipación del indio decretada el 5 de julio de 1854* (Lima: José María Monterola, 1856), 20.

in psychological and physical vitality.[27] "With secular oppression," Lorente stated, "comes the deterioration of the body and the gifts of the spirit; the physiognomy of certain Indians provides an air of the decrepit races; there is a total absence of vigor, a lack of the freshness that animates races full of youth and promise."[28] The millennial oppression of Inca "theocratic communism" reduced men to machines and paved the way for colonialism. Only the passing of "several generations" could cleanse Indians of their lethargic and torpid spirit. In the immediate future the republic could not count on them as citizens.

Lorente's *Pensamientos sobre el Perú* (Thoughts about Peru) (1855) situated Indians at the margin of civilization and brimmed with disparaging adjectives: "They lie in ignorance and are cowards, indolent, incapable of realizing the benefits [of civilization], without feelings, shiftless, thieves, have no respect for the truth, hold no elevated sentiment, vegetate in misery and in worries, and live in drunkenness and sleep in lasciviousness."[29] Indians were a repository for all negative values, the mirror image of whites. It is difficult to find an earlier influential writer who served up such openly racist and aggressive discourse against Indians – and this from a forward-thinking, radical figure for the period. In Lorente's view Indians had degenerated to animal level: "Someone once said: Indians are llamas that speak."[30] Although a certain prudence led him to attribute the reference to others, he did not clarify or deny it. Yet Indians were not just any llama but rather a "stupid llama." A similar image circulated among Andrés Santa Cruz's intellectual enemies during the years of the Peru-Bolivia Confederation (1836–39), but this racist discourse crystallized around the middle of the nineteenth century, along with the recomposition of the upper class.

Castilla – the most important caudillo of the nineteenth century, the architect of republican public administration, and a hero to the military – also subscribed to that view. Castilla believed the solution to the national problem was immigration, the incorporation of "robust, hard-working, and moral men whose noble race would merge with

[27] Gonzalo Portocarrero, "La historia del Perú en la divulgación escolar," unpublished manuscript.

[28] Sebastián Lorente, *Historia de la civilización peruana* (Lima: Imprenta Liberal, 1879), 147. See also his *Historia del Perú, compendiada para el uso de los colegios y de las personas ilustradas* (Lima: Aubert y Loisseau Editores, 1866).

[29] Sebastián Lorente, *Pensamientos sobre el Perú* (Lima: Universidad Nacional Mayor de San Marcos, 1967), 23.

[30] Ibid.

ours and improve it."[31] It was a purely biological vision of society. Idealized immigrants were the negation of Lorente's portrait of Indians. They should be white, western, and European, such as the handful of Tyroleans who set up in Pozuzo or the Basques in Talambo. But they were exceptions. The immigrants then entering Peru were mostly Asians, whom Castilla considered even weaker and more slothful than Indians. They went to work on haciendas but ended up fleeing to towns and cities where, "mixed in with our natives, they pervert their character, degrade our race, and infuse people, especially youth, with the embarrassing and repugnant vices that control almost all of them."[32] The number of Chinese piled into boats traveling from Macao to Callao increased yearly during Castilla's two administrations. Uprooted and residents of a country whose language they did not speak, Chinese immigrants unwittingly contributed to racism just as slaves were gaining their freedom. Racism convinced Peru's economic and intellectual elites that their rule was justified, no matter how violent it was.

About the same time, in 1847, the reconquest of the Amazon region began when Castilla authorized a military expedition that penetrated the central jungle by "blood and fire."[33] After establishing a fort in San Ramón, the group embarked on frequent punitive expeditions. Settlers began to arrive and natives revolted as in the eighteenth century. On one occasion they ambushed an official naval commission. Benito Arana commanded a retaliatory expedition in 1866. The region of the Mountain of Salt became a military zone with the civilized on one side and "savages" on the other. What Pablo Macera called "a horrific war of extermination" began, although the press did not deem it worthy of news coverage. Some sectors of the Peruvian population experienced racism in dramatic ways.

Violence continued playing a central role in social control. Chinese immigrants and Amazon natives experienced as much open violence as Indians faced daily on haciendas. As racist discourse solidified, a significant percentage of public expenditures went toward military purposes – 48 percent in 1849, 37 percent in 1852, and 51 percent in 1862.[34]

[31] Fernando de Trazegnies, *La idea de Derecho en el Perú republicano del siglo XIX* (Lima: Pontificia Universidad Católica del Perú, 1980), 177.

[32] Ibid.

[33] Nelson Manrique, *Mercado interno y región. La sierra central 1820–1930* (Lima: Desco, 1987), 111.

[34] Javier Tantaleán, *Política económica-financiera y la formación del Estado: siglo XIX* (Lima: CEDEP, 1983), 195.

Army ranks grew to about 10,000. However, internal military structure reflected the fissures in Peruvian society. More than 80 percent of troops were stationed in Lima and Callao, and the social composition of officials and enlisted men differed sharply. Indians and mestizos – forced into service and lacking what one English observer called "esprit de corps" – served as soldiers. According to him, "the majority of officials, especially in higher ranks, are descendants from old Spanish colonizers, and for that reason they have little in common with their men."[35]

It is hardly surprising that such an army crumbled against a foreign invader. When the War of the Pacific with Chile broke out in 1879, political crisis and disorder helped trigger pent-up conflicts. When Chilean troops reached the Cañete valley, the Chinese joined the invading army, not to defend the Chilean flag but rather to sack and attack Peruvian haciendas. Despite little incriminating evidence, Limeños blamed the Chinese for a fire in Chorrillos when Chilean troops occupied it in January 1881. Almost immediately, vengeful retaliators in Callao sacked Chinese businesses and killed more than a few immigrants.

Peru's defeat caused intellectuals such as Manuel González Prada to question a republic that excluded the indigenous population and did not recognize its citizenship rights. But many others blamed Peruvian failure and frustration on Indians' inferiority and the burden they represented to national development. Chile defeated Peru, the thinking went, because the former had fewer Indians and more Europeans. The military campaign against the Mapuches before the war even helped train Chile's army. In 1881, during the occupation of Peruvian territory, a University of Arequipa professor blamed the defeat on unproductive mestizaje between Spaniards and Indians. In 1894 Javier Prado y Ugarteche insisted on the "pernicious influence that inferior races have exercised in Peru." Francisco García Calderón envied countries such as Chile and Argentina that were free of "depleted races."[36] In 1897 Clemente Palma spoke for many Peruvian intellectuals when he affirmed that "the Indian race is an old and degenerate branch of the ethnic trunk from which all inferior races emerge. They have all the characteristics of decrepitude and ineptitude for civilized life. Lacking character, endowed with a mental life that is almost null, apathetic, and

[35] Celia Wu Brading, ed., *Testimonios británicos de la ocupación chilena en Lima* (Lima: Editorial Milla Batres, 1986), 92.

[36] Jeffrey Klaiber, "Los 'cholos' y los 'rotos': actitudes raciales durante la guerra del Pacífico," *Histórica* (Lima) 2:1 (July 1978), 27–37, quote on 34.

without aspirations, they are not adaptable to education."[37] In the 1920s, philosopher and university professor Alejandro Deustua stated without qualification that "Peru owes its misfortune to the indigenous race."[38]

When German traveler Ernest Middendorf visited Huaraz in 1885 – shortly before a peasant rebellion threatened the city – he sensed the tension between Indians and whites: "The conflicts between different races cannot be solved on the basis of principles of justice, and racial wars are always wars of extermination."[39] If we take Pardo, Palma, and Deustua seriously, their ideas framed the so-called Indian problem in definitive and antagonistic terms.

Help Wanted

In *Pensamientos sobre el Perú*, Lorente included a text entitled "El cholito." In it he reveals a curious secret: "When one leaves for the sierra, ladies from Lima do not fail to request a *cholito* and a *cholita*, and at times they ask for so many that you would think they were found in fields by the dozen."[40] What was a cholito? The diminutive form of cholo was a synonym for "Indian boy," generally an orphan or outsider destined for domestic service. Lima's *El Comercio* published employment ads seeking a boy or girl to work in a certain position, as seen in this ad: "A married couple without children is urgently seeking a male or female cook and a handmaid."[41]

The earliest editions of *El Comercio*, founded in 1839, contained only two pages, but they included a section of brief ads that cost four reales for the first run and two reales for subsequent ones. Artisans offering their services, requests for teachers, announcements about fugitive slaves, teachers offering language lessons – ads such as these provide a window on daily life in Lima. Frequent classified ads sought domestic employees for a specific task such as coachman, laundry woman, and wet nurse. One such announcement stated, "Seeking a well-behaved cook to work

[37] Clemente Palma, *El porvenir de las razas en el Perú* (Lima: Torres Aguirre, 1897), 15.

[38] Alejandro Deustua, *La cultura nacional* (Lima: Universidad Nacional Mayor de San Marcos, 1937), 68.

[39] Ernest Middendorf, *Perú. Observaciones y estudios del país y sus habitantes durante una permanencia de 25 años*, vol. 3 (Lima: Universidad Nacional Mayor de San Marcos, 1973), 53.

[40] Lorente, *Pensamientos sobre el Perú*, 29.

[41] *El Comercio* (Lima), January 3, 1859.

in a family home; the person who wishes to hire himself out for this purpose should inquire at this printing office."[42] Readers saw ads for fugitive, lost, or abducted cholitos and cholitas, or those lured away by another patron. These ads appeared in the mid-1840s and even more frequently in the 1850s. There were two or more in each edition. It was rare, however, to find an ad seeking a cholito per se. The ads referred to servants already working in Lima, perhaps recruited outside the city by a powerful relative (prefect or landowner), or by an occasional traveler to the sierra such as Lorente. Domestic service appeared to be an extension of *pongaje* or personal service that peasants performed in the hacienda house.

Servant descriptions were symptomatic of how the upper class and middle sectors viewed the Other. Almost all servants were minors, predominantly boys. Although names were rare, ads frequently provided physical characteristics – even dental details at times – and almost always described their clothing. These were either nameless people or objects with first names only. Here are examples from the late 1850s:

> "Today a *serranito* named José from Huaraz has fled from the house next to the stables of Mr. Gárate, No. 649. He is hatless and shoeless and wearing a shirt with faded blue stripes. The person who returns him will receive a reward."[43]

> "Notice: Last night a seven- or eight-year-old boy named Gregorio fled from his master's house. He is of Indian caste, fat, round face, pug-nosed with scars on his forehead; he speaks Spanish with great difficulty, being a native of an Ayacucho province. He left wearing a purple shirt, grey wool pants, with no hat or shoes."[44]

> "Interesting notice – Any person who found a boy at 12:30 yesterday, July 29, we prevail upon you to go to 109 De la Riva Street for a nice reward. His description is: thick lips, big head, chubby, brown-skinned, and is four years old."[45]

> "Notice – Yesterday, Monday the ninth, a ten-year-old girl named Flora fled from the store at 155 Inquisition; the person who has her is warned to turn her over immediately if he or she does not

[42] *El Comercio* (Lima), December 2, 1839.
[43] *El Comercio* (Lima), August 7, 1858.
[44] *El Comercio* (Lima), January 4, 1858.
[45] *El Comercio* (Lima), August 3, 1858.

> want to face the consequences resulting from hiding her from the police, for the girl's employer who raised her is like her mother."[46]

Servants were part of domestic life and like members of the family on occasion, although on an inferior level. This apparent paternalism allowed employers to justify free labor and even corporal punishment. Nonetheless, frequent ads indicated that many servants resisted and fled. Lima's population of 55,000 in 1836 doubled in the next thirty years. Accelerated demographic growth, which must have disconcerted Limeños, made the city a good place in which to flee, find alternative work (perhaps in another house), or hide. Employers sometimes suspected that servants left to work for other masters. It is plausible that urban growth or changes in living standards increased demand for servants, as Lorente's story seems to confirm. Like slaves during the colonial period, the number of servants per household was an external sign of wealth.

Servants did not go unnoticed by European travelers. Middendorf depicted domestic servitude as characteristic of Lima, observing that the

> domestic service of a household is composed of at least three people: a cook, a butler or *mayordomo*, and a girl or assistant to the señora. The servants are generally cholos or zambos, with the exception of the cook, who is frequently Chinese and, in exceptional cases, French. In the richest homes there is additionally a doorman, a second mayordomo who helps the first in setting up the dining table, a kitchen assistant or dish washer, a laundry woman, a seamstress, and as many female servants as the number of children demands.[47]

Although Middendorf was describing Lima after the Chilean occupation, there is no reason to think there were fewer servants during the guano period before the war.

Domestic service was stratified. On one side were those with specific jobs or special training; on the other side were general laborers who almost exclusively performed manual tasks. The former had existed for a long time and worked for the wealthiest families; the latter were also employed by middle-class homes and even families with fewer resources.

[46] *El Comercio* (Lima), August 1, 1858.
[47] Middendorf, *Perú*, vol. 3, 176.

Servants replaced slaves after emancipation in 1854. After the beginning of the republic, the number of slaves declined significantly in Lima. Once freed, few continued as servants. The Chinese who arrived in Callao mostly worked on haciendas and very rarely in households, perhaps because the paternalistic ties that families had established with cholitos were not possible with new immigrants. Masters or employers often knew their servants from a young age and at times even their parents. What stands out above all, however, was that they were minors; some went forcibly to Lima and were unable to return to their families, creating an uprootedness that led to total dependence. Like Gregorio, described above as slow to learn Spanish, many spoke Quechua or Aymara and barely knew a few Spanish words. Employers were not interested in educating them, and a marked accent or the inability to speak their masters' language was another form of social differentiation.

Although racism colored politics and even the interpretation of Peruvian history, it was also part of the structure of daily life. Lima children learned it at home at an early age by observing how their parents treated cholitos. Servants might be the same age as their employer's children and at times even played with them. The cholito was an outsider in a growing city, tethered by rigid dependency ties and forced to attend to the requirements, requests, and demands of his employers – a manifestation of total power inside the domestic realm. About the only way out of such submission was flight, although there were extreme alternatives. Crimes that especially shook Lima involved servants with several years of service who killed their employers.

According to the 1876 census, domestic service was the most important activity in Lima: 6,460 inhabitants worked as domestics. If we include launderers, coachmen, nursemaids, grooms, and errand boys, the number reached about 9,000, 19 percent of the overall population and between 20 and 30 percent of the "working population."[48] Women slightly outnumbered men. We do not know the ethnic breakdown. However, when in 1908 the number of servants grew to 14,274, about 19 percent of the working population, the majority were indigenous. Next came mestizos, a few "yellows" (Asian), and even fewer blacks.[49]

[48] Perú, Ministerio de Gobierno, *Censo General de la República del Perú formado en 1876*, vol. 6 (Lima: Imprenta del Teatro, 1878).

[49] Perú, Dirección de Salubridad Pública, *Censo de la Provincia de Lima (26 de junio de 1908), decretado y levantado durante la administración del Excmo. señor don José Pardo* (Lima: Imprenta de la Opinión Nacional, 1915).

Domestic service was a cholo occupation. The relationship between *señores* and Indians in Andean haciendas constituted the paradigm of Peruvian racism. Such a relationship reproduced itself in the urban domestic context. Lima was the center of diffusion for racist ideology.

However, urban servitude was not a new phenomenon. We find its antecedents in the Lima convents that employed a large number of servants, among them children turned over as apprentices in artisan workshops. We also see servants working alongside slaves in private homes as early as 1613. Of the 1,978 Indians included in the indigenous register that year, 451 were servants, including 274 men and 177 women. Around 90 percent were single, and minors predominated. Here we see uprootedness similar to that of the 1850s: 47 percent of servants did not belong to an encomendero or were under the rule of a cacique.[50] More than a century later, the 1771 register for the Lima barrio of Cocharcas included 244 servants and 4,332 Indians. Forty-seven percent of those servants worked in houses with one servant, and one household had nineteen domestics.[51]

Domestic servitude, therefore, was an institution as old as the city itself and served as a mechanism for the reproduction of the colonial legacy. But a structure that survives relatively unchanged until today solidified in the 1850s along with an explicit racist discourse. At that historical moment domestic service not only increased as a result of slave manumission but coincided with the emergence of a "cholitos" market. Cholitos were the acute manifestation of the symbiosis between social class and caste. Domestic servant and cholo were synonymous, but even worse, cholo was a disparaging term, at times equivalent to a dog, always a person of low social condition, the offspring of a defeated and inferior race condemned to subjection. At least, that's what their masters believed.

[50] Noble David Cook, *Padrón de los indios de Lima de 1613* (Lima: Seminario de Historia Rural Andina, 1968).

[51] Mauro Escobar, "Un padrón de Lima – 1771," *Revista del Archivo General de la Nación* (Lima), 6 (1984).

CHAPTER 8

The Utopian Horizon

Indigenismo, APRA, and Mariátegui's socialism emerged in the 1920s and served as the pillars of Peruvian intellectual life for the rest of the century.[1] *For all their differences, each was a tributary of the Andean utopia and subverted an ideological order that until then was dominated exclusively by the oligarchy. How did this happen? The answer lies not just in the history of ideas or changing collective mentalities; more than discourse, the crisis of the oligarchic system originated on the ground in the form of rebellions and rural uprisings in southern Peru. For some it was the long-awaited rebirth of the Andean world – for others, the feared "caste war."*

Local Power

In 1912 a young Limeño with an aristocratic name and author of a brilliant history thesis journeyed to the southern sierra. Armed with books and maps, José de la Riva Agüero traveled by steamship from Callao to Mollendo and then took the train to Puno. From there, accompanied by a friend from Lima, muleteers, and various servants, Riva Agüero left the high plains for a three-month tour through Cuzco, Apurímac, Ayacucho, and up to the Mantaro Valley. The journey of a 27-year-old intellectual who preferred to travel in Peru instead of Europe was so unusual that it demanded a written

[1] APRA stands for Alianza Popular Revolucionaria Americana, a continental movement founded in México in 1924 by Peruvian exile Víctor Raúl Haya de la Torre. It has existed in Peru since the mid-1920s, and in 1930 the "Partido Aprista Peruano" was founded [Editors' note].

account. Five years later Riva Agüero wrote *Paisajes peruanos* (*Peruvian Landscapes*).[2]

For Riva Agüero, the landscape evoked the past. The very mention of Jaquijahuana, the Ayacucho pampa (upper highlands), the Vilcas ruins, and the Cocharcas sanctuary recalled the chronicler Fernando de Montesinos and Alonso Carrió de la Vandera (known as Concolorcorvo). Riva Agüero's erudition, however, did not equip him to discover the inhabitants of those territories. He documented a sierra without Indians, an empty landscape, a sort of cemetery. Although he considered Cuzco "the heart and symbol of Peru," the city in which he began his account filled him with melancholy and dismay. From the sixteenth century on, "slow agony" characterized the history of Cuzco. Little by little its population declined until it resembled a regal tomb. Riva Agüero wondered: "Is the essence of our most representative city oppressive sorrow, horrendous tragedy, and unrelenting prostration?"[3]

Around the same time, Pedro Zulen, a Limeño writer of Chinese origin moved by the indigenous situation, planned to publish a collection of his passionate articles – not of historical nostalgia but of contemporary fervor.[4] Although his "Gamonalismo y centralismo" was never published, the title words became central themes in Peruvian intellectual debates. In some ways José Carlos Mariátegui (1894–1930) published Zulen's book thirteen years later, for some of the best pages of his *Siete ensayos de interpretación de la realidad peruana* (*Seven Interpretive Essays on Peruvian Reality*) were precisely an attack on gamonalismo and a vote against suffocating centralization.[5]

What is gamonalismo? The term gamonal was a Peruvianism coined in the nineteenth century that likened landowners to parasitic plants. Another version suggested a "gamonal was the worm that corroded the tree of the nation."[6] Beyond passionate overtones, however, the term conveyed the existence of local power: privatization of politics, fragmentation of authority, and control over a town or province. The middle classes or peasants of the interior knew the powerful as mistis (lords,

[2] José de la Riva Agüero, *Paisajes peruanos* (Lima: Instituto Riva Agüero, 1995).

[3] Ibid., 16.

[4] Letter from Pedro Zulen to Blanco Fombona, Archivo Zulen (BNP), Correspondencia.

[5] José Carlos Mariátegui, *Siete ensayos de interpretación de la realidad peruana* [1928] (Lima: Empresa Editora Amauta, 1978), translated by Marjory Urquidi as *Seven Interpretive Essays on Peruvian Reality* (Austin: University of Texas Press, 1971)

[6] *La crítica*, 1:25 (February 24, 1918), 5; BNP, "Memoria administrativa," Apurímac, 1890–92 (Prefectos).

señores). In theory they were white or considered themselves as such; in socioeconomic terms they usually were landlords or landowners, owners of estates, haciendas, and other properties. In other instances they were merchants and political authorities. Some might be all of the above.

Mistis commonly exercised their power in two complementary spaces: within the hacienda through relationships of personal dependency or asymmetrical reciprocity, and outside the hacienda with the winking consent of central power. An example of the latter case was the Trelles family of Abancay, who demonstrated that control extended all the way to a departmental capital. The state needed gamonales to control the indigenous masses excluded from voting and other liberal democratic rituals and whose customs and language greatly differentiated them from urban residents. No common ideology or culture permitted the oligarchic upper class – merchants, bankers, and modern landowners from coastal cities such as Lima or Trujillo or from cities midway into the sierra such as Arequipa – to communicate with peasants. A national consensus was impossible. Difficult Peruvian geography and a deficient road system exacerbated the divide. After independence in 1821, the separation between coast and sierra was so great that it was more profitable to bring peons from faraway China than from interior Peru and to import wheat from Chile or California rather than Huancavelica. Urbanization was just beginning to appear; of the 4 million inhabitants in 1900, an estimated 3 million or more lived in towns of fewer than 2,000. Without gamonales it was impossible to control a country with these characteristics.

Gamonalismo emerged with the collapse of the colonial state. In the eighteenth century three groups shared rural power: the provincial magistrate (corregidor), who administered justice and oversaw a jurisdiction equivalent to a province in the post-independence period; the Indian chieftain (kuraka), who was directly responsible for the indigenous population; and the priest, who not only shepherded souls but also responded to specific economic interests through the parish (*curato*). The Bourbon Reforms replaced provincial magistrates with intendentes and *subdelegados*, but these new authorities were never as effective as their predecessors and disappeared with the advent of the republic. At the same time, the Spanish abolished chieftainships (kurakazgos) and the noble titles of the indigenous aristocracy after the Tupac Amaru revolution. Although the measure was not immediately implemented, indigenous leaders eventually disbanded and lost rights, goods, and status. The power of priests similarly diminished with the retreat of the Church in the countryside, due to the elimination of the tithe and the reduction of rents and properties of both the religious orders and the bishopric. As the clergy began to concentrate in urban centers, countryside churches were frequently abandoned, with only their decorations, paintings, and objects of silver remaining as vestiges of an earlier period. Gamonales inherited the power that the provincial magistrate, the kuraka, and the priest previously shared. The consolidation of gamonal power took place early in some areas, but not until the twentieth century in other places such as Cailloma.[7]

Luis Aguilar, a contemporary of Zulen's, used to say that all gamonales had political aspirations: "[T]he gamonal is a congressman, subprefect, judge, or mayor." But access to public office was granted in most cases by land ownership.[8] Private control of the hacienda was fundamental, and the gamonal was not an absentee landowner. He knew the peasants and shared their habits and customs. Like the Quiñones and Luna families of Azángaro and Acomayo, respectively, it was not unusual for gamonales to speak Quechua. This was compatible with the fact that hacienda land was divided between the owner and the peasant sharecroppers: the *runa*, *colono*, or *yanacona* worked misti lands for usufruct rights. The landowner in turn granted protection from the state (taxes and military drafts) and provided essential but scarce products such as aguardiente and coca, as well as medicines and occasionally farming implements. In exchange, peasants performed personal service in the master's house or special tasks such as wool transport. Kinship relationships and paternalism buttressed these exchanges. Depending on the situation, the misti was treated as either the father or the child of his subjects, always spoken in the diminutive; the peasant in turn was a helpless soul in need of protection. Christian doctrine, with its mandate that some ordered and others obeyed, reinforced these arrangements. Authority was personal: the señor had a first and last name and related individually to his peasants. Lands rotated according to usufruct agreements each year. Peasants accepted an immobility that guaranteed them land possession and forced them to forge marital alliances among themselves. Such endogamous practices tied to *compadrazgo* – the señor or the overseer of the hacienda was almost invariably the godfather in baptisms – ensured workforce subjugation. The wealth of a landlord depended more on the number

7 Nelson Manrique, *Colonialismo y pobreza campesina. Caylloma y el valle del Colca, siglos XVI-XX* (Lima: DESCO, 1985).

8 Luis Aguilar, *Cuestiones indígenas* (Cuzco: Tip. El Comercio, 1922), 112.

of peasants he controlled than the crops and cattle produced by the hacienda.

As hacendado lineages developed, the system fostered a sense of permanence and social stasis. In fact, mistis resisted innovation and seemed impervious to outside change and even more so to change within. Mariátegui and others born at the turn of the century reached adolescence with the strange sense of living far removed from the hectic rhythm of European progress. Monotony and boredom characterized daily life within oligarchic society. Rigid social structures that prevented social mobility fostered tedium. This resulted from the association between class and ethnicity: whites were gentlemen (señores), Indians were peasants, and the roles were not interchangeable.

Nonetheless, closer scrutiny revealed instability. Gamonales did not constitute a homogenous group; to the contrary, disputes among them were all too frequent. Neither law nor custom guaranteed their newly acquired local power, which was nebulous and undefined. Thus, in 1886 in the Apurímac district of Talavera, the prefect blamed not political or electoral motives but rather an "implacable hatred" between the Tello and Alarcón families for a number of injuries.[9] Justo Alarcón's death provoked the sacking of Tello's houses in retaliation. Decades later in Canchis, Cuzco, the Cisneros family feuded with the Fernández clan.[10] In such disputes landowners mobilized the colonos of their haciendas into veritable armies. No colonial landowner ever enjoyed comparable power. State disintegration after the War of the Pacific (1879–83) contributed to this phenomenon. Guerrilla groups, some led by landowners, formed to confront the Chilean army, which penetrated all the way to Cajamarca in the north and Ayacucho in the south. Armed groups remained so strong in the years after the war that in 1886 the Huanta prefect lamented that his authority was subject to "the capricious will of guerrilla commanders."[11] Indeed, enduring clashes between the Lazo and Urbina families appeared to represent Huanta's entire political history.[12]

[9] Archivo del Ministerio del Interior (hereafter AMI), Prefecturas, Abancay, March 30, 1886.

[10] *El Tiempo* (Lima), April 13, 1918, 3.

[11] AMI, Prefecturas, Ayacucho, November 22, 1886.

[12] José Coronel, "Don Manuel Jesús Urbina: creación del colegio de instrucción media Gonzales Vigil y las pugnas por el poder local de Huanta," unpublished manuscript, 217–37.

Not surprisingly, landowners attacked each other. In 1920 in the La Convención valley, the brothers Oré, owners of the Lairochaca hacienda, attacked the Paucartamba estate and nearly killed owner Joaquín Tió.[13] The hacienda peons accompanied the assailants. There was no clear difference between attacks and banditry. In fact, the weakness of the state served as the backdrop for both. Prefects complained about the lack of weapons, the limited number of policemen, and the deplorable jail system. Bandits were typical characters in those days. Songs and stories immortalized Luis Pardo, the best-known bandit who roamed the area around Chiquián, in the department of Ancash. Other prominent bandits were Morón and his gang in the Ica valleys, Lino Ureta in Cañete, and Adolfo Rondón, whom police in Moquegua, Puno, and Cuzco pursued for more than thirty years. His raids extended all the way to La Paz, Bolivia.[14]

The social bandit who stole from the rich and gave to the poor was an exception. More often bandits engaged in pure criminality, and as Eric Hobsbawm noted, it was common to attribute cruelty to Andean bandits. Legend blamed them for everything from the brutal treatment of victims to cannibalism.[15] In the imagination of some, the bandit shared characteristics with the *pistaco*, a type of armed and mounted highland vampire who lay in wait to extract fat from his victims. In some cases bandits were landowners who staged punitive expeditions or established control through terror. In others, bandits were outsiders, migrants, or local mestizos, such as the five "famous bandits" who attacked Sicuani estates, or Ramón Flores, an unmarried, twenty-five-year-old small farmer accused of stealing livestock in the Cuzco province of Paucartambo.[16] Livestock rustling was the most frequent charge against Cuzco inmates; in March 1916, for example, seven of eleven people on trial were rustlers. Banditry appeared endemic to the high provinces around Espinar. The Supreme Court was "alarmed by the simultaneous and growing development of highway robbery in certain areas of the Republic, which awakens and agitates the worst

[13] ADC, Corte Superior de Justicia, legajo 87, 1920.

[14] *El Tiempo* (Lima), October 5, 1917, 4; Basadre, *Historia de la República*, vol. IX, 208.

[15] Eric Hobsbawm, *Bandits* (London: Weidenfeld and Nicolson, 1969). See also José Varallanos, *Bandoleros en el Perú* (Lima: Imprenta López, 1932).

[16] ADC, Corte Superior de Justicia, legajo 80, 1919; and ADC, Corte Superior de Justicia, legajo 78, 1919.

instincts of depraved spirits and spreads unrest and distrust in the cities and countryside." It sent Cuzco an official communiqué addressing it.[17] The conclusion was correct: Gamonalismo did not stabilize rural order as much as Lima might have believed, and insecurity reigned. Authorities, judges, and prefects at times simply confirmed crimes or violent acts without being able to determine culprit or motive. A July 1919 appeal in the Cuzco province of Paruro claimed "that stampeding and revenge-thirsty mobs have committed the greatest excesses."[18]

Seventh-day Adventists also contributed to instability. They arrived at the end of the nineteenth century, settled in Puno, and, unlike Catholic priests who confined themselves to cities, fanned out across the countryside and established schools. They focused on the upper provinces and introduced shepherds to Bible reading.[19] Adventists instructed Indians scorned by mistis that they were citizens who needed to shed their "ignorance" and demand due rights. Adventists soon clashed with the official Church, above all when they urged peasants not to bother taking care of the local temple or paying fees to priests.[20] Adventist schools in Puno came to enroll 3,500 students, 44 percent of the department's school-age population. The phenomenon paralleled a rise in education in the twentieth century, a virtual revolution that significantly advanced literacy. Teachers gradually became common figures in rural areas.

Teacher presence in turn was related to the emergence of new middle sectors. Intermediary groups emerged between gamonales and Indians that did not always serve as mediators. Commercial development partially explained this trend, especially in the southern areas. Alongside large wholesale merchants connected to commercial houses such as Ricketts, Forga, and Grace appeared small, itinerant merchants, retailers, many of Arabic origin erroneously called "Turks." Some settled permanently, and even today Sicuani's Plaza de Armas is home to the spacious stores of merchants who arrived at the end of the nineteenth century. The populations of Sicuani, Ayaviri, Puno, Juliaca, and other

[17] ADC, Corte Superior de Justicia, legajo 82, 1919, Lima, April 13, 1918.

[18] ADC, Corte Superior de Justicia, legajo 82, 1919, Paruro, July 8, 1919.

[19] Laura Hurtado, "Cuzco, iglesia y sociedad: el obispo Pedro Pascual Farfán de los Godos (1918–1933) en el debate indigenista," BA thesis, Pontificia Universidad Católica del Perú, 1982, 32. See also Dan Hazen, "The Awakening of Puno: Government Policy and the Indian Problem in Southern Peru, 1900–1955," PhD dissertation, Yale University, 1974.

[20] Atilio Sivirichi, "Diez horas con Francisco Mostajo," *La Sierra* (Cuzco) 1:5 (May 1927), 38–9.

southern cities increased. The sons of merchants became the lawyers, doctors, and journalists who formed new urban groups.[21] A key reference for them was the University of San Antonio Abad of Cuzco, which a progressive rector of North American origin, Albert Giesecke, restructured after his appointment by President Leguía in 1912. Giesecke initiated his students in the analysis of contemporary social reality and shortly after his arrival conducted a city census.[22] That year the university's 170 students included Luis Valcárcel, a Moquegua native who wrote a thesis on agrarian property in Cuzco. New critical ideas emerged, and even Cuzco's bishop, Monseñor Pascual Farfán de los Godos, supported them. Perhaps in competition with the Adventists, Farfán's pastoral letters expressed concern for Indians, distancing himself from former Church members who were readily inclined to side with gamonales.

Accustomed to viewing Indians as submissive and acquiescent, mistis did not foresee threats to their dominance. In 1920 a Cuzco lawyer referred to "that wretched aboriginal race, today so debilitated, ignorant, and without the faintest trace of dignity."[23] Racism was fundamental to gamonal mentality: races existed, some superior to others, and the hacienda colono had to look up to the misti, venerate him, and address him as though he were begging. The gamonal, meanwhile, spoke with a stentorian and commanding voice. One group was on foot, the other on horseback; one was barefoot, the other wore tall boots. Some gamonales grew attached to these helpless children, got drunk with them, and participated in their fiestas; others, however, were prone to violence, sexual abuse, and even the branding of their peons.[24] This combination of racism and paternalism made the relationship between mistis and Indians ambiguous; gamonales shifted from one attitude to the other with impunity. Furthermore, rural social dynamics did not remain confined to the hacienda but migrated with servants to urban homes. A Lima deputy compared Peruvian Indians to "redskins" and demanded their extermination. With the decline of the colonial indigenous aristocracy, *Indian* and *peasant* became synonyms for *savage*, the antithesis of civilization and the western world. Writer and journalist Manuel

[21] José Deustua and José Luis Rénique, *Intelectuales, indigenismo y descentralismo en el Perú, 1897–1931* (Cuzco: Centro de Estudios Rurales Andinos Bartolomé de Las Casas, 1984).

[22] Alberto Giesecke, "Censo del Cuzco," *Boletín de la Sociedad Geográfica de Lima* (Lima) 29 (trimester 3–4), 142–67.

[23] ADC, Corte Superior de Justicia, legajo 83, 1920.

[24] ADC, Corte Superior de Justicia, legajo 90, 1921.

Beingolea, referring to an Indian woman in 1909, stated, "Savagery is portrayed in her physiognomy, in her distrustful and timid attitude. It does not reveal intelligence, imagination, or reason, not even common sense."[25]

Francisco García Calderón's *Le Pérou Contemporain* (Contemporary Peru) provided a similar point of view. The author considered Peru a Latin country and dismissed its pre-Hispanic history. In his view mystery and ignorance forever shrouded the Incas and all earlier civilizations: "The age of that race is not known." Unable to ignore the majority Indian population, he described them in the final pages as "a nation dominated by a sad and profound atavism."[26] They were old but without history, a contradiction he resolved by calling them a "people of aged children." This pristine racism was concomitant with gamonalismo. As local power took root in the sierra and Lima witnessed the short-lived expansion of guano commerce in the mid-nineteenth century, artist Luis Montero captured the apparent decline of Andean utopia in the painting "The Funeral of Atahualpa" (1861–68). It depicted two separate worlds: to the right the Spanish, all men in armor, standing gallantly; and to the left Indians, nearly all women in horizontal positions. The only male Indian was Atahualpa, who lay dead but with his head still attached, contrary to the mythical account.[27] About the same time, and from an apparently different perspective, Puno intellectual and "friend of the Indians" Juan Bustamante imagined Indians as wretched and prostrate, fleeing cities reserved for mistis and seeking refuge in the deepest valleys or the craggiest mountains, where they lived "abandoned by society, humbled brow, nearly naked; there, their children are born and die without any idea of the nation and its laws."[28]

Indians were the Other, condemned to silence and as expressionless as stones. The elite saw them as an undifferentiated mass whose only salient feature was their empty gaze. Ventura García Calderón's masterly 1919 short story, "La venganza del cóndor" ("Revenge of the condor"),

[25] Manuel Beingolea, "Psicología de la mujer India," *Contemporáneos* (Lima) 1:8 (July 28, 1909), 345.

[26] Francisco García Calderón, *Le Pérou Contemporain* (Paris: Dujarric et Cie., 1907), 357.

[27] Roberto Miró Quesada, "Los funerales de Atahualpa," *El Caballo Rojo* (Lima) 183 (November 13, 1983), 10–11. See also Mirko Lauer, *Crítica de la artesanía* (Lima: Desco, 1982), 140.

[28] Juan Bustamante, *Los indios del Perú* (Lima: J. M. Monterola, 1867), 36.

captured misti views of Indians.[29] The narrator admits with disappointment that "never have I known if when punished they see us with anger or compliance." The punishment, he informs us, is the difficult art of kicking an Indian awake. An Indian who suffered a captain's whip gets his revenge on the road to Huaraz by hurling boulders from above. It was the same Indian who earlier appeared given only to crying and gaining sympathy, but who "was spying with his impenetrable look." And it was the same fear of rocks moving and becoming weapons that loyalist generals experienced in the highlands during the War of Independence. The white man – at first overly proud and sure of himself, with his revolver, boots, and horse – is ultimately impressed by the unfading Andes and later by Indians, then referred to in the plural: "[P]erhaps between them and the condors there is a dark pact to take revenge upon the intruders, who are us."[30] A stranger in his own country, Ventura García Calderón, like his brother Francisco, lived removed from Peru in voluntary exile. The guilt and dark fear that saturated his fiction are also found in earlier administrative documents from provincial authorities. In 1887 in Andahuaylas, for example, the subprefect warned that rebellious Indians might unite with those of other provinces such as Huanta and Cangallo; and a Huaraz subprefect feared no fewer than 10,000 rebel Indians in the event of an uprising and an "incalculable" number who would unite thereafter.[31] Authorities, who believed unity and an incomprehensible language worked in the Indians' favor, feared that at any moment they might unleash a bloody and devastating "race war" against minority whites.[32] As mistis alternated between violence and paternalism, they constructed an image of Indians as either resigned and passive or vengeful and bloodthirsty. Either way, they occupied a world apart, excluded from the nation and beyond the borders of the civilized world.

A Seismic Wave

Racism was not unanimous in a society with ideological fissures. Mariátegui expressed a different world view in one of his first newspaper articles, which he wrote under the pseudonym "Juan Croniqueur," about the unexpected arrival of a number of Christianized Campa Indians in

[29] Ventura García Calderón, *Cuentos peruanos* (Madrid: Aguilar, 1961).

[30] Ibid., 62–8.

[31] AMI, Prefecturas, Ayacucho, April 1887, and Huaraz, May 1887.

[32] AMI Prefecturas, Apurímac, May 13, 1886.

Lima. After interviewing them he displayed an unusual cultural relativism: "To the savages, the civilized must be as exotic as the savages are to the civilized. This is undeniable. Our hats and adornments must seem as ridiculous and extravagant to them as their techniques are to us."[33]

The author was the same young man who felt alienated from the rigid, stilted, immobile society that confronted him but at the same time was thrilled by the progress that automobile speed and airplane acrobatics represented. He sought alternatives. A childhood ailment predisposed Mariátegui to observation. He directed his gaze to daily life, to the supposedly aristocratic customs of Lima, and to the political life manifested in tedious parliamentary debates. Day after day his journalistic chronicles depicted a society utterly lacking unpredictability, a narrow horizon where everything was regulated and there was little room for imagination. Nothing occurred off script. Juan Croniqueur's verse captured that malaise: "An indolent apathy that prevents me from fighting/and submerges me in the sterile weariness of dreaming."[34] In other words, tedium.

Yet an unusual character appeared unexpectedly in the Lima press: General Rumi Maqui, the alleged organizer of an attack in late 1915 on a Puno hacienda. The action launched a long struggle for the restoration of the Inca empire. Authorities captured him in April 1916 and turned him over to the military on treason charges. His case demonstrated that Indians were not just on the margins of the Peruvian nation but also were challenging it. A reporter for the Lima magazine *Variedades* and other journalists begrudged Rumi Maqui the title of "General." They did not support or defend him, and they thought the notion of a twentieth-century Tahuantinsuyo was a grotesque trick not to be taken seriously. He was a caricature and not some fearsome character worthy of respect.[35]

Authorities moved the supposed Rumi Maqui to Arequipa for trial, but the "dethroned restorer of the Inca empire," as *El Tiempo* scoffed, escaped and disappeared without the slightest clue. Except for a letter, there was no trace until May 1917, when it was reported that he might have been living in Bolivia. However, his ghost still prowled the Andes. Rumi Maqui followers in Nazca threatened "to kill all the rich." Indians of the Ailla community supposedly solicited his help in attacking a

33 Juan Croniqueur, "Entre salvajes," *La Prensa* (Lima), July 19, 1914, 2.

34 *Lulú* (Lima) 1:3 (July 28, 1915), 26.

35 *Variedades* (Lima), May 1916, 624.

hacienda in Sandia, and he reportedly was present during an uprising in Huancané. A biographical article entitled "An interesting report on the new Inca of Peru" appeared in April 1917.[36] Joking began to fade. That same month a report on a Puno riot wondered about Rumi Maqui's presence. Fear spread, and officials sent infantry and other troops to Puno. *El Tiempo* observed: "Taking up the matter of the now-legendary General Rumi Maqui, we should say that his presence as the leader of indigenous agitation is not confirmed, but it would not be surprising if it is, because his ideas in favor of Inca imperialism and his profound hatred for gamonalismo are known all too well."[37] Peruvians began taking him seriously. Although officials never again found him, his actions grew in the collective imagination. Years later a seal and a flag appeared as emblems of the restoration of Tahuantinsuyo. A photo supposedly depicting his top military commanders began to circulate, and oral tradition held that in December 1915 Rumi Maqui had called out to Indians from all over the south, from Abancay to La Paz, for a great rebellion against gamonalismo. Today the Puno Peasant Federation carries Rumi Maqui's name. Some have compared his deeds to Emiliano Zapata's campaigns in Mexico. A researcher as careful as Robert Paris referred with absolute certainty to an army of "several thousand rebellious Indians" who for three years wandered about the Puno altiplano.[38] From one hacienda assault to a prolonged guerrilla struggle – that was Rumi Maqui's trajectory in collective memory.

Juan Croniqueur was one of the first to take Rumi Maqui seriously. The contrast between Rumi Maqui and politicians of the era was notable. He was not a prudish salon character, but a man of action who bore no resemblance to typical political caudillos. Juan Croniqueur felt a natural affinity for the elusive Rumi Maqui, who seemed to blend into the Arequipa, Puno, and Cuzco mountains and day after day made fools of José Pardo's government. But Rumi Maqui embodied the contrast between savage and civilized. Juan Croniqueur wrote: "General Rumimaqui, who among us was simply Major Teodomiro Gutiérrez, among the Indians is the Inca, the restorer, and other remarkable and transcendental things."[39] It was 1917, and Juan Croniqueur's

[36] No citation provided in the original [Editors' note].

[37] *El Tiempo* (Lima), April 24, 1917, 1; and May 6, 1917, 7.

[38] Robert Paris, "Para una lectura de los 7 ensayos," in José Aricó, ed., *Mariátegui y los orígenes del marxismo latinoamericano* (Mexico City: Siglo XXI, 1978), 317.

[39] *El Tiempo* (Lima), January 17, 1917, 1.

enthusiasm for Rumi Maqui coincided with his excitement for "*bolcheviquis*," synonymous with revolution and socialism. In Europe, change came from Russia; in Peru, it came from Puno. Tedium ruptured, and cracks appeared in the oligarchic order. The "seismic wave" originated in places least expected, in areas farthest removed from Lima, the most backward territories in the country. This opened new possibilities for Mariátegui, who saw that the old could become the new. Almost intuitively, he discovered a different meaning for tradition. If for oligarchic intellectuals such as the García Calderón brothers, tradition was synonymous with the colonial era, for Rumi Maqui the only past worth preserving in Peru was the pre-Hispanic world that Lima either ignored or deemed forever lost. The Incas unexpectedly became flesh and blood. Mariátegui, who traveled outside Lima only once for a brief trip to Huancayo, began to discover a hidden and neglected aspect of Peru: an Andean world not destroyed by European invasion and that still weighed heavily on the present.

For mistis, Rumi Maqui was the embodiment of the feared caste war. Some indigenista writers, on the other hand, challenged what they considered a landowner invention. Dora Mayer accused Lizares Quiñones, an Azángaro gamonal, of concocting the Samán rebellion to "ruin a town."[40] Luis Felipe Luna argued that hacendados propagated "the ridiculous utopia of race conflict, of a restoration of the Inca empire" to imprison Major Gutiérrez, whose only crime was defending Indians.[41] Historian José Tamayo Herrera contended that Luna was a spokesman for Azángaro landowners throughout his long parliamentary career, and he hypothesized that the Rumi Maqui rebellion was a product of conflicts between landowners, who also invented the legend of the Tahuantinsuyo restoration.[42] Augusto Ramos Zambrano, a Puno historian who produced the most complete study of the rebellion, rejected that argument.

Was Rumi Maqui real or imagined? Teodomiro Gutiérrez Cuevas apparently assumed the pseudonym Rumi Maqui ("Hand of Stone" in Quechua). Photographs revealed a man with a well-groomed mustache

[40] This was a movement that took place in the village of Samán reportedly led by Rumi Maqui [Editors' note]; Dora Mayer, "La historia de las sublevaciones indígenas en Puno," *El Deber Pro Indígena* (Lima), 4:48 (September 1917); and 4:49 (October 1917).

[41] Basadre, *Historia de la República*, vol. IX, 206.

[42] José Tamayo Herrera, *Historia social e indigenismo en el altiplano* (Lima: Ediciones Treintaitrés, 1982), 214–15.

wearing an official cavalry uniform. His concern for peasants dated to his first stay in Puno at the beginning of the century. In 1913 the government named him "special commissioner" to report on the Quechua-speaking populations of the high plains. Landowners did not look favorably upon the report he presented to President Guillermo Billinghurst in December.[43] They vilified him, none more than Lizares Quiñones. We do not know if their alarm was justified, because the text was lost in the coup that toppled the Billinghurst government, and we only know of it by references. A prison interview and a signed letter to the daily newspaper *El Pueblo* of Arequipa after he fled on January 29, 1917, are Gutiérrez Cuevas's only surviving direct testimony. In the letter he proclaimed himself an enemy of gamonalismo, a supporter of a Peru-Bolivia union, and a pacifist. He denied attempting to restore the Tahuantinsuyo: "I have never taken part in any revolution; my hands are not stained with my brothers' blood; never have I committed a crime, not even the slightest offense. God knows it. He reads the depths of my heart."[44] Gutiérrez cited his arrest at home as evidence – had he participated in the San José rebellion, logically he would have hidden. His escape from the Arequipa jail, the letter he sent days later, and his subsequent disappearance demonstrated that he had the ability to simply vanish.

Besides this testimony, there are the documents Rumi Maqui signed. Historian Mauro Paredes published one dated November 1, 1915, that named Santiago Chuquimia as the Phara authority. Augusto Ramos Zambrano found one dated November 8 that named someone else as the "restorer of Samán." And, finally, Manuel Vassallo discovered in the hands of Azángaro peasants a document that named Buenaventura Itusaca as the restorer of Ccalla; the assumed date was May 1914, but a reproduction shows that in reality it was 1917, when Gutiérrez supposedly was in Bolivia.[45]

Why did all this have to be the work of just one character? Why did Gutiérrez and Rumi Maqui have to be the same person? Ramos

[43] Jorge Basadre, *Introducción a las bases documentales para la historia de la República del Perú con algunas reflexiones* (Lima: P.L. Villanueva, 1971) and Luis Bustamante, "Mito y realidad: Teodomiro Gutiérrez Cuevas o Rumi Maqui en el marco de la sublevación campesina de Azángaro (1915–1916)," BA thesis, Pontificia Universidad Católica del Perú, 1987.

[44] Reprinted in *El Tiempo* (Lima), January 12, 1917, 3–4.

[45] Manuel Vasallo, "Rumi Maqui y la nacionalidad quechua," *Allpanchis* (Cuzco) 11–12 (1978), 123–7.

Zambrano stated that "it is unquestionable that between August and September 1915, in one of the Samán communities (*parcialidad*) and in the presence of numerous leaders, Gutiérrez Cuevas proclaimed himself restorer of the Tahuantinsuyo, adopting the sonorous and meaningful name of General Rumi Maqui."[46] However, Ramos Zambrano offered no evidence other than oral testimony from descendants of two supposed Rumi Maqui deputies. Although the interview with them was not dated, it is fair to assume that it was done at a time when Rumi Maqui's fame was already widespread. On the other hand, Ramos Zambrano provided evidence of others who used the same name. In November 1915, an Indian proclaimed himself "descendent of the famous Rumi Maqui"; another, or perhaps the same one, christened himself with that *nom de guerre* and issued manifestos. That same month, a journalistic account signed in Juliaca referred to a crazy Inca who lived in Vilcabamba, assembled an army of 3,000 men in Puno, and was planning to punish a spurious Inca named Rumi Maqui.[47] Pages earlier we saw how Rumi Maqui's "incendiary torch" continued illuminating the high plains in early 1917. All this suggests a collective pseudonym, another of the imaginary Incas that appear repeatedly in Andean history.

Rumi Maqui responded to opposing interests and expectations. For some landowners he represented the dreaded caste war and vengeful spirit of Indians; he provided others the justification to levy taxes and annex property at the expense of peasant communities. Some believed that only an outsider could shake Indians out of their passivity. And some had a score to settle for Gutiérrez Cuevas's celebrated 1913 report. On the opposite side, a certain messianic hope once again seemed to inspire Azángaro peasants, who were active in organizing meetings. Lima intellectuals such as Mariátegui – who experienced a romantic rejection of oligarchic society through Rumi Maqui but without visualizing a credible alternative to it – also contributed to the legend. They did not accept the "rules of the game," but it did not seem possible to toss them out either. The *civilista* "dynasty" that ruled Peru – as Juan Croniqueur

46 Augusto Ramos Zambrano, *Rumi Maqui* (Puno: Instituto de Investigaciones para el Desarrollo Social del Altiplano, 1985), 52. This is the most important and carefully written work on the subject. See also Antonio Rengifo, "Semblanza del mayor de caballería Teodomiro Gutiérrez Cuevas, defensor calificado de los indios y enemigo de los gamonales," *Álbum de oro del departamento de Puno*, vol. 8 (Puno: Editorial Los Andes, 1981).

47 Ramos Zambrano, *Rumi Maqui*, 53–4.

ironically noted – appeared eternal until Rumi Maqui interrupted the line of succession.

Rumi Maqui appeared to fulfill Marx's formula of "finding the newest in the oldest." The past inspired a revolution that was not an ephemeral caudillo uprising or a fleeting peasant guerrilla group. If the character did not exist, he must be invented. Erudite and useless digressions did not interest Mariátegui. Rumi Maqui or Gutiérrez Cuevas? What mattered was what he represented: the possibility of social change and insurrection. Years later Mariátegui wrote, "The Inca past has entered a new history, recovered not by traditionalists but by revolutionaries. In this lies the defeat of colonialism . . . The revolution has vindicated our oldest tradition."[48]

The Messengers

Those hopes and fears, social revolution and caste war, appeared to come true a few years later. Between 1919 and 1923, about fifty rebellions took place in Peru's southern Andes. The epicenter was the Puno and Cuzco highlands, but the expanding wave of a veritable social earthquake reached Ayacucho and even Cochabamba, Bolivia.[49] The Tacna and Moquegua highlands, some Huancavelica provinces, and the La Convención valley to the east of Cuzco also were among the affected zones. Six Peruvian departments experienced unusual peasant agitation that some argue was comparable to the independence wars. However, during the 1780 Tupac Amaru revolution, Spanish loyalist forces controlled Ayacucho and Apurímac, and insurgents in that period failed to recruit peasants from Cailloma or Espinar, all rebel areas in the 1920s. The 1920–23 map of social unrest instead recalls the 1814 revolution in which the Angulo brothers organized three armies that marched from Cuzco toward Ayacucho, Arequipa, and La Paz. A century later the stage was the same, but rebellion began not in an urban center but in various rural locations: Santiago de Pupuja, Zepita, Taraco, Acora, Huallpan, Pinaya, Azángaro, Carango, Espinar, Canas, Sullupa, Aymaraes, Lauramarca, Haquira, and Quiñota.[50] Rebels attacked haciendas, did

[48] José Carlos Mariátegui, *Peruanicemos al Perú* (Lima: Amauta, 1970), 121.

[49] Rosalind Gow, "Yawar Mayu: Revolution in the Southern Andes 1860–1980," PhD dissertation, University of Wisconsin, 1981.

[50] Among many others, see Gow, "Yawar Mayu"; Tamayo Herrera, *Historia social e indigenismo*; Wilfredo Kapsoli and Wilson Reátegui, *El campesinado peruano:*

not respect boundaries, and invaded and occupied land. In other cases, heavy or unscrupulous fiscal burdens, arbitrary political demarcations, pressure to move provincial or district capitals, merchant usury, and broken political promises apparently provoked uprisings. Although newspapers reported "horrible massacres," the conflicts did not claim many lives. Taraco apparently lost thirty people, but Pinaya just twelve, Acora four, and Azángaro one. Two exceptional cases were Huancané and Jesús de Machaca, in Bolivia. In Huancané, soldiers and police reportedly killed 150, the vast majority peasants, apparently shot to death with no judicial proceeding.[51] Historian Herbert Klein and others cite a March 1921 "massive uprising" in Jesús de Machaca that authorities quelled at the cost of "several hundred villagers." Like all rebellions during those years, this uprising was brief and, allegedly, without clear goals.[52]

But can we validate this? At first peasants from indigenous communities were the principal actors in the rebellions, but later tenant farmers from haciendas such as Lauramarca or Ccapana joined in. This important change went unnoticed at the time. Even José María Arguedas, with his deep understanding of peasant life, lamented – as late as 1958, the year he published his novel *Deep Rivers* – colonos' submission and resignation. That situation had begun to change in some southern haciendas as early as the 1920s. Colonos organized, in some cases forming unions, and wrote or requested reports to be sent to Lima. But almost immediately they took direct action by occupying land and refusing to carry out

1919–1930 (Lima: Universidad Nacional Mayor de San Marcos, 1987); Reátegui, *Explotación agropecuaria y las movilizaciones campesinas de Lauramarca, Cusco, 1920–1960* (Lima: Universidad Nacional Mayor de San Marcos, 1974); Laura Maltby, "Indian Revolts in the Altiplano, 1895–1926," BA thesis, Harvard University, 1972; Jorge Flores Ochoa y Abraham Valencia, *Rebeliones indígenas quechuas y aymaras* (Cuzco: Centro de Estudios Andinos, undated); Hazen, "The Awakening of Puno"; Manuel Burga y Alberto Flores Galindo, *Apogeo y crisis de la república aristocrática* (Lima: Rikchay Perú, 1980). My essay responds to Dan Hazen's relevant criticism of my book, *Arequipa y el sur andino: ensayo de historia regional (siglos XVIII-XX)* (Lima: Editorial Horizonte, 1977). Hazen criticized the lack of "an explanatory model of peasant mobilization." See his review in *Annales* (Paris) 5–6 (September–December 1978), 1210.

[51] Instituto de Estudios Aymaras, Chucuito (Peru), Biblioteca, "Sublevación de Huancané" (unpublished manuscript). I thank Diego Irrarazábal for this reference.

[52] Herbert Klein, *Historia general de Bolivia* (La Paz: Editorial Juventud, 1982), 214–15.

duties and personal services. The conflict did not center exclusively on land. The colonos rebellion called peasant servitude – the very foundation of gamonalismo – into question. The system was not as solid as it appeared, and its very structures began to erode.

Rebellions occurred during a critical juncture in the southern Andes. At the end of the nineteenth century in the highlands of Puno and Cuzco, Arequipa commercial capital, dedicated primarily to sheep and camelid wool exportation, reorganized regional space. It did so by creating a branch network and a system of wool traders who reached even the haciendas and communities farthest removed from urban centers. The formation of new haciendas, the acquisition of others, and the expansion of areas that landowners directly controlled, inside or outside their estates, accompanied the growth of wool exports. Increased production in a low-tech agrarian economy required extensive exploitation, which meant acquiring more land and livestock. Wool quality posed another problem. Peasant livestock, called *huaccha*, produced spotted wool, and mixed-breed sheep carried a parasite that spread animal diseases within haciendas and thwarted flock improvement. Landowners, foremen, and latifundia administrators linked to mercantile capital launched an offensive against huaccha. It was not easy for peasants to give up their livestock – first, because they wanted to continue as peasants and not wage earners, and second, because wool from mixed-breed sheep was most suitable for their looms and allowed them to dispense with dyes. That silent conflict laid the groundwork for the great rebellion: the struggle between landowner economy and peasant economy.

Hostility began with mistis who participated in the regional market and who considered themselves modernizers and entrepreneurs. For landowners, the introduction of capitalism meant consolidating and increasing hacienda lands; for peasants, it meant dispossession, more work, and less time for their own parcels and flocks. Between 1909 and 1924, the number of shepherds in the Azángaro village of Picotani declined from sixty-nine to fifty-seven as the hacienda grew from 56,834 to 133,437 acres, the number of sheep increased from 26,000 to 32,000, and the number of llamas, alpacas, and vicuñas grew from 214 to more than 1,000. Thus, in 1909 there were 376 sheep per shepherd; fifteen years later the average was 562.[53]

[53] Data from research by Clemencia Aramburú using sources from the Archivo del Fuero Agrario. [This archive is now housed in Peru's Archivo General de la Nación. Editors' note].

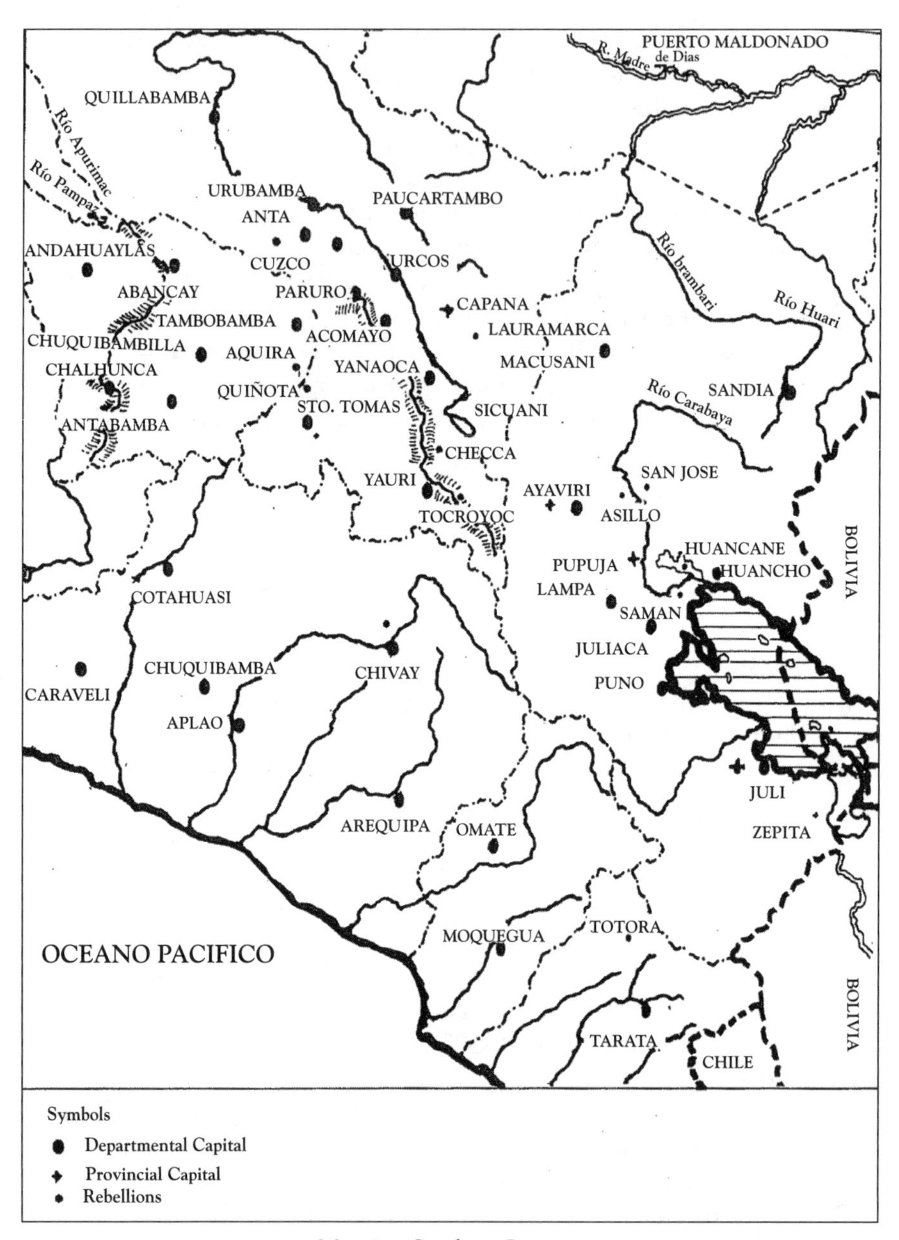

Map 8.1. Southern Peru.

The reciprocity and mutual exchanges that traditionally regulated relations between hacendados and peasants demanded respect for rules that did not change. Mistis who wanted to cease being traditional landlords and become modern landowners broke the implicit pact. They demanded more work of their Indians and tried to appropriate land and pastures from tenant farmers. Haciendas launched an offensive inside and outside their boundaries against community lands. Peasant response was not automatic. Although mistis always feared rebellion, it only broke out in 1919, when Augusto B. Leguía took power in Lima, challenged previous oligarchic governments, and announced reforms. Ultimately it was more talk than action, but it enabled peasants to identify cracks in the state apparatus. Leguía, following up on a request by Puno intellectual José Antonio Encinas, appointed Ernesto Roca, Humberto Luna, and Alejandro Franco to a parliamentary commission charged with traveling to Puno to produce a report about the peasant situation. The Gutiérrez Cuevas precedent comes to mind. The government also created an Indian affairs office within the Ministry of Development, legally recognized peasant communities that presented titles, and in May 1922 established the Patronato de la Raza Indígena (Council on the Indian Race), presided by the archbishop of Lima. All these changes encouraged Indians from a hacienda as far away as Ccapana, Cuzco, to organize, send a commission to Lima, and present its demands before Leguía himself. Decades later the community still preserved a photo capturing the Indians' visit to the Governmental Palace. Leguía, who often spoke of the long-suffering "race of Manco," inaugurated a monument to the mythical founder of the empire, flavored his speeches with Quechua (although he did not speak the language), and made June 24 the Day of the Indian, a national civic holiday. His demagoguery did not please all landowners, especially in such a racist environment as Peru in the early twentieth century.

Leguía's rise coincided with falling wool exports and prices in the southern economy after World War I. Although the city of Arequipa bore the crisis silently and nearby villages such as Aplao witnessed some unrest, "the rebellion spread as rapidly as the crisis" in wool-producing areas.[54] In September 1919, unrest began to spread to peasant communities and estates; in September 1921, it reached haciendas. Peasants took over Lauramarca, the Saldívar family property that covered

[54] Manuel Burga y Wilson Reátegui, *Lanas y capital mercantil en el sur. La Casa Rickets, 1895–1935* (Lima: Instituto de Estudios Peruanos, 1981), 49.

more than 148,000 acres, and occupied it until 1928. In some parts of Azángaro, mistis never recovered their land, and hacienda expansion at the expense of communities ceased all over the south. Although rebellion did not completely do away with gamonales, it seriously challenged their control. Regional middle sectors who backed peasants, viewed as eventual allies in their dispute with gamonales, were another essential factor. Small merchants who continued to acquire wool in Lauramarca under peasant occupation belonged to this group.

However, the tenant farmer rebellion was not simply a response to political and economic crisis. Years earlier there was isolated unrest when, for example, peasants in Chuyugual (in Huamachuco) began to "completely disobey the orders and will of the master and his employees. They roundly refuse to pay the subleases for the land they occupy – as is custom – and don't want to sign any contracts with the current administrator of the estate, Sr. Sedano."[55] Changes brought about by outside processes such as capitalist development or middle-sector radicalization were not solely responsible for the rebellion. Transformations in peasant outlook, previously submissive and always aligned with landowners, require further study. I'd like to suggest that a point of departure was the War of the Pacific (1879–83), when two peasant armies formed in the central highlands to confront the foreign invaders. One organized spontaneously and recruited within indigenous communities; the other formed as part of the landowner mobilizations that Mariscal Andrés A. Cáceres initiated. The conflict mobilized Junín, Huancavelica, and Ayacucho tenant farmers, who were forced to roam highland areas for as many as four military campaigns. The two armies ended up merging.[56] At the same time, peasant goals displaced nationalist agendas; they occupied haciendas, and the struggle for land continued after the war. A few years later, the 1894–95 confrontation between popular caudillo Nicolás de Piérola and the Cáceres government led to the formation of montonero and guerrilla groups composed of landowners and tenant farmers from as far away as Húanuco and Piura. In a true rural and provincial mobilization against the capital, the groups joined in Lima to confront the Peruvian army and defeated it after three days of combat. Thus, haciendas and colonos, through montoneras and civil wars,

[55] *Archivo Zulen* (BNP). Rodríguez to Joaquín Capelo, January 27, 1915.

[56] Nelson Manrique, *Las guerrillas indígenas en la Guerra con Chile* (Lima: Centro de Investigación y Capacitación, 1981).

engaged national politics. Colonos no longer toiled in complete isolation. When reciprocity ties broke and economic crisis struck years later, peasants were attentive to political changes and were waiting for an opening. They believed it came in 1919.

From then on landowners' fears grew. In Cuzco they formed the League of Southern Landowners, which convened a regional congress to discuss what peasants intended to do and how to confront their attacks. They believed Indians from the punas would invade the cities, and in some places such fears seemed to materialize. In 1921 Sicuani was full of fearful mistis who had abandoned their properties. Mistis believed that what Indians "now intend is to sack haciendas, burn populations, exterminate mistis, divide up territorial property and livestock, destroy everything, and restore the Tahuantinsuyo and the worship of the Sun."[57] The same year, as Lima celebrated the centennial of the proclamation of Peruvian independence, Tocroyoc peasants shouted protests against gamonales and cheers invoking the Incas as they attacked the village.[58] Arequipa's *El Pueblo* closely followed events, and *El Heraldo* predicted doom: "A serious threat exists that could produce an uprising of Indian communities, instigated by outside elements to establish communism; daily news reports lead one to think that they are indeed preparing a communist movement with frightful consequences for those who have land in that region."[59] Fears of a massive uprising made destruction, communism, and Inca society synonymous.

Were these dire predictions unfounded? It is true that Domingo Huarca led a rebellion in Tocroyoc, but in places such as Huancané (1923), landowners appeared to be behind the rebellions. Gamonales employed the so-called return to Tahuantinsuyo to argue that Indians did not desire to be Peruvians, thus justifying hacienda expansion and land appropriation. Peruvian historians José Deustua and José Luis Rénique called attention to the imaginary dimension of these rebellions. Journalists and some indigenista intellectuals also contributed to this invention. From the beginning of the century, books, theses, and articles examined the communist nature of the Inca Empire. Any peasant rebellion inspired by the past evoked the restoration of a supposedly

[57] Burga and Flores Galindo, *Apogeo y crisis*, 124.

[58] Jean Piel, "Un soulèvement rural péruvien: Tocroyoc (1921)," *Revue d'Histoire Moderne et Contemporaine* (Paris), 14 (October–December 1967). See also Piel, *Capitalisme agraire au Pérou* (Paris: Anthropos, 1975).

[59] *El Heraldo* (Arequipa), April 7, 1920.

egalitarian peasant order. Luis Valcárcel articulated this in his 1927 book *Tempestad en los Andes* (*Tempest in the Andes*), a work plagued by such definitive phrases as "culture will radiate once again from the Andes" and "the indigenous proletariat awaits its Lenin."[60] In connection to the 1919–22 rebellions, those phrases were not purely rhetorical, and what was a source of fear for mistis represented hope for intellectuals such as Valcárcel: Indians would descend from the highlands to the cities to create "a new Peru," in Mariátegui's words.

But could rebellions sustain a messianic spirit? And what relationship was there between these desires and fears and reality? This raises the issue of historical sources. We lack testimonials in which peasants expressed themselves directly. Landowners, journalists, judges, prefects, and other authorities almost always spoke for them in local and national newspapers, prefectural reports, and judicial proceedings. More than the persistence of ethnic differences, the veil of silence over peasant life throughout the republican period explains the absence of Indian voices in historical records. Peasant culture became defensive and took refuge in lies and muteness. The racist stereotype of the "lying Indian" was grounded in reality. Speaking, telling the truth, and sharing information provided those in power with new charges and accusations. Indians saw mistis as foreigners and, even if they were submissive and respectful in public, they called these outsiders names, mocked, and scorned them when speaking Quechua with other colonos.[61] A comparison of 1920 legal testimony with similar colonial documents underscores the lack of judicial protection for communities under the republic. Peasants expected little from an appearance before a judge; Cuzqueño Martín Chambi captured one such instance in stirring photographs. Any declaration might incriminate them. After all, they were not citizens. Knowing that mistis perceived them as inferiors, Indians feigned slowness and lack of understanding and provided ridiculous alibis.

One of the first uprisings occurred in Vilcabamba, in the province of La Convención, where Indians attacked Manuel Condori's hacienda,

[60] Luis Valcárcel, *Tempestad en los Andes* (Lima: Editorial Minerva, 1927) [Editors' note].

[61] Rodrigo Montoya, "El factor étnico y el desarrollo andino," in Alvaro Ortiz Saravia, ed., *Estrategias para el desarrollo de la sierra* (Cuzco: Universidad Nacional Agraria La Molina y Centro de Estudios Rurales Andinos Bartolomé de las Casas, 1986), 309–26.

destroyed fences and cultivated areas, and threatened to kill the owner. Condori filed suit, accusing community peasants of rioting. They denied the charge and reminded authorities of an ongoing legal dispute over land Condori reportedly seized years earlier. Months passed between accusations and appeals to Cuzco's Superior Court of Justice. Finally, in 1922, the prosecutor concluded that three years had passed "without clarifying the events or the guilt of the accused."[62] This was not simply ineffective administration of justice. Older conflicts, banditry, and rural criminality complicated relationships. In Ccollpa, Santo Tomás, in the Espinar highlands, community peasants claimed that colonos from the Cuatro Esquinas hacienda attacked and raped two women. But charges coincided with the hacienda administrator's plan to turn over livestock to Ccollpa peasants, force them to graze them on their land, and thus turn them into colonos.[63] In another case Indians from the Viscochoni farm in Colquepata (Paucartambo) rebelled. Charging that Indians "do not recognize him as owner," Wenceslao Díaz claimed a group surrounded him and that an Indian woman brandishing an immense knife approached him "intending to grab and kill him and drink chicha from his skull."[64] Díaz filed a criminal complaint with the Superior Court for "attempted homicide." Similar threats in those months supposedly invoked an old Inca war song: "We will drink from the traitor's skull/we will make a necklace of his teeth,/from his bones we will make flutes,/out of his skin we will make a drum;/afterward we will dance."[65]

Although there were no great massacres, specific violent acts heightened misti fears. On June 30, 1921, Leopoldo Alencastre and two boys were headed to his Checca farm in the high provinces of Cuzco. They stopped at the Moroccoyo hacienda to sleep because they feared an attack by Indians "who in bands of hundreds had crowned the hills since June 24." That night Indians surrounded the hacienda house and killed Alencastre, beating him with clubs, a broken sabre, and a *ranckana* (an Andean hoe). Troops arrived the next day, and after several hours of fighting, the bodies of twenty-four Indians littered the field. Besides two carbine rifles, the peasants were armed with only slings, hoes, clubs,

[62] ADC, Corte Superior de Justicia, legajo 79, 1919.

[63] ADC, Corte Superior de Justicia, legajo 84, 1920.

[64] ADC, Corte Superior de Justicia, legajo 83, 1920.

[65] Sebastián Salazar Bondy, ed., *Poesía Quechua* (Mexico City: Universidad Nacional Autónoma de México, 1964), 35.

and whips, hardly weapons for the massacre that mistis feared. Despite appearances, Alencastre's death was not a coincidental or unforeseen act of vengeance. Days earlier Indians had taken over the highlands (alturas), where, according to a judge, authorities later found

> conveniently distributed piles of stones carried from the river, ready to be thrown by slings, and entrenchments made of large rocks and in faraway sites where it was not possible to move stones from the river, they have broken up clumps and carried them in alcohol cans to second- and third-line trenches; an inspection of those places reveals that the Indians had been camping there several days because all around they found campfires for cooking their grub, empty bottles of alcohol, and food.[66]

The judge added that investigators found numerous shell casings (although slings caused most wounds inflicted by Indians) and cited documents proving a link with Indians from Puno. A comparison of these testimonies suggests it was neither a spontaneous eruption nor a great conspiracy. When authorities detained eighty-three peasants from the Checca event, their silence deprived the judge of evidence. That and perhaps the threat of a greater rebellion led to reprimand and release. Checca peasants did not participate in subsequent unrest in the provinces of Langui and Espinar.

The rebellion, however, had an unexpected epilogue. Andrés Alencastre, a son of the dead landowner, dedicated himself to studying Andean culture and published among other texts an article in collaboration with Georges Dumezil about ritual fighting; Quechua poems that one critic compared to those of Arguedas; and a monograph on social organization in the "high provinces" that addressed the uprising that killed his father: "The first of July of that year my father lost his life at the hands of natives; the tragic event was a powerful incentive for me to study and understand the deep socioeconomic problems that are awaiting resolution in Peru."[67] In July 1984, Alencastre met a similar fate in a

[66] ADC, Corte Superior de Justicia, legajo 90, 1921.

[67] Andrés Alencastre, *Kunturkanki. Un pueblo del Ande* (Cuzco: Editorial "Garcilaso," undated). Under the pseudonym of Kilku Wark'a, Alencastre also published a book of poems in Quechua entitled *Yawar Para* (Cuzco: Editorial "Garcilaso," 1972); and *Dramas y comedias del Ande* (Cuzco: Editorial "Garcilaso," 1955). In one play in the latter work, a hacienda is converted into a collective farm after a confrontation between a father and his son, who says, "I don't want to be a landowner" (71).

spot near where his father died: he burned to death when his house was set on fire. Authorities took the presumed culprits to Cuzco, and as I was reviewing judicial cases in the departmental archive, I attended a radio interview that Centro Bartolomé de Las Casas journalists conducted with those peasants. What followed was the same silence of the 1920s. All repeated the same implausible alibi: suddenly the house caught fire and no one could put it out. They did not care if it sounded convincing. Months later accounts of the event circulated in the Canas highlands: "I'm sure the perpetrators took him as a symbol, as a 'man of authority' (*hombre principal*), and by his own will he might have requested that they leave his heart in the earth as a payment (*pago*) to the blessed mother of life." In that region, pago is a ritual homage to the earth that consists of sacrificing a lamb, extracting its heart, and depositing it on the "pachamama."[68]

Most of the 1920s uprisings in the Andes began in September and continued through October and November, when the dry season ends and rains begin. September is the month of regeneration on the Andean calendar, a time to expel evil and plagues from villages.[69] Rebels participated in a ritual that showed up in archival documents, if one reads them carefully. Leaders used conch shells (*pututos*) and horns to convene comuneros and colonos for assemblies and meetings in remote locations, such as those in Checca before the elder Alencastre arrived.

But most important, as Manuel Burga discovered, was the *rama*, an effective underground organization of colonial origin. Communities pursued litigation against mistis before attacking haciendas. This happened, for example, in the Totora hacienda in the upper reaches of Tacna. Legal disputes required money for court proceedings, travel by community leaders to cities, and lawyer fees. Preparations for planned land invasions also required money. The sight of Indians "busy collecting funds" concerned landowners. Some peasants said collection was voluntary; others, perhaps to explain away their contributions, claimed

68 "Razas, clases sociales y violencia en los Andes," *Sur* (Cuzco, 1985). Testimony collected by Sonina Salazar in Yauri, September 27–28, 1984.

69 Manuel Burga, "Los profetas de la rebelión," in *Estados y naciones en los Andes*, J.P. Deler and Y. Saint-Geours, comps., vol. 2 (Lima: Instituto de Estudios Peruanos and Instituto Francés de Estudios Andinos, 1986), pp. 463-517; Anne Marie Hocquenghem, "L'iconographie mochica et les rites de purification," *Baessler-Archiv* (Berlin), vol. 27 (1979), 211 ff.

they were forced to give. Few admitted that behind the collection was the rama, around which the leadership core of the rebellion formed. Who were the leaders? In their study of 1922 uprisings in Haquira and Quiñota, Ricardo Valderrama and Carmen Escalante distinguished three types of leaders: old monolingual Quechua speakers from the community's traditional structure; young literate leaders with experience outside the community; and leaders of armed groups, the organizers of rifle and sling attacks.[70] In a community near San Pablo in Sicuani, *ramalistas* or rama organizers were a combination of old and young leaders. Here are a few bios: Buenaventura Sicos, single, no children, 25 years old, carpenter, literate; José Ccuro, married, 28 years old, literate; Vicente Puma, married, one child, farmer, 45 years old, illiterate; Mariano Mamani, married, four children, 70 years old, illiterate.[71] The biography of one of the principal Haquira leaders is revealing. Esteban Hilla Pacco, nicknamed Wamancha ("Young Falcon"), learned Spanish after his parents gave him up to be a servant in the house of a shady lawyer in Tambobamba, where he trained himself reading the articles of the constitution. He wrote the list of demands that all comuneros later signed.

Leaders from the heart of the peasant movement met others from cities. These included José Carmona, who operated in Vilcabamba ayllus and was known as "dispute manager and defender." Carmona was a *tinterillo*, a lawyer without degree who knew judicial codes and laws and could write. Tinterillos at times charged excessively for their services – a whole body of indigenista literature has disparaged them – but at times, when they came from the community or had relatives there, they joined peasant leaders. Members of the Tahuantinsuyo Pro Indigenous Rights Committee (Comité Pro Derecho Indígena Tahuantinsuyo) also came from the city. They were young lawyers, teachers, and journalists who advised peasants and peddled a vague anarchism or a type of romantic socialism. They were convinced the Andean past – communist and rural – remained a viable alternative to gamonal control. Leguía ended up banning the Committee in 1924. Earlier he had created a rival group, the Patronato de la Raza Indígena. Mistis did not welcome these groups, which in their eyes unconditionally supported peasants and

[70] Ricardo Valderrama and Carmen Escalante, *Levantamientos de los indígenas de Haquira y Quiñota* (Lima: Seminario de Historia Rural Andina, 1981), 14–15.

[71] ADC, Corte Superior de Justicia, legajo 93, 1921.

eroded their authority. In January 1923, a complaint presented before the Cuzco prefect stated that Indians attacked the commissions charged with collecting contributions and that "the only weapon with which to commit their daring assaults was the unconditional support of the Patronato Indígena, which does not grasp Indians' treachery."[72]

A predecessor, the Pro Indigenous Association (Asociación Pro-Indígena), founded by twenty-year-old student Pedro Zulen from the University of San Marcos, established a relationship between intellectuals and peasants. It sought to support Indians' complaints and demands, assign lawyers to defend them free of charge, and establish investigative commissions. It planned a broad national survey and reports on the condition of Indians in every province. A central committee in Lima organized a network of informants, correspondents, and delegates or messengers throughout Andean cities, especially Puno, Azángaro, Cotahuasi, Acomayo, Cora Cora, and others in the south. One member was Juan José del Pino, a lawyer and a correspondent in Huarochirí and Ayacucho. While passing through Huanta in 1914, he attempted to rally editors of the local newspaper, *El Estandarte Católico*, to support the Pro Indígena group. Many joined out of sympathy for Indians. Delegates traveled constantly throughout the country. Arturo Delgado wrote from Oyón that "at the end of last month, I made a special trip to the capital of the province, where I conducted some business and solicited more supporters. I was able to address complaints I received, which reveals the ascendance that the Association is achieving."[73] The inverse also occurred when peasants traveled to Lima to directly present their complaints. In the capital, provincial migrants formed clubs that served as another nexus between the Association and the country's interior. A truly national network formed. One session chosen at random is telling: On Friday, August 22, 1913, the Paucartambo delegate sent an appeal, Indians from Huancrachuco forwarded case records, and the community in Barranca denounced looting. There were also declarations from Huánuco peasants forced into free labor and reports on the Cabana jail, abuses in Puno, and an appeal against the Chongos governor.[74] This covered the whole country. The Asociación Pro Indígena was

[72] ADC, Corte Superior de Justicia, legajo 98, 1923.

[73] Archivo Zulen, BNP, Arturo Delgado to the Asociación Pro Indígena, August 2, 1913.

[74] Archivo Zulen, BNP, a session of the Asociación Pro Indígena, August 22, 1913.

the precursor to a political organization.[75] Its delegates, or messengers, witnessed efforts by a young generation to meet the peasant world and organize moral indignation against gamonalismo.

The Force of Myth

Was the restoration of the Inca empire a real alternative in 1920? There is no evidence to suggest that peasants formulated such a program. However, landowners undoubtedly were convinced a "true caste war" was at hand, and some Lima and provincial intellectuals believed highland unrest portended long-awaited Andean rebirth.

Mariátegui left for Europe when the great rebellion had scarcely begun. On October 8, 1919, he boarded a ship in Callao bound for La Rochelle, France, by way of New York. He left convinced that Peru needed a new political language and that old words were empty. Conservative and liberal meant nothing, because the old parties had run their course, and Peru had to create "new associations capable of acquiring effective popular force."[76] Mariátegui stayed in Europe for three years and seven months. In Paris he met Henri Barbusse. He went to Genoa, Rome, Florence, Venice, and Rome again. He read, but above all, he observed the European scene, attentive to new phenomena such as the worker takeover of Turin factories, the spread of Soviet influence, and the foundation of the Italian Communist Party. Mariátegui continued on to Berlin and traveled around Germany before boarding a ship in February 1923 in Antwerp, Belgium, bound for Peru. He imbibed the same intellectual climate as young authors such as Gramsci, Korsch, Lukács, Bloch, and others who promoted critical Marxism. The work of Georges Sorel, an early critic of progress with a fervor for union organization and a belief in the transformative role of violence, was a crucial reference for that group. Unlike the García Calderón brothers, Mariátegui did not allow Europe to dazzle him, perhaps because from the outset he was convinced of the differences between them and us. He went to observe, like savages watching the civilized in a

[75] Wilfredo Kapsoli, *El pensamiento de la Asociación Pro-Indígena* (Cuzco: Centro de Estudios Rurales Andinos Bartolomé de Las Casas, 1980).

[76] José Carlos Mariátegui, "La reorganización de los grupos políticos," *Nuestra Epoca* (Lima) 1:2, July 6, 1918, 2.

way that recalled his encounter with the Campa Indians in Lima.[77] He later said that in Europe he discovered Peru. Distance was necessary to elucidate the language and popular forces that Peruvian society demanded.

Mariátegui returned when the southern rebellions were ending, but he educated himself on the unrest through indigenista intellectuals such as Valcárcel, Romero, and Churata and especially through his links to participants in those struggles. In 1923 Lima hosted an indigenous congress that reflected, if belatedly, the advocacy of the Tahuantinsuyo Pro-Indigenous Rights Committee: defense of community, abolition of free labor, demand for schools, and freedom of assembly and worship.[78] The program suggested Adventist influence, but its most striking feature was its antifeudal content. At this event Mariátegui met Ezequiel Urviola.

Urviola was an exceptional character because he attempted to push the principles of indigenista intellectuals to their limits. He traded suit and tie for poncho and sandals. He mingled with high plains peasants, who venerated this hunchbacked, unkempt young man who demanded powder and dynamite to destroy haciendas. At the indigenous congress he argued that there was continuity between Domingo Huarca, Juan Bustamante, Tupac Amaru, and Atahualpa. Mariátegui noted similarities between the Azángaro and Huancané rebellions, the Atusparia uprising in Ancash, and the Tupac Amaru revolution. It confirmed his youthful intuition that Rumi Maqui represented an alternative national tradition. Indians were not submissive and cowardly, as some oligarchic intellectuals portrayed; on the contrary, at no moment during the colonial or republican periods had they ceased rebelling against feudalism.

Urviola embodied the new Indian who, immersed in his own Quechua tradition, also understood Western culture. He associated with Zulen and perhaps leaned toward anarchism, but in 1923 he proclaimed himself socialist. He did not move beyond the Andean utopia, as Kapsoli erroneously argued, but attempted to combine it with socialism.[79] In that lay his originality. Mariátegui claimed that

[77] See pages 161–2.

[78] Agustín Barcelli, *Historia del sindicalismo peruano*, vol. 1 (Lima: Editorial Hatunruna, 1972), 178.

[79] See Kapsoli, *Ayllus del sol*, 115.

Urviola, who died in January 1925, "represented the first spark of a coming fire."[80]

Intellectuals who placed too much hope in fire and dynamite were not the only ones to view the 1920s rebellions as part of a larger history. At the same time in Bolivia, peasant groups tried to recover the remains of Tupac Catari, the Aymara leader of the 1781 movement, from land a hacienda had seized from communities.[81] Today Domingo Huarca is as real for Tocroyoc peasants as Rumi Maqui is for Puneños. Peasants tell stories about the latter, and a play dramatizes mistis dragging him behind their horses, killing him, and cutting off his head.[82] The plot evokes Tupac Amaru's decapitation in 1572 and Tupac Amaru II's quartering in 1781. The syncretism of popular memory reveals the persistence of tradition.

Myth continued to live in the Andes. More than just memory, the material life of communities sustained peasant struggles. In the twentieth century, communities still maintained Inca society's collective relations to such an extent that socialism, embraced by intellectuals and workers from cities and mines, gained followers from the rural masses, that is, the majority of the population. It was a European idea capable of fusing with Andean traditions; that's why Urviola could herald the country of the future. Socialism, more than mere ideological discourse, was the form myth acquired in contemporary times. Mariátegui wrote in 1925, "The strength of the revolutionaries is not in their science but in their faith, in their passion, in their will. It is a religious, mystical, spiritual force. It is the power of Myth."[83] That power had the capacity to shake Peru to its very foundations.

Although Mariátegui did not write extensively about Inca society, arguments about agrarian communism were central to his work at large. According to him, the Incas did not use slaves, their society was not feudal, and the term "socialist" was a blatant anachronism. Their society combined state organization, collective appropriation of goods and products, and developed agriculture. It was not primitive communism

[80] José Carlos Mariátegui, "Prólogo," in Valcárcel, *Tempestad en los Andes*, 10. [Editors' note].

[81] Silvia Rivera, "Luchas campesinas contemporáneas en Bolivia: el movimiento 'Katarista': 1970–1980," in René Zavaleta, ed., *Bolivia hoy* (Mexico City: Siglo XXI, 1983), 129–68.

[82] Centro Bartolomé de Las Casas, Cuzco, interview with Tocroyoc peasants. Radio program, cassette No. 13, Chumbivilcas, side A.

[83] José Carlos Mariátegui, *El alma matinal* (Lima: Amauta, 1960), 22.

but rather agrarian communism. This suggested a peculiar historical formation: while Europe marched from slavery to feudalism, collectivism persisted in the Andes. The Spanish interrupted that history, but the collapse of the Inca state did not destroy ayllus, kinship groups whose silent and prolonged struggle persisted through peasant communities. Twentieth-century Peruvian society would be incomprehensible to Europeans. Capitalism emerged in cities, some mining centers, and coastal plantations; colonial feudalism endured in highland haciendas; and peasant communities reproduced ancestral forms of appropriating nature. All stages of historical evolution could be identified at once, from primitive men in the Amazon region to the modern proletariat.

To change such a society, a transformative project must combine new and old. That did not mean that Soviet communism equated to Inca communism. In a dispute with writer Mario Aguirre Morales, Mariátegui addressed this issue:

> Aguirre begins with the idea that autocracy and communism are two irreconcilable terms. The Inca regime, he posits, was despotic and theocratic and thus not communist. But historically, communism does not mean individual liberty or popular suffrage. Autocracy and communism are incompatible in our age but they weren't in primitive societies. Today a new order cannot renounce any form of modern society's moral progress.[84]

Socialism superseded the liberal idea; the democracy he glimpsed in the Soviets was the opposite of bourgeois parliamentarism. The idea thus was not simply to prolong an Andean tradition – agrarian communism – but to integrate it into the construction of a new society, projecting it toward the future. The return of the Inca was a romantic idea, but it could not change society. It was akin to challenging the republic with slings and lances; it needed a European catalyst, an explosive import represented by Marxism in the field of ideas.

Mariátegui's thinking – along with a large part of Peruvian culture in the 1920s – was a tributary of the Andean utopia. In this lay its irreducible character, the peculiarity of his Marxism. What made it possible? Religion represented common ground, a place of privileged encounter between Mariátegui and the Andean world. In 1923, Víctor Raúl Haya

[84] Mariátegui, *Siete ensayos*, 79–80.

de la Torre's leadership emerged from demonstrations against the consecration of Peru to the Sacred Heart of Jesus.[85] Mariátegui refused to participate in this sort of baptism of the new generation. He was not anticlerical. Although he criticized the actions of the Mexican ecclesiastical hierarchy, his writings on Miguel de Unamuno and Mahatma Gandhi demonstrated that he always valued religious sentiment. Religion for him was personal. Writing about the poet Alcides Spelucín, Mariátegui admitted that his own soul had searched for God since his youth, tempted by the infinite and the adventurous. Religion was also collective, the passion that moved multitudes and conferred upon them force and conviction, like those carriers of the Señor de los Milagros who so moved him during his days as Juan Croniqueur.[86] But like socialism, religion needed to be re-created in the Andes: "Communism is essentially religious. What causes misunderstandings is the old sense of the term."[87] Mariátegui would have fully agreed with the philosopher Mariano Iberico, who in *El nuevo absoluto* (The New Absolute) signaled that "the fundamental meaning of socialism consists in the feeling that man needs to be saved, redeemed."[88] The difference for Mariátegui was that salvation was not an abstract notion, but a worldly and collective one. Socialism was the millennial, the utopian: "The countless army of the humble, of the poor, of the wretched has resolutely set off toward the Utopia that Intelligence, in its generous, fecund, and clairvoyant moments, has conceived."[89]

In Mariátegui's Peru, Christianity was not the same religion the Spanish had introduced. First, the institutional power of the Church had declined considerably. Second, its earthly power also had waned as religious property passed to lay landowners. Third, the Church no longer monopolized ideology and culture. Fourth, variations of Christianity – minority groups such as Adventists, Evangelicals, and Presbyterians – managed to have a significant presence. In the 1920s Pastor John Mackay introduced Haya de la Torre to Bible reading. Mariátegui not only enrolled his oldest son in the school Mackay directed, but also

[85] The plan to consecrate Peru to the Sacred Heart of Jesus was conceived by President Leguía as a way of winning over the Catholic masses. [Editors' note].

[86] See José Carlos Mariátegui, "La procesión tradicional" [1917], in *Escritos Juveniles*, vol. 2 (Lima: Biblioteca Amauta, 1992), 139–45 [Editors' note].

[87] Mariátegui, *Siete ensayos*, 264.

[88] Mariano Iberico, *El nuevo absoluto* (Lima: Editorial Minerva, 1926), 222–3.

[89] José Carlos Mariátegui, *La escena contemporánea* (Lima: Amauta, 1960), 158.

visited him frequently. The Christian doctrine that attracted Mariátegui was not the supposedly rational orthodoxy of Thomism, but rather the passionate impulses of the mystics, removed from hierarchies and blended with the multitudes. For him, religion seemed borne of immense sentiment and implied the search of a limitless horizon.

In a country with such cultural contrasts, it was difficult if not impossible for Lima intellectuals to approach peasants on their own terms. A bridge, a mediation, was necessary. For Mariátegui, the importance of the indigenista movement was that it offered the possibility of connecting Marxism with the Andean world. Indigenismo was a heterogeneous current, to be sure, at times made up of authors with overly diverse qualities and projects, but they articulated "a state of mind, almost a state of consciousness of the new Peru."[90] Mariátegui came to their defense in February 1927 when Luis Alberto Sánchez attacked them for "excessive improvisation and rhetorical display among more than a few of the Indians' defenders."[91]

Mariátegui answered Sánchez by arguing that the lack of program and unified will were not necessarily deficiencies in a movement as young as indigenismo. He did not believe in the fruitfulness of unanimity; to the contrary, diverse voices, polemics, and debates would elaborate a program that was not the starting point but rather the result of collective enterprise. And not just intellectualism mattered. There had to be a place for passion, for the mysticism and messianism of "the postwar generation" that Valcárcel embodied. In his response to Sánchez's "indigenista mishmash," Mariátegui enunciated with total clarity the political project that he had advanced since his return from Europe:

> What I affirm on my own is that upon the confluence or amalgamation between indigenismo and socialism, no one who looks at

[90] José Carlos Mariátegui, "El indigenismo en la literatura nacional," *Mundial* (Lima), January 21, 1927.

[91] Sánchez, an agile journalist and literary critic, and a future member of the Aprista party, had written several books that gave him an air of precocity. Though he was not a Hispanist, Sánchez kept his distance from apostles and redeemers. Some saw certain whims favorable to the Leguía regime that tarnished his independence, but he was clearly not a right-wing intellectual at that time, and Mariátegui never asserted the contrary during their intense, two-month debate in the Lima magazine *Mundial*. I do not share the opinion of Luis Enrique Tord, who attributes "equal reformist intentions" to Mariátegui and Sánchez. See *Tord, El indio en los ensayistas peruanos, 1848–1940* (Lima: Editoriales Unidas, 1978), 80.

> the contents and essence of those things can be surprised. Socialism orders and defines the demands of the masses, of the working class. And in Peru the masses – the working class – are eighty percent indigenous. Our socialism thus would not be Peruvian – neither would it even be socialism – if it did not show solidarity, first and foremost, with indigenous demands.[92]

This was a public admission of his beliefs (*confesión de parte*). Not all indigenistas were socialists, but Mariátegui believed his project reflected reality. In his prologue to Valcárcel's *Tempestad en los Andes*, Mariátegui argued that "socialism appears in our history not by chance, imitation, or fashion, as superficial spirits suppose, but rather as historical fatalism."[93] It was Peru's destiny. Through socialism, the country could complete its transformation into a nation, fusing new with old and ideas from Europe – the best of the West – with Peru's historical tradition.

Sánchez's much-anticipated response appeared in the following edition of *Mundial*. He admitted lacking a political affiliation, but he attacked indigenismo's rhetorical inconsistency and posed a series of questions to his adversary:

> Tell me, do you believe that in the opposition between coast and sierra and in the indigenous community there lies a solution, and that the community is an autochthonous organization? Do you not see in it the colonialist legacy that you denounce? Do you not involve the cholo in the movement? Could you not approve a movement of total and non-exclusionary vindication?[94]

In response, Mariátegui insisted on the necessity of a "Peruvian socialism" and underscored the origin and revolutionary impulse of nationalism in colonial nations. He concluded that his references to working classes did not distinguish between Indian and cholo or between coast and sierra, that in 1927 Peru, a foremost priority was to confront the Indian problem to eliminate feudalism and servitude. The debate did not end there. Sánchez charged back and repeated the community questions that Mariátegui brushed aside. Sánchez questioned the efficacy of an institution that was a "remote parody of an autochthonous

92 Manuel Aquézolo Castro, ed., *La polémica del indigenismo* (Lima: Mosca Azul Editores, 1976), 75.

93 Mariátegui, "Prólogo," 13.

94 Aquézolo Castro, ed., *La polémica*, 81. [Editors' note].

organization."[95] By then the spirits of both polemicists were exasperated and the debate became repetitive. Mariátegui titled his following article "A finite polemic" ("Polémica finita") and Sánchez, "More on the same" ("Más sobre lo mismo"). Sánchez's repetition of questions about the community was a skillful polemical maneuver. He did not hazard an opinion and put his adversary at his mercy, awaiting a response. Mariátegui avoided a difficult situation but dodged questions to do so.

The debate left open one key question: could the indigenous community sustain Peruvian socialism? Little was known then about peasant communities. In 1905 a partial figure for twelve provinces pointed to 548 communities with a population of 219,000. Indigenistas assumed that indigenous social relations were collectivist and were convinced of their pre-Hispanic origins, but in 1927 there were barely a hundred recognized communities in the whole country. Abelardo Solís calculated 1,562 communities, a number quite removed from reality. In 1987 there are about 5,000 recognized communities. Lacking empirical data, observing peasants from the outside and in confrontation with the oligarchic intelligentsia, indigenistas followed only their hopes and desires. They ignored the fact that other peasants helped defeat the 1920s rebellions. In 1923, gamonales troops reappeared. In Haquira, the subprefect, governor, mayor, and notable residents – all mistis – formed a group with eight policemen and 300 Indians to confront rebels, using the same weaponry (slings and stones) as their enemy, but spreading terror through rape, massacres, and the sacking of properties.[96] In Yanaoca, policemen and peasants were willing to teach rebels a lesson. Retaliation lacked a central command. Groups in villages organized to attack communities, but along the way unforeseen rivals intercepted them. Surprise and ambush were the weapons of choice. This suggests that the colonos rebellion had limits. Many runas remained loyal to mistis and even risked their lives for them. A familiar phenomenon in Andean history reappeared: Indians fighting Indians.

Gamonal armies took on a life of their own for several months. Peasants abandoned their plots and lived on what they could take with them. Pursued rebels acted similarly. Was this guerrilla warfare or banditry? All of this happened amid confusion and with impunity, in isolated punas and mountain passes, where the dominion of some over others

[95] Ibid., 90. [Editors' note].
[96] Valderrama and Escalante, *Levantamientos*.

hinged on violence. It was difficult to distinguish between opposing groups. On occasion, the 1921 attacks on haciendas were also attacks against the colonos plots. The misti Washington Ugarte, in an appeal presented before a judge, described the following situation in Santo Tomás:

> Adrián Lanllaya, José López, and other Indians of the community of Ppisacphuyo, known and renowned ringleaders of mutinous and rebellious Indian hordes, have been committing all types of crimes and abuses in the communities of Incuta, Picutani, Alhuacchuyo and others. They are burning and laying waste to private properties such as those I bought from Ceferino Enriquez in Incuta. They are usurping others that in weeks past they marked out and delineated by themselves, without authorization, such as the lands between Picutani and Alhuacchuyo, called Sura, in an extension of its four square leagues, annexing them in fact to Cootacca. There another gang of rebels is stealing and assaulting livestock, like my two cows and calves they just snatched from shepherd Mariano Alferes, five horses from shepherd Bernabé Hanampa, a cow from shepherd Mariano Aphaya, and almost daily llamas, sheep, etc. On public roads they assault my employees and dependents, from whom they take whatever they carry on them; they even attempted to strangle Juan Carrillo when he was carrying a condor to this village; [and] in all the shrines or passes they lie in wait to abuse and steal whichever of my dependents passes near them.[97]

While the Indians of Picutani rebelled against the Santo Tomás mistis, those of Pisacpuyo instead rushed to their defense and insulted the comuneros who were ready to attack them. It was not difficult for Ugarte to gather a group of "boys" to burn and destroy the huts of Picutani peasants.

The notion of "caste war" does not hold up under close scrutiny. It was not a struggle, in a strict sense, of mistis against Indians. Mistis confronted rebels, but there were Indians in both groups. At times one community fought another; at others, colonos battled comuneros. And there were conflicts within communities themselves. The introduction of capitalism heightened old tensions. The internal market penetrated and fragmented communities and initiated processes of social differentiation, which was more advanced than indigenistas thought. In the

[97] ACD, Corte Superior de Justicia, legajo 82, 1920.

southern high provinces, wool exports did not rest solely with haciendas; production by communities was increasingly important. They seemed to have been even more efficient and profitable businesses than large estates. This quietly undermined mistis' power and explained the mercantilization of villages around Lake Titicaca and the development of a great urban center in Juliaca, a rival city to traditional Puno. Fairs were no longer annual but weekly events. Commercial and monetary flows were conduits that integrated Andean spaces and spurred migration, another contributing factor to greater peasant mobility. Obviously, these developments demanded an expanded road network. In 1925 peasants in Puquio (Ayacucho) bored through the hills in twenty days to build a road to Nazca and the ocean, reducing travel time from four days on horseback to just six hours. This was not an isolated case. Even more than mistis, peasants took advantage of trucks to transport their products to the marketplace.

Commercial agriculture also brought with it product specialization. In the communities of Chancay and Huarochirí it appeared to force early land privatization beginning in the 1890s. Town council minutes recorded an agreement to suppress collective usufruct rights and divide plots. The process was not as rapid in Cuzco, but in 1920 in the Sicuani community of Pucamachay, a conflict arose between peasant families who wanted to privately cultivate their land and communal authorities who defended periodic redistribution and land rotation according to collective criteria. Documents stated that land should be assigned to "each community member, according to his merits and service record; for example, preference goes to those who pay more contributions, those who carry out civil and religious responsibilities, those who punctually attend public work parties, and other merits that are more or less easily known by the authority."[98] Some viewed this egalitarian peasant world as an alternative to the country's woes, but rather than spreading down to and transforming the coast, that world was threatened by the very capitalism that made cities, newspapers, and universities possible. It produced a new encounter between the Andes and the west, without the pathetic features of the sixteenth-century civilizational clash, but perhaps more subjugating. Capitalism tends to homogenize, the development of an internal market eliminates localisms and traditions, and particular habits are sacrificed to a greater common language. Schools, a factor in earlier peasant mobilization, propagated new values. The

[98] ADC, Corte Superior de Justicia, legajo 84, 1920.

presence of Adventists had mundane effects. The growth of literacy underscored the backwardness of Quechua and Aymara. The whole Andean culture was on the defensive.

Was Sánchez correct in the questions he posed Mariátegui? The debate pitted the intellectual versus the political, reality versus ideology. In 1927 Mariátegui agreed with Sánchez that indigenismo was not a cohesive movement but an attitude, an attempt to discover the key to Peru in the Andean world, to distance Peru from Europe, look toward the interior, revive tradition, wrest it away from conservatives, and assign it new content. To do all that it was necessary to unite indigenismo with politics.

Socialism obviously did not originate in Peru. It was a European import like sugarcane, to use Mariátegui's metaphor, one that required adaptation and cultivation. Indigenous multitudes and Andean cultural traditions offered a privileged terrain. Inconsistency or error aside, Mariátegui intuited something that only later became all too evident to historian Jorge Basadre, who said that "the most important phenomenon in twentieth-century Peruvian culture is the heightened awareness about the Indian among writers, artists, men of science, and politicians."[99] Without rebellions – real or imaginary – would that new consciousness have been possible?

What Mariátegui conceived in the political realm, poet César Vallejo attempted in the imagination. Vallejo sought a new type of writing, forged at the confluence of cosmopolitanism and nationalism, two currents of Peruvian literature that rarely coincided. The result was *Trilce* (1922), a vanguardist text inscribed within indigenismo. Its very title signaled its originality. Mariátegui viewed Vallejo's poetry as the "dawn" of national literature. The same amalgamation was necessary for socialism: to combine popular impulse with external influence, the Andean with the universal, cosmopolitanism with "rootedness in the land, in the province, in the most familiar and immediate."[100]

Mariátegui was not the only one who approached indigenismo from a political position. Regionalism and, after 1928, Aprismo, were other attempts at merging indigenismo and politics. Manuel Seoane, who later became a prominent Aprista leader, expressed enthusiasm for the

[99] Jorge Basadre, *Perú: problema y posibilidad*, 2nd edition (Lima: Banco Internacional del Perú, 1978), 292.

[100] Washington Delgado, *Historia de la literatura republicana* (Lima: Rikchay Perú, 1980), 118.

Resurgimiento group, founded in Cuzco in 1925, and maintained that "the old imperial city had to be the cradle of a vindicationist movement."[101] He echoed Valcárcel in citing the "proletarian" role of the provinces against the "centralism of the capital." Combating gamonalismo meant challenging Lima: the dominion of the capital over the interior lay in local power, in the articulation between gamonalismo and centralism that Zulen denounced. The memory of imperial Cuzco emerged in opposition to Lima. Even before the student movement in Córdoba, Argentina, Cuzco served as a stage for university reform when San Antonio Abad students mobilized in 1915. When reform reached Lima's University of San Marcos and students organized into a national federation, they convened their first congress in March 1920 in Cuzco. There among others were Manuel Seoane and Haya de la Torre, who visited the south at the very moment when peasant rebellions were spreading. In a 1928 letter to the magazine *La Sierra*, Haya admitted that "Cuzco transformed the national youth as it transformed me two years earlier. For that reason I am a citizen of Cuzco because I believe that the new man within me appeared in the beginning of my youth during my long years of residence in Cuzco."[102] Although his stay there was not that long – he was secretary of the prefect from August 1917 to April 1918 – that emotion compelled him to invoke Tupac Amaru II and the Andean rebellions in *Por la emancipación de América Latina* (*For the Emancipation of Latin America*).[103] He believed he had discovered a tragic and rebellious Indian who secretly harbored a clear intuition of his own destiny: "Is there more unequivocal proof than the hundreds who die in silent heroism in those dark massacres, which in recent years happen almost every three months?"[104] Not surprisingly, Mariátegui referred glowingly to the book and found it logical that, since both departed from the same premises, they arrived at the same conclusions.

Their alignment, however, did not last long. In 1928, when Haya de la Torre was in Mexico, he launched his presidential candidacy – supposedly from Abancay – with support from the nonexistent Partido

[101] Manuel Seoane, "Carta al grupo Resurgimiento," *Amauta* (Lima), 9 (May 1927), 37.

[102] Víctor Raúl Haya de la Torre, "Carta de Haya de la Torre a La Sierra," *La Sierra* (Cuzco) 2:18 (June 1928), 6.

[103] Víctor Raúl Haya de la Torre, *Por la emancipación de América Latina* (Buenos Aires: Gleizer, 1927) [Editors' note].

[104] Ibid., 68.

Nacionalista Libertador (Nationalist Liberation Party). Rather than merely opposing Leguía's reelectionist efforts, Haya aspired to form an armed group to seize power. A resemblance to the onset of the Mexican Revolution was obvious. Rumi Maqui also springs to mind. Mariátegui did not object to taking power by force: Influenced by the Bolsheviks, he was convinced that attacking the state was an unavoidable imperative. The question, however, was timing, actors, and form. Haya's desire to lead a revolutionary movement from abroad and to invent a party and army where there were none seemed to Mariátegui to repeat the most repugnant vices of Peruvian petty politics (*politiquería*). Deception and caudillismo could not lead to an effective transformation of the country.

For Haya, politics above all was action. Revolutionary praxis did not require the kind of discussions or debates in which Mariátegui and Sánchez engaged. Haya imagined Aprismo as a sort of "Red Army," disciplined, hierarchical, and commanded by a lucid intelligentsia capable of leading the way. It was essential to count on a select group of conspirators. "There is no need to lose heart," he wrote in a 1926 letter to Eudocio Ravines. "Five Russians moved the world. The twenty of us can move Latin America."[105] Although he penned those words with Lenin in mind, his words evoked Salaverry's daring, Castilla's campaigns, and Piérola's montoneras – in short, Peruvian caudillismo.[106] A letter to Esteban Pavletich stated with greater clarity that "the people always follow representative men."[107] Haya viewed himself as the incarnation of Peru's destiny, a providential actor called to lead.

The Andean past inspired Haya's rhetoric. The Chavín condor was the party symbol for APRA, and beginning in 1930 Apristas unfurled the supposed Tahuantinsuyo flag, made up of all the colors of the rainbow, at party demonstrations. Later during his clandestine period, Haya used the pseudonym "Pachacútec" and called his refuge "Incahuasi." But for Aprismo the Andean became associated only with the messianic – the

[105] *Archivo Mariátegui*. Haya de la Torre to Eudocio Ravines, London, October 17, 1926. For expanded treatment, see Alberto Flores Galindo, "Un viejo debate: el poder," *Socialismo y participación* (Lima) 20 (1983), 15–41.

[106] Flores Galindo refers here to Felipe Santiago Salaverry, Ramón Castilla, and Nicolás de Piérola, all Presidents of Peru during the nineteenth century [Editors' note].

[107] Haya de la Torre to Esteban Pavletich, London, April 27, 1926, cited in Pedro Planas, *Los orígenes del Apra. El joven Haya*, 2nd edition (Lima: Okura Editores, 1986), 147.

arrival of the messiah (or the man, to use Haya's terminology) destined to save the country. From his followers he demanded, even more than doctrinal understanding, a blind faith capable of "moving mountains" and shaking oligarchic Peru. Many took the cult of leadership to the extreme; poet Roberto Souza Martínez, for example, addressed Haya in these terms: "You are the light that illuminates the path/that was once dark in this country so exploited."[108]

For Mariátegui, on the contrary, understanding Marxism as the myth of our time was to view revolution as a collective act, a creation of the masses, a translation of their impulses and passions. In reference to the leadership core, the intelligentsia who articulated the utopian project, he pointed out that the root of the term *elite* was "elect." Recalling the dreadful experience of Italian fascism, Mariátegui rejected the idea that someone could designate himself boss or leader. To avoid dictatorship, revolution cast workers as the true protagonists. It had to spring from the interior of the country, and Marxism had to find expression in Quechua. Utopia expanded its horizon toward the future. The utopian and the messianic, however, remained opposite notions, two ways to confront national problems, two projects for locating Peru's hidden key and transforming the country. One trusted the creativity of the masses to set the course from below, beginning with communities and villages. The other awaited the providential man to illuminate the path from above, leaving nothing to debate, nothing to imagine. Messianism required only faithful followers within an authoritarian structure. In return, messianic parties could claim the attributes of realism, effectiveness, and a close link with the country's political traditions. The others sought to build on a different tradition: Andean collectivism. The debate raised the old question: what was the community? Was it a reservoir of popular democracy, or a corporate and hierarchical organism? Were peasants protagonists of their own history, or followers of whoever incarnated messianism?

There was another component to the differences between Haya and Mariátegui. Although Aprismo appropriated elements of Andean culture, it aimed to modernize the country, advance capitalism, and shake up the routine world of peasants. Mariátegui, however, sought an intersection between socialism and the indigenous community, which he did not consider an obsolete institution condemned by historical design.

[108] Burga and Flores Galindo, *Apogeo y crisis*, 201.

The two were debating the future of Andean culture: Aprista messianism would drag the country toward modernity; Mariátegui's utopianism believed a different future could exist. Was utopia becoming a synonym for impossible? Were these the ramblings of a handicapped intellectual removed from practice, as Haya accused Mariátegui of being?[109]

Whereas for some the state formed the nation, for others civil society, inspired by popular uprisings, had maintained its independence. We are not interested in convening an historical tribunal to declare a winner of this debate. We should leave it as it actually ended, that is, as an unfinished discussion.

This chapter began with Riva Agüero's 1912 trip to the Peruvian sierra. The resulting *Peruvian Landscapes* was published posthumously in 1955. Three years later, another rite-of-passage account, *Los ríos profundos* (Deep Rivers), told the story of a mestizo boy named Ernesto whose imagination was shrouded in magic. The natural landscape acquired an unusual dimension in José María Arguedas's narrative: It sprang to life and became a medium that conveyed feeling. As the book progresses, Indians, such as the women who assault Abancay, become more prominent in the text. Beyond the obvious differences between travel account and novel, between essay and fiction, we are confronted by two opposing sensibilities. One formed in Lima and found itself in a strange and incomprehensible environment when it arrived in the sierra. The other sprang from the Andean interior – Andahuaylas, where Arguedas was born in 1911. Besides the class, cultural, and ethnic differences that separated Riva Agüero and Arguedas, there was an important time lapse between 1912 and 1958. In the interim came the 1920–23 rebellions, Mariátegui's polemics, and the emergence of Aprismo and communism. All this transformed Peruvian intellectuals and rendered obsolete the sonorous and elegant prose of turn-of-the-century writers such as Riva Agüero. Readers demanded a different narrative style, and new ways to understand Peru emerged.

A frequent image in Peruvian literature is the identification of Indians with stones. It is an ambivalent image. On one hand it signifies persistence, tenacity, the ability to endure. On the other hand it suggests silence, lack of expression, even the inability to understand. Stones evoke pre-Hispanic constructions – mythic Andean beings turned to

[109] Crippled in one leg since he was a young boy, Mariátegui spent his final years with both legs amputated, confined to a wheelchair. [Editors' note].

stone, gods who moved gigantic rocks. It plays on white fears by recalling boulders unleashed against Spanish loyalists or the stone that seals indigenous vengeance. In *Peruvian Landscapes*, Cuzco stones convey nothing more than "the funereal charm of its outdated monuments."[110] In *Deep Rivers*, however, stones acquire movement and life, like the Incas themselves, threatening the invaders who built their houses on top of them – Cuzco mistis, the real or imagined heirs to Pizarro.[111]

In the opening pages of *Deep Rivers*, Ernesto and his father are talking in front of Inca stonework:

– Papa, every stone is talking. Let's wait a moment.
– We won't hear anything. It's not that they're talking. You're just confused. They get into your mind and disturb you.
– Each stone is different. They are not chiseled. They're moving.
He took my arm.
– They seem to be moving about because they're all different, more different than field stones. The Incas made the stones out of mud. I've told you that many times.
– Papa, it seems as if they're walking, that they move about and then become still again.
I hugged my father. Leaning against him, I contemplated the wall once more.
– Is someone living in the palace? – I asked again.
– A well-born family.
– Like the Old Man?
– No. They're well-born, and at the same time misers, but not so miserly as the Old Man. Not like the Old Man! All the gentry of Cuzco are misers.
– Does the Inca allow them to live there?
– The Incas are dead.
– But not this wall. If the owner's a miser, why doesn't the wall swallow him up? This wall can walk; it could rise up into the sky or travel to the end of the world and back. Aren't the people who live in there afraid?[112]

[110] Riva Agüero, *Paisajes peruanos*, 14.
[111] Magdalena Chocano, "La palabra en la piedra: una lectura de Martín Adán," *Socialismo y participación* (Lima) 32 (December 1985), 85–93.
[112] José María Arguedas, *Deep Rivers*, translated by Frances Horning Barraclough (Austin: University of Texas Press, 1978), 8–9.

The dialogue pits Inca (capitalized, singular), the organizing principle of the world, against incas (lowercase, plural), historical beings who were unmistakably dead. Hope remained that the besieged men, the underdogs symbolized in the stones with which the Spanish built the walls, would move, march toward the "ends of the earth," and become besiegers themselves.

CHAPTER 9

The Boiling Point

Peasant movements again took the Andean stage in the 1960s. On the surface these battles were different: Indians fought for land and the abolition of servile burdens, not the return of the Tahuantinsuyo. But in reality the older and deeper question of power in the countryside underlay these demands. This power struggle played out through class warfare but also was depicted in José María Arguedas' stories and essays.

And I see (like everyone) the passing of the ship of death.
Antonio Cisneros[1]

Arguedas

José María Arguedas published his first book, *Agua* (Water), in 1935. Those three short stories launched a literary corpus that extended spatially from village and community to provincial capital and department and eventually to Peru at large: city and country, bourgeoisie and peasantry, mistis and Indians. No writer had ever attempted a similar undertaking. Literary critic Antonio Cornejo Polar identified in Arguedas's literary trajectory a reflection of Peruvian economic evolution – the easing of fragmentation, capitalist penetration, and the slow construction of an internal market.[2] It was difficult for people living in the Andean

[1] Antonio Cisneros, *Monólogo de la casta Susana y otros poemas* (Lima: Instituto Nacional de Cultura, 1986), 15.

[2] Antonio Cornejo Polar, *Los universos narrativos de José María Arguedas* (Buenos Aires: Losada, 1973).

interior to acquire, in 1935, an all-inclusive image of Peru. Peasants, Arguedas recalled, did not identify with national symbols such as the flag and national anthem, whose meaning was lost on them. However, commercial flows, expansion of the road network, urbanization, and migration ended the Andean population's relative immobility that began with demographic decline in the sixteenth century. Four centuries later, however, Peru's population surpassed pre-Hispanic levels, and Andean people from the upper highlands and Quechua valleys descended to coastal cities. Migrants formed cities, such as Chimbote, where only fishing villages existed before. The changes that made it possible to think and imagine Peru as a totality set the rhythm for Arguedas's work.

Critics have argued that his work successfully observes Peru from within the Andean world. Arguedas claimed he embarked on his literary adventure out of exasperation with the erroneous and superficial image of Indians that some writers presented. He wanted to show how they really were, a task that demanded the invention of new language. Critic Martin Lienhard has posited that Arguedas's purpose was even more ambitious: The author was not just an interpreter of Andean popular culture but indeed a subversive expression of that world.[3] In his most pessimistic moments, Arguedas paradoxically imagined himself as the troubadour of a world in decline. Lienhard argued just the opposite: through Arguedas, Andean culture appropriated western literary forms (the short story and the novel), transformed stagnant language, and established a radically original body of work, an entirely new discourse, a mixture of fiction, personal testimony, and essay, all masterly condensed in *El zorro de arriba y el zorro de abajo* (*The Fox from Up Above and the Fox from Down Below*).[4]

Ruggiero Romano warned us against separating Arguedas's fiction from his other work. Some ignore the fact that Arguedas was also an anthropologist who wrote numerous articles and essays on folklore and popular art. He was passionate about ethnology, and we have him to thank for a revalorization of Ayacucho altar pieces (retablos), the rediscovery of the mythical Inkarri cycle, and solid studies on peasant

3 Martín Lienhard, *Cultura popular andina y forma novelesca* (Lima: Tarea, 1981).

4 José María Arguedas, *The Fox from Up Above and the Fox from Down Below*, translated by Frances Horning Barraclough (Pittsburgh: University of Pittsburgh Press, 2000). The book was incomplete at the time of the author's death. The first edition was published in 1971 [Editors' note].

communities.[5] He established a counterpoint between social science research and fiction, and at times the two converged, as seen in his last novel. Arguedas went to the coastal city of Chimbote to study Andean migration and discovered unexpected materials about migrant culture; he thus began to conceive a new novel. Everything became mixed in a sort of boiling pot, as he wrote in a February 1967 letter to anthropologist John Murra (see appendix). That letter betrayed the strong tensions and conflicts that at times overwhelmed Arguedas. Personal experience, his relationship with his father, a difficult connection with his stepmother, his journeys in the Andes, his student days, the search for a political path, and imprisonment, all appeared time and again in his stories.

It is difficult to separate Arguedas the ethnologist from Arguedas the novelist, and to separate both from Arguedas the person. The mutually sustaining elements of fiction, social commentary, and autobiography in his work after *Agua* seemed to contrast before fusing into the most original Peruvian literary product of our time. What image of Peru does Arguedas convey? How was that dreadful country that he attempted to portray in 1935? His stories do not necessarily give us access to the real Peru, but rather to the country as lived and experienced through personal biography – that is, to social reality glimpsed from the inner world of a sensitive soul who wishes to map a territory and find a place in it. But what is that territory like?

In his early short stories, between "Warma Kuyay" (1933) and "Orovilca" (1954), Arguedas sketched a rural environment in which two opposing groups – mistis and Indians – silently struggle for centuries. Mistis are the lords, the whites and mestizos who rule and wield power, the hacienda owners and political authorities who need Indian labor "to be able to live" (p. 129).[6] For some Indians, mistis are synonymous with "respect" (p. 61), but generally they are "annoying" (p. 60), "bad" (p. 9), and "corroded by envy and betrayal" (p. 129). Indians, by contrast, live in communities and dedicate themselves to daily work. They are "good" (p. 95), but perhaps for that reason the majority accept misti domination and resign themselves to silent suffering. They seem

[5] These texts are comparable in page numbers to the five volumes of his complete literary works. See the bibliography by Mildred Merino de Zela, "Vida y obra de José María Arguedas," *Revista Peruana de Cultura* (Lima) 13–14 (1970), 127–78.

[6] This and the following references (page numbers in parentheses) are from José María Arguedas, *Obras Completas*, vol. 1 (Lima: Editorial Horizonte, 1983).

cowardly, incapable of looking mistis in the eye, fearful before the whip. This portrait seems to apply to hacienda Indians, but not to those who live apart, such as the Utej or the Tinkis. Mistis control them by pitting them against those groups that are hacienda captives, such as the Ak'olas and Lukanas.

There is no communication between mistis and Indians. One group speaks Spanish and the other Quechua. They have different customs. They despise each other. The only mediating agent is unrelenting misti violence, a private and daily form of abuse that police and authorities approve (p. 129). To rule is to physically beat, which reaffirms domination. Indians, including those who are cowards, feel profound hatred, an intimate rage that grows and grows but never goes beyond the individual (p. 98): "A man can be as fulfilled by anger as by love" (p. 33). Individual rebellion takes place through certain characters, but collective rebellion – that is, an Indian uprising against mistis – is little more than a fantasy, as seen at the end of the short story "Los escoleros" ("The students"): "But hatred continues to boil with more force in our chests, and our anger has grown bigger and bigger . . . " (p. 113). "Agua" ends in a similar way:

> Alone on that dry hill that afternoon, I cried for the comuneros, for their little farms scorched by the sun, for their hungry little animals. Tears filled my eyes; the clean sky, the pampa, the tile-like hills were trembling: the Inti, bigger and bigger, . . . was burning the world. I fell, and in the church, kneeling on the dry grass looking at *tayta* Chitulla, I begged him:
>
> Tayta: I hope rulers everywhere die! (p. 76).

Hatred is supplication, the hope that one day an immense fire brings an end to an unjust and brutal order, that Indians will no longer occupy the bottom. This order not only exploited Indians but also subjected them to daily humiliation. The only way to turn this world upside down is to transform hatred into collective passion and to transfer fear to the powerful. That is the only way to break the "total domination" of body and soul that mistis exercise: "Weeping, at such an altitude, or a fire – a great fire! – would disrupt the world" (p. 180). Rebellion appears impossible, but if carried out, it would acquire cosmic dimensions. Although these stories take place in Ayacucho villages, in provinces that border Ica and Arequipa, near Puquio, Arguedas believes the reality he portrays is valid to the entire highlands. Nuance disappears in Andean villages. The sides are clearly demarcated and confront each other with "primitive cruelty." A 1950 essay explained, "There are only two classes of people there who represent two implacable and essentially different worlds" (p. 79), that is, mistis, who imagine themselves superior, and Indians, who despite their resignation have learned to resist. They wait, but for what, for whom, and until when?

Arguedas offers a dual vision, the image of the "small village burning from the fire of love and hate" (p. 78). He presents misti against Indian, hatred against love, weeping against fire. These counterpoints coincide with an older cosmovision that divides reality between the world above and the world below, the condor and the bull, the *huamani* (the divinity that inhabits the hill) and the lake. Does Arguedas invest Andean images with pre-Hispanic significance? His narrative is filled with first-person passages, which convey a sense of confidentiality. Where does Arguedas fit in the secular conflict between mistis and Indians? Distanced from the mistis whom he rejects, Arguedas experiences three distinct moments in his relationship with Indians: First are solitude and abandonment, which cause him to imagine himself at the bottom of a "dark ravine" (p. 9), living without hope, crying, until, in a second moment, he joins the Indian world and finds inclusion among comuneros: "And a tenderness without equal, pure, sweet, like the light of that mother peak illuminated my life" (p. 11). Arguedas later said he found protection among Indians after he was thrown out of a hacienda house. He learned Quechua and indigenous customs. Some critics argue that the Andean in his work appears in feminine images, such as the absent mother who represents the Quechua language. Life among Indians appears to resolve personal and social identity problems. Later, according to this version, Arguedas the writer was a natural interpreter of the Andean world. Although in speeches and conferences he often agreed with that assessment, in personal conversations he lamented an inability to imagine even his own mother.[7] Yet wasn't his mother identified with the Andean?

Only in appearance does Indian acceptance ease his initial solitude. Arguedas realized he could not participate in their fiestas and customs, that he could not become just another in the group. "I remained outside the circle, embarrassed, forever defeated" (p. 7). Successful integration

[7] Personal confession to Jaime Guardia, cited in Roland Forgues, *José María Arguedas: del pensamiento dialéctico al pensamiento trágico. Historia de una utopía* (Lima: Editorial Horizonte, 1989), 25.

would have created one more Ayacucho comunero and robbed us of an influential writer. Failure, however, sent him on a path toward creativity. This is the third moment. As Indians find surprising bliss in their fiestas, the narrator is happy nowhere despite his efforts. Sadness and weeping reappear, and solitude persists. He lives "bitter and pale" (p. 12), unable to find consolation for his life as an "orphan," an "outsider," a "man without a father or mother." He is not an Indian and cannot become one by will or choice. In a rigid world, one is born an Indian or a misti. At best, Arguedas was a "fake mak'tillo" (p. 102). He was the son of a lawyer, born in the sierra, scion of gamonales whom he rejected even though he was not Indian, inhabitant of that nebulous and intermediate realm where mestizos resided. In his early stories a world divided between mistis and Indians left no space for mestizos, the absent ones who would only appear in *Yawar Fiesta* (1941) and later anthropological essays. In his texts on central highland communities or Huamanga popular art, mestizos seem to herald the future of a country in which Andean and western worlds fused.[8] Yet when Arguedas returns to fiction and passion asserts itself again, mestizos find little space in a world that does not allow for a middle ground. It is either resignation or rebellion, weeping or fire. Mestizos are then reduced to the individual, that is, the narrator's soul.

"Orovilca," the first Arguedas story set on the coast in Ica, captures that isolation. The narrator's experiences and sentiments take center stage. Arguedas narrates in first person his impressions as a boarding student who is "a recent arrival from the Andes." A classmate named Salcedo stands out. He is a precocious young man, unusually knowledgeable, who is also interested in plants and animals and does not reject the realm of the magical. Forced to fight a strapping student named Wilster, Salcedo ends up on the ground, beaten and defeated. Too proud to go back and face his classmates, he leaves the boarding school and loses himself among nearby sand dunes. Nobody could find him. Only the narrator knows that Salcedo had walked toward the ocean, following the tracks of a golden fish, a sea nymph that travels the desert and disappears among the oases. Salcedo was not an Indian, but he listened to

[8] José María Arguedas, *Formación de una cultura nacional indoamericana* (Mexico City: Siglo XXI, 1977). Politically, Arguedas fluctuated between radical positions (which made him close, at different times, to the Communist Party, Trotskyist leader Hugo Blanco, and the radical group known as Revolutionary Vanguard) and enthusiasm for reformist movements (such as the first Belaúnde administration [1963–68] or the beginnings of the military revolution in 1968).

their stories and could hear the silence of the punas beckon from 13,000 feet up. Arguedas wrote: "They listened to me like a delirious child, like a child addicted to apparitions and inventions, like all those who live among the deep rivers and immense mountains of the Andes" (p. 186).

The short story is a metaphor for another Arguedas project: the construction of his identity through the pursuit of Andean myths. In the letter to Murra, he showed enthusiasm for the publication of old manuscripts and the translation of the stories gathered by Father Ávila in Huarochirí at the beginning of the seventeenth century.[9] In the last years of his life, Arguedas inspired anthropologist Alejandro Ortiz to edit a collection of Andean myths, and he himself had prepared various collections of stories and short stories.[10] But where would the mythical lead? In "Orovilca," Salcedo was lost forever; no one could find him: "The sea by the Orovilca area is desert, useless; no one wanted to look where only the condors swooped down to devour large pickings" (p. 186). Earlier Arguedas hinted at a possible outcome: "[W]alking in the desert on the loose sand is a sure way to find death" (p. 178).

His identification with peasant and indigenous worlds makes him subordinate his personal destiny to the fate of Andean culture. Arguedas believed that his justification and salvation hinged on his capacity to penetrate the Andean world, understand it, and pour it into his stories. That's why he felt so wounded when, at a 1965 colloquium after the publication of his novel *Todas las sangres*, critics and sociologists questioned the veracity of his portrait of Peruvian society. They told him the Peru he depicted no longer existed, that the country had changed drastically, that the peasants he imagined in Huancavelica did not live there, and that if they still existed in parts of Ayacucho or Cuzco they were no longer the majority. Yet there was no reason for Arguedas to take into account their objections. He had not written a sociological study, and fiction had its own rules. But Arguedas, as he stressed in

[9] Flores Galindo refers here to the campaign against idolatries that Father Francisco de Avila led in Huarochirí. Arguedas edited a collection of documents gathered by Avila as *Dioses y hombres de Huarochirí* (Lima: Instituto de Estudios Peruanos, 1966). See Chapter 2 of this book for more information about Avila's campaign [Editors' note].

[10] See, for example, José María Arguedas and Francisco Izquierdo Ríos, *Mitos, leyendas y cuentos peruanos* (Lima: Ediciones de la Dirección de Educación Artística y Extensión Cultural, 1947); Arguedas, ed., *Canciones y cuentos del pueblo Quechua* (Lima: Editorial Huascarán, 1949); Arguedas, ed., *Ollantay. Cantos y narraciones Quechuas* (Lima: Patronato del libro peruano, 1957) [Editors' note].

a debate with Argentine writer Julio Cortázar, was not a professional writer. He belonged to a milieu in which the intellectual division of labor was not greatly developed. More than anything, he was convinced the imagination provided a way to understand an intricate country such as Peru. Essay and novel, thesis and description were not disconnected in his works. Therefore he could not ignore challenges to his truthfulness, and on the night after the conference he wrote in his diary:

> My home destroyed by slow and progressive incompatibilities between my wife and me; convinced just today of the futility and impracticality of making another home with a young lady whose forgiveness I beg; my book ("Todas las sangres") shown by two wise sociologists and one economist to be negative for the country – there is nothing else for me to do in this world.[11]

Intellectual debate that was cold and distant to other writers touched a more intimate chord in Arguedas. But he did not give in to defeat and continued with his internal struggle: "I am fighting like hell," he wrote to Manuel Moreno Jimeno the following year:

> You can't imagine how much this struggle takes out of me. Do you remember when we made our first trip to the Andes and I, at age 22 or 23, did not sleep even a wink for something like seven days? Where did that insomnia come from? This bout, which has lasted months and months, comes from a whirlwind of causes. My life is changing, parts of its foundation – the most intimate of them – have crumbled in on me, and I am building others with infinite effort. But if I succeed in getting over this I surely will produce new things. In Chimbote and in Puno I have seen the Peru of these days and its force almost doubles me over. I must grow to reach the height of that energy, of that terrible force that moves worlds and on many fronts breaks and bleeds.[12]

Was there a force that moved worlds? Arguedas was trapped in ambivalence. At times it seemed that for him the Andean world was condemned to disappearance, toppled by capitalism and progress, but at other times he saw capacity to resist, to give birth to a transformative force capable of moving stones (remember *Los ríos profundos*), shaking the earth, and

[11] *¿He vivido en vano? Mesa redonda sobre* Todas las sangres, *June 23, 1965* (Lima: Instituto de Estudios Peruanos, 1985), 67.

[12] Letter to Manuel Moreno Jimeno, quoted in Forgues, *José María Arguedas*, 22.

making the mountains walk as in the final passage of *Todas las sangres*. If the Peru he portrayed in this novel was false and did not exist, his hope was unfounded. That the novel sought a discourse about the future of the country was lost on sociologists; they did not hear the millenarian resonances that fill its pages, the hope for social revolution. Concepts and categories insulated sociologists from reality. Arguedas, on the contrary, confused his own life with those debates: "I feel terror at the same time as great hope."[13]

The Crisis of Andean Feudalism

In 1964, the year *Todas las sangres* was published, the demands of 300,000 peasants for land, schools, and salaried pay plunged the Peruvian Andes into tumult. In the span of a month, peasants attacked haciendas in the Cuzco districts of Paucartambo and Urcos and occupied small farms near Huancayo; comuneros from Oyón entered the latifundio Algolán; and similar events occurred in Huancavelica, Ayacucho, and Apurímac. The northern department of Cajamarca was also in turmoil. Agrarian agitation already had arrived in coastal valleys, where peasants occupied haciendas in Chancay and Callao, near Lima.[14] Unlike the 1920–23 unrest in the south, the 1964 rebellion spread throughout most of the country. The only exception was the department of Puno, whose inhabitants were still recovering from a devastating drought ten years earlier. A self-proclaimed reformist and antioligarchic administration had just come to power.[15] At first the regime ignored peasant mobilizations, but conservative parliamentary sectors called for order and the restoration of authority. They warned that peasants were challenging Peru's power structure, a rigid system in which some ordered and others obeyed.

The immediate antecedents of these events emerged between 1945 and 1948. After a prolonged ebb in peasant struggles that included the 1930s international financial crisis, organized peasants sought the

[13] *¿He vivido en vano?*, 68.

[14] Comité Interamericano de Desarrollo Agrícola, *Tenencia de la tierra y desarrollo socio-económico del sector agrícola: Peru* (Washington: Unión Panamericana, 1966). For a broad bibliography on these mobilizations, see Pedro Gibaja, "Los movimientos campesinos en el Perú o la frustración de una revolución agraria (1945–1964)," MA thesis, Pontificia Universidad Católica del Perú, 1982, vol. 4.

[15] The author is referring to the first administration of Fernando Belaúnde Terry (1963–68) [Editors' note].

legal recognition of their communities, formed unions within haciendas, and established the Peasant Confederation of Peru. Seizing an opening under the democratic administration of José Luis Bustamante y Rivero (1945–48) and influenced by the Aprista Party, the movement began in the central sierra and followed a strictly legal course: peasants dusted off papers and property titles, turned to lawyers and consultants, and demanded the return of usurped land. Many of these legal disputes dated to the seventeenth and eighteenth centuries. A classic example was the centuries-old confrontation between the Sicaya community and the Laive hacienda over ownership of eleven pastures. As a rite of passage, central sierra community peasants had to demonstrate knowledge of original town boundaries. Lawsuits against haciendas helped reaffirm these memories. This first stage of peasant mobilization could be considered reformist. Peasants constrained their actions to legal channels and, through litigation, began to recuperate history and acquire identity through memory. General Manuel Odría's reactionary 1948 coup interrupted the process, but the dictatorship had barely ended when peasant mobilization began anew.

New communities demanded recognition, and legal proceedings against haciendas resumed. In 1957 in the Cuzco jungle provinces of La Convención and Lares, hacienda colonos organized unions in valleys that produced coffee, tea, and coca. In 1961, the newly formed Cuzco Departmental Confederation united 214 local peasant sections. Marches and assemblies included those by peasants from the highlands and warm valleys who marched to Sicuani or Cuzco to present demands. The following year, unions from the La Convención valley demanded land for peasants and an end to servitude. They occupied seventy haciendas, paralyzed the valley, and imposed a type of Agrarian Reform Law – authored by Hugo Blanco, a Trotskyite affiliated with the tiny Revolutionary Leftist Front (FIR) – that essentially abolished the hacienda. The initiative resonated with peasants elsewhere. Colonos occupied their parcels, resisted free services, and formed unions in Silque, Compone, Ollantaytambo, and Písac. The uprising appeared to reverse the course of the Vilcanota River from lowland La Convención toward highland Cuzco. Landowners felt threatened. Could the Andes become another Sierra Maestra?[16] At that point, peasants from the

[16] Sierra Maestra is the name of the eastern mountains of Cuba where Fidel Castro led the guerrilla movement that would eventually topple dictator Fulgencio Batista [Editors' note].

La Convención valley suffered repression. Some Blanco collaborators attempted to organize resistance, robbed banks, and sought weapons, but with little effect. Blanco, isolated and unarmed in La Convención, ended up in Cuzco's La Almudena jail and then transferred to Tacna, where he faced trial and possibly the death penalty. The trial made Blanco famous. Before his capture, according to anthropologist John Earls, some La Convención peasants began to identify him with the Inca. Although it went no further, it was the first encounter between Andean culture and Marxism. Conscious of this confluence, Blanco believed exploitation was not just economic: "They destroy our culture, our Quechua, our Aymara, our Guarani, our yaraví, our aesthetic values. They spit on us, as the tayta says."[17] Those themes reappeared in Blanco's correspondence with Arguedas when the former was imprisoned on the penal island of El Frontón.

In 1963, a transitory military junta declared agrarian reform in the La Convención valley, but it was too late. Agitation did not stop in Cuzco.[18] It continued into the central sierra, where Aprista influence declined and a communal movement formed under the leadership of Genaro Ledesma. The most significant clashes were between the livestock division of the Cerro de Pasco Corporation and neighboring communities such as Urauchuc, San Pedro de Cajas, Vilca, and Rancas. The North American company owned eleven haciendas covering almost 1,483,000 acres appropriated from peasant lands between 1920 and 1950. The Laive, Algolán, and Antapongo haciendas also endured attacks from the communities and internal pressure from colonos. The central sierra movement was more mestizo than in the south and specifically targeted land recovery.[19] Protagonists came from communities that had experienced significant modernization, including division of labor, commercial crops, and increased technification. Electricity, for example, arrived in Muquiyauyo in the 1920s. Illiteracy declined. But in the south, demands appeared linked to centuries-old indigenous oppression and included an ethnic dimension. According to Howard Handelman, "It could be useful to think of the Cuzco peasant movement as part of a

[17] Hugo Blanco, *Land or Death. The Peasant Struggle in Peru* (New York: Pathfinder Press, 1972), 133. Yaraví is an Andean music genre whose antecedents have been traced to the Harawi, an Inca musical and poetic tradition [Editors' note].

[18] Decree 14444, April 6,1963.

[19] Howard Handelman, *Lucha campesina en los Andes* (Lima: Cuadernos del Taller de Investigación Rural, Pontificia Universidad Católica del Perú, 1978).

long historical tradition of indigenous rebellion against the cultural and economic domination of whites (or mestizos)."[20]

Even though both central and southern movements followed "legal" channels, the latter were more radical. Peasants struggled for land and fought to abolish secular oppression. Lucila Goycochea argued that these struggles challenged Indian-misti relations. The following testimonies confirm this. The first was a communication from peasants of Pitumarca, near Sicuani, to hacendado Nicolás Delgado:

> The peasant union of Rata, Pitumarca, writes to let you know that we peasants who were colonos until recently, enslaved by your hacienda, have formed a union and organized; we are also informed and we know that current laws condemn all methods of exploitation and humiliation that we peasants suffer. For that reason our union is legally established.
>
> Likewise we use this opportunity to inform you that from this day forward we will not work in your hacienda because constitutional laws and other legal mechanisms protect us.

In assemblies and in discussions with landowners and police, peasants sometimes expressed their goals more crudely, as seen in a letter from landowner Gregorio Velásquez to the Pitumarca subprefect:

> With great cynicism the invaders have told me that they are taking over all "misti" goods and that they will go to civil war if necessary, and addressing my pleas, as if they were the owners of the invaded land, have designated a small fraction of pasture land so I can keep my livestock for a few days.[21]

Peasants from communities with access to the market and productive specialization were better informed about national politics and more inclined to seek social change. Peasants on haciendas, on the other hand, had trouble believing that hierarchies and society might change, that misti power could be challenged. When they came to accept these ideas, however, they were not satisfied with limited demands and even surpassed those of comuneros.[22]

[20] Ibid., 46.

[21] Francisco Durand provided me a photocopy of these documents.

[22] I base these reflections on the important study by Julio Cotler, "Haciendas y comunidades tradicionales en un contexto de movilización política," *Estudios Andinos* (Lima), 1 (1970), 127–48.

Researchers Virginia Vargas and Virginia Guzmán identified 413 movements reported in Lima newspapers from 1956 to 1964. Pedro Gibaja concluded that in 249 of those movements, the principal objective was land; only 58 targeted salaries, and 106 addressed diverse issues such as freeing leaders from jail, establishing schools, and protesting repressive measures.[23] Protagonists came from Indian communities in 222 movements (54 percent), which helps explain why the mobilization of choice was land occupation in 215 cases (52 percent). For landowners, these actions were "invasions," but peasants saw them as "recoveries." More recently, others referred to them as "seizures" ("*tomas*"). Historian Eric Hobsbawm identified three types of land that peasants occupied: vacant land on fringe agriculture areas such as the high jungle; land in litigation with previous legal battles or doubts over boundaries; and land with a known owner, in which case seizure represented a serious challenge to private property. The most frequent were the second type, which reaffirmed the importance of legal tactics in these struggles.[24]

Organizers planned and discussed occupations in advance through massive assemblies. They began at dawn when long columns of peasants – men and women, children and elderly, carrying flags, accompanied by drums, bugles, and conch shells (*pututos*), shouting encouragement in Quechua – cut wires or broke property boundaries, entered haciendas, and occupied land belonging to them. Peasants did not carry weapons. The threat of "civil war" notwithstanding, they did not seek to physically confront mistis. They respected hacienda houses and were tolerant toward hacendados, even allowing them to keep livestock and giving them grazing areas, as seen earlier in the Velásquez case.[25]

Unions were the organizing structure for colonos' uprisings, which were probably more numerous than Lima newspapers reported. Between 1945 and 1947, 16 percent of new unions formed in the countryside; between 1956 and 1961, the percentage was relatively unchanged at 14 percent. However, between 1962 and 1968, the percentage grew to 20 percent and served as the platform for the 1963–64 peasant mobilization. Besides traditional external attacks on haciendas, internal

[23] Gibaja, "Los movimientos campesinos," 833.

[24] Eric Hobsbawm, "Peasant Land Occupations," *Past and Present* (London), 62 (1974), 120–52.

[25] For a description, see Hugo Neira, *Los Andes: tierra o muerte* (Madrid: Editorial, ZYX, 1972).

pressure grew from colonos who appropriated their own parcels. Possession became property.

How did peasant unionization and the recovery of land change Andean agrarian structure? One of the most visible results was the growth of peasant small property. As Hobsbawm argued,

> There is good evidence that some time between June 1963 and February or March 1964 the bulk of the state owners and lords in the central and southern highlands decided to cut their losses, faced with a general peasant mobilization and began to liquidate their assets and think in terms of compensation for expropriation under some sort of agrarian reform.[26]

Handelman signaled that 75 percent or more of families who in 1965 benefited from agrarian reform under Belaúnde's first government obtained land through occupation. During those years, Chiquián and Puquio landowners abandoned their properties, selling or taking with them what they could. The Andean countryside was decapitalized.

Agrarian agitation forced many Andean landowners to parcel out haciendas or sell them entirely. This particularly affected traditional haciendas and, to a lesser degree, large livestock ranches. The deterioration of traditional haciendas was already under way and weakened their ability to resist the peasant "avalanche." Observers called parcellation "private agrarian reform," and some newspapers advocated it to appease peasant struggles. This type of reform appeared in diverse regions. According to *La Prensa*, in 1961 the owner of a Cajamarca hacienda divided his property into lots; a short time later another newspaper announced parcellation of 8,575 acres in Chancay, 2,226 in Ate-Rímac, 5,609 in Huaura, 2,224 in Chillón, 652 in Lurín, 1,483 in Huarmey, and 8,659 in Casma. By the end of 1963, a Trujillo hacendado announced the sale of 17,297 acres for agrarian reform.[27]

The Catholic Church and religious orders undertook perhaps the most significant sell-off in Andean places as diverse as Cajamarca and Cuzco. In 1963 in Cuzco, Monseñor Carlos Jurgens ordered "the parcellation of all rural lands of our archdiocese, which will be allocated to peasant families under favorable economic conditions to be determined

[26] Eric Hobsbawm, "Peasants and Politics," *Journal of Peasant Studies* 1:1 (1973), 3–22, quote from 11–12.

[27] *La Prensa* (Lima), October 15, 1961; *El Comercio* (Lima), October 13, 1961; *La Crónica* (Lima), October 15, 1963.

Table 9.1. *Type of Ownership among Minifundista Farmers (in Thousands of Acres)*

	1961	%	1972	%
Owner	677	65.4	927	68.4
Renter	114	11.0	55	4.1
Feudatario (sharecropper)	66	6.4	70	5.2
Comunero	55	5.3	72	5.3
Other forms	35	3.4	11	0.8
Mixed forms	88	8.5	220	16.2
Total (thousands of acres)	1,035	100.0	1,355	100.0

Source: Oscar Dancourt, "Aspectos económicos de la lucha campesina (1957–1964)," typescript, Programa de Ciencias Sociales, Pontificia Universidad Católica del Perú (Lima, n.d.)

later." Church lands, whose extension at the beginning of the twentieth century surprised Cuzco indigenista writer Luis E. Valcárcel, dwindled to 1,394 parcels in 1972 covering 2,807 acres, that is, about two acres per parcel.[28] This program, clearly triggered by peasant mobilization, allowed the Church to avoid conflict with peasants. The Church severed ties with landed property and stripped hacendados and latifundistas of political and ideological support. It is also important to recognize the impact of encyclicals (such as the 1891 *Rerum novarum*). If not particularly progressive in Europe at that time, the diffusion of supposedly equitable capitalism was subversive in the Andes. It recommended "fair" salaries, the very mention of which was potentially explosive in areas where landowners paid no salary. What's more, peasant struggles forced many provincial priests to rethink the Church's social positions. To that point it had served landowners, but could it continue doing so? That question partly explains the progressive nature of the Church in the southern Andes since the 1960s.

Along with parcellations, another parallel process was the increase in the number of lots within haciendas. Hacendados in Silque-Ollantaytambo claimed that in the 1960s, shepherds refused to descend to haciendas, a *de facto* appropriation of attached lands used for usufruct farming. A consequence of land division was the increase in the *minifundio*, a sign of peasant economic growth. Table 9.1 shows an increase in minifundista farmers (peasants who owned fewer than 12 acres). It is interesting to note changes that took place within minifundistas. As the number of *arrendatarios* (renters) and *feudatarios* (sharecroppers) decreased, the number of comuneros remained stable, and owners and

[28] Asunción Marco supplied these references.

mixed ownership increased. Among other things, leased land became owned land.

The acquisition of "new lands" does not explain the expansion of peasant economies between 1961 and 1972. Minifundistas did not expand agricultural borders, which remained virtually stationary. Dancourt argued that peasants acquired land through the retreat of the landowner economy due to "the generalized peasant uprising that developed between 1957 and 1964." Landowner retreat was one of the most important outcomes of peasant battles.

What did landowners do when faced with land occupation and agrarian unionism? Better yet, what could they do? The answer: very little. The reason: They lost power.[29] Landowner debilitation was reflected in the "relative tolerance" of the state, including police forces, toward land occupation. Let's look at two scenarios from the conflict between the Cerro de Pasco Corporation and the communities. First, in September 1960 the Urahuchuc community "invaded" lands on Quilla, a hacienda the Corporation owned. The invasion was the dénouement of litigation between community and company that began in July 1957 and resulted in a ruling against comuneros both by the Superior Court of Junín and the Supreme Court of Lima. With a "rebellious attitude against the Supreme Court ruling," however, comuneros occupied the disputed land on September 7–8, 1960. The company turned to the Junín prefect, who recommended following determined legal proceedings. Company officials, however, demanded compliance with the judicial ruling, which meant ordering action against peasants. The prefect claimed he lacked the necessary authorization. The Cerro de Pasco Corporation had little choice but to take its fight to the highest levels of the state in Lima, which produced a favorable outcome for the company. A document from Cerro archives stated that on September 19, the company "insisted again by telephone that the prefect take action because Urahuchuc, emboldened by the passive attitude of the authorities, was completing a larger invasion. Officials responded that they had instructions from the Director of Government to complete an investigation to verify if our claims were true." In Lima, the company tried unsuccessfully to speak with the Director and Minister of Government before managing to talk with other officials, who remained noncommittal or acknowledged only that they were investigating.[30]

[29] Martínez Alier, *Los huacchilleros del Perú.*

[30] *Archivo del Fuero Agrario* (Lima), Cerro de Pasco document, report by Guillermo Rosas, La Oroya, September 20,1960.

In the version of events presented by the Cerro official, even the office of the Minister of Economy, Pedro Beltrán, dragged its feet on the company's request. The prefect, traditionally a position at the beck and call of hacendados, also chose not to act. This response would have been unimaginable a few years earlier. The local and national political power of the company was gravely weakened. And if this occurred with one of the three largest mining companies in the country, it must have happened with hacendados as well. On the other hand, it is interesting to observe how official hesitancy opened new possibilities for the "invaders." In the first months of the Belaúnde government (1963), state tolerance was even greater.

For that reason, land occupations could be democratically and openly debated. This helps us understand the pacifism that characterized occupations. Organizers announced them in advance, and frequently police attended as spectators. That is precisely how the Vilca community's "invasion" of the hacienda Cochas, which also belonged to the Cerro de Pasco Company, happened in 1963. The administrator wrote in an internal memorandum:

> [L]ikewise on November 15 lieutenant Pedro Heredia, accompanied by ten civil guards, arrived to try to contain the invasion, with the detachment remaining on the Pachachaca bridge with the idea of halting the invasion. On November 16, in front of the whole civil guard, the community of Vilca began to invade, passing just a few meters away from the troops, with all of them conversing with the invaders.[31]

Similar events occurred in other Andean places. Policemen and "invaders" took their positions and nothing more happened, much to the exasperation of landowners. These scenes encouraged other potential "invaders." Andean history offers multiple examples of brutal violence against peasants. So what changed? What stopped the state from deploying repressive forces in the service of latifundistas? Three developments were essential: (1) the weakening of landowners and the various forms of local and national power they previously exercised, due to capitalist development, the appearance of new groups within the dominant class such as an industrial sector, the expansion of the internal market, and the increase in state apparatuses; (2) the decline of agriculture's

[31] *Archivo del Fuero Agrario* (Lima), Cerro de Pasco document, F. Isaacs, July 1, 1964.

participation in Peruvian gross domestic product resulting from industrialization and urban growth; and (3) the fact that landowners were no longer indispensable allies to the state and even became a liability, given their role in perpetuating backwardness and creating social tension.

Faced with peasant agitation, the Peruvian ruling class had the unprecedented foresight to make concessions in areas that were not vital to its reproduction as a class. General repression against peasants only occurred when hacendado demands peaked. On the other hand, "invasions" threatened to go beyond the rural milieu and in fact already represented a challenge to the very notion of private property. In 1964, when the executive branch decided to use violence in the countryside at parliament's behest, peasants in some places already had met some objectives such as land acquisition.

The following year, as peasant agitation halted, the Movimiento de Izquierda Revolucionaria (MIR, Leftist Revolutionary Movement) and the Ejército de Liberación Nacional (ELN, National Liberation Army) attempted to organize guerrillas in Cajamarca, Junín, Ayacucho, and Cuzco, with the first of them prematurely dismantled. What began in June 1965 ended tragically at year's end when the army found, surrounded, and annihilated those guerrilla columns. The military shot and killed guerrilla leaders such as Máximo Velando, Guillermo Lobatón, and Luis de la Puente and threw their bodies from helicopters. Those leaders were unable to blend in with the Andean population – winning peasant confidence required patience – and weapons arrived late. That in part explained why political organizations failed to connect with peasant movements.

If peasant rebellion did not eliminate mistis, it took a steep toll. In many places, the old masters had to leave their haciendas, migrate to Lima, and enter urban commerce. The 1969 Agrarian Reform law, substantially more radical than the one Belaúnde's first administration enacted in 1963, finished the job.[32] Private ownership of land was no longer the means of support for local power. Gamonales faded into the past. However, new agrarian reform did not empower peasants; instead, it attempted to replace the deteriorated power of hacendados with that of state officials, blocking any possibility of autonomous peasant mobilization. This statist project did not always succeed, particularly in the most

[32] Decree 17716, issued by the nationalist military junta that came to power October 3, 1968 [Editors' note].

backward and depressed Andean areas where land reform arrived much later than on the coast. Moreover, the entrepreneurial model of reform promoted large estates. Haciendas had to maintain or expand their size by annexing land or acquiring communal properties in litigation. Ownership changed, but property structure did not. Those who traditionally fought haciendas – the comuneros – were not the biggest beneficiaries. Unequal land distribution continued despite peasant movements that were still active in 1969. The disappearance of landowners, therefore, did not necessarily lead to a substantial change for peasants and generated a "power vacuum" in the countryside. Narcotraffickers, local merchants, small landowners who managed to escape agrarian reform, and state officials attempted to fill the void in some places. In 1980, economic backwardness and the power vacuum created conditions for the public emergence of a little-known group from the heterogeneous Peruvian left whose name quickly achieved messianic resonances: the Shining Path (Sendero Luminoso).

We must examine the Shining Path within the context of the limits and possibilities of the 1960s peasant movements and particularly the question of power. These issues reappeared in 1974 in the southern province of Andahuaylas, where under the direct influence of Marxist parties such as Vanguardia Revolucionaria (Revolutionary Vanguard), land occupations ignited conflict between peasants and the military government. Movement leaders were sons of mistis or urban middle-class families, such as Lino Quintanilla and Julio César Mezzich, who were willing to carry on the "march to the people" that other young people from their generation merely talked about. They established themselves in Andahuaylas, learned Quechua if necessary, married peasants, and became comuneros. With the exception of Blanco and a few others, such figures had been scarce in 1964. But a decade later they faced the same problem: Even if occupations were successful and peasants acquired the land they demanded, did this change power relations in the countryside? Would mistis no longer scorn Indians? The challenge was to initiate a "long march" from the most backward area of the country to take power. Not everyone framed the problem in those terms. For the majority of the left, the political horizon did not transcend the most immediate demands such as land acquisition, a signed agreement with state authorities, and then a new slogan. Leftist groups were accustomed to denunciation and organizing stoppages and strikes, but were incapable of imagining an enduring offensive and an assault on power. The left grew in number of militants and sympathy during the military regime (1968–80), but miners' marches on Lima, local demands, and national work stoppages did not offer a valid alternative to military rule. Ultimately, the only alternative was to support a project that emerged from within bourgeois sectors: the call for elections and the formation of a Constituent Assembly.[33] The most "ultra" and "radical" hardliners refused to participate, however, in what can be interpreted as a display of *voluntarismo*. Whether they realized it or not, they represented a sector of the population absent from electoral processes. People who left their ballots blank or did not vote made up 35 percent of the electorate in 1980.[34] Within those numbers lurked the Shining Path's clandestine militants, plotting a different project.

The possibility of a revolutionary project understood as an inversion of the world began to circulate again in 1974 in Andahuaylas. We find that sentiment not in fliers, agreements signed by political leaders and authorities, or even accounts by the protagonists themselves. Rather, we must listen to *huaynos* of the period, sprinkled with violence and rage, expressing a desire to end servitude and personal dependency: "[I]t doesn't matter that you are someone/whom I love,/it doesn't matter that you are someone/whom I am courting. Even if you call me brother!/I will throw you in the river/I will push you into the abyss!"[35] Years later, in 1979, children from a barrio of the old hacienda Toxama in Ayacucho brought together violence and hope in the harsh words of another huayno:

> We have lost much time going around in circles/but it won't last forever, peasant brother/in the town of Manchaybamba/rich and poor will confront one another/and among all the poor/we will make you spin around, we'll trap you/as if you were the thief fox./Just wait to see,/exploiter (murderer) of my people,/when I become a fox/I will make you die (I will kill you). When I am like the (big) fox /I will make you lose (I will reduce you) I will disappear you.[36]

33 Jorge Nieto, *Izquierda y democracia en el Perú* (Lima: Desco, 1983).

34 *Ausentismo electoral: tendencias* (Lima: Servicios Populares, 1985), 4.

35 Lino Quintanilla, *Andahuaylas: la lucha por la tierra* (Lima: Mosca Azul, 1981), 131. On Andahuaylas, see Abdón Palomino, "Andahuaylas, 1974: un movimiento de reivindicación campesina dentro del proceso de reforma agraria," *Allpanchis* (Cuzco) 11/12 (1978), 187–211, and Rodrigo Sánchez, *Toma de tierras y conciencia política campesina* (Lima: Instituto de Estudios Peruanos, 1981).

36 Diego García-Sayán, *Tomas de tierras en el Perú* (Lima: Desco, 1982), 272.

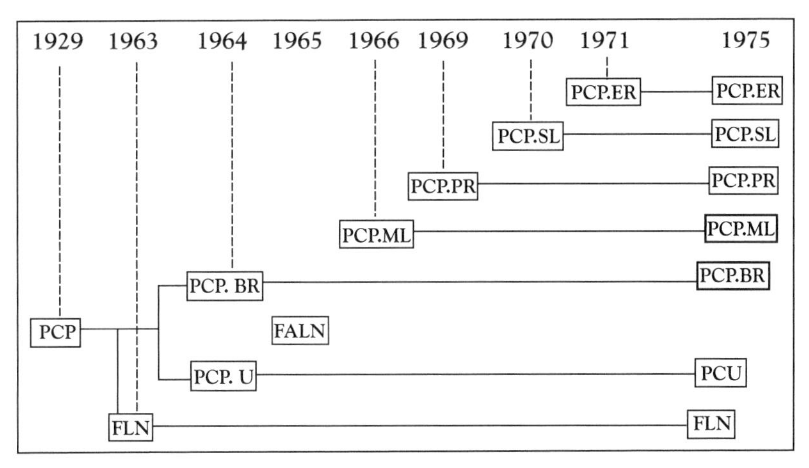

Figure 9.1. The Peruvian Communist Party and Its Divisions. *Source:* Ricardo Letts, *La izquierda peruana* (Lima: Mosca Azul Editores, 1981), 60.

Black and Red

In the 1978 elections for a Constituent Assembly that was meant to mediate the so-called transfer of power from military to civilian rule, the left received a surprising 28 percent of valid votes. The only important antecedent was the 15 percent that the coalition Unidad de Izquierda gained in Lima in 1967. Although leftist ranks had grown considerably, multiple ideological influences and debates dating in some cases to 1928 (the year José Carlos Mariátegui founded the Socialist Party) and in others to 1965 (the year the MIR guerrillas started) kept the Peruvian left heavily fragmented into at least twenty organizations. Ricardo Letts identified four "basic branches": the Communist Party, Revolutionary Vanguard, the MIR, and the FIR (Frente de Izquierda Revolucionaria).[37] According to Letts, Communist party fragmentation began in 1963 with the Sino-Soviet split, which spawned seven organizations within a decade (see Figure 9.1). The number of Maoist groups and militants was significant. In no other Latin American country did the Chinese revolution wield such influence. One of those parties adopted the slogan, "Following the Shining Path of José Carlos Mariátegui," as a subtitle for its publications.

It is not our purpose to write a history of the Peruvian left, and even less the development of Marxism in Peru. Shining Path proclaimed

[37] Ricardo Letts, *La izquierda peruana* (Lima: Mosca Azul Editores, 1981). [Editors' note].

itself a follower of Mariátegui thought, but although there are some similarities, there are many more differences. As seen in his debate with Víctor Raúl Haya de la Torre, Mariátegui did not accept the idea of an authoritarian project. Identified with the most rigid and dogmatic positions on the left, Shining Path characterized Peru as a semifeudal country in which hacendados and gamonales persisted as the main pillars of a bureaucratized state that was barely achieving, through military-implemented reforms, incipient and slow capitalist penetration. For Shining Path, the path to power required an armed struggle from the countryside to the cities. Perhaps for that reason its militancy concentrated in one of the most backward departments in the country, Ayacucho, which seemed to confirm earlier theories. The majority of the population were peasants; the capital, Huamanga, had no more than 60,000 people and lacked industry and large-scale commerce; artisans predominated; exchange still relied heavily on muleteers; and bartering was not unusual in a cultural environment where Quechua effectively resisted Spanish. However, it had a large university with more than 6,000 students, not including the 2,000 applicants and 1,000 incoming students in 1980. The San Cristóbal National University in Huamanga enjoyed an exceptional faculty that included foreign scholars the caliber of Tom Zuidema, John Earls, Billie Jean Isbell, Jürgen Golte, and Jan Szeminski and Peruvians such as Marco Martos, Antonio Cisneros, Luis Lumbreras, Carlos Iván Degregori, and Jaime Urrutia, who joined intellectuals such as Efraín Morote Best, an exceptional scholar of Andean folklore. An explosive contrast developed between the expansion of the intellectual horizon and economic backwardness. The university weakened the influence of the Ayacucho clergy. For the lower classes, poverty was no longer natural or acceptable; among the well-to-do, a rebellious and moral indignation emerged in the face of poverty. Years later Morote Best's response to an incisive question about Shining Path violence reflected this state of mind:

> [O]bserve the orgy of corruption that saturates the country, the feast that bloats some and the famine that destroys others; talk with people who go about on foot; observe those on horseback. Listen, but don't just hear; observe, but don't just look. That way you will surely find an explanation for the violence in the same way I explain it to myself. And if you do not want present-day explanations, reread the Gospel of Matthew 21:12–13 and you

> will find the millenarian explanation of an anger that many men around the world consider saintly.[38]

Huamanga professors and students were interested in local reality in a way other universities were not. They traveled, visited estancias and communities, and conducted field work. Numerous theses examined Pampas River communities. The dominant attitude was clearly visible in Antonio Díaz Martínez's 1969 book, *Ayacucho: hambre y esperanza* (*Ayacucho: Hunger and Hope*).[39] This was a peculiar mix of travelogue (notes on a professor's trips with his students), essay, and sociological analysis – a "pilgrimage in search of wisdom," as the author confessed – that at times asked specific questions: "Corrugated asbestos sheeting, cement, and iron contrast with the cold and sober beauty of the upper highlands. Are adobe, ichu [grass], tile, stone, and mud not good materials for an architectural style that, at once beautiful and functional, could also preserve the most characteristic native features?"[40] On other occasions he clung to answers rooted only in personal conviction:

> Might one day the native communities and the true owners of these lands have possession again? They could. Might they find the biological-emotional equilibrium they had in the past? They could go even beyond that. Might they escape the mechanistic and utilitarian Western culture that colonizes them day after day? They will be creators of their own destiny. Will the selfish thesis of population control conceived by Vogh, P. Moussa, and other neo-Malthusians triumph? They will erase all the principles of class society.[41]

From one of the most backward spaces in Peru emerged the possibility of changing world history. When China's political orientation changed, the problem was not just to destroy class society in Peru, but rather to change the world: "To the men of today, to the men who breathe, struggle, fight, to them has fallen the responsibility of eliminating all reactionaries from the face of the earth, the most illustrious and grandiose

[38] "Cómo se encendió la mecha," Gustavo Gorriti's interview with Efraín Morote Best in *Caretas* (Lima), 733 (January 31, 1983).

[39] Antonio Díaz Martínez, *Ayacucho: hambre y esperanza* (Ayacucho: Ediciones Waman Puma, 1969). The author would die in the massacre perpetrated against Shining Path inmates in the Lurigancho prison on June 18, 1986.

[40] Ibid., 40.

[41] Ibid., 117–19.

mission ever assigned to any generation."[42] The ideology of "Gonzalo," the nickname of their leader Abimael Guzmán, would guide them. Perhaps these ideas sound less absurd if we consider that they sprang from what was once the center of a great pre-Hispanic empire. Fifteen miles from Huamanga was Huari, the capital of a realm by the same name between the seventh and eleventh centuries A.D., the first Andean state formation whose territory extended from the Bolivian altiplano to the central Peruvian coast. Once this empire disappeared, the ethnic group Chancas took its place, establishing itself on both sides of the Pampas River. Centuries later the Incas came to dominate the sierra only after defeating them. That was when the Incas moved mitimaes to the Pampas region. Once the colonial order was established, the Spanish used Huamanga as an intermediate point between Lima and Cuzco and a stronghold against Inca incursions from Vilcabamba. The construction of thirty-three temples and the establishment of convents and monasteries bolstered the religious importance of the city. Commerce, mining in Castrovirreyna and Huancavelica, and above all land ownership supported the population. Hacendado lineages were formed and acquired special prestige with the founding of Peru's second university in their city.[43]

The Republic ushered in what now appears to be the permanent decline of Huamanga and the region. Various transverse routes uniting cities and raw-material centers with ocean ports supplanted the traditional longitudinal route that crossed the Andes from the Mantaro Valley toward Cuzco and Upper Peru. This created the central circuit that linked Huancayo with Callao, the southern circuit that connected Arequipa with Puno and Cuzco, and minor routes such as the Loma, Puquio, and Chalhuanca axis. In many places this spatial reorganization was synonymous with commercial agriculture, urbanization, and monetary circulation. For Ayacucho, as Carlos Iván Degregori has argued,

[42] Abimael Guzmán, "Somos los iniciadores." Speech before the members of Shining Path's "1st Military Academy" (April 19, 1980). http://www.blythe.org/peru-pcp/docs_sp/iniciad.htm. The change in China that Flores Galindo refers to was the ascension to power of Deng Xiaoping, widely interpreted as a move against the most radical versions of Maoism represented by the so-called Gang of Four. The Shining Path of Peru was aligned with the latter [Editors' note].

[43] Carlos Iván Degregori, *Sendero Luminoso: los hondos y mortales desencuentros* (Lima: Instituto de Estudios Peruanos, 1985); Manuel Granados, "La conducta política. Un caso particular," MA thesis, Universidad Nacional San Cristóbal de Huamanga, 1981.

this process represented the amputation of Huamanga-controlled territories such as Puquio, as well as the onset of neglect and isolation. It reduced the region primarily to the provinces of Huamanga, La Mar, Huanta, Víctor Fajardo, and Cangallo. Capitalism signified poverty and backwardness in a region with no roads or electricity – a fragile generator illuminated the city until only a short time ago – and decreasing resources. Many saw Shining Path as a regional movement and a defensive reaction against capitalist modernity.[44] The fact that important Shining Path leaders came from the impoverished provincial aristocracy and that the group localized its actions in the Ayacucho countryside reinforced this perception.

Armed conflict began May 17, 1980, when members of the Shining Path seized Chuschi and symbolically burned ballot boxes.[45] Until that moment the town, located about seventy-five miles from Ayacucho, was unknown in Peruvian political geography. In 1961 its 1,000 or so inhabitants subsisted in poverty; only a few anthropologists had visited it. Few knew that during the colonial period Chuschi was the governmental seat for seven communities and, as in other Pampa River towns, a region where vertical ecology, dual organization of space, compadrazgo (fictive kinship), and reciprocity persisted.[46] Shining Path actions accelerated between 1980 and 1984. According to official statistics, it committed 219 "attacks" in 1980, 715 in 1981, 891 in 1982, 1,123 in 1983, and 1,760 in 1984. A mapping of those attacks demonstrates that Shining Path was not a strictly regional phenomenon. What was the nature of these "attacks"? In 1980 and early 1981, Shining Path blocked highways, assaulted estates and mines, destroyed tractors, attacked stores and warehouses, set off explosions, severed railway lines and bridges, and above all, blew up electrical towers that caused the infamous "blackouts" (*apagones*) in Huamanga, Lima, and the whole central region. Immediately following a blackout, Shining Path carried out other actions, some symbolic, such as the illumination of San Cristóbal – a hill that presides over Lima and remains a religious pilgrimage destination – with torches representing the hammer and sickle. Other actions included the

44 Degregori, *Sendero Luminoso*, 26.

45 The first presidential election in Peru since 1963 was scheduled for the next day, May 18, 1980. [Editors' note].

46 Billie Jean Isbell, "Parentesco andino y reciprocidad. Kuyaq: los que nos aman," in Enrique Mayer and Giorgio Alberti eds., *Reciprocidad e intercambio en los Andes peruanos* (Lima: Instituto de Estudios Peruanos, 1974), 111–12.

unfurling of red flags on streets, public buildings, and towers. In those early months Shining Path surprised and disconcerted observers because it destroyed but did not kill. It was a bloodless guerrilla war.

Shining Path was like a lightning bolt across a clear sky. There is no better image for a movement that appeared just when most of the left was choosing an electoral path and accepting the minimum rules of the "democratic game," when sociologists and economists were presenting the image of an increasingly modern country with irreversible urbanization, a nearly extinct peasantry, and salaried or semiproletarian popular classes. It seemed the "Andean" was disappearing amid "depeasantization." If a revolutionary movement ever broke out in Peru, it was expected to occur in new cities. The rural guerrilla was unimaginable in a country in which peasants were abandoning the countryside and where steep and uncultivated landscape offered no hiding places. When Shining Path militants spoke of armed conflict, opponents lightly and even sarcastically dismissed it. It became the topic of debates in San Marcos and San Cristóbal de Huamanga university classrooms. And on top of that, where would they get weapons?

The use of dynamite in the construction of highways, tunnels, and bridges as well as mining made it a logical weapon for insurgents. It could be used to prepare bombs and hurled with the *huaraca*, the traditional sling that all Andean children know how to use. The first dynamite attacks seemed to reveal a group willing to demolish, to destroy any symbol of modernization. Some observers recalled Luddites and anarchists in the early stages of the European labor movement; others evoked traditional revolutions against everything western and modern. The political right and the government did not resort to nuanced interpretation: these were "terrorists," a soulless new species that spread like a plague throughout the world, inspired by "Marxist" and "totalitarian" ideologies, and willing to take power using crime and assassination. This discourse was in place even before Shining Path's first victim. The Belaúnde administration did not care to understand guerrillas and their motivation, only to eliminate them.[47]

Understanding their mindset was difficult. The movement did not claim responsibility for its actions, did not use propaganda, jealously guarded leader anonymity, did not produce books, fliers, or manifestos, and did not present a political program. Anthropologist Juan Ansión

[47] Fernando Belaúnde Terry's second administration began in July 1980 [Editors' note].

argued that this peculiar style paradoxically spoke volumes: because Shining Path "considered itself representative of a world stripped of speech, the only thing left is action."[48] This silence seemed to draw the Shining Path close to the marginalized and excluded Andean majority who, since the sixteenth century, had been deprived of its right to speak.

In the few available Shining Path texts, one would expect to find orthodox Maoist discourse, like that of other leftist organizations before 1980 that even reproduced Chinese metaphors. In effect, Shining Path's prediction of a great fire in the Andes, similar to the one that spread from Yan'an across the Chinese plains, echoed that influence. At the same time it was trying to locate the struggle (of which they considered themselves the "initiators") within Peruvian historical tradition, recalling peasant rebellions and evoking Juan Santos Atahualpa, Tupac Amaru, and even heroes they considered bourgeois such as Admiral Miguel Grau and Francisco Bolognesi, martyrs in the war with Chile (1879–83). Documents such as "We are the Initiators" (April 1980) articulated a history that was to unfold in clearly defined and opposite stages. One narrative subsumed them: a long past that preceded armed conflict, and a new era inaugurated under the Marxist guidance of Comrade Gonzalo, who was comparable, in their view, to Marx, Lenin, and Mao. Darkness versus light, black versus red: those were the images we saw in one of the few known Shining Path fliers. The black area was subdivided into two parts: on the left, images of inmates and the prison; the right side contained two sections, with guerrillas in Andean clothing on top and army and police forces committing massacres and ripping bodies apart at the bottom. There were no divisions of the red area, just one image centered around a rising red sun, fluttering flags, and a crowd carrying signs celebrating the Communist Party of Peru, Shining Path's official name. Ansión suggested that such fliers reflected Andean thought structure: Dualism reemerged and fused with political discourse. He does not offer a value judgment but simply believes he is verifying a natural phenomenon: because the Shining Path came from Andean territories, they offered a peculiar reading of Marxism. They did not see revolution as Marx or Lenin envisioned it, but rather as synonymous with Pachacuti: "[E]verything inverts, that which was above is below and that below, above; the night becomes day and day, night;

[48] Juan Ansión, "¿Es luminoso el camino de Sendero?," *El Caballo Rojo* (Lima) 3 (June 6,1982), 108.

men turn into stone but also from stones comes a new generation."[49] Destroying towers, darkening cities, and illuminating the nearby hill with torches announced a shining, hopeful future born amid prevailing darkness, misery, and exploitation.[50] It was old against new, a world turned upside down. The anonymous faces on the pamphlet's red side would recover their country and sweep away exploiters.

However, a discourse that furthered pre-Hispanic concepts was not uniquely Andean. Dualism was present in deeply rooted Christian images in the Andes as seen in the Apocalypse and final judgment. Among the precursors of that discourse was Gabriel Aguilar, whose image of Peru evoked that in the stories of Arguedas.[51] That dualism appeared to directly inspire metaphors in Shining Path documents: "[T]he besieger will be besieged, the would-be annihilators will be annihilated, and the would-be victors will be defeated." It evoked not only Arguedas's references to the Spanish conquest and the western offensive against the Andean world, but inevitably the Apocalypse: "[A]nd finally the beast will be corralled, and as we have learned, the thundering of our armed voices will make them tremble in fear."[52] Rodrigo Montoya argued that Shining Path struck a chord in one aspect of Peruvian reality, namely, the resentment harbored by a majority scorned for the color of its skin, its poor use of Spanish, its way of dressing, its poverty: "[I]t incarnates Andean anger against old and secular oppression."[53] But that anger, more than reflecting peasants themselves, captured the deferred and many times silenced rage of mestizo intellectuals. Arguedas was one of them. Rage was the other side of racism.

Shining Path militants, that is, the mid-level leaders, were not exactly illiterate. Many prisoners accused of terrorism were college educated (38.5 percent) or high school graduates (37.7 percent); a few only

[49] Ibid.

[50] Juan Ansión, "Essais sur le pensée andine et se reinterprétation actuelles dans la region d'Ayacucho (Pérou)," PhD dissertation, University of Louvain, 1984. See also Ansión, *Desde el rincón de los muertos*.

[51] Gabriel Aguilar was a mestizo accused of an anti-colonial conspiracy and executed in 1805. His dreams were the subject of a chapter, "Los sueños de Gabriel Aguilar" ("Gabriel Aguilar's Dreams") included in the original Spanish edition of this book and left out in this English translation [Editors' note].

[52] Guzmán, "Somos los iniciadores."

[53] Rodrigo Montoya, "Izquierda Unida y Sendero: potencialidad y límites," *Sociedad y Política* (Lima) 13 (August 1983), 35.

attended early grade school (17.5 percent) and even fewer had no education (6.3 percent).[54] However, we must handle these figures with care. While inequalities in income distribution have grown in Peru, the democratization of education has made access to schools and universities possible for children of peasants, small merchants, and artisans. These students make up the majority of Andean young people, a group westernized by education and migration. They are the contingents of new mestizos, frustrated participants in a history dating to the Spanish conquest. The similarities between mestizo young people of today and Garcilaso in the sixteenth century are obvious; in both cases they appeared "deprived of everything," forced into "vagrancy" and "depredation," condemned to become "men with destroyed lives," those who in the 1560s were protagonists of "rebellions" without hope.[55]

But Shining Path militancy was not reduced to groups from the impoverished provincial aristocracy or frustrated mestizos; these people encountered others coming directly from the peasant world, such as Huamanga comuneros from the banks of the Pampas River. Unlike the 1965 guerrillas, the 1980 combatants were not alienated from the rural world, where they were born, had relatives, and learned Quechua. For that reason they successfully recruited peasants, although they also resorted to forced enlistment. From the beginning, Shining Path was a vertical and authoritarian organization convinced it was delivering a message that all should follow. Messianism is authoritarian: you take it or leave it. There is no in between. But in the majority of cases, especially early in their struggle, recruitment appeared voluntary. To those enlisted, Shining Path did not offer highways, food, and schools but rather something more ethereal that paradoxically justified the greatest sacrifices: all power. To the poorest (the favorite recruits) and most disenfranchised belonged a shining future.

Upheaval had struck the Ayacucho region. Some peasants believed that Pachamama refused to tolerate any more earthly suffering and that the world had to change. Entire towns unfurled the red flag and turned "Shining," willing to march to Huamanga or Lima, not to beg but to expel the exploiters and establish a new order. They attacked police posts. In some cases police hunkered down and patrolled only the urban perimeter during daylight hours. Jesús Saldaña, the only priest in the region, told a *Caretas* reporter in Pampa Cangallo: "[A]t night the

[54] *El Comercio* (Lima), April 7, 1985.
[55] No citations provided in the original [Editors' note].

children of the shadows come out. At night they mobilize and during the day they are camouflaged in the hills." Saldaña was forced to move from one place to another, but did not spend nights among policemen out of fear of being labeled an "informant" ("*soplón*").[56] The priest symbolized a church that had abandoned the countryside. The stage on which Shining Path imposed itself was the small village with no gamonal, its temple in ruins, and its police post demolished, all the trappings of a power vacuum. Beginning in 1982 "red zones" appeared, communities where Shining Path forces found shelter and protection. With spreading fear came concerns that departmental capitals would end up surrounded, under siege, and condemned to hunger. The Shining Path ordered peasants to sow and harvest only the most basic foodstuffs. The idea was to sever ties with the market and plunge cities into certain and prolonged agony.

Shining Path appeared to fulfill the hope that pulsed through Arguedas's stories, to transform anger and individual bitterness into collective hate or a great fire. The *terrucos* – as the terrorists were called in the region – at first destroyed only goods and property. In 1980, political violence in the whole country caused just three deaths. In 1981, eleven more died, including six policemen. But the following year deaths spiked to 151, including 65 civilians and 47 *Senderistas*. What happened? The declaration of a state of emergency in several provinces, intervention by police special units, and Shining Path violence against rustlers, usurers, and local authorities increased violence. Shining Path threatened, publicly tried, and whipped or executed offenders. It sought to maintain an iron grip on territories it liberated, and it tolerated no dissent. There were reports of particularly cruel acts, but they appeared, in the early stages of the insurrection, more spontaneous than planned, including two of the first civilian deaths attributed to the Shining Path in the Ayacucho region. During an assault on a Cangallo hacienda on December 24, 1980, "The peasants, motivated by revenge, first blindfolded their victims and then with a razor blade cut the ears off the farmer and owner of the hacienda house, Benigno Medina del Carpio, who then was beaten to death along with Ricardo Lizarbe."[57] During land seizures in 1974 in Andahuaylas, leaders wishing to avoid confrontation with the state prevented such violent acts. But convinced of the necessity

56 *Caretas* (Lima) 774 (April 18, 1983), 14.

57 Piedad Pareja, *Terrorismo y sindicalismo en Ayacucho* (Lima: Imprenta Ital Perú, 1981), 94.

of a "great peasant hurricane," Shining Path did not attempt to control excesses. It appeared unconcerned about the social costs of war. The revolution – like pachacuti or Apocalypse – carries with it weeping, pain, suffering, and death. The old had to be destroyed to make room for the new. Terror as an instrument in political struggle stood out. In 1982, the year Shining Path organized the largest popular Ayacucho mobilization ever during the funeral of guerrilla militant Edith Lagos, the group attacked Huamanga's mayor and killed an anthropologist, the director of the local branch of the National Culture Institute. Such acts found no approval in the city.

Confronted with one of the most corrupt governments in our republican history, with Aprismo in crisis and the left in check, Shining Path was at its peak in 1982. Marxism expressed itself with a Quechua accent, as in the time of Hugo Blanco and agrarian unionism, but now there was guerrilla warfare, not confined to one valley but spread throughout a country plunged into devastating economic crisis. Shining Path threatened ten of Peru's twenty-four departments. The movement offered power to the poorest in the countryside. But how many were willing to follow? Not all Andean communities were like Chuschi. Backward towns where llama herders (*wamani*) and folk healers (curanderos) ruled and reciprocity persisted might reject western civilization and progress. But comuneros such as those from Huayopampa (Chancay), Muquiyauyo (Jauja), and Puquio (Lucanas) had access to modernity and opted for western schools, electric lights, highways, and trucks. For them progress was a palpable reality; power, only an illusion. They had something worth preserving.

Shining Path reminds us of characters, images, and projects from Arguedas's narratives. However, we must remember that as an anthropologist studying Mantaro Valley indigenous communities, Arguedas was enthused about mestizo peasants who displayed an entrepreneurial spirit and reconciled modernity with the Andean world. In the Mantaro Valley, capitalism and peasantry were not mutually exclusive. The Andean and western worlds did not conflict. Upon receiving the Inca Garcilaso de la Vega prize in 1968, Arguedas stated that "the currents of the two nations can and should unite."[58] Violence and hate would disappear. A comunero slogan might have been "let there be no anger" ("*que no haya rabia*"). But many aspects differentiated the Mantaro

[58] José María Arguedas, "No soy un aculturado," included in *El zorro de arriba y el zorro de abajo* (Madrid: ALLCA, 1996), 257. [Editors' note].

Valley from other Andean spaces – there was a free peasantry, not attached to the land, dating to colonial times; haciendas had not taken over communal property; mercantilism and commercial agriculture appeared early; muleteers traveled throughout the region, where there were commercial fairs; mining developed; and there was permanent articulation with Lima. Other regions remained outside the internal market and were synonymous with backwardness and deterioration, such as the Colca Valley in the south, the Pampas River in Ayacucho, and the Chaupiwaranga pass in the central sierra.

Appendix : Letter from Hugo Blanco to John Murra[59]

Lima, 10 February 1967

Dear John:[60]

Gordon just gave me a copy of the Iñigo Ortiz's *visita*.[61] I am pleased that my name appears in the first sentence. As you well know I am not given to self promotion, but as a human being with a heart I am happy to be in good company in documents we must not let disappear. It was exciting seeing the cover; I enjoyed browsing through the book. I read your presentation and a few pages more and realized that this document must be very important for historians and all those who attempt to study Peruvian people, but it saddened me to think I will only read it in fragments. For years I have had incurable reading fatigue, especially for documents like this that require a lot of time and are read only by those who provide us intellectual work. With this volume your bonds with Peru are strengthened and are more apparent. In fifteen days at the most Ávila will appear, and you well know that without you this book would not exist.[62] But none of this exempts you from the main obligation of affection that you have with us. It occurs to me that your

[59] Letter from José María Arguedas to John Murra. Archivo José María Arguedas, Editorial Horizonte. A few years ago, Sybila Arredondo, Arguedas's widow, authorized me to publish this letter in the journal *Allpanchis* (Cuzco) 17–18 (1981), 164–6.

[60] John Murra (1916–2006) was a renowned ethnohistorian and author of numerous books about the Andean world [Editors' note].

[61] Iñigo Ortiz de Zúñiga, *Visita de la provincia de León de Huánuco en 1562* (Huánuco: Universidad Nacional Hermilio Valdizán, 1967), ed. John V. Murra [Editors' note].

[62] José María Arguedas, *Dioses y hombres de Huarochirí* (Lima: Instituto de Estudios Peruanos, 1966) [Editors' note].

struggle against the inexplicable – or better yet, almost invincible – forces that make your hands stiff while writing your main work are like those I confront in trying to accept happiness, to find pleasure in that which, after enjoyment, the darkest materials of the subconscious transforms into a source of the most disturbing depression. I was terribly sick; fortunately Sybila is a wonderful woman. No one can imagine how she attends to and cleanses my soul, even when in my darker moments I see her at times as the cause of many of my anxieties. I am fighting fiercely. I miss you. I do not have a single friend who is suffering or who has suffered and can accompany me. My psychiatrist is a fat cholo who is in formidable health. He almost always tells me the same thing; he lacks subtlety and artfulness but he has faith in me.

I have been in Chimbote for fifteen days. It is almost exactly like Lima; it has something like forty shanty towns; seventy percent of the population is of Andean origin; the mass of highland immigrants is proportionally greater than Lima's and Chimbote does not have the traditional Creole aristocracy; that mass of people who still live separated from the coastal population, tries to assimilate to it by less painful channels than in Lima. I have worked feverishly for fifteen days, always believing that death was creeping up on me. However, except for Huancayo, never have I felt life's flow so powerfully. What a science ethnology is! I am intuitive, but I apprehend well what I have heard from people like you, and I sense problems, and before analyzing them I live them. Sybila was with me and the kids for eight days. We worked hard. I have recorded some interviews. Bravo is impressed with this material and has enthusiastically approved my continuation of the work.[63] I felt very guilty that the money was for folklore and I was doing an ethnological project. I am going to give you some bits and pieces:

> We have collected data on 3,645 fishermen and 3,840 industrial workers. I have conducted five interviews with men of Andean origin about their lives in Chimbote and before they arrived in this port. One of the subjects, Don Hilario Mamaní, the captain of a nearly 120-ton boat, was illiterate until age 30. Now he is a leader of sorts, very *sui generis*, married twice with women from the coast. They said it was not possible, that no one would get a recorded testimony of his life. I largely did it and it is a priceless document.

[63] Most likely Jorge Bravo Bresani, then a scholar at the Instituto de Estudios Peruanos [Editors' note].

I have formulated some hypotheses. In Chimbote there are no provincial clubs; the organization is the shanty towns. Coastal and highland inhabitants, despite active social and commercial exchange, still remain as differentiated strata; the *serranos* tend to assimilate (*acriollarse*) and do it without the difficulties of Lima because the social environment is much more accessible. The mass of serranos already acclimated are industrial workers and fishermen; new arrivals take jobs more directly related to the needs of the salaried masses: marketplace workers, porters, hotel servants, etc. But as the Chimbote myth continues to spread – the myth that it is the center of enrichment for the serrano (many have managed to lead a wasteful life) – the avalanche of serranos continues and there are people who live in the most horrific misery. In the end it opened unthinkable perspectives for a general ethnological report about Chimbote and provided materials for my novel. It will be called "Pez Grande" ("Big fish").[64] I am very encouraged even though insomnia weakens me.

As for the project on the fourth centennial of the *Visita* by Garci Díaz de San Miguel, I don't see it creating excitement to the point that we gain funding and support. Cueto himself removed from the budget the funds for the maintenance of the Convenio.[65] It was good in part because they have now included me in the budget of the university itself. I won't be constantly anxious over the possibility of unemployment, but on the other hand I will not have research funding. Of the S/. 250,000 from last year S/. 120,000 remains, which we will use this year to buy necessary furniture and to finance my stay for some five months in the sierra collecting myths, legends, stories, and general information, all of which we have talked about. What worries me now is how in the coming year I am going to find seven free months to write the novel. If I manage to get better I can write something on Chimbote and Supe that would end up like a strong liquor made of the substance of Peru's present scalding state, its ebullition, and the burning materials with which liquor is made. My best psychiatrist is Sybila, but I would like to visit Viñar in Montevideo.[66] That's for the day I win the lottery; tomorrow I travel to Puno.

[64] The novel would be posthumously published as *El zorro de arriba y el zorro de abajo* [Editors' note].

[65] Carlos Cueto Fernandini (1913–68), a well-known educator and philosopher, was Minister of Education between 1965 and 1968 [Editors' note].

[66] Marcelo Viñar, a Uruguayan psychiatrist and one of the specialists who treated Arguedas's depression [Editors' note].

CHAPTER 10

The Silent War

Historians cannot and should not disregard the present. How can we write about Andean utopia without addressing the violence that today rocks the region of Huamanga, an area that once served as the stage for Taqui Onqoy? As in the eighteenth century, violence again attempts to shroud itself in incomprehension. Therefore you must turn to critical method, the central element of historical reasoning: compare sources, consider their veracity, reconstruct events, establish a chronology, and finally, do not avoid moral judgment.[1]

> We must side with the oppressed on every occasion, even when they are in the wrong, though without losing sight of the fact that they are molded of the same clay as their oppressors.
>
> E.M. Cioran[2]

Between May 1980 and December 1982 – that is, the thirty-two months between the occupation of Chuschi and peasant outbursts, including police interventions, executions, and Shining Path terrorist acts – political violence in Peru claimed 165 lives and wounded 204. In 1983 deaths multiplied to 2,282 and the number of wounded increased only slightly to 372. There were two types of victims: state officers and civilians. The first were policemen, military forces, and authorities; the second were civilians and Senderistas (or terrorists). We combine these latter two groups because an undoubtedly high but unverifiable percentage of those

[1] I here admit my debt to two historians – Moses Finley and Pierre Vidal Naquet – who studied European antiquity but whose work always responded to current political issues.

[2] E. M. Cioran, *The Trouble with Being Born* (New York: Viking Press, 1976), 127. [Editors' note].

Table 10.1. *Political Violence in Peru, 1980–1984*

Year	1980	1981	1982	1983	1984	Total
Attacks	219	715	891	1,123	1,760	4,708
Deaths						
Police forces	—	6	30	51	54	141
Armed forces	—	—	1	8	15	24
Authorities	—	—	8	23	34	65
Civilians	3	4	65	802	1,042	1,916
Senderistas	—	1	47	1,398	959	2,405
Total	3	11	151	2,282	2,104	4,551
Wounded						
Police and armed forces	2	8	101	135	111	357
Authorities	—	—	5	8	—	13
Civilians	7	10	52	224	279	572
Senderistas	—	—	19	5	55	79
Total	9	18	177	372	445	1,021
Disappeared (*)				245	168	414
Clandestine burial sites (*)				133	183	316
Prisoners (**)		23	46	81	105	255

(*) Approximate figures
(**) These figures include only prisoners from Izquierda Unida and independents.
Sources: Amnesty International, APRODEH, *El Comercio* (April 7, 1985), *Hoy* (May 19, 1985), *El Nacional* (April 20, 1985), DESCO Database.

deemed terrorists have been considered so without reliable evidence. In 1983 civilian deaths represented 96.4 percent of the total; state deaths were 3.6 percent. By comparison, civilians made up 61.6 percent of wounded; state wounded were 38.4 percent. The numbers demonstrate that violence against the state maintained the previous pattern (many were left wounded after violent attacks) while state violence changed dramatically: armed forces did not want to leave wounded victims who could eventually testify as witnesses. In 1982, 47 dead and 19 wounded victims were considered Senderistas; in 1983 the figures were 1,398 and 5, respectively. Total deaths in 1984 were 2,104. In 1983 and 1984 combined there were 4,386 deaths, 96 percent of total victims in five years of political violence (see Table 10.1). The character of political violence clearly changed in 1983. What happened that year?

In 1983 deaths did not increase gradually – there were 175 in January, 344 in February, 157 in March, 466 in April, 671 in May, and 187 in June.[3] The intensity and the volume of political violence seemed

[3] These figures are from the data bank maintained by Desco, Centro de Estudios y Promoción del Desarrollo (Lima).

to increase almost automatically in the new year. What happened between December 1982 and the early days of 1983? On December 21, a decree turned over internal order in Ayacucho and Andahuaylas to the armed forces. The army entered December 28, and Andahuaylas and Angaraes were added to the list of provinces already in a state of emergency, which included Huamanga, Huanta, La Mar, Víctor Fajardo, and Cangallo. The body of a La Mar teacher kidnapped by *sinchis* (countersubversive Civil Guard forces) turned up on January 9 on the banks of the Apurímac River. Arrests, extrajudicial "trials," and mock executions began. In 1983 the state and repressive forces introduced two new practices: disappearances and the use of clandestine graves, revealingly called *botaderos* ("dumps"), poorly covered pits in which the dead piled up. Families reported 245 credibly documented disappearances. Amnesty International estimated more than 1,000 disappearances up to 1984. There were probably more if we consider that some peasants, out of fear or illiteracy, did not go through reporting procedures. To report a disappearance was to admit that the Shining Path virus, a sort of plague, had infected a family. Many bodies found in secret cemeteries had died of a bullet to the head, indicating execution by an organized force, but at times explosions, burning, or decomposition destroyed bodies or rendered them unidentifiable. The actual figures likely surpassed the very conservative number of 316 (see Table 10.1).

More important than quantity, however, was the dramatic change in violence after the entrance of the armed forces. A new strategy created this change. The communities were the bases of support for Shining Path, whose guerrillas hid among peasants. They carried out Mao's metaphor and became fish in water. The military had to poison the water and render it intolerable as a refuge. It could not repeat the 1965 strategy – isolating a guerrilla column and decimating it – because in the Pampas and Huanta regions it was impossible for a Peruvian military official to distinguish peasant from subversive. The military was forced to accept one of Shining Path's terms for war: a long, patient, protracted struggle. Helicopters and modern military weaponry were useless. What's more, outside army or navy units with few Quechua-speaking officials might be seen as a foreign occupying force, so direct combat was not feasible. That prompted a strategy to limit military casualties and shift the costs of war to civilians. The goal was to recruit peasants, bring them into formation, make them celebrate the flag and army, protect them, promise to satisfy some immediate necessities, and then throw them against Shining Path. They were called "montoneros" and, like their predecessors during independence, had to scavenge their own weapons – spears, knives, rocks, slings – for hand-to-hand combat. One of the most modern armies in Latin America promoted eighteenth-century tactics and weaponry.

However, protection and handouts were not enough to compel men to fight. Two other factors intervened. First, military studies demonstrated that the comunero world was hardly homogeneous; on the contrary, multiple internal conflicts separated wealthy communities from poorer ones, shepherds from farmers, men from the higher reaches from those in warm valleys. There were old land disputes and interethnic rivalries. The military knew it had to immerse itself in this history to discover which communities harbored Shining Path guerrillas and then recruit natural rivals. Second, with what later were called "counterguerrilla" bases, the military attempted to set all groups against each other: terrorists against montoneros, subversives against the civil defense, red flags against white flags. A fundamental strategy was to tolerate no neutrality. Anticommunism became central. According to the military, a communist was not only someone with leftist ideas, but anyone concerned with human rights or who opposed the military strategy. If a community did not wish to be destroyed, it had to demonstrate loyalty by arming itself and apprehending guerrillas. And it was not enough to claim fealty; communities had to offer proof. And so they did, such as the seven supposed Shining Path boys (between ten and fifteen years old, according to photos) who were apprehended and hanged January 21, 1983, in Huaychao.[4] The army had barely arrived when it implemented this strategy, obviously a campaign carefully planned inside an office using maps and executed with knowledge of the terrain. The ensuing massacre was calculated and premeditated.

Days before the Huaychao executions, the magazine *Caretas* published a report on army commandos and a cover photograph of an officer yelling with a fierce expression, knife in hand and ready to charge, blood covering his face, chest, arms, even his hair. A report described training methods. A series of photos captured a man in indigenous clothing

[4] Later, during the trial motivated by the Uchuraccay case, suggestions and presumptions emerged that conflicted with the first version of events: military forces and not comuneros from Huaychao knew who killed the seven young people. Four of them were shot to death in Huaychao; the others were killed in nearby villages and later moved to that community, where *Caretas* photographed them. Javier Diez Canseco, *Democracia, militarización y derechos humanos en el Perú*, 2nd edition (Lima: Servicios Populares, 1985), 68.

armed with a submachine gun and standing in the doorway of a house in the mountains; in the two ensuing photos, the commando attacked and killed him and then entered the house and killed two more. Although the images suggested the dead were Shining Path, they dressed like any other Indian, mestizo, or inhabitant of the Andean highlands. The report illustrated how in this society, as in many others, people were trained to kill in the most rapid and efficient way without rationality. Realistic training obliged enemies to dress like Indians and mestizos. The army understood the struggle against subversion as an internal war, like the French in Algeria or North Americans in Vietnam. Internal war was colonial war, but for good or bad, in Peru colonizers and colonized were part of the same country.

An effective internal war required other strategies. To ideologically isolate Shining Path, the military characterized militants not as guerrillas or political combatants but as "terrorists," synonymous with "criminals." What treatment do criminals deserve? Society must protect itself by excising the tumors that threaten it. Although there was no official death penalty in Peru, beginning in 1980 authorities effectively employed it against inmates, fugitives, and reputedly dangerous criminals who fell in police ambushes. If authorities killed criminals in Lima streets, why not do the same with terrorists far away in Ayacucho? Another method transplanted from cities to the countryside was torture. In fact, "prisoner" in Peru was practically synonymous with "tortured." In Chimbote, far from the emergency zone, an investigation concluded that authorities tortured more than 90 percent of inmates.[5] Police posts apparently knew no other interrogation methods. Beating prisoners, submerging them in water, hanging them, even using electrical shocks were methods so mundane and quotidian in Peru that they did not provoke surprise or indignation. Perhaps that explains why it was left to a Canadian priest to produce one of the few studies (and denunciations) of inmate torture. In early 1980, riots broke out in Lima prisons against growing mistreatment. A February 13 rebellion in Lurigancho jail left fourteen seriously injured; six days later, forty-eight prisoners went on hunger strike. There were more disturbances on August 15 and another hunger strike against torture on November 6 in Lurigancho. A confrontation between rival groups in El Sexto jail that

[5] Of those arrested in Chimbote, 92.8 percent "answered affirmatively to having been mistreated and/or tortured." Richard Renshaw, *La tortura en Chimbote* (Chimbote: IPEP, 1985), 139.

claimed thirty-two deaths ushered in 1981; riots erupted in Lurigancho on May 30, July 5, and September 9.

From the beginning of the military counterinsurgency, authorities employed Lima prison procedures in the emergency zone, but their use intensified in 1983. Calderón Rojas, a peasant from Apurímac, testified: "I was detained in my home and that day they tortured me in various ways: water boarding, *pita*, parrot's perch."[6] We could cite many other instances. Those procedures in turn returned from Ayacucho to Lima, where treatment of common prisoners and accused terrorists hardened. In December 1983, Lurigancho prisoners, supposedly protesting disciplinary measures, rebelled, and two alleged Shining Path inmates died; eleven days later, officials shot to death eight delinquents and a nun (taken as hostage) outside the same prison as they attempted to flee. When El Sexto inmates rioted the following March, police forces squelched the disturbance at a cost of no fewer than twenty deaths. In these two cases, police used weapons at their discretion, left no injured, did not accept surrender, and attempted no dialogue, even at the expense of hostages.

Until January 1983, observers armed with cameras and pens were walking around Ayacucho. Their presence was unsettling. Under the pretext of reporting, they could become witnesses, so the army began harassing them. On January 7, correspondents working in Ayacucho protested the violent way in which the army impeded their jobs. On January 26, eight journalists and a guide were killed in Uchuraccay. The army's version was that they were members of the Shining Path or at least people assumed to be so, because they traveled to the region with a red flag, which emergency zone commander General Clemente Noel repeatedly exhibited. Peruvian novelist Mario Vargas Llosa presided over an official investigation whose extensive report – which dedicated only a few lines to the crime – concluded that the journalists died from misunderstanding: Uchuraccay community Indians confused them with terrorists.[7] However, Indians were in contact with police; sinchis visited them several times, and they had links with Huaychao comuneros

[6] APRODEH, "Relación de Casos," typed report.

[7] Literally, this line says: "The Commission is under the relative conviction that the journalists were attacked without warning, massively, without any dialogue, and by a multitude inflamed by a mixture of fear and rage that gave them a ferocity unusual in their daily lives and normal circumstances." *Informe de la comisión investigadora de los sucesos de Uchuraccay* (Lima: Editora Perú, 1983), 15. Some

who a few days before hanged the seven Shining Path boys; days later, the same comuneros attacked other villages considered red. On February 1, they sacked Balcón.[8] The journalists' deaths helped the antisubversive strategy; with a few exceptions, no reporter ventured outside the city of Huamanga from then on. For the 1983–84 deaths, the official version was the only version. Laconic press reports provided only the number of victims – ten, twenty, fifty deaths – with no other details. Few journalists repeated the "mistake" of going to the countryside to report news or seek an alternative version.[9] In February 1983, *El Diario de Marka* director José María Salcedo covered the journalists' route from Ayacucho to Uchuraccay and was the first to observe confrontations among communities. Back in Lima he published the headline "Civil War among Communities," which at that moment appeared sensationalist.

On March 17, the first battalion of army veterans (*licenciados*), some 1,000 men, was officially organized in the upper reaches of Huanta, near Uchuraccay and Huaychao. At the same time, a sort of psychological war began that attempted to depict Abimael Guzmán and Shining Path members as vampires, pistacos whom peasants must kill without compassion to prevent the evil from spreading. New communities attacked

photos developed later proved the existence of a dialogue before the crime. The commission spent barely a few hours in Uchuraccay. Its members arrived by helicopter accompanied by army officers. To give apparent scientific support to their "relative and absolute convictions," two anthropologists and a psychoanalyst, none of whom spoke Quechua, served as advisors. The conditions described were incompatible with even minimally serious and responsible "field work."

In the absence of a serious investigation, it only affirmed old convictions. The idea of violence as misunderstanding was not new: Vargas Llosa had actually used it in his novel *La guerra del fin del mundo* (1981, *The War of the End of the World*). Another stereotype was imagining Andean men in a world apart, with its own rules and laws that were necessary to leave untouched: one could not blame anyone in Uchuraccay for the deaths because the campesinos were treated as "minors." This helped protect the allies of the military command. As subsequent events confirmed, the commission played a role in a cover-up, no matter what the will of its members was.

8 *Amnístia Internacional – Perú* (London: Amnistía Internacional, 1985), 17.

9 "Everything appears to suggest that the first error – which in no way excuses those of others – was committed by the very colleagues who undertook the expedition." *Caretas* (Lima), February 7, 1983, 15. "Error" is a euphemism when it comes to explaining nine deaths.

Shining Path bases.[10] In Lucanamarca, a relatively prosperous ranching community like Uchuraccay, six young people died by hanging. Shining Path responded with a belated attack in April: according to the official version, 40 militants and 100 peasants killed between 45 and 67 area peasants. On the opposite bank of the Pampas River, the army occupied the community of Totos between April 5 and April 16. Inhabitants told the public prosecutor in Lima that they had suffered torture and mock executions and that eight peasants had died. Shining Path executed thirty peasants in Huancasanccos and killed the Chuschi mayor. A communal patrol from the community near Urancancha attacked the Espite community in the Pampas region; detainees turned over to armed forces later appeared on the list of disappearances. Responding with a primitive form of terrorism on July 11 in Lima, Shining Path dynamited the central offices of the ruling party. War continued in the upper reaches of Huanta and Tambo. Twelve Shining Path members reportedly died at the hands of the army and paramilitary forces on October 4 in Santa Rosa. When the latter left the village, Shining Path returned and killed seven peasant collaborators. Like the military, Shining Path also permitted no neutrality. The war proceeded thus in the following months. Military forces and comuneros from Ocros, Chumbes, and Ccamarca – district capitals with a larger population – attacked the communities of Tanta, Huaracayocc, and Manzanayocc, in the district of Concepción, province of Cangallo, between July 9 and July 19, 1984. Afterward, peasants reported six disappearances and the destruction and sacking of property. A similar story played out when navy troops and Huamanguilla comuneros attacked the community of Ccarhuace three times between September and December 1984.

The "terrucos" responded not against the armed forces, who generally remained barricaded in their garrisons, but against those who, by choice or force, fought on the front lines. Shining Path's war against the state became an atrocious civil war in which communities faced off against each other, in which the dividing line was not rich against poor or

[10] The information we use is based on journalistic material ordered and codified in the Desco data bank and its weekly reports, newspapers and magazines (especially *Caretas*), and information gathered by institutions such as APRODEH (Asociación Pro Derechos Humanos), CEAS (Comisión Episcopal de Acción Social), and Amnesty International. Aldo Panfichi helped gather this information.

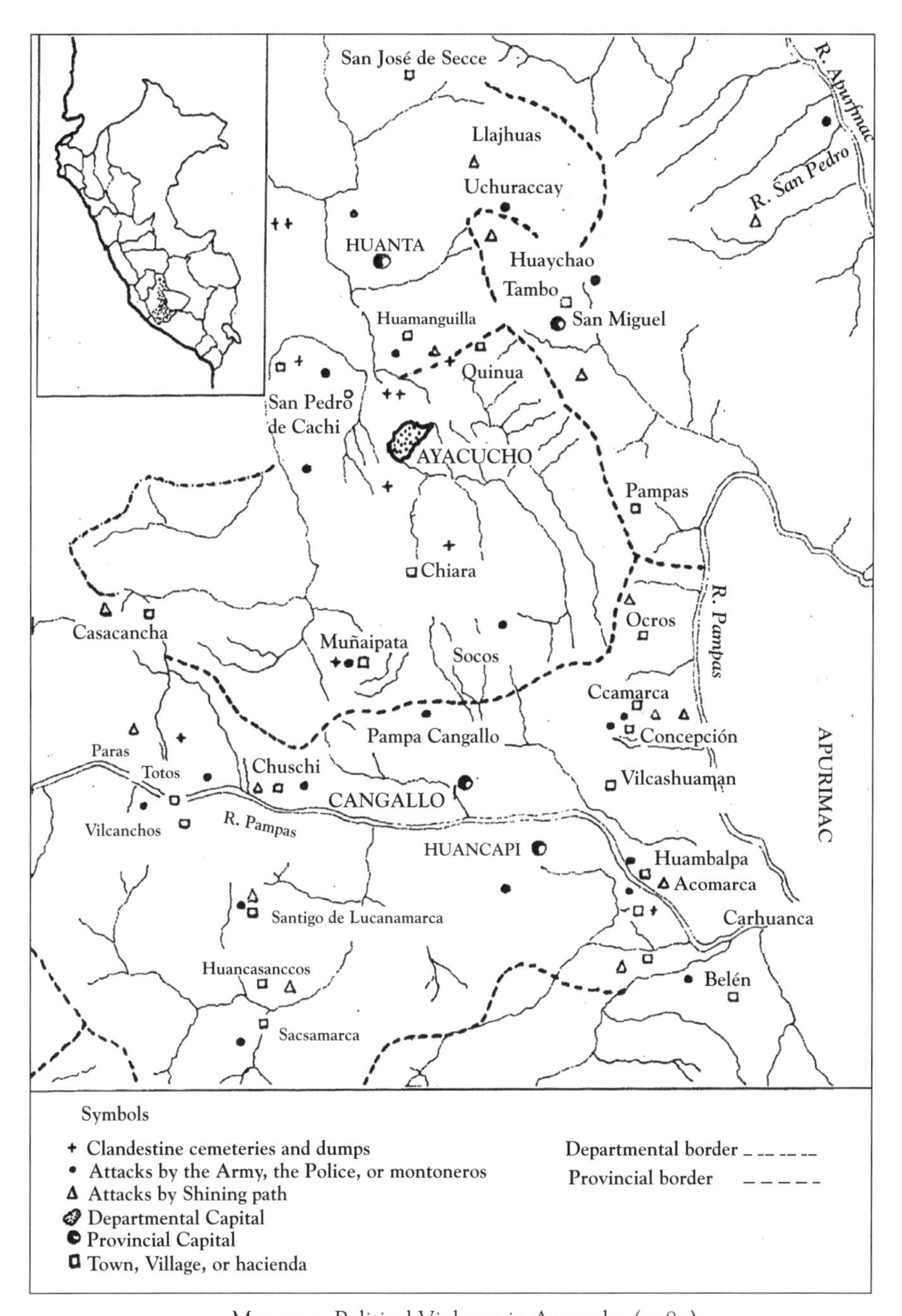

Map 10.1. Political Violence in Ayacucho (1983).

white against Indian, but Manzanayocc against Ocros. In this way, water turned into a swamp.[11]

Conflicts between communities were well known in the region. Barely a small river separated Chuschi, where Shining Path began its insurgency, from neighboring Quispillata; the two communities, however, were rivals and antagonists. "The rivalry," wrote Antonio Díaz Martínez in 1969, "is very old and originated in the possession of the communal lands of the upper highlands. Both communities say that the small hill that divides their pastures belongs to them. What is certain is that they have never been able to establish the true boundaries. In 1960 an armed conflict between the two groups broke out and some comuneros died."[12]

The army hoped Shining Path would slowly bleed to death, but with nothing more than official data, it is difficult to judge the efficacy of that strategy. Iquicha community Indians were on the winning side in 1814; the same was not the case ten years later when they fought for the defeated royalists. And now? Beyond arguing who won and lost, there were more than 4,000 civilian and Shining Path deaths and 24 military casualties. The social cost of the war was not even a matter of concern. What's more, military leaders suggested that this horrifying number of deaths was meant quite literally to muddy the water. There was no distinction between combatants and civilians. Neither were age and sex relevant. The majority of victims were young peasants. In July 1985, of the 345 prisoners who belonged to Izquierda Unida, a legal leftist coalition, or were considered independent, 60 percent were from the emergency zone, 48 percent were peasants, 12 percent were students, and 43 percent were thirty years or younger. Of the 427 disappearances, 22.7 percent were farmers and 18.5 percent were students.

It was comunero against comunero, peasants on both sides of a war in which at best we learned the name of the victim but not the victimizer. Generally, we have only official sources for Shining Path attacks against communities. Shining Path silence, the military siege, the absence of journalists and social scientists from areas where not even the Red Cross would go – all conspired to create a silent war. Although a flier confirmed the attack, the number of dead and wounded in Lucanamarca, the first village that Shining Path attacked, came exclusively

[11] This is a reference to the Maoist metaphor "The people are like water and the red army is like fish." [Editors' note].

[12] Díaz Martínez, *Ayacucho: hambre y esperanza*, 146

from *Caretas*. But the military command authorized this report, which was produced under conditions similar to those of the Uchuraccay commission.

The number of deaths we can report, therefore, is only an approximation of reality. On occasions the figures were larger or smaller, depending on how they fit military strategy. The actual number was irrelevant. Given the difficulties of muddying the waters, the military opted without hesitation for extermination to turn the region into a desert. Shanty towns and largely abandoned villages inhabited by orphans were the consequences of the strategy. In March 1983 only 42 elderly people out of Huambalpa's 3,000 inhabitants remained. The only option for peasants who were not Shining Path militants or montoneros was to flee as soon as possible to a refugee neighborhood in Ica or Lima (about 10,000 people to date) unless a blind faith (like that held by some evangelicals) allowed them to remain and defy all tribulation.[13]

The war, however, did not play out only in Ayacucho. To date twenty-six provinces are in a state of emergency (see map 10.2). Except for Mariscal Cáceres, the latest to be added to that category, all belong to the central sierra (departments of Pasco and Huánuco) and southern sierra (Huancavelica, Ayacucho, and Apurímac). In those areas, peasants are the majority and Andean forms of production persist. Between the central and south is the Mantaro Valley, where Arguedas found signs of a peasant bourgeoisie, which appeared to remain at the margin of the war. The southern area corresponds to the Taqui Onkoy map in the sixteenth century. Although Ayacucho continues as the epicenter of this social earthquake, it has affected 1,496,714 inhabitants in an area that covers 34,358 square miles; in the southern departments, it touched 995,255 inhabitants in an area encompassing 27,334 square miles.

Language followed an itinerary similar to that of deaths. "Shining Path" became "terrorist," which later became synonymous with "Ayacuchano," which in turn meant anything that was Indian or mestizo, dressed poorly, and spoke deficient Spanish. To say you were "Ayacuchano" was to admit breaking antiterrorist law. At the end of 1984, the war was an assault by the western part of Peru against its Andean counterpart. The number of deaths, wounded, and disappearances betrayed the often hidden reality of a country in which some

[13] José María Salcedo, "Zona de emergencia: el proceso de la paz," *Quehacer* (Lima) 37 (1985), 70–85.

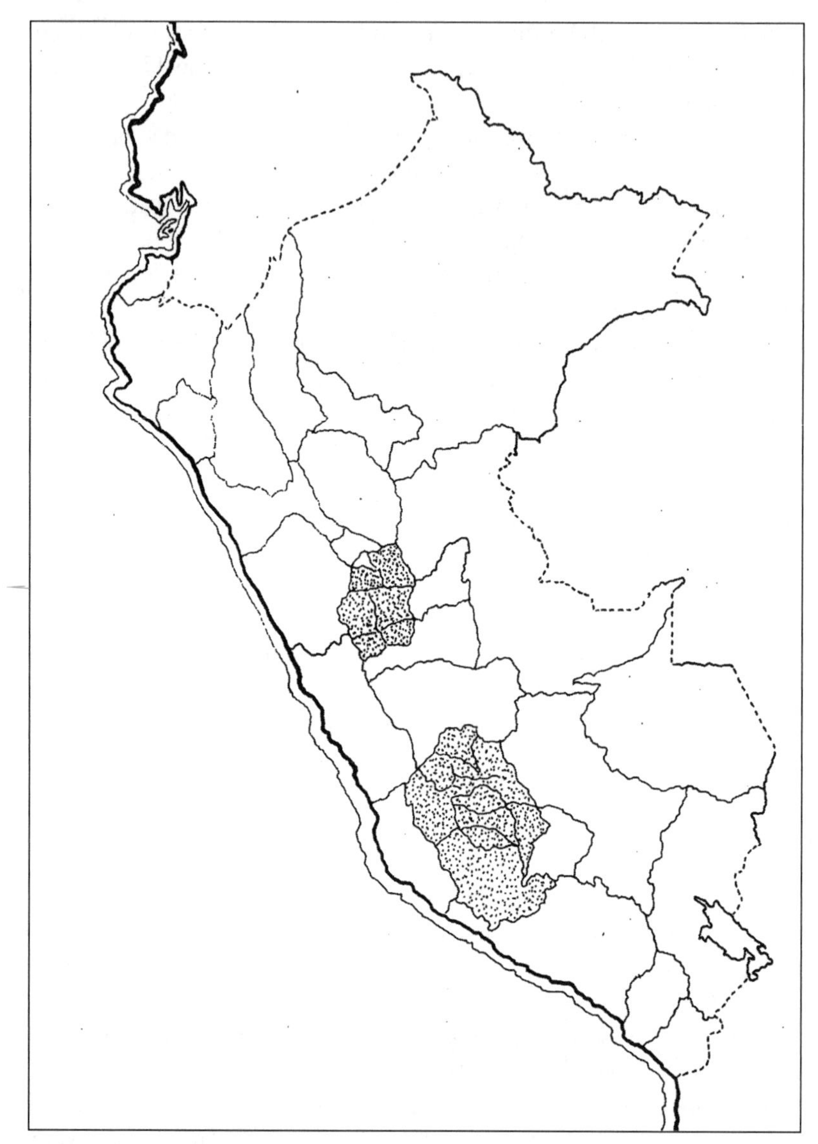

Map 10.2. Peruvian Provinces under State of Emergency and Military Control (1984).

citizens were more equal than others and racism contaminated human relations. It is a problem as old and as deeply rooted as violence. If torture, more than a thousand disappearances, indiscriminate killing, and forced migration due to fear and terror happened in a system that calls itself democratic, in which parliament, churches, universities, and professional guilds are in full activity, then the title of a Julio Ramón Ribeyro short story was still relevant in 1985: "The skin of an Indian is cheap." The war happened over there, far away in Ayacucho or in Huánuco, where deaths were numbers and not people with whom we identified. In the Andes, in the past, the Christian metaphor of the dead returning to life at the end of time served to inspire more than one hope; perhaps it still does.

CHAPTER 11

EPILOGUE

DREAMS AND NIGHTMARES

This epilogue is intended to avoid misunderstandings. To write about the Andean utopia is not to present it as necessarily valid or as an alternative to the present. I do not deny sympathy for some of its proponents (they wanted change), but I do not share the same projects. The thesis of this book, therefore, is not that we continue searching for an Inca. What we need is a utopia sustained by the past and open to the future, one that helps us rethink socialism in Peru.

Dead past never buries the dead.
The world will have to be changed, not the past.
M. I. Finley[1]

Utopia, by definition, is outside time and space. However, the Andean collective imagination ended up placing ideal society in the period before the arrival of Europeans. That is the fundamental argument of these essays. A long pre-Colombian history was identified exclusively with the Inca empire, and a world with inequality and oppression was transformed into a homogenous and just society. The Incas, converted from a dynasty into a singular, came to symbolize a time when society belonged to its previous and rightful owners. The idea of the Inca's return was charged with messianic and millenarian resonances. Such ideas sustained rebellions in the Lima sierra in 1666, Juan Santos Atahualpa's central jungle uprising in 1742, and Tupac Amaru's "great rebellion" in

[1] Moses I. Finley, *Economy and Society in Ancient Greece* (London: Chatto & Windus, 1981), xxvi.

the southern Andes in 1780. Understanding Andean utopia is essential for explaining social movements – but in the twentieth century, how relevant is the utopian horizon?

At the beginning of the twentieth century, upper-class intellectuals believed the question of Peruvian identity was settled; the answer lay in the past. There was a national soul, but defining it privileged unity over diversity. One country, one nation, one state. The past conditioned the future. Although different cultural traditions existed in Peru, synthesis held the keys to the future and moved a discourse about mestizaje to center stage. These ideas were best incarnated in individuals. José de la Riva Agüero, author of this historical paradigm, initiated contemporary studies about Inca Garcilaso (1915). Raúl Porras (1936) and others viewed conquistador Francisco Pizarro as the "founder" of the country. By then, mestizaje identified itself with Hispanic tradition, perhaps as a consequence of indigenismo, its rival current. What emerged amid bitter debates was a dual Peru, but one in which "indigenous" was an abstraction. The idea of national unity was displaced from the past to a hypothetical future. It is still in the making today. Uniting the Spanish and the Indian was proposed as the path toward collective identity.

Although critical of Riva Agüero and his contemporaries in the so-called Generation of 1900, later intellectuals were trapped in the same paradigm. This began to show cracks in the 1960s, when demographic growth and migration revealed Peruvian plurality. Ethnohistory emerged, harkening to Julio C. Tello and Luis E. Valcárcel but finding new expression with John Murra (1955) and Tom Zuidema (1964). Stefano Varese's study of the Campas presented a different history that broke with previous notions of Spanish and Indian time. José María Arguedas's fiction depicted a country in which the clash between the modern and traditional forged new cultural expressions. Similarly, Alfredo Torero argued that the Andean world was profoundly heterogeneous, as seen in the varieties of the Quechua language. Another Arguedas disciple, Rodrigo Montoya, found the persistence of diversity in Quechua peasants. Nelson Manrique, a student of Torero's, used regional history in the central sierra to delineate different economic spaces and distinct cultures.

What emerges, therefore, is the image of a diverse society. These authors challenged the idea of one nation in formation. Why not several nations? Diversity, after all, is more democratic than homogeneity. As Néstor García Canclini argued, "By developing and systematizing our ignorance of what is different, commercial standardization trains us to live under totalitarian regimes, in the most literal sense in which they differ from those democratic: because they suppress plurality and submerge everything into a uniform totality."[2] Around 1962, writer Luis Loayza lamented that Peruvians lacked a "national type," an easily identifiable figure such as the Argentine *gaucho* or the Chilean *roto* (poor city-dweller). That missed the point. The real challenge was finding not one but several national types. Identity did not demand a single response. Plurality lay at the heart of the Andean utopia.

Although diverse social sectors have shared conceptions of the Andean utopia, it is frequently associated with peasant history. Thus, its future appears precarious in a society in which the countryside and peasants are increasingly less important. In 1876 more than 70 percent of the population lived in rural areas. In 1961 the percentage dropped to 67 percent. Today it is probably less than 50 percent, although placing the rural-urban divide at populations less than 2,000 is debatable in a country in which peasants tend to assemble in villages. Numbers aside, the tendency toward a shrinking rural population is undeniable, and it reflects growing rural poverty, the increase in uncultivated fields, stagnation, and even the retreat of the agricultural frontier because of little and poorly utilized land. Capitalist development does not necessarily mean proletarianization in Peru, but it uproots and dismantles peasant societies as in other areas of the world. Modernity and progress come at the expense of the traditional world. The market demands uniform habits and customs so workers and employers can understand each other. The number of Quechua speakers is shrinking. So is the use of traditional food, fabric, and tiled roofs, replaced by pastas, synthetic fibers, and aluminum. Antibiotics force the retreat of epidemics and relegate traditional medicine to the folkloric. We do not wish to idealize the past, for only those never exposed to typhus could lament the construction of roads or medical posts. Not to oversimplify, but we can ask what tradition and Andean utopia tell us about the present and future. Are these fossilized ideas that only "archaeology" can address?

In the 1960s, Peru appeared on an irreversible path toward modernity. Social scientists increasingly believed we were living in a capitalist country in which the internal market was expanding, peasant numbers were decreasing, and traditional cultures were in their final throes. The 1980s crisis undermined these ideas. We discovered a facet of Lima that

[2] Néstor García Canclini, *Transforming Modernity: Popular Culture in Mexico*, translated by Lidia Lozano (Austin: University of Texas Press, 1993), 67.

was much less modern, represented, for example, by unemployed people and followers of religious sects. Above all, the crisis meant seriously deteriorated living conditions. Nationally up to 50 percent lived in poverty and 35 percent in extreme poverty, unable to solve food, housing, clothing, and health problems. Sixty percent between the ages of one and five were undernourished. From the point of view of the poor, the crisis questioned not just a political regime or capitalist development but the very imposition of western civilization dating to the European encounter in the sixteenth century. Coming from a continent devastated by periodic famines, Europeans were surprised to discover food stored in Andean state deposits. Historian Henry Kamen argued that for Europeans, "The only indisputable fact is that the great mass of the people lived perilously close to a level of food consumption that threatened their very existence."[3] Centuries later the situation reversed itself.

The Andean utopia emerged as a response to the identity problem after the defeat in Cajamarca and the cataclysm that European invasion unleashed. Myths were powerless; you had to understand history. The Indians and peasants who led nativist rebellions lived this problem, but so too did groups rejected by Spaniards and Indians: mestizos, the illegitimate children of the conquest, the product of the collective orgy that was the arrival of the Spanish hordes. Beyond their uncertain ethnic condition was their difficult insertion into the labor market, leading to vagrancy, unemployment, and marginalization. They were stereotyped as troublemakers given to unrest. They were the minority in the sixteenth century and more than 20 percent of the population in the eighteenth century. By the 1940 census, the last that utilized racial categories, mestizos were grouped with whites, and the two constituted more than 53 percent of the population. Mestizos likely outnumbered Indians and were the largest population group. Urbanization and migration have led to an increase in mestizaje in Peru, what Aníbal Quijano and José Varallanos called *cholificación*.[4]

For people without hope, the Andean utopia challenges a history that condemned them to the margins. Utopia denies modernity and progress,

[3] Henry Kamen, *The Iron Century: Social Change in Europe 1550–1660* (New York: Praeger Publishers, 1971), 38.

[4] Aníbal Quijano, *Dominación y cultura. Lo cholo y el conflicto cultural en el Perú* (Lima: Mosca Azul Editores, 1980); José Varallanos, *El cholo y el Perú. Introducción al estudio sociológico de un hombre y un pueblo mestizos y su destino cultural* (Buenos Aires: Imprenta López, 1962) [Editors' note].

the illusion of development understood as westernization. Until now, it has led to the destruction of the traditional world and the failure to replace it with developed society. The model of a raw-material export economy did not work, and it seems too late to try Taiwan's path. Maybe all that remains is to look again toward the interior, to agriculture and Andean people, to find a development plan that does not bring rural neglect and peasant ruin. It must preserve cultural plurality and recover traditional practices, astronomical knowledge, water use, and so on. Populism? Romanticism? This does not mean transposing the past into the present. Without shunning highways, antibiotics, and tractors, it mandates development that does not cause futile suffering to future generations. That's the myth that José Carlos Mariátegui demanded.

The word *myth* is not always positive; it can also signify authoritarianism and violence. Nightmares as well as dreams fill the history of utopia. In messianic movements, salvation depends less on how people exercise freedom than on revealed truth; in its name, one can withstand any sacrifice and justify all atrocities. The conquest of the millennium demands an Apocalypse. These traditions connect to a world that has not produced capitalism, with its misery and obsession with progress, or spawned democracy. Recognition of the past does not mean acceptance. Seeking its lessons and applying them to the future does not mean prolonging it. A socialist project salvages foundations, columns, and bricks from the old society and combines them with a new framework. The key issue is how to combine the old with that which does not yet exist. Only in this way will socialism be truly unprecedented in Peru. Therefore it requires a distinct utopia in which the past does not close the horizon, one that allows us to understand our history, construct a collective identity and, above all, change society.

It should be clear, therefore, that we are not advocating the Andean utopia. History should liberate us from the past, not seal us off – as Quijano argued – within "longue durée" prisons of ideas. The creations of the collective imaginary are instruments over which people should never lose control. If people are controlled by ghosts, it is impossible to confront the future. The challenge is to create new ideas and myths without jettisoning the past. If the theme of Andean utopia is relevant today, it is because there is more than one similarity between present circumstances and those that generated the idea in the first place. Peru at the end of the 1980s faces a new confrontation between the Andean world and the west – that is, modernity, capitalism, and progress. The 1920s produced a similar encounter. Going back in time, historical crossroads in the sixteenth, eighteenth, and twentieth centuries were crucial to the production of utopias in the Andean area. But besides another iteration of that encounter, the end of the twentieth century represents a moment in which Andean culture is precarious and on the defensive, threatened by the tendency toward homogenization that the internal market and capitalism always seek to impose. Andean, however, is no longer exclusively synonymous with terms such as Indian, sierra, and rural. Massive migration has generated an unprecedented influx of Andean people to the coast. Valcárcel's prediction in *Tempest in the Andes* came true, but without the apocalyptic overtones. These people demand a new response.

Millenarianism and messianism loom in Peru because politics here is not just a secular activity. Like so many other things in this society, religion and even the irrational condition it. Utopias summon passions capable of dragging or leading the masses beyond the immediate, inducing attempts to take the sky by storm or snatch fire from the gods. But this type of mystique easily turns into fanaticism and the dogmatic rejection of those who do not share it. Underlying it is an authoritarian current that generates its own violent outbursts. In 1947 in the Cuzco village of Coporaque, 52-year-old peasant Silverio Arovilca argued that "the only way to reform and reorganize the (Inca) empire is the extermination of all whites; the hatred of mestizos was so great that one could not even look at a white dog because they said it was the spirit or soul of the Spanish, and that to get rid of both you had to kill them."[5] The citation illustrates the rejection of mestizos but also recognizes change as the suppression of the ruling sector. In a way, that is the inversion of the postindependence social order. Accumulated hate fuels rebellion, but it does not necessarily lead to a different society. The efficacy of the dominant class is measured by its capacity to introduce its values and ideas to the dominated. When this is achieved, it might foster the hope of final victory: that is, that a new order and new agents might end up reproducing old authoritarianism.

In 1965, Arguedas turned a story he heard from a Cuzco peasant into "The Pongo's Dream" ("El sueño del pongo"), which appears to confirm these fears. The relationship between gamonal and pongo, based on exploitation and daily humiliation, can change, but only when outside factors intervene. At the end of the story, "our great Padre San Francisco" orders the master to lick the excrement-covered servant.

[5] Archivo del Museo de la Cultura Peruana, Cuzco, legajo 46–65.

Reality inverts. The exploiter is on the bottom and the dominated on top. The characters change, but humiliation persists. Old structures continue.

The pongo's dream is compatible with the Andean conception of "pachacuti." But socialism seeks not just change, but the construction of a new order, which was absent from the pre-Hispanic cosmovision. That is the only solution for eliminating the exploiter and exploitation.

Passion, although necessary, often does not allow us to get too far. Throughout the history of millenarian and messianic movements, fanatics throw themselves against superior forces without a strategic plan. A state of permanent tension impels them to seek the most rapid solution possible. The mystique that gives messianic and millenarian movements their moral force can also become its weakest flank. As Eric Hobsbawm argues, "without being imprinted with the right kind of ideas about political organization, strategy and tactics and the right kind of programme, millenarianism inevitably collapses."[6] But we could expect a different outcome if millenarian mystique connects with modern socialism, with its capacity to organize, produce strategic programs, and ability to adapt to short term political changes – in other words, if passion joins forces with Marxism and its reasoning capacity. That is an explosive mix against a backdrop of poverty and the rule of a few. History guarantees nothing, but at least this mix might generate a more consistent and less ephemeral movement than those abandoned to their own devices.

Andean utopia condensed strong passions. Although in its history the written and conscious reside alongside the oral and spontaneous, it appeals above all to sentiment. It ends up mingling with collective mentalities and assumes some features that George Rudé attributed to "inherent" ideologies, capable of pushing people to rebellion but always with uncertain and limited results. In a comparison of popular revolts, Rudé concluded that those ideologies "cannot bring them all the way to revolution, even as junior partners of the bourgeoisie."[7] Perhaps he exaggerates, but it is true that passion is not enough: radical change requires alternatives and projects, plans and programs.

6 Eric Hobsbawm, *Primitive Rebels: Studies in Archaic Forms of Social Movement in the 19th and 20th centuries* (Manchester: Manchester University Press, 1971), 106–7.

7 George Rudé, *Ideology and Popular Protest* (Chapel Hill: University of North Carolina Press, 1995), 26.

Glossary

Adoratorio Place of worship, often remote
Aguardiente Distilled spirit, usually of sugar cane
Alcabala Excise tax
Altiplano High plain, between the ridges of the Andean sierra
Aprismo The APRA political party and its movement
Apu Mountain god or spirits
Ayllu Kin-based unit of social organization in the Andes
Botadero Literally "garbage dump," but used also to refer to clandestine burial sites
Camachico President of an ayllu
Caudillaje Strong-man politics
Ceja de selva Rain forest of the eastern Andes
Chapetón Derogatory term for Spaniard
Chicha Corn beer
Cholo Urbanized or acculturated Indian
Chuncho Term for jungle native, often derogatory
Civilista Member of the Civilista Political Party, 1870s through 1920s
Cofradía Religious brotherhood or confraternity
Colla (*see* Qolla)
Colono Service tenant on haciendas
Compadrazgo Ritual or fictive kin
Comunero Member of Indian community
Consolidado Recipient of fraudulently high payoff on internal debt in the 1850s
Converso A Jewish or Muslim individual who converted to Catholicism
Corregidor District governor in colonial period

Curaca (*see* Kuraka)
Curandero Healer or shaman
Cushma Woven cotton tunic worn in the Amazon
Doctrinero Parish priest, usually member of the regular clergy
Encomendero A holder of an *encomienda*
Encomienda Grant of Indians, mainly as tribute payers, in early colonial period
Forastero Indian living in a town other than where he or she was born
Gamonal A town strongman or landowner who used his power and authority to abuse Indians, with whom he often shared cultural practices
Hacendado Owner of a hacienda; landowner
Hechicero Sorcerer or witch doctor
Hidalgo Gentleman or member of the petty nobility
Huaca Local or regional sacred site and divinity in the Andes
Huaccha A campesino who has no land; a poor person; orphan
Huaico Landslide caused by torrential rains in the mountains
Huamani (or Wamani) Mountain lord believed to act as guardian of grazing flocks
Huaraca Andean sling
Huari Collection of ethnic groups that occupied the Peruvian central and central-north highlands preceding the Inca state
Huayno Andean rural folk music and dance
Idolatría Idolatry, worship of idols
Indiano A person born in the Indies (America). It is also used to refer to a Spaniard who came to America and became rich.
Indigenista A non-Indian who worked to alleviate indigenous marginalization and oppression
Inkarri A colonial-era myth about an Andean messiah who one day would return and overthrow the Spanish invaders
Intendente Provincial governor
Kuraka Indian chieftain
Latifundista Owner of a large estate or latifundio
Llacuaz Central Andean coastal-western valley group that moved into the higher puna lands of the Huari
Machay Cave tomb
Mallqui Mummified ancestor
Marrano Derogatory term for a Spanish Jew who converted to Christianity to escape persecution
Mascaipacha Royal tassel worn on the Inca king's forehead; ornamental Inca headpiece
Mestizo(a) Person of mixed Spanish and Indian ancestry

Misti Quechua variant of mestizo meaning white-skinned person or lord; denotes power

Mita Forced indigenous labor, often through rotational labor drafts

Mitimae Forced colonist or settler

Montoneros Irregular military forces composed mostly of peasants

Obraje, obrajillo Andean textile mills

Pachacuti A period of radical and dramatic social changes, or the leader who fosters those changes. The ninth Inca according to certain accounts of the Inca Empire

Pachamama Mother earth

Paititi A mythical place in eastern Peru, considered the "lost city of the Incas," where some believe they retreated after the Spanish conquest

Pallas Indigenous women of noble origin

Panaca A family of royal lineage

Pistaco, pishtaco A mythical character, usually depicted as a foreigner, who attacks members of the local population

Pongo An indigenous serf attached to a hacienda and subjected to non-economic forms of exploitation

Puna Highest altitudes in the Andes

Pututo An instrument made from a sea shell or cow horn

Qero Ceremonial vase.

Qolla (or colla) A princess or a queen in Inca times

Reparto de mercancías (or reparto) The forced sale of goods imposed by colonial authorities on indigenous people

Retablo Artistic boxes that represent daily life events among Andean communities

Runa Quechua for "the people"

Senderista A member of the guerrilla group known as "Sendero Luminoso" (Shining Path)

Serrano An inhabitant of the highlands (the "sierra")

Sinchi Member of a special antisubversive police unit

Tahuantinsuyo The Inca empire

Tambo A rest and storage area found in Andean roads during the Inca Empire

Taqui Dance

Tayta (or Taita) Father or fatherly figure

Terruco A pejorative/colloquial term for "terrorist" in late-twentieth-century Peru

Tinterillo An informal lawyer and legal intermediary, savvy in legal trickeries

Trajinante An itinerant trader in the Andes

Visita A process established by the Spanish crown to monitor the administration of its colonial possessions

Voluntarismo The idea that individual and collective will could overcome all obstacles to social transformations

Wamani The deity or protective spirit of the mountains

Yanacona A serf during the Inca Empire; later, a sort of share-cropper working for a landowner

Yunga Forest region east of the Andean highlands. Also, the people living in that area

Author's Acknowledgments

The research behind the essays included in this book was carried out thanks to the financial contribution of the UNESCO to Project No. 2277, "Andean utopia," that I submitted with Manuel Burga. The Instituto de Apoyo Agrario and its directors, Juan Mendoza and Víctor Caballero, offered the necessary infrastructure for writing it. This is a center that promotes rural and peasant development but is also receptive to intellectual work.

Numerous conversations and debates with different people over the course of several years have nurtured this book: Manuel Burga, Heraclio Bonilla, Pablo Macera, Henrique Urbano, Gonzalo Portocarrero, Magdalena Chocano, and César Rodríguez Rabanal and the members of his seminar at the Pontificia Universidad Católica del Perú. The ideas presented in this book were discussed in courses I taught in the Social Sciences department of that university. I should mention students such as Fanni Muñoz, Elizabeth Acha, Víctor Peralta, José Coronel, Aldo Panfichi, Javier Flores, and Eudocio Sifuentes. Gustavo Buntinx and Luis Eduardo Wuffarden taught me about colonial art. The Centro de Estudios Bartolomé de las Casas (Cuzco) offered me the possibility of discussing some of these ideas with Cuzqueño students in August 1984. I traveled through the territories of the Tupac Amaru rebellion thanks to the collaboration of Abdón Palomino.

I would like to mention in particular the incisive critiques I received from Ruggiero Romano. Cecilia Rivera was another careful reader of this manuscript. Sofía Jiménez did the typing with enthusiasm and intelligence, at times from unintelligible drafts, and at times under extreme pressure. Luis Caballero drew the maps and Edwin Lazo took the photographs.

The original version of this book was awarded the Casa de las Américas prize in Havana, Cuba, which was a source of happiness for me for two reasons. First, because of the institution and the country that awarded me the prize. Second, because a committee comprising intellectuals from different Latin American countries demonstrated that they did not share the misgivings and attacks that supposedly orthodox Marxist critics had launched against my previous works. This is a book that originates in Marxism but then makes its way into the inner world (and establishes a dialogue with psychoanalysis) and deals with inventions, imaginary spaces, myths, and dreams. None of this prevents this book from offering, without interruption, a political discourse.

I have introduced some changes to the original version. Both Chapter 2 on the extirpation of idolatries and the Epilogue are new. In the latter, I have summarized my conclusions in an attempt to avoid capricious interpretations of my work.

I should broaden the list of people who have given me generous comments or made specific observations that have allowed me to correct mistakes, among them Javier Champa and Efraín Trelles. The chapter, "The Tupac Amaru Revolution and the Andean People," was presented at the Seminario Permanente de Investigación Agraria (SEPIA) in Piura, in October 1985. "The Utopian Horizon" (Chapter 8) benefited from criticism and debates at an encounter of historians of the Andean world organized by the Instituto Francés de Estudios Andinos in 1984. The text on communities and doctrines (Chapter 2) was presented in September 1986 at an event in Chiclayo organized by the Centro de Estudios Sociales "Solidaridad". Finally, "The Boiling Point" (Chapter 9) was nurtured by the dialogue with the interdisciplinary team that Fr. Jeffrey Klaiber brought together to study violence and the moral crisis in Peru, which was sponsored by the Tinker Foundation.

I express my gratitude to all of them.

Lima, January 15, 1986.

Editors' and Translators' Note

We would like to express our gratitude to Cecilia Rivera, Alberto Flores Galindo's lifelong *compañera*, for her continuous support of this project. The late Maruja Martínez, a long-time collaborator of Flores Galindo, deserves our appreciation for her friendship and her meticulous work in the preparation of the author's *Obras Completas*, which proved to be extremely helpful. Stuart Schwartz's enthusiasm for the translation of this book was the initial motivation behind this effort. We thank him for his enduring support and endless patience. A word of thanks is also due to the many friends and colleagues, in Peru and elsewhere, who have expressed interest in this project over the years and have helped keep the legacy of Flores Galindo's work alive. Many among them answered our questions about obscure terms or read parts of the translation. Our editor at Cambridge University Press, Eric Crahan, helped us bring this project to completion with his professional advice and scrupulous guidance. Our deepest gratitude, however, is to the author himself, whose intellectual prowess, passion for history, and warm friendship were instrumental in shaping our careers as historians.

This has been a truly collaborative effort. Charles Walker and Willie Hiatt took on the main responsibility of translating the text into English, and Carlos Aguirre revised it thoroughly. All three shared the responsibility of checking references and finding citations in the original language. Hiatt offered sharp comments on the introduction's draft written by Aguirre and Walker. The three of us compiled the glossary.

We have not included in this translation Chapter VI of the definitive Spanish edition of this book (Lima: SUR. Casa de Estudios del Socialismo, 2005), entitled "Los sueños de Gabriel Aguilar" ("Gabriel

Aguilar's dreams"). A selection of this chapter has been translated into English. See "In Search of an Inca," in Steve Stern, ed., *Resistance, Rebellion, and Consciousness in the Andean Peasant World, 18th to 20th Century* (Madison: University of Wisconsin Press, 1987).

CA, CW, WH.

Addenda to the 1988 Edition

This new edition of *In Search of an Inca* includes three new chapters: one on Juan Santos Atahualpa that discusses the degree to which messianic and millenarian ideas were able to change the course of things; one on the Tupac Amaru rebellion in the context of the Spanish colonial empire; and one on racism, the other side of the Andean utopia. With them, the ideas presented in this book are more clearly stated. These new essays, like all the other ones, can be read independently, even if the connections between them are clear. All the materials have been revised to eliminate errors or imprecise references, which are almost inevitable when one deals with such varied themes and periods. I must thank especially Scarlett O'Phelan and Fernando Lecaros for their help in this effort. I hope that this is the definitive version of this book.

I also want to mention the conversations with Juan Martínez Alier at his home in Cerdanyola. Goni Evans typed the corrections and the new materials with enthusiasm and diligence. Maruja Martínez helped me organize the bibliography, and Mónica Feria assisted me with corrections (typographic and otherwise). The space for debate that we have opened in "Sur. Casa de Estudios del Socialismo" has been essential to carry on these efforts. Chapter 7 uses materials from an ongoing research project on racism and violence in nineteenth-century Peru. Finally, I want to express my thanks for the intellectual and financial support offered by CONCYTEC (Lima) and the Social Science Research Council (New York).

Lima, February 26, 1988.

Index